Portugal in the Twenty-First Century

Portugal in the Twenty-First Century

Politics, Society, and Economics

Edited by Sebastián Royo

LEXINGTON BOOKS
Lanham • Boulder • New York • Toronto • Plymouth, UK

Published by Lexington Books
A wholly owned subsidiary of The Rowman & Littlefield Publishing Group, Inc.
4501 Forbes Boulevard, Suite 200, Lanham, Maryland 20706
http://www.lexingtonbooks.com

Estover Road, Plymouth PL6 7PY, United Kingdom

Chapter 3 was originally published as "Portugal's semi-presidentialism (re)considered:
An assessment of the president's role in the policy process, 1976–2006," by Octavio
Amorimi Neto and Marina Costa Lobo, in *European Journal of Political Research* 48,
no. 2 (March 2009). Reprinted by permission of Wiley-Blackwell.

Chapter 8 was originally published as "Portugal and Spain in the EU: Paths of economic
divergence (2000–2007)," by Sebastiàn Royo, in *Analise Social* 195 (2010): 209–54.
Reprinted with permission.

Chapter 9 was revised from António Gaucho Soares's "The Europeanization of
Portugal," published in *European Societies* 12, no. 3 (2010): 317–37. Reprinted by
permission of Taylor & Francis Ltd.

British Library Cataloguing in Publication Information Available

Library of Congress Cataloging-in-Publication Data

Royo, Sebastián, 1966–
    Portugal in the twenty-first century: politics, society, and economics / edited by
Sebastián Royo.
        p. cm.
    ISBN 978-0-7391-3755-0 (cloth : alk. paper)—ISBN 978-0-7391-3756-7 (pbk. : alk.
paper) — ISBN 978-0-7391-3757-4 (electronic)
    1. Portugal—Politics and government—1974–2. Portugal—Politics and
government—21st century. I. Title. II. Title: Portugal in the 21st century.
JN8509.R69 2011
320.9469—dc23   2011030970

Printed in the United States of America

To my twin brother, Pepe. I miss you so much.

Contents

List of Figures

List of Tables

Acknowledgments

This book originated at a panel about Portugal that I organized in 2008 for the Iberian Studies Group of the American Political Science Association. The papers presented at the panel looked at developments in Portugal during the first decade of the twentieth century. The panel generated a stimulating discussion among all the participants, which led to the idea to edit them in a book. In order to provide an overall overview of development in the country I commissioned additional papers to include the foreign relations of the country, as well as its sociological evolution, hence the delay in the publication of this project.

The book would not have been possible without the extraordinary contributions of all the authors included in this volume. I want to express my most sincere gratitude to Michael Baum, Teresa de Almeida Cravo, Ana Maria Evans, Robert M. Fishman, Miguel Glatzer, Marina Costa Lobo, Pedro C. Magalhães, Octavio Amorim Neto, and António Costa Pinto. I could not have asked for a better group of colleagues to work with. They are among the best social scientists working on Portugal related issues. They have been inspiring and patient with all the bumps that we have hit along the way with this project.

The foundations of this book were built while I was a student at Boston University when I started working on corporatism in Southern Europe. This research opened my eyes to beautiful Portugal, a country of which, despite being born in neighboring Spain, I knew little about. Since then I have had the opportunity to visit it multiple times and I have learned about its spectacular history, culture, and people. I have come to love it and I now consider it a home away from home. In addition to the contributors to this volume, there are many people that have helped me to learn about Portugal; my thanks go to António Barreto, Jorge Braga de Macedo, Nancy Bermeo, António Dornelas, Maria da Paz Campos Lima, Paul C. Manuel, Reinhard Naumann, Marino Regini, Luís Salgado de Matos, Luís Campos e Cunha, José Da Silva Lopes, Francisco Seixas da Costa, Nuno Monteiro, Rui Machete, Alan Stoleroff, and Philippe Schmitter for their support and encouragement of my research on Portugal. They not only provided valuable, insightful information but encouraged me during all the stages of my research. They have also been instrumental in helping me get access to relevant policy makers, union and business leaders, and scholars.

Over the years my thinking about political science issues has been influenced by many people. I would like to acknowledge the insight of the following people: Joaquín Almunia, Michael Baum, Nancy Bermeo, Katrina Burgess, Cesar Camisón, William Chislett, Carlos Closa, Xavier Coller, Francisco Conde, Pepper D. Culpepper, Alvaro Cuervo, Roberto Dominguez, Omar Encarnación, Miguel Angel Fernández Ordoñez, Bonnie Field, Robert Fishman, Ana M. Guillén, Mauro Guillén, Paul Heywood, Peter Hall, Kerstin Hamann, Diego Hidalgo, Richard Locke, Paul C. Manuel, Andrew Martin, Cathy Jo Martin, Felix Martin, Jesús de Miguel, Andrew Moravcsik, Fernando Moreno, Carlos Mulas, Victoria Murillo, Rafael Myro, Juan Díaz Nicolas, Emilio Ontiveros, Andrés Ortega, Sofía Pérez, Charles Powell, Marino Regini, George Ross, Joaquín Roy, Mark Rush, Vivien Schmidt, Philippe Schmitter, Ben Ross Schneider, Miguel Sebastián, Kathleen Thelen, Pablo Toral, Mariano Torcal, and José Ignacio Torreblanca.

Drafts of my chapters in this book have been presented at academic conferences, including meetings of the American Political Science Association, the International Studies Association, and the Conference of Europeanists. I want to thank all the people that participated in those panels for their valuable insight and comments.

My research was greatly facilitated by the active collaboration of the people that I interviewed for this project. The list of people who assisted with my field research in Portugal includes former cabinet members, business leaders, entrepreneurs, union leaders, scholars, and national and regional administration officials. They were all extremely generous with their time and interest. Anna Decatur, Joseph Guay, and Emily Fritz-Endres have been extremely helpful in providing editorial and research assistance for the book. It would not have been completed without their help, and I am indebted to them.

This book would not have been possible without the help and inspiration of a number of people. I owe a great debt of gratitude to the institutions and people who have supported my research over the years. In particular I would like to thank my colleagues and students in the Government Department at Suffolk University for providing a supportive environment, as well as my colleagues and students at the Suffolk University Madrid campus. Working with them has been an extraordinary experience. Their motivation and inspiration have been crucial.

The Minda de Gunzburg Center for European Studies at Harvard University, in which I am an affiliate and co-chair of the Iberian Studies Group, has also been an exceptionally supportive institution for my research. I want to thank Peter Hall for his constant guidance and inspiration. I also want to thank David Blackbourn, Patricia Craig, Charles Maier, and Andrew Martin.

During the past five years I have had the fortune to work as associate dean of the College of Arts and Sciences at Suffolk University for Dean Kenneth Greenberg. Ken is not only my supervisor, but an extraordinary person as well. He has been a mentor and an inspiration, and I have learned a lot from him. Ken represents all that is special about Suffolk University: the commitment to learning, passion for education, dedication to students, and devotion to people. He has been incredibly supportive throughout my career at Suffolk, and I am forever indebted to him for all the opportunities that he has given me. I feel enormously privileged to work for him and to count him as a dear friend. I would also like to thank all the members of the CAS Dean's Office. I am very fortunate to work with an amazing group of people at Suffolk University.

On a more personal note I would like to thank all the members of my family. My parents have always been incredibly loving and supportive. Early on, and more so than they probably know, they sparked my interest in politics around the dinner table. They are my role models and have always been supportive. My brother Borja has always been a champion of my work and is now turning into a political scientist himself. My daughters Abigail, Andrea, and Monica have been a joy and a constant source of happiness. I feel obliged to ask forgiveness for the way my research imposes on them, and I want to express my deepest appreciation for the way that they enrich my life with their love, warmth, humor, and liveliness. Last but not least, I want to thank my wife Cristina. We have shared nineteen extraordinary years, and she is an exceptional wife, mother, and professional. Cristina continues to bear the brunt of my professional activities and my travel, yet she still continues to provide emotional and intellectual support. She is my rock, and she is the best thing that ever happened to me. Nothing that I have achieved, including this book, would have been possible without her love, patience, dedication to her family, incredible hard work, and support.

When I started this book my twin brother, Pepe, was diagnosed with liver cancer. For almost three years he bravely fought a devastating illness. He passed away on May 18, 2010. At a time when we overuse the word hero, Pepe was a true hero. The way he lived his life was an inspiration to all of us who had the privilege to know him. His wit, passion for people, sense of humor, unbound energy, professionalism, creativity and innovation, as well as his joy for life and his unrequited devotion to his family, friends, and colleagues will be forever missed.

Pepe was not only the smartest, kindest, and most generous person that I have had the privilege to know, but more importantly he was (and still is) the most influential person in my life. We shared everything and he always led the way. I would not be who I am without him, and I would have never accomplished anything without his love, motivation, leadership, inspiration, and constant support. He has left such a profound void in my life, but he finished the task he came to fulfill in this lifetime. I believe that he will always be near, helping and supporting me. I miss him dearly, but I know that the world is a much better place for him having been here. I dedicate this book to him.

Sebastián Royo
Boston, Massachusetts
March 2011

1

Introduction: Crises e Oportunidades em *Tempos* de *Mudança* (Crisis and Opportunities in Transition Times)

Sebastián Royo

The year 2011 marks the twenty-fifth anniversary of the accession of Portugal to the European Community (now European Union), and the thirty-seventh year anniversary of the Carnation Revolution of 1974, which re-established democracy in the country. After decades of relative isolation under authoritarian regimes, the success of the processes of democratic transition paved the way for full membership in the European Community in 1986 (Royo and Manuel 2003). For Portugal and their EC partners, this momentous and long awaited development had profound consequences and set in motion complex processes of transformation.

The purpose of the book is to reflect on what has happened in Portugal during the last three decades. It seeks to examine the legacies of authoritarianism on the democratization process, as well as address issues related to the integration of Portugal into the European Union with the perspective offered by twenty-five years of membership. It analyzes how far the country has come since 1974, in order to better understand where it is headed at the dawn of the twenty-first century. In this regard, a primary goal of this book is to examine the impact of the combined processes of democratization and European integration on Portugal from an economic, social, institutional, and cultural standpoint.

This book offers an up-to-date assessment of political, sociological, and economic issues in Portugal. Drawing on research by leading scholars, it provides original analyses of the development of Portuguese politics, sociology, and economics since the transition to democracy and the accession to the European

1

Union. It examines the legacies of the democratization process; analyzes the impact of EU membership in Portugal; explores the challenges that the country faces at the dawn of the twenty-first century; and finally, considers the lessons for other countries from the integration of Portugal into the EU, which provides insight into the legal, political, economic, institutional, and cultural challenges and opportunities involved in such a complex undertaking.

This book challenges the interpretation that the responses of European countries to the pressures associated with globalization and the process of European integration are uniform. Contrary to this prediction, it shows that in Portugal, globalization and European integration have promoted rather than undermined alternative domestic responses. While technological changes, capital market integration, and post-industrialization have affected the balance of power between governments and private actors and have triggered new political realignments, they also have influenced the interests and strategies of the actors and have led to new strategies and patterns of change.

Historical Background

The pattern of Portuguese history has been described, crudely, as a graph shaped like an upside-down V. The graph rises, bumpily at times, through six hundred years under the Romans, seven hundred years partly under the Moors, and a century of empire-building, to the peak of Portuguese power in the sixteenth century. After that it is downhill almost all the way. The riches of the American and African colonies were squandered in wars, and a vast empire was gradually lost, leaving Portugal poor and powerless. In Portugal, the years following the assassination of the king in 1908 and the subsequent overturn of the monarchy were a period of political chaos, which led to forty years of authoritarian rule under Salazar and Caetano. After the 1974 Carnation Revolution, the line on the graph has turned upward again. The Portuguese democratic transition was a turbulent period and it included a revolutionary period, but it culminated in the establishment of a parliamentary democracy. These developments were followed by the country's progressive return to the international arena—where it had been relatively isolated during the dictatorship—bringing a new era of modernity.

Portugal held its first-ever democratic elections on April 25, 1975. With over 90 percent of the voters turning out, Mario Soares's *Partido Socialista* (PS, or Socialist Party) scored a stunning victory with 37.87 percent of the vote. Francisco Sá Carneiro's *Partido Popular Democrático* (PPD, or Popular Democratic Party) finished second with 26.38 percent of the votes, and the *Partido Comunista Português* PCP (Portuguese Communist Party) was a distant third with 12.53 percent (Manuel 1996, 99). Successive elections reinforced the tendency toward bipolarization (see Table 1.1).

The Portuguese economy has also undergone a deep transformation since the 1950s. Whereas industrialization took place slowly, this process accelerated in the 1950s and 1960s when agricultural employment declined rapidly and

Table 1.1 Electoral Results in Portugal (*Assembleia da República*), 1975-2009 (%)

Date	PCP/Left Block	PS	PPD/ PSD	AD***	CDS/ PP ****	PRD**	CDU*	Other
1975	12.53	37.87	26.38	----	7.0%	----	----	8.45
1976	14.35	34.87	24.38	----	16.0	----	----	5.7
1979	18.8	27.3 ⟶		42.52 ⟵		----	----	5.9
1980	16.75	26.65 ⟶		44.91 ⟵		----	----	5.6
1983	18.07	36.12	27.0	----	12.56	----	----	3.3
1985	15.49	20.77	29.87	----	9.6%	17.92	----	4.0
1987	12.14	22.24	50.22	----	4.44	4.91	---	8.8
1991	----	29.1	50.43	----	4.4	----	8.8	4.9
1995	----	43.9	34.00	----	9.1	----	8.6	4.4
1999	2.44	44.1	32.3	----	8.3	----	9.0	6.4
2002	2.74	37.79	40.21	----	8.72	----	6.94	1.62
2005	6.35	45.03	28.77	----	7.24	----	7.54	2.103
2009	9.81	36.56	29.11	----	10.43	----	7.86	2.99

Sources: Ministério da Administraçao Interna and Presidência da República Portuguesa, Eleiçóes para a Assambleia da Republica, Lisbon.
Notes: *CDU: Coligação Democrática Unitária (Unitarian Democratic Coalition), a coalition between the Partido Comunista Português (PCP), Movimento Democrático Portugues (Portuguese Democratic Movement, MDP) and the Partido Ecologista Os Verdes (Ecologist Party The Greens).
** PRD: Partido Renovador Democrático (Democratic Renewal Party), created by outgoing president Eanes to stay involved in politics.
*** AD: Aliança Democrática (Democratic Alliance), a coalition between the PSD and the CDS.
**** CDS: Partido do Centro Democrático Social (Social Democratic Center Party); and Partido Popular (Popular Party), a conservative party.

industrialization surged. Industrialization was first driven by import-substitution policies. Portugal's access to EFTA in 1959 produced a shift in economic policy based on the opening of the economy to attract foreign investment. Low wages and taxes, coupled with Portugal's geographic location and its colonial markets, fueled foreign investment in the 1960s and contributed to the transformation of the Portuguese economy. Tertiarization accelerated in the 1960s, and the service sector became the most important sector of the economy in the 1970s and 1980s.[1] This process of modernization accelerated with the country's integration into the European Community after 1986 (see Table 1.2).

However, the long-standing authoritarian regime prevented Portugal from joining European institutions and kept the country on the fringe of the integration process that began in Europe after World War II. In the not-too-distant past an adage claimed that Europe ended in the Pyrenees at the southwest corner of France. This was based on certain truths. Portugal (and Spain) was not a participant in the twentieth century's second major military confrontation. This historical isolation provided the nation's authoritarian and traditional sectors with the necessary shield against perturbing foreign influences, including the consolidation of liberal democracy. Rephrasing a tourism motto that became very popular in Spain in the 1960s, Iberia was "different," both in the eyes of the other Europeans and in the mentality of the Portuguese establishments.

In the second half of this century, the European Community epitomized in the eyes of the Portuguese citizens the values of liberty, democracy, and progress absent in the country. In addition, Portuguese entrepreneurs knew that their only future lay in Europe. Belonging to the European club was a mission not to be questioned. The European Economic Community, however, stipulated the democratic pre-conditions for entry, so the incentive for democratization was clear. Hence, the emergence of a democratic regime in the second half of the 1970s paved the way for the successful consideration of these countries' application for membership by the European Community. After years of relative isolationism and long and often protracted negotiations, the country became a full member of the European Community in January 1986. This was a crucial decision.

The country joined the European integration process with the hope that it would help consolidate its newly established democratic institutions, modernize its outdated economic structures, and finally, normalize relations with its European neighbors. People in Portugal saw EC membership as a form of political maturation. It would also help to align the politics of the country with their European counterparts and to accelerate the Europeanization and democratization of its antediluvian political structures. The urgent need for this development was highlighted by the stark environment in which it took place: one of the worst economic recessions experienced by Portugal since the 1950s, in a political context deeply marked by the instability of the institutions that had been established during the democratic transition (Royo and Manuel 2003).

Entry to the EU has so far brought many advantages to Portugal. Indeed, Portugal has benefited extensively from the EU's cohesion policies, which have contributed to improve the country's physical infrastructure and capital stock. At

Table 1.2 Economic Performance, Portugal, 1986-1997

Subject Descriptor	Units	1986	1987	1988	1989	1990	1991	1992	1993	1994	1995	1996	1997
Gross domestic product, constant prices	Percent change	3.32	7.632	5.34	6.649	7.859	3.37	3.13	-0.687	1.489	2.307	3.619	4.186
Output gap in percent of potential GDP	Percent of potential GDP	-6.133	-2.858	-1.704	0.699	4.433	3.977	3.486	-0.637	-2.374	-3.213	-2.729	-1.598
Gross domestic product based on purchasing-power-parity (PPP) share of world total	Percent	0.378	0.392	0.396	0.407	0.427	0.436	0.442	0.432	0.425	0.421	0.421	0.422
Inflation, average consumer prices	Percent change	11.666	9.402	9.58	12.611	13.37	11.428	8.863	5.93	4.971	3.969	2.934	1.892
Unemployment rate	Percent of total labor force	8.603	7.126	7.069	5.059	4.225	4.138	3.86	5.127	6.34	7.2	7.2	6.7
General government net lending/borrowing	Percent of GDP	-10.462	-8.624	-4.283	-3.413	-6.911	-8.048	-5.169	-8.179	-7.478	-5.147	-4.581	-3.545
General government structural balance	Percent of potential GDP	-7.518	-7.266	-3.54	-3.718	-9.069	-10.022	-6.792	-7.874	-6.373	-3.743	-3.405	-2.852
Current account balance	Percent of GDP	3.218	0.96	-2.01	0.267	-0.239	-0.833	-0.178	0.256	-2.303	-0.117	-3.476	-5.833

Source: IME: *World Economic Outlook*, 2010

the same time Portugal's trade with the Community has expanded dramatically over the past two decades, and foreign investment has flooded in. One of the main consequences of these developments has been a reduction in the economic differentials that separated the country from the European average. For instance, since 1986, Portugal's average per capita income has grown from 56 percent of the EU average to about 79 percent. The culmination of this process was the country's (largely unexpected) participation as original founder of the European Monetary Union (EMU) in 1999.

From a social and cultural standpoint, the effects of integration have also been significant. As part of its decolonization and democratic transition, Portuguese people embarked on new processes of self-discovery. They have begun to come to terms with their own identities, while addressing issues such as culture, nationality, citizenship, ethnicity, and politics. Decolonization and integration into Europe have greatly influenced these developments. At the dawn of the new millennium it would not be an exaggeration to say that the Portuguese have become "mainstream Europeans" and that many of the cultural differences that separated the country from its European counterparts have faded as a consequence of the integration process.

Integration, however, has also brought significant costs in terms of economic adjustment, loss of sovereignty, and cultural homogenization. European integration has had, and will continue to have for the foreseeable future, a profound effect on Portuguese society. It has had an impact on issues such as national identity, the sustainability of welfare institutions, and the adjustment of political and economic structures. Under the terms of the accession agreement signed in 1985, Portugal had to undertake significant steps to align its legislation on industrial, agriculture, economic, and financial polices to that of the European Community. The accession agreement also established significant transition periods to cushion the negative effects of integration. This meant that Portugal and Spain had to phase in tariffs and prices and approve tax changes (including the establishment of a VAT) that the rest of the Community had already put in place. In a second phase, this process also involved the removal of technical barriers to trade and the implementation of the necessary economic policies to become a member of the European Monetary Union. These requirements brought significant adjustment costs to the Portuguese economy. These developments are analyzed in this volume.

Objectives of this Book

With this book I hope:
1. To examine the legacies of the democratization process
2. To analyze the impact of EU membership in Portugal
3. To examine the challenges that the country faces at the dawn of the twenty-first century

4. That the integration of Portugal into the EU will provide insight into the legal, political, economic, institutional, and cultural challenges and opportunities involved in such a complex undertaking.

What is Unique About this Book?

a. The focus on Portugal. There are very few books published in English that examine Portugal's transformation over the last two decades and the challenges that the country faces in the new millennium.

b. The incorporation of the Portuguese European integration experience—which to date has been studied almost solely from the standpoint of the literature on political transitions to democracy—into the literature on European political economy.

c. The analysis of the consequences of the combined processes of democratization and European integration from a multidisciplinary standpoint. It will cover political, economic, social, historical and sociological issues.

d. The study of the effects of European integration in new democracies. The Portuguese experiences with European integration offer two of the few instances in which integration took place in an economic, political, and institutional context markedly different from that of the other European states. Therefore, one of this book's key objectives is to explore the impact of European integration on democratic consolidation.

e. The analysis of the sociological consequences of democratization and European integration. As mentioned above, from a social and cultural standpoint, the combined effects of democratization and European integration on Portuguese society have been significant. As a result, Portugal embarked on new processes of self-discovery, addressing issues such as culture, citizenship, and ethnicity. Integration into Europe has greatly influenced these developments.

f. The study of the impact of democratization and accession into the EU for the Portuguese economy and its social policies. EU membership initially brought its own problems for the Portuguese economy. While, the difficulties of the 1980s and early 1990s were successfully overcome, new challenges have emerged in the new millennium. As mentioned before, entry to the EU has so far brought many advantages to the country: it has benefitted extensively from the EU's cohesion policies, and membership has contributed to trade growth with the EU, which has expanded dramatically over the last two and a half decades. The culmination of this process was the country's participation as original founders of the EMU in 1999.

g. The examination of the economic, social, institutional, and cultural challenges of these undertakings and the lessons for other countries.

While integration has had very positive effects, the process of integration has also brought significant costs in terms of economic adjustment, loss of sovereignty, and cultural homogenization. Furthermore, EU integration does not guarantee success. Indeed, Portugal has suffered an intense economic downturn since 2004 and has experienced serious budgetary and fiscal problems that have hampered economic growth.

Theoretical Contributions

This book will be of interest to scholars and students working on comparative politics and comparative political economy. Political economy literature extensively examines the effects of economic integration on domestic policies, institutions and economic performance. This book will be of interest to political economists focusing on these issues because it seeks to push forward this theoretical concern by examining an empirical puzzle that has received little attention in comparative politics literature: the impact of European integration and economic liberalization on southern European peripheral economies. The book will be also of interest to comparativists because it considers the Portuguese experiences in light of various arguments developed in recent literature on European political economy, none of which is found to offer a fully convincing explanation of the Portuguese case.

In addition, this book should also be of interest to scholars working on issues related to the process of European integration. It not only examines the impact of integration from a comparative standpoint but also from a multidisciplinary one. The book's contributors are specialists from different areas of the social sciences: political science, history, sociology, and economics. This project might also be of interest to Europeanists because the Portuguese case offers one of the few instances in which European integration took place in an economic, political, and institutional context markedly different from that of the other European states. In addition, the integration of Portugal will provide insight into the legal, political, economic, institutional, and cultural challenges and opportunities involved in such a complex undertaking.

Furthermore, Portugal has been the object of study by comparativists interested in the country's successful democratic transition in the 1970s and 1980s. In this literature, Portugal often appears as a model "dual transition" country that has successfully combined economic adjustment and democratization. This literature, however, has neglected important signs of failure—e.g., the high comparative levels of inflation or the fiscal problems—in the economic strategies pursued by post-Salazar governments. This project sheds further light on the impact of European integration and its implication in the country's economic performance and democratic consolidation. Therefore, the book will also be of interest to scholars focusing on the impact of economic integration and liberalization on democratic consolidation and economic adjustment strategies.

Finally, this volume provides an original series of analyses of the development of Portuguese politics and economics since the accession to the European Union. Drawing on the research by established scholars, it will offer an up-to-date assessment of political and economic issues in Portugal and will be essential reading for those who want to understand contemporary Portugal.

Portugal at the Dawn of the New Century

Crisis

The book's contributions were developed before the global financial crisis hit Portugal in 2008. The impact of the crisis, however, needs to be addressed. Sebastián Royo's chapter provides an overview of the Portuguese economy's performance during the decade prior to the crisis and analyzes the economic divergence with neighboring Spain (and with Europe in general). Unfortunately, since the period analyzed in that chapter, economic conditions have deteriorated further in the country, and it is expected that this year (2010) the economy will contract 2.6 percent.

As analyzed by Royo, in the run-up to the launch of the Euro in 1999, the advantages of European Monetary Union (EMU) membership were clear as Portugal benefitted from low interest rates and low inflation, which encouraged economic growth. Portuguese businesses benefited as well from the increase in cross-border trade, lower transactions costs, and from the stability of using a global currency.[2] However, as in other Eurozone countries, membership may have offered too much protection by shielding the country against attacks (financial markets failed to distinguish among Eurozone countries), and therefore allowed successive Portuguese governments to avoid the necessary reforms that would have fostered the country's productivity and competitiveness; and making it possible for them to postpone the necessary measures to reduce fiscal imbalances.[3] This led to poor economic performance, particularly during the last decade (starting in 2000).

Indeed, the sluggish performance is not a recent phenomenon (see Table 1.3). Since 2000, Gross Domestic Product (GDP) growth has been the second lowest in the Eurozone after Italy (an average of less than 1 percent). This low growth has affected living standards, which have stagnated in terms of the European average: per capita GDP was the same in 2005 as in 1998 at 79 percent of the EU average. As opposed to Spain—which benefited from the decrease in interest rates and experienced a long period of growth—Portugal's growth rates were stagnant, and it did not benefit from a housing or consumer boom. At the same time, credit based consumption has converted Portugal into one of the world's most indebted countries: fifteen years ago (1995) the external debt represented 10.6 percent of GDP, by 2010 it has increased to 100 percent of GDP.

By the time the global crisis reached Portugal, the country was already en-
cumbered in 2009 by high debt (90 percent of GDP), weak competitiveness,
high unemployment (10.5 percent), stagnant growth (it contracted by 2.7 percent), and low savings rates (7.5 percent of GDP versus 20 percent in Spain),
which is a better proxy to measure a country's ability to pay down its debt than
the debt-to-GDP ratio. Unemployment reached almost 11 percent in May 2010
and it is not expected to fall much below 10 percent in the short term (see Table
1.3).

Yet, while Portugal has avoided the property market collapse that Spain has
faced since 2008 (in Spain the construction boom added 2.8 million houses in
Spain over five years, of which only 1.5 million were sold according to Morgan
Stanley), the country is still suffering from the poor management of public fi-
nances. The combined effect of increasing spending to address the effects of the
crisis and failing tax revenue saw the budget deficit increase from 2.8 percent in
2008 to a record 9.3 percent in 2009. Some of this is a historical problem. For
instance, public sector employees are virtually guaranteed a job for life regardless of performance, which makes it hard for young people to find jobs or gain
promotion.

Despite the structural reforms that Portugal undertook in recent years to reduce the public sector, raise the retirement age, and change the social security
system, the global crisis precipitated a new serious financial crisis: the increasing cost of financing the debt and the mounting difficulties to generate tax revenues (intensified by fears that Greece might have to default on its debt and that
this would have a contagion effect in Portugal[4]) made it difficult to meet the
country's fiscal obligations, thus forcing the government to implement tough
austerity measures.[5] These have included: cutting spending and raising taxes
(including a 1 percent increase in the Value Added Tax scales to 21 percent);
imposing an additional surcharge of 2.5 percent to the largest companies and
banks; increasing incomes taxes by up to 1.5 percent (1 percent raises for workers with monthly salaries of up to 2.375 euros, and 1.5 percent for those with
higher salaries); and establishing new tolls in free highways; freezing civil service wages for four years and cutting the salaries of politicians and top managers
from public companies by 5 percent; reducing social spending and cutting military investment by 40 percent; and reversing plans to delay deficit reduction
measures.[6] The overall objective is to reduce the public deficit to 7.3 percent in
2010 and to 3 percent by 2013.

The effects of the crisis have been manifested in the unstoppable increase in
unemployment, which has been particularly severe in the construction and transformation industry sector (78,000 employments destroyed in one year), but also
in large commerce and the financial sectors. The regional impact has also been
uneven: Algarve (13.6 percent) and the northern part of the country (12.5 percent) are the regions that have been affected the most.

The deteriorating fiscal situation and markets' doubts have been compounded by the country's loss of competitiveness since it adopted the euro in 2000.
Portugal, which has largely based its economy on low labor costs, was hit hard

by the EU's eastward expansion and the loosening of trade barriers with Asia. Indeed, the lack of competitiveness, globalization, the disproportionate growth of the Asian economies, and the Eastern European EU enlargement provoked in Portugal a drastic fall of investment in the industrial sector, which remained somewhat hidden because of the benefits from European funds and short-term growth, which in turn contributed to disguise the lack of competitiveness.[7] Some sectors, like textiles, have been particularly hit: the industry has experienced a 32 percent fall in exports in the last nine years (2000-2009). In 2009 alone, more than 2000 companies went bankrupt in the country, of which 150 were textile. In areas like Braga, unemployment has exceeded 15 percent.

The lack of competitiveness problem has been further compounded by the increase in unitary labor costs, which rose 19 percent between 2000 and 2007 (22 percent in Greece). Hence, Portuguese exporters have been losing market share since it joined the euro, which forced the government to borrow from abroad to finance its balance of payment deficit and thus increased the debt. Dealing with the lack of export competitiveness, which has been one of the leading causes of low growth, is one of the country's main challenges. This will be even more difficult in the absence of devaluations (despite some complaints about the negative effects of the euro on exports and the loss of control over monetary policies, most Portuguese understand that the cost of exiting the Eurozone would be catastrophic) and, in the context of austerity measures that will act as a severe brake on growth, will make it even more important for the small export sector to grow rapidly.

Slow progress towards competitiveness is a serious concern, and it is particularly troublesome at a time in which some investors have been abandoning the country in a context of worrisome budgetary cuts. Many of the obstacles to doing business in Portugal remain: the tax system's instability and lack of clarity (exacerbated recently by successive rounds of tax rises and budgetary cuts); the unpredictability and slowness of the judicial system (a recent judgment over a VAT dispute was handled down sixteen years after the events took place); labor laws, considered by employers as too rigid and protective of workers; and the many complaints about the bureaucracy and attitudes of Portuguese toward work, often characterized by delays, unreliability, and languor. Some worry that there is too much emphasis on knowledge-based industries and not enough on niche sectors such as ceramics or clothing, where Portugal could excel.[8] Companies also complain about the disconnect between public investments and the competitive needs of companies. For instance, Autoeuropa, an auto-part company that works with Volkswagen and the leading Portuguese exporter, complains that they were never consulted about the decision to build a high-speed train link between Portugal and Spain (which is currently paralyzed for lack of resources) and has already announced that they do not plan to use it. Finally, they also complain about the lack of support for Small and Medium Enterprises (SMEs)— which are suffering the brunt of the lack of finance from banks and financial institutions—and the excessive centralism of the government. Regions like Porto

and Braga feel increasingly discriminated against because the largest infrastructure projects are concentrated around Lisbon.[9]

A central problem, as analyzed in greater detail in Goucha Soares' and
Royo's chapters, has been the poor levels of educational attainment. Despite
significant improvements (over the last fifty years the percentage of the population who complete secondary education has gone up from 1.3 percent to 63.2
percent, 35 percent receive university degrees, and 80 percent receive preschool
education, compared with 1 percent in 1960) and increasing investment in education, comparable to most Western countries, educational outcomes are well
below average and have added to the slow growth and lack of competitiveness.
In 2008, 31 percent of students abandoned secondary schools early (40 percent
in 2004), one of the highest rates in Europe. According to a 2006 OECD report,
the educational achievements of fifteen-year-old Portuguese students in math,
reading and science, were among the lowest of the thirty-one OECD member
countries. Moreover, fewer than half of the twenty-five to thirty-four year olds
have been educated beyond the ages of fifteen or sixteen (the average in the
OECD is 80 percent); and for the fifty-five to sixty-four year olds the percentage
is less than 15 percent. The main reason for the dismal performance, according
to this report was not insufficient spending but the system's low efficiency.[10]

In the end, the crisis has exposed the weaknesses of the country's economy
and economic model. Despite the last two decades' significant progress and
achievements, the Portuguese economy still faces serious competitive and fiscal
challenges. Unfortunately, the country's early economic success in the first decade and a half since it joined the EU fostered a sense of complacency, which
allowed for a delay in the adoption of the necessary structural reforms. While
there has been significant progress, Portugal still has considerable ground to
cover to catch up with the richer EU countries and to improve its economy's
competitiveness. Given the existing income and productivity differentials with
the richer EU countries, Portugal must continue to intensify the reform process.

In sum, as examined in more detail throughout the book, the recent experience of the country shows that EU and EMU membership have not led to the
implementation of the structural reforms necessary to address these challenges.
On the contrary, as suggested before, it can be argued that EMU has contributed
to the economic boom fueled by record-low interest rates, thus facilitating the
postponement of necessary economic reforms, which is a domestic challenge of
national policies. Indeed, economic reform has to be a domestic process led by
domestic actors willing to carry it out.

Fortunately, concerns about the government's ability to confront the crisis
(it lost its absolute majority in the last general election of September 2009) did
not materialize.[11] On the contrary, as opposed to Spain where the opposition
conservative party has systematically refused to support the Socialist government's measures to deal with the crisis, the Portuguese Socialist government has
received support from the opposition's conservative Social Democratic Party
(PSD), led by new leader Pedro Passos Coelho, who agreed to back the govern

Table 1.3 Economic Performance, Portugal, 1997-2011

Subject Descriptor	Units	1998	1999	2000	2001	2002	2003	2004
Gross domestic product, constant prices	Percent change	4.852	3.841	3.925	2.016	0.759	-0.805	1.516
Output gap in percent of potential GDP	Percent of potential GDP	0.34	1.545	3.114	3.081	2.071	-0.242	-0.011
GDP based on purchasing-power-parity (PPP) share of world total	Percent	0.431	0.433	0.429	0.428	0.42	0.402	0.387
Inflation, average consumer prices	Percent change	2.213	2.167	2.807	4.41	3.677	3.257	2.508
Unemployment rate	Percent of total labor force	4.95	4.4	3.925	4	5	6.25	6.65
General government net lending/borrowing	Percent of GDP	-3.372	-2.792	-2.966	-4.321	-2.889	-2.953	-3.383
General government structural balance	Percent of potential GDP	-3.527	-3.439	-4.819	-5.67	-5.117	-5.124	-5.464
Current account balance	Percent of GDP	-7.053	-8.464	-10.241	-9.9	-8.093	-6.103	-7.578

Continued...

Subject Descriptor	Units	2005	2006	2007	2008	2009*	2010*	2011*
Gross domestic product, constant prices	Percent change	0.91	1.368	1.872	0.043	-2.678	0.293	0.653
Output gap in percent of potential GDP	Percent of potential GDP	-0.208	0.181	1.171	0.404	-2.578	-2.39	-2.047
GDP based on purchasing-power-parity (PPP) share of world total	Percent	0.373	0.361	0.35	0.34	0.333	0.325	0.315
Inflation, average consumer prices	Percent change	2.129	3.043	2.425	2.651	-0.902	0.841	1.088
Unemployment rate	Percent of total labor force	7.6	7.65	8	7.6	9.455	11.004	10.338
General government net lending/borrowing	Percent of GDP	-6.051	-3.941	-2.652	-2.751	-9.334	-8.729	-7.537
General government structural balance	Percent of potential GDP	-5.995	-3.999	-3.193	-3.496	-7.813	-7.062	-6.515
Current account balance	Percent of GDP	-9.481	-10.029	-9.429	-12.115	-10.057	-8.976	-10.165

Note: *Estimate. Source: IMF, *World Economic Outlook,* 2010

ment's austerity measures, in exchange for some concessions like a 5 percent cut in politician's pay. However, despite these tough measures the country could notavoid having its debt downgraded by ratings agencies (Fitch and Standard & Poor) over doubts about its ability to cut its deficit, and over comparisons with Greece's situation. Consequently the country's borrowing costs have soared.

A positive development has been the fact that these painful measures have not been accompanied by the social unrest that has taken place in other countries, such as Greece. Indeed, strikes and protests are relatively infrequent, and Portugal still has one of the lowest crime rates in the EU (thirty-eight crimes per year per one thousand inhabitants versus an average in the EU of fifteen per sixty-nine). Indeed, Portugal still defines itself as a country of *brandos costumes*,[12] or "mild ways," in which tolerance, aversion to polarization, and acquiescence are historical patterns. This trait is manifested in many ways.[13] While millions still support the Catholic Church and thousands participated in open-air masses during Pope Benedict's last visit in May 2010 (and this despite the fact that only 18.7 percent say that they practice the religion and 10.3 percent are regular churchgoers), a month later, thousands mourned the death of the Nobel laureate Pedro Saramago, a fervent self-confessed anti-Catholic and Communist. The first gay couples were married (the law legalizing gay marriage was approved in January 2010 with very mild opposition, despite the fact that according to polls only 30 percent of Portuguese people support same sex marriage); and the government decriminalized in 2001 the personal use and possession of all drugs, which has had no averse results on drug consumption rates that remain among the lowest in the EU.

Despite these developments, there is a growing sense of pessimism among Portuguese people; their worry increases, but no one can say exactly why. In the words of one of Portugal's leading humanists and intellectuals, José Gil, who has been named by the prestigious French journal *Le Nouvel Observateur* as one of the twenty-five greatest thinkers of the world:

> It is not only a financial, economic, competitiveness, and social crisis, it is a crisis of the soul. . . . We are afraid, but we do not know exactly of what. We know that we are going to lose quality of life, which we will need to make significant sacrifices. The middle class and the low middle class do not yet know how their lives will change. For the poor, of which there are many, over two million, there is no future. Summer vacations are near and most people will try to enlarge the parenthesis. However, when they return they will encounter a different panoramic. Everything will be more expensive: bread, electricity, water. . . . Everything that conditions our life will be more expensive, a lot more. The social climate will deteriorate and the consequences are unpredictable, because for the first time Portuguese people will be forced to confront reality. Will citizens listen to these warnings and modify their life style?[14]

Opportunities

Despite this somewhat negative outlook there are strong reasons for optimism.[15] Recent economic data has been encouraging: Portugal grew 1.1 percent in the first quarter of 2010, among the highest rate in the EU and fiscal revenue has been above target. The government is fully committed to cut the deficit to 2 percent of GDP in four years. Furthermore, the Socialist government, as outlined in chapter seven, has been a reformist government since taking office in 2005, and has undertaken important structural reforms in areas such as education: compulsory schooling was increased in 2009 from nine to twelve years; children in primary school are now taught in English (English as a second language is now compulsory from the age of six) and given a laptop computer (as of July of 2010 more than four hundred thousand laptops have already been distributed); entrepreneurship has been introduced in the schools curriculum; and the government approved in 2005 a 2.4 billion euros plan to rebuild and modernize secondary schools, which have been equipped with high-speed fiber-optic internet connection. Despite fierce resistance from the unions, the government was also committed to passing teacher assessment processes, which were finally approved after a compromise with the unions. One of the most significant reforms may have been the provision of vocational training in secondary school, an area that for historical and ideological reasons had been underdeveloped in the country. As a result, in 2010, 180,000 of Portugal's 351,000 secondary students are enrolled in technical training courses that will equip them with specific skills for the job market. Finally, in order to tackle the school drop-out problem the government has focused on adult education and it has introduced a program, *Novas Oportunidades* (New Opportunities), that offers adults and school dropouts the possibility to complete their secondary education. This program has proved to be a great success, and in the past five years (2004-2009) one million people have registered for courses.[16]

The government has also reformed the pension system: public sector workers who have been retiring at sixty will now retire at sixty-five, and the reform introduced a sustainability factor that gives employees the option of working longer or receiving lower pensions. At the same time, it has also cut back the Portuguese public administration (a historical challenge) reducing the number of civil servants between 2005 and 2009 by 10 percent, or 73,000, and reducing the public sector wage bill from 14.8 percent of GDP to below 12 percent. The government has also pushed for the reform of the frustrating paper-based bureaucracy and over the last five years it has developed new online and face-to-face services to citizens and businesses under a new initiative called Simplex, the Program for Administrative and Legislative Simplification. The main objective of this initiative is to cut red tape, make bureaucratic tasks simpler for citizens and investors, and to do as much as possible online through "e-government." While there are still problems (it works far better receiving than disbursing, and it has yet to displace the system of paperwork and licensing), the results so far have been satisfactory because it has generated greater efficiencies, it has made it easier for Portuguese citizens to deal with bureaucratic tasks, and it has contributed to the reduction in the civil service's size. Even the OECD has praised the new system. Finally, the government has also established a central procurement agency, the ANCP or National Public Procurement Agency, which operates largely online to cut the costs of government procurement operations. Businesses seem to be satisfied with this new procurement system, and this initiative has made it easier for the government to find better prices for goods and services. As a result, in 2010 it is expected to save 150 million euros in a 1.2 billion euro budget.[17]

Furthermore, the revision of labor laws in 2008 has also made the labor market more flexible (according to the OECD Portugal's labor laws are now closer to Germany's and more flexible than France's). In addition, the government has increased investment in research from 0.7 percent of GDP to 1.55 percent, overtaking Spain and Ireland, and the country now has 7.6 researchers for every one thousand workers—one of the highest rates in the EU. It has also sought to reduce dependence on imported oil and has invested in making the country a pioneer in green energy (70 percent of the country's electricity consumption has been generated from renewable sources in 2010), including the launching of the first European national recharging network for electrical cars, which draws on Portuguese technology developed for intelligent bank cards and prepaid mobile phone systems, and the rolling-out of an electric car project being developed by the local consortium of technology and energy companies, Mobi.E. The electric cars will be available by the end of 2010, and the government plans to offer tax breaks, direct subsidies and generous trade-in deals, including a five thousand euro grant for the first five thousand buyers, to encourage drivers to switch to electric cars. Under the government plan, the country seeks to produce 31 percent of its energy needs from renewable energies (in 2010 it only produces 20 percent). Finally, the government has also developed a technology plan that seeks to improve productivity, and it has supported the digital economy, pushing Portugal to move from sixteenth to first place in the World Bank rankings of e-government in just five years. Prime Minister Socrates challenged anyone "to show [him] a country that has been more reformist during the past five years."[18]

In addition, important efforts are being made to move the country's traditional industries up the value-added chain into design, branding and higher technology production. Despite stronger global competition, Portugal still remains an attractive destination for Foreign Direct Investment (FDI). In addition to EU membership, the country has good communication and transport infrastructure, and the mild climate attracts international staff. Moreover, Portuguese companies are also rising to the challenge. Portugal has 848,000 more small-and-medium-sized companies than any other Western European country, and they provide 82 percent of its employment (more than 40 percent work at micro-enterprises with less than ten employees) and 68 percent of its value added. Despite the pressure throughout Europe to consolidate and create bigger companies as a way to allow them to carry out global operations, attract finance (an acute problem for SMEs, which are very dependent on bank credit, particularly in the current economic context in which banks are forced by new rules on bank capital to hold more capital in reserves), and also to increase the value of European exports, Portuguese SMEs are seizing new opportunities.[19] Seeing few prospects of domestic consumption or public investment growth, as well as the faltering situation of their main export markets in Spain, France, and Germany, they are increasingly looking for opportunities abroad, particularly in their former African and American colonies.[20]

Portugal is also emphasizing the significance of the "Lusophone triangle," which links Portugal with Europe and the expanding economies of its former colonies in South America and Africa. These markets are growing faster (in 2008 Angola grew 13.2 percent, Cape Verde 5.9 percent, and Mozambique 6.8 percent) than the world economy (2.9 percent), and hence their demand for quality goods, services and infrastructure is also increasing. Because of the historical, linguistic and economic ties with their former colonies, Portuguese firms are ideally positioned to take advantage of this growth, and also to serve as gateways for companies who want to expand their business in these countries. Consequently companies such as Sonae (manufacturing and services), Pestana (tourism), Millennium BCP (banking), Mota Englil (construction), and Galp (oil) are expanding their operations in African markets. As a result, Portuguese exports to non-EU countries have been growing rapidly from 15 percent of the total to more than 27 percent in the last decade (2000-2010), and more than ten thousand Portuguese companies are doing business with Lusophone Africa, investing more than one billion dollars in Angola between 2007 and 2009 (Portugal has become the country's biggest foreign supplier, overtaking China). Brazil has also become a strategic market for Portuguese firms. These links have not only boosted Portuguese exports, they have also encouraged inward investment into Portugal, thus helping alleviate some of the pain caused by the global recession.

Portuguese companies view this geographical diversification not merely as a search for new growth markets, but as an important driver of technological innovation and marketing development. Portuguese firms are realizing that they can no longer compete with low-cost manufacturing centers in Asia, northern Africa, and Eastern Europe, and that they need to raise their standards and value added options. As a result, textile and clothing manufacturers and shoemakers, two of the traditional strong production sectors in the country, are developing more efficient production techniques and producing more sophisticated designs and higher quality products than ever before. Textile and footwear manufacturers have grouped around the northern towns of Felguiras, Santa Maria de Feira, and the Vale do Ave area to form one of Portugal's most important industrial clusters. Portuguese shoes, considered traditionally as cheap and of poor quality, are now the second most expensive in the world after Italy; and the Spanish Inditex, the world's largest integrated clothing company, is using Portugal as one of its main production bases. The textile sector, aware of the need to further nurture talent and develop infrastructure, is setting up the foundations for sustainable growth, with initiatives to promote local designers abroad, develop overseas contacts, and create a fashion institute, as well as education programs and schools geared specifically to the sector.[21]

This development has expanded to other economic sectors. As part of the country's push toward renewable energies described earlier, a new industrial cluster focused on wind energy has emerged in the country's northwestern border with Spain around the town of Viana do Castelo. This cluster includes five new factories and a consortium of leading international companies (including the Spanish Endesa and the German Enercon), as well as eleven refitted production and service centers. They have invested 220.3 million euros and created nearly two thousand jobs, and in addition to exporting state-of-the-art gearless turbine and towers set-ups around the world, they also generate 3,500 MW of wind power. As a result of these initiatives, exports in the energy sector have increased 100 percent in the first quarter of 2010 (compared with an increase of 28 percent in Portuguese exports), and Portugal is exporting—for the first time ever—more technology-based goods and services than it is importing.[22] Finally, Portugal is also expanding and diversifying its tourist sector, emphasizing the country's natural landscapes, local gastronomy, wineries, historic sites, culture, and golf courses, while moving into new areas such as medical tourism (wellness resorts, cosmetic surgery centers), nature, and sports. This is a crucial sector for the country, and it is expected to increase its contribution to GDP from 14.4 percent (or 24.2 billion Euros) in 2010 to 16.9 percent (or 43.7 billion) by 2020.[23]

Finally, some cities like Porto have been actively developing new economic alternatives that will provide sustainable foundations for growth. Porto is determined to become the country's creative region and to promote the development of creative industries to overcome the crisis and create new employments. The city has made a registry of companies that are devoted to eleven creative areas: publicity, architecture, artisan and jewelry, filmmaking and video, and design and music, among others, which employ over twelve thousand people and have an annual business of 816 million euros.[24]

In sum, while it is undeniable that the challenges facing the country are daunting, Portugal is moving again in the right direction. Until recently, EU and EMU membership was all about the benefits. Now the terms are unquestionably different, as Portugal has to face the pain of life in Euroland and adjust to this new reality. Yet, there has been significant progress and hence strong reasons for optimism.

Structure of the Book

The book has been divided into three main sections: political and sociological aspects, economic and social aspects, and foreign affairs. The book chapters will identify the basic changes in Portugal's economy and society that occurred as a result of the democratization, decolonization, and European integration process-es. They will also assess the impact that these changes have had on the "quality" of Portuguese democracy and the country's economic, political, and social de-velopment.

The book's first section deals with political and sociological issues. In chap-ter 2, Marina Costa Lobo, António Costa Pinto, and Pedro Magalhães examine the legacies of the authoritarian past on contemporary Portuguese democracy. They examine the main political institutions of Portuguese democracy—the electoral system and the executive legislature—and their evolution since the democratic transition. According to their analysis, the "rules of the game," which were agreed to in 1976, largely reflect the historical and political circum-stances of the transition period. This period was characterized by a strong pres-ence of the military in the country's political life, an ascendancy of the Left, and a strong cleavage concerning the future nature of the political regime. At the same time, they examine the transformation of the Portuguese party system, which they claim has been the main political development of the last thirty years. This transformation has in turn contributed to the process of democratic consolidation. Yet they show that despite the success of the new regime, there have been constant calls for institutional reforms during the democratic period. They conclude the chapter with an overview of the recent major debates on the nature of the political regime.

In chapter 3, Marina Costa Lobo and Octavio Amorim examine the policy-making role of Portugal's chiefs of state in the country's semi-presidential re-gime from 1976 to 2006. This analysis is important not only because Portugal is one of the longest-standing semi-presidential democracies, but also because it has been relatively overlooked in the English-language scholarly literature. Moreover, there is an unsolved controversy regarding the nature of the country's system of government. In fact, some influential studies tend to downplay the president's role, and contend that Portugal should be considered a parliamentary system. They show how party system changes in the mid-1980s gave rise to single-party majority cabinets, which in turn considerably strengthened the prime minister, to the detriment of the president.

Ana Evans examines in chapter 4 how Portuguese political parties have ad-justed to the challenge of multivariate governance. In particular, she analyzes how Portuguese political parties have adapted to the changing institutional make-up and decision-making processes of the European Union (EU), focusing on their behavior in the European Parliament (EP). The main objective of this chapter is to assess the political alliances that parties build in the supranational sphere, the extent to which such alliances are conditioned by the specific institu-tional character of the EU's multilevel governance, and their effects upon the capability by party leaders to achieve their most desired goals. Based on a bat-tery of interviews with EP staff and with former and current members of the European Parliament (MEPs), she examines the reasoning driving the choices by Portuguese political parties for group affiliation in the EP during the period between the entry of Portugal in the (then) EC in 1986 and at the end of the fifth EP legislature in 2004.

Chapter 5 deals with the issue of national identity. Michael Baum and Miguel Glatzer examine the country's transformation in the last four decades and its impact on national identity. The chapter provides an overview of some of the main structural changes in Portuguese society, economy, and politics during the period from 1960 to 2008 and offers some reflections on the impact of these changes on the concept of national identity. They show that while there may be disagreement and debate about the relative success of Portugal's convergence with European norms in every social, political and economic domain, there is nearly unanimous agreement on the country's singularly rapid transformation over the past forty years. According to them, this transformation from a poor, still significantly rural and illiterate authoritarian country with imperialistic dreams, to a proud democratic member of the European Union, the Eurozone club, and one of the twenty-eight most developed countries in the world by 2000, must surely rank as one the great transformations of the twentieth century. Baum and Glatzer show that Portugal is no longer a backward-looking country of emigrants and examine how the combined processes of modernization and Europeanization have transformed Portugal into a destination country that is significantly more urbane, diverse, and multi-ethnic than before. This chapter addresses the following questions: What impact have these changes in Portuguese society had on national identity? How do the Portuguese see themselves and the foreigners among them? How has national identity been (re)constructed with the Portuguese diaspora?

The second part of the book deals with economic and social aspects. Antonio Goucha Soares examines the impact of the European integration process in chapter 6. This chapter provides an overview of the main transformations in Portugal since the European accession. Goucha Soares shows how the accession to the European Union allowed Portugal to benefit from the so-called European structural funds and how the massive financial transfers helped the country achieve the modernization of its physical infrastructures and improve the quality of public services provided in different areas, such as education, health, and social security. However, he also shows the negative impact of the fiscal constraints associated with the adoption of the Euro and, more recently, the consequences of Eastern European enlargement. Finally, he identifies the reasons that have caused convergence with the Union to slow down since the beginning of this century, focusing in particular on the macroeconomic imbalances, the widening lack of trust, the unsuitable functioning of the rule of law, and the problems raised in the field of education and training when compared to other European Union member states.

Chapter 7 looks at Portugal's migration experience. I present an overview of the Portuguese migratory experience over the last five decades and show how Portuguese emigration has been an integral part of the country's history. At the same time, the social, cultural, demographic, and economic impact of immigration has grown exponentially in the country over the last two decades. Hence the chapter examines the evolution of migration flows to the country, as well as the consequences of this development. It also analyzes the reasons that have converted Portugal into a net recipient of immigrants.

I close this section of the book in chapter 8 with an analysis of Portugal's somewhat disappointing economic performance since the turn of the century. During the last decade (until 2008) Portugal's economic performance has lagged behind its close neighbor Spain. I explain the reasons for this divergence by examining the integration experiences of Portugal and Spain in the European Union in order to study how integration has affected their economic structures and economic performance. I analyze the relationship between regional integration, economic growth, and economic reforms in the Iberian countries, and in particular, look at the impact of European Monetary Union (EMU) integration in the Portuguese and Spanish economies. I conclude that while the overall benefits of EMU membership have been undeniable to both countries, their economic policies have diverged, and this has impacted their performance. The examination of these cases will show that the process of economic reforms has to be a domestic process led by domestic actors willing to carry them out.

The book's final section and chapter deal with Portugal's foreign policy and its place in the world. Teresa Cravo analyzes Portugal's foreign relations at the dawn of the new century. This chapter covers the period between Portugal's accession to the European Union in 1986 and 2008. According to Professor Cravo's analysis this has been a transformational period in Portuguese foreign policy. The colonial question was undoubtedly the central issue in Portugal's foreign relations until the 1970s. Since then, however, the combined processes of decolonization, democratization and European integration have radically transformed the country's foreign policy priorities. European integration and democratization have led to the development of new relations and ties with other countries. Portugal's place in the world has changed, shifting from Africa to Europe. Without denying its Atlantic vocation, Portugal's strategic option is now Europe. This chapter examines these developments.

Robert Fishman concludes the book with a magisterial analysis of the themes for which Portugal provides a valuable vantage point to scholars and intellectuals, which makes the country such a fascinating case study.

Notes

1. By 1988 agriculture represented 20 percent of total employment but only 6 percent of GDP; industry 35 percent and 38 percent; and services 44 and 56 percent respectively.

2. Ralph Atkins, "The gain, then the pain, of life in euroland," in *Financial Times*, Wednesday 14 July 2010, 2 (special section on Portugal).

3. Other analysts have blamed the lack of reforms on the country's conciliatory approach and its tendency to back away from radical solutions and solve problems only

partially. See Peter Wise, "Aversion to social unrest is a double-edged sword," in *Financial Times*, 14 July 2010, 2 (special section on Portugal).

4. It seems pretty clear that Portugal is not Greece: public debt is not as high, there are no questions about the working of the country's tax collection system, or the reliability of its data/statistical services. However, in the context of the global financial crisis, markets and speculators were not discriminating and Portugal suffered their wrath. This was one of the reasons that led to the announcements of the 750 billion Euros stabilization plan in May 2010.

5. "Portugal se suma al ajuste con una subida general de impuestos," *El País*, May 14, 2009.

6. The Portuguese parliament voted on March 25, 2010 a four-year austerity program that aims at lowering the deficit to 2.8 percent of GDP in 2013, a cut of about 9 billion euros. On May 13, 2010 the government announced yet another tax increase and budget cuts to save 2.1 billion Euros and reduce the deficit to 7.3 percent of GDP in 2010 (down from the current 9.3 percent). As noted elsewhere, in contrast to Spain, where the government has struggled mightily to get support from other parties, these measures had the support of the leading opposition party, the Social Democratic Party.

7. "Portugal no quiere ser Grecia," interview with businessman Rui Moreira, *El País*, June 6, 2010.

8. Victor Mallet, "Business frustration and obstacles remain," *Financial Times*, July 14, 2010, 3 (special section on Portugal).

9. "Portugal no quiere ser Grecia," *El País*, June 6, 2010.

10. Peter Wise, "Must do better to catch up with European Peers," *Financial Times*, July 14, 2010, 3 (special section on Portugal).

11. Peter Wise, "Campaign to speed up slow growth," *Financial Times*, July 14, 2010, 1-2 (special section on Portugal).

12. This was the title of a classic Portuguese film that depicts the stiffing atmosphere of Portuguese society during the Salazar dictatorship. Fortunately the country has changed dramatically since them, starting with the role of women in society: nowadays more women graduate from university than men.

13. Wise, "Aversion to social unrest," 2.

14. "Portugal no quiere ser Grecia," *El País*, June 6, 2010.

15. Wise, "Campaign to speed up slow growth," 1-2.

16. Wise, "Must do better to catch up with European peers," 3.

17. Victor Mallet, "Web is yet to displace system of paperwork and licensing," *Financial Times*, July 14, 2010, 5 (special section on Portugal).

18. From "Severe test of inveterate optimist," *Financial Times*, July 14, 2010, 3 (special section on Portugal).

19. Richard Milne, "Small size hides uncomfortable truth," *Financial Times*, July 14, 2010, 4 (special section on Portugal).

20. Peter Wise, "Effort to exploit ties with former colonies pays dividends," Peter Wise, *Financial Times*, July 14, 2010, 3 (special section on Portugal).

21. Mark Mullingan, "Local talent raises its game," *Financial Times*, July 14, 2010, 4 (special section on Portugal).

22. Mark Mulligan, "Green technology at heart of state policy," and Peter Wise "Electric car in the vanguard of mobility," *Financial Times*, July 14, 2010, 5 (special section on Portugal).

23. Jill James, "There is more than just golf," *Financial Times*, July 14, 2010, 5 (special section on Portugal).

24. "La creatividad, industria alternativa," *El País*, June 6, 2010.

2 The Political Institutions of Portuguese Democracy

Marina Costa Lobo, António Costa Pinto, and Pedro Magalhães

Portugal initiated the so-called "Third Wave" of democratization in 1974 (Huntington, 1991) after more than forty years of authoritarianism. The "rules of the game" which were agreed to in 1976 largely reflect the historical and political circumstances of that period, which was characterized by a strong presence of the military in the political life of the country, an ascendancy of the Left, and a strong split concerning the future nature of the political regime. The major political development in the last thirty years has arguably been the transformation of the Portuguese party system, which has in turn fundamentally contributed to the process of consolidation. Nevertheless, as we shall see, calls for institutional reform have been a constant during the democratic period, acting as an indicator of the shifts in political consensus and the tensions that persist concerning the design and effects of Portuguese political institutions.

In what follows, the main political institutions of Portuguese democracy are presented, both in terms of how they were devised in the 1976 Constitution and how they have evolved. Then, the electoral system is described, and the effects it had on the party system and governmental majorities are discussed. Next, the executive power and governmental majorities are set in the context of the counterweights that exist in the political system. As we shall see, Portugal is a country where comparatively few counterweights exist to governmental action. In that light, the importance of membership in the European Union, which occurred in 1986, becomes even more apparent. The chapter ends by giving an overview of the recent major debates on the regime's nature.[1]

The Making of Portuguese Democracy

On April 25, 1974, a bloodless military coup put an end to almost five decades of dictatorship (1926-1974). Unshackled by international pro-democratizing forces and in the midst of the Cold War, the coup led to a severe state crisis that was aggravated by the simultaneous processes of transition to democracy and decolonization of what was the last European colonial empire.[2]

The comparative literature on transitions to democracy has always incorporated the Portuguese case; however, some of its characteristics, particularly the role of the military, the crisis of the State, and the dynamics of the social movements, constitute elements that are difficult to integrate into the comparative analysis of democratization. As Juan Linz and Alfred Stepan have noted, "we all too often tend to see [Portugal] in the framework set by later transitions processes,"[3] forgetting the greater degree of uncertainty and the extreme conflict path of a regime change that, according to some authors, "was not a conscious transition to democracy."[4]

The Portuguese dictatorship's nature tells us little about the country's transition to democracy. Salazarism was close to the Linzian ideal-type of authoritarian regime: it was a regime that survived the "fascist era," and was not too dissimilar from the final phase of neighboring Spain's Franco regime, despite its single party being weaker and its "limited pluralism" greater.[5] The singularity of the dictatorship's collapse resides in the military intervention by the captains—a rare, if not unique, case in the twentieth century. The colonial war that was being waged by the regime on three fronts—in Angola, Mozambique and Guinea-Bissau—from 1961 onward made them protagonists in the country's political transformation. In 1968, Salazar was replaced by Marcello Caetano, who initiated a limited and timid regime "liberalization" that was swiftly halted by the worsening Colonial War. The inability of Salazar's successor to resolve some of the dilemmas caused by the war provoked the coup d'état in April 1974. This was a military coup conducted by a "non-hierarchical" military, which had a political program that promoted democratization and decolonization.

Although disconnected from the military officers that led the coup, the prior existence of a semi-legal and clandestine opposition to Salazarism was of crucial importance. It constituted a political option legitimized by the struggle against dictatorship. The replacement of Salazar by Marcello Caetano in 1968 due to health reasons gave rise to a two-year liberalization process, and although it was cut short, it allowed for the consolidation of a "liberal wing" of dissidents opposed to the dictatorship. The creation of SEDES (*Sociedade para o Desenvolvimento Económico e Social*) in 1970 further consolidated this dissident "liberal wing."[6] Thus, despite the surprising action of the military, there were alternative elites who had close connections with various sectors of civil society and who were ready to play a leading political role in the democratization process.

Unlike Spain's *ruptura pactada*, Portugal underwent a transition without negotiations or pacts between the dictatorial elite and opposition forces. However, there is no direct causal link between this marked discontinuity and the subsequent process of radicalization: other transitions by rupture did not cause comparable crises of the state. As we will show below, the simultaneous democratization and decolonization processes was one factor of the crisis. Decolonization also triggered the conflict that broke out soon after the regime's collapse between select conservative generals and the Armed Forces' Movement (MFA: *Movimento das Forças Armadas*), which planned and executed the coup. This conflict was at the root of the military's generalized intervention in political life following the dictatorship's overthrow.

The mobilization of diverse anti-dictatorial forces was crucial in the first days after the 1974 coup. It was especially important in the immediate dissolution of the most notorious institutions of the New State, as well as in the occupation of various unions, corporatist organizations and municipalities. Some of the military elite, the leaders of several interest groups, and a part of the first provisional government sought the rapid establishment of a presidentialist democratic regime immediately following the convocation of elections.

The institutionalization of the MFA transformed it into the dominant force behind the provisional governments. The "interweaving of the MFA in the State's structures" and its emergence as an authority for regulating conflicts, which substituted, dispersed and paralyzed the classic mechanisms of legitimate State repression, prevented "the re-composition of the State apparatus."[7] This was the main factor explaining why, in the Portuguese case, the movement for the dissolution of institutions and purges exceeded those of classic purges in transitions by rupture and, in many cases, came to be a component of the transgressing social movements.[8]

Indeed, the "revolutionary period" of 1974 to 1975 was the most complex phase of the transition if one considers the transition as the "fluid and uncertain period in which democratic structures are emerging," but in which it is still unclear what kind of regime is to be established.[9] During these two years, powerful tensions emerged within Portuguese society, but they began to subside in 1976 when a new constitution was approved and the first legislative and presidential elections were held.

The disagreements over the nature of decolonization, which was the initial driving force behind the conflict between the captains who had led the coup and General Spínola and other conservative generals, led to the emergence of the MFA as a political force. This subsequently opened a space for social and political mobilization that exacerbated the state's crisis and perhaps explains why the moderate elites were incapable of directing, "from above," the rapid institutionalization of democracy. Many analyses of the transition rightly emphasize the powerful "revitalization of civil society" as a factor leading to the process of radicalization. As Philippe Schmitter notes, "Portugal experienced one of the most intense and widespread mobilization experiences of any of the neo-democracies."[10] However, this mobilization developed in parallel with and in the presence of this protective cover; it is difficult to imagine this mobilization developing otherwise.

The strength of the MFA, and of the military more generally, led to it exercising considerable leverage in order to be included in the nascent political system. Throughout that period, early attempts at the "presidentialization" of the regime were soon followed—after a failed coup attempt in March 1975—by a "First Pact" between the parties and the military about the future content of the Constitution. This pact, signed two weeks before the scheduled 1975 elections for a Constituent Assembly, gave the military a veto power over the future constitutional text, severely constraining the work of the freely elected members of the constituent assembly. It even imposed the constitutionalization of an "Assembly of the Movement of the Armed Forces" formed by military officers; an assembly that participated in the indirect election of the head of state.

It was at this time that the parties that were to represent the right and center-right—the Social Democratic Center (CDS: *Centro Democrático Social*) and the PPD—were formed. A great effort was made to exclude from these parties any persons associated with the New State and find leaders with democratic credentials. Indeed, the CDS, which integrated sectors of Portuguese society that espoused conservative authoritarian values, was on the verge of being declared illegal up until the first elections for the Constituent Assembly on April 25, 1975.

The overthrow of General Spínola, along with the MFA's shift to the left and the implementation of agrarian reforms and nationalization of large economic groups, were symbols and motors of an ever-worsening state crisis that was sustaining powerful social movements. The MFA's decision to respect the electoral calendar was a significant factor in the legitimization of the democratic regime and the realization of these elections as scheduled greatly enhanced the position of the moderate political parties.

It is too simplistic to consider the "hot summer" of 1975 simply as an attempt by the Portuguese Communist Party (PCP: *Partido Comunista Português)* to impose a new dictatorship with the support of the Soviet Union. Naturally, the democratic political elite made much of this argument in its founding discourse, but this does not provide a full explanation of events. The situation was more complex: conflict was fed by the development of strong grass-roots political organizations such as the workers' commissions, and the growing challenge posed by the extreme left during the crisis and its influence within the military. The importance of internal divisions within the armed forces in driving these events forward means that they cannot be explained as part of a "programmed conspiracy."

Portuguese society began to polarize with the emergence of an anti-revolutionary (and anti-Communist) movement in the north of the country. It was in this context of increasing mobilization, that on November 25, 1975, moderate MFA officers organized a successful counter-coup that toppled the radicals. The Socialist Party (PS: *Partido Socialista*) and the PPD backed the moderates, leading mobilizations in Lisbon and Oporto, with the former opening a rift with the communists that would become a central divide in the left-wing segment of the political spectrum. In the provinces to the north of the River Tagus, the hierarchy of the Catholic Church and local notables supported parish level mobilizations, with the local military authorities remaining neutral and/or with them being complicit in the activities. As elements of the extreme right— military officers and civilians alike—began to mobilize, the anti-left offensive became violent. Attacks were made on the offices of the PCP and the extreme left and associated unions. Right-wing terrorist organizations emerged, such as the Democratic Movement for the Liberation of Portugal (MDLP: *Movimento Democrático para a Liberação de Portugal*), and the Portuguese Liberation Army (ELP: *Exército para a Libertação de Portugal*).

Following this counter-coup that neutralized the radical left-wing military, a new settlement between the parties and the military followed, the so-called "Second Pact." This included the direct election of the president of the Republic by universal suffrage, but under stringent conditions that were imposed by the moderate and hierarchical military, which had now gained control of power. Among those conditions was the imposition of an "implicit military clause,"[11] through which the major parties, the center-left Socialist Party and the center-right Social-Democratic Party, would endorse a particular candidate in the next presidential elections, to be selected by the military Council of the Revolution (CR) itself.

From 1974 to 1975, Portugal experienced significant foreign intervention not only in diplomatic terms, but also affecting the formation of political parties, unions and interest organizations, as well as shaping the anti-left strategy that evolved over the "hot summer" of 1975. The Portuguese case was a divisive issue in international organizations, within the North Atlantic Treaty Organization (NATO) and in the European Economic Community (EEC), affecting relations between these two organizations and the Socialist Bloc countries led by the Soviet Union.[12] All evidence makes it clear that from 1974 to 1975, Portugal was an issue of "international relevance."

Caught by surprise with the coup, the international community, and the United States in particular, focused on supporting democratic political forces of the center left and right in Portugal, as well as on intervening in the rapid process of de-colonization, particularly in Angola.[13] The same post-Second World War methods deployed to deal with Italy were used in the Portuguese case. The moderate political parties were financed by the U.S. administration, which together with the international organizations of the European political families— these often mediating the U.S. role—also supported the training of party cadres. The impact of foreign aid, however, was limited. They were drowned out by the powerful political and social mobilization led by the left, an economy strongly marked by a large nationalized sector, as well as capital flight and the actual flight of members of the economic elite from the country. Although domestic political factors played a critical role in enabling both the triumph of moderate civilian forces and the final withdrawal of the military from the political arena, international support and perspectives of EEC membership were more important than the early literature on the transition suggests.[14]

The nature of the transition left several legacies to the political system. First, the presence of the military, which had been determinant for the demise of the *Estado Novo*, demanded a stake in the new regime. After difficult negotiations, an important role was found for the military within the institutions to condition the political system until at least 1982. Second, the authoritarian right-wing nature of the *Estado Novo*, and especially the radicalization of the transition, guaranteed an ascendancy for the left-wing parties within the party system. Nonetheless, the conflicts between Socialist and Communist parties during the transition rendered any coalitions between the two major parties on the Left unviable. Finally, during the transition period, the radicalization of political actors and society centered on the nature of the regime and became a fundamental split within Portuguese politics which, as we shall see, served to diminish other social and political divides among the electorate. We now turn to the executive power, how it was created, and how it has changed in the last three decades, bearing in mind the authoritarian and transition legacies to the democratic regime.

Executive Power

In the Portuguese case, the choice of a semi-presidential system is central to understanding how executive power was conceived and how it developed. Duverger defined this model of government as having a constitution with two main characteristics: a president elected by direct universal suffrage that has considerable powers and a prime minister and ministers possessing executive and governmental powers that are responsible to parliament.[15] Duverger's definition has been found wanting on one major aspect, namely due to the fact that it is unclear what "considerable presidential power" means.[16] More recently, Elgie reformulated Duverger's criteria by eliminating that phrase. According to Elgie, a regime is semi-presidential whenever the president is popularly elected on a fixed mandate and co-exists with a prime-minister and a government which are responsible to parliament. From these constitutional norms, a variety of political practices may emerge, ranging from a president who is a mere figurehead to one who dominates the executive branch. The outcome will depend on three types of factors: namely, the events which surrounded the creation of the regime; the constitutional powers granted to the main political bodies and the nature of the parliamentary majority; and the president's relationship with that majority.[17] Next, we will analyze Portuguese executive power in light of these three factors.

All constitutions are necessarily a product of the time and circumstances in which they are designed, embodying the wishes and fears of their framers, both current and historical. The Portuguese Constitution of 1976 was no exception. It was a compromise document, agreed upon by the two main political actors who emerged from the revolutionary period of 1974 to 1976; namely, the military and the parties that competed to determine the workings of the state and government.[18] In fact, the Constitution was drafted by a Constituent Assembly working under constraints imposed by the military (the Armed Forces Movement), thus crystallizing a particular moment of Portuguese political history and conditioning the polity's subsequent development.[19] When the Constitution was amended in 1982, the 1976 balance-of-forces had evolved considerably due to the decline in the power of the military, of revolutionary activists, and of the left in general. Thus, the temporary ascendancy of the military explains the choice of semi-presidentialism. Looking at the successive proposals made by the different parties in the Constituent Assembly, Lucena points out that initially none of them called for a semi-presidential regime. That choice came about as a result of the second pact between the military, and the parties signed in 1975—that is, from the pressure to include the military in the nascent political regime, and from an implicit agreement that the first president would be a military officer.[20]

That he would be elected by popular suffrage meant that in the medium term, the presidential office might become partified, thus holding the promise of a partisan, civilian president in the future. In the short-term, however, the concession made by political parties that the first president should be a military officer meant that the presidential office would combine both electoral and revolutionary legitimacy.

The military's importance in the transition towards democracy was prolonged not only by General Eanes' election to the presidency in 1976 but also via the creation of the Council of the Revolution (CR), presided by Eanes himself. This body was given extensive powers: it had exclusive legislative powers concerning the organization, functioning, and discipline of the armed forces, and could approve international agreements on military matters via decree-laws.[21] Article 149 underlines the independence of the CR by stating that all of its decree-laws have the same validity as laws of the Assembly or of government decree-laws. This reserved power is a watered-down concession of what the MFA demanded in the First MFA-Parties Pact signed in 1975; a military assembly that would have equal legislative powers to those of an elected assembly. The CR was also the guarantor of the fulfillment of the Constitution, i.e., the defender of the "conquests" of the revolution (Art. 146, 1976 version), and could make recommendations to this end, as well as declare government decree-laws unconstitutional if they did not serve the revolutionary ideals. Given the extensive social guarantees and the economic stipulations set forth in the Constitution, the CR had potentially considerable leeway in constraining government policies. Thus, this was a *sui generis* constitutional court with a mandate to ensure that the revolutionary ideals were not discarded but actively pursued after 1976. Linz and Stepan date the consolidation of Portuguese democracy from 1982, when this institution was dismantled.[22]

The president was granted veto powers over both parliamentary and government diplomas. A presidential veto cannot be overturned if the diploma has governmental origin. When it is a parliamentary diploma it can be overturned by a second vote by an absolute or a two-thirds majority of members of Parliament (MPs) depending on the nature of the law. The president can also request that the constitutionality of both parliamentary or government diplomas be verified, either *ex ante* or *ex post*.[23] Despite these powers, the 1976 Constitution placed the government at the helm of policy-making, and of public administration.[24] Other institutions however—the presidency, the parliament, and the Council of the Revolution—enjoyed powers that constrained the overall steering function of government. It is necessary to take into account the initial weakness of the State and the party system, and the confluence of the revolutionary and democratic legitimacies to gauge the scope of the functions and competencies of the president—namely, his role as constitutional guarantor, as head of the armed forces, and the representative of the nation.[25]

The president had the power to nominate the prime minister after considering the electoral results. This article (Art.136, 1976 version) gives an indication of the *potential* power of the president: if no majority can be found in Parliament, the president can try to engineer a majority himself, as was the case in 1978. Moreover, the equal responsibility of government to the presidency and the Assembly meant that the president could withdraw his political confidence in a government, i.e., force it to resign, even if it enjoyed the support of the Assembly. In fact, at least until 1982, the government was at the intersection between the two legitimacies laid down in the Constitution: the military-revolutionary vs. the party-pluralistic, represented respectively by the President of the Republic and the Council of the Revolution on one hand, and the Assembly on the other.[26] The government's difficulty in asserting its power was a reflection of the struggle of these two tendencies inherent in the Constitution, especially while there was no majority in the Assembly.

There were also some important provisions that were meant to protect the government of the day from a fragmented parliament. For example, a new government did not need to present a motion of confidence to Parliament once it was sworn in, thus facilitating minority or presidential governments.[27] The minority clause was introduced at the bequest of the Socialist Party, which expected to win the elections but without a majority, and rejected the idea of coalitions.[28] To dismiss the government, two motions of censure had to be approved by an absolute majority of the Assembly deputies within a thirty-day period.[29] Although the government had to resign if its program was rejected by a simple majority in the Assembly, or if a motion of confidence was not approved, the Assembly itself would be dissolved by the president if it passed a motion of censure or rejected a government's program three consecutive times.

Six years after the adoption of the Constitution, it was revised, with the favorable votes of the right wing government parties—the PSD, CDS, and the PPM (Popular Monarchist Party) and the Socialist Party (PS). The goals of this major revision were twofold: to circumscribe the powers of the president and to subordinate the military to partisan political power. Thus, the Council of Revolution was extinguished and its powers were re-distributed among other institutions which were set up (all dominated by the parties), namely, a consultative body for the president (the Council of State) and a Constitutional Court to defend the Constitution. Concerning presidential powers, article 136 was reformulated, limiting the president's powers to dismiss the government "to ensure the regular functioning of democratic institutions."[30] Still, his ability to dissolve Parliament was preserved, although certain time limits were imposed; namely, the *Assembleia* could not be dissolved in the first six months following legislative elections, in the last six months of the president's mandate, nor if a state of emergency had been declared.[31]

From a comparative perspective, the 1982 constitutional revision decreased the constitutional powers of the president considerably, placing it below the average presidential powers in semi-presidential regimes.[32] However, it seems that the consensus surrounding the effective decrease in presidential powers may have been overstated. It seems they have been argued based not only on the decrease in constitutional powers per se but also on the changes in the party system which produced stable government majorities. Following General Eanes's two mandates (1976-1980; 1980-1986), Mário Soares, historic leader of the Socialist Party, became the first civilian president of Portuguese democracy. Soon after taking office the right-wing PSD won the first of two absolute majorities (1987-1995). Thus, Mário Soares's presidency, which lasted between 1986 and 1996, was almost wholly held in *cohabitation* with a single-party majority government. From 1987 until 1995, stable single-party absolute majorities, coupled with a president who saw himself as a referee and a facilitator rather than a policy-maker, combined to frame the Portuguese president as an interested and even active observer, but not as the locus of executive power, which rested firmly with the prime minister and his government.

The following president, socialist Jorge Sampaio, also served two mandates (1996-2001; 2001-2006). His presidency coincided with the beginning of single-party minority Socialist governments led by António Guterres. Thus, between 1996 and 2001, both the government and the presidency were held by the Socialist Party. Following António Guterres's resignation at the end of 2001, elections were held and a right-wing coalition government was formed between the PSD and the CDS. Following a return to political instability in 2002-2004, however, President Sampaio was able to determine both government formation and to dissolve Parliament. Thus, experience from 2002 to 2004 suggests that constitutional powers still allow great presidential power at times of government instability and caution against a minimalist interpretation of the president's role in the political system.[33]

The transformations in executive power which have occurred over the last three decades have served to extricate the military from the political system, and to subordinate them clearly to the civilian power. Thus, the events which surrounded the creation of the regime led to a curtailment of presidential power in the medium-term, namely with the 1982 revision of the Constitution. Indeed, in that revision, presidential powers were circumscribed, especially regarding the power to dismiss government. The ensuing nature of parliamentary majorities (i.e., the concentration of votes in the two center parties) has made single-party governments the norm since 1987 and has served to strengthen the prime minister vis-à-vis the other institutions.[34] Nonetheless, presidential powers remain operational at times of political instability, as the end of the Sampaio presidency clearly demonstrated.[35] Moreover, all presidents have actively used their power to refer legislation to the Constitutional Court and their power of veto to influence policy-making, as will be discussed below. Clearly, the changes in the party system underpin the evolution of executive power, and these are accounted for next.

The Electoral and Party Systems

The rules that constitute the electoral system of the Portuguese Parliament have remained mostly stable ever since they were designed for the election of the constituent assembly in 1975, in the first fully democratic elections following the 1974 military coup that put an end to authoritarian rule. On the one hand, Portugal has preserved untouched since the use of a proportional representation (PR) formula in the conversion of votes into seats. On the other hand, it has also maintained a closed-list system, in which voters merely choose between parties who present a list of candidates for all seats available in the district, and seats are attributed to candidates in proportion to votes obtained and in the order established in the proposed list.

The adoption of these particular rules during the Portuguese transition to democracy seems to be linked to a common factor: the absolute novelty and lack of institutionalization of most political parties that emerged immediately before or after the 1974 coup. On the one hand, in the absence of a clearly dominant party able to impose particular rules, and with parties uncertain about their future electoral support in the forthcoming elections, the option they predictably agreed upon was one that allowed them to hedge their bets, i.e., a PR system.[36] On the other hand, with the exception of the Communist Party, all other parties lacked any significant local roots or a national political organization. Thus, parties' monopoly over the presentation of candidates and national control over the composition of party lists emerged as a potentially useful instrument of leadership strengthening and centralization.[37]

There are some limitations, however, to the extent to which the use of a PR formula has allowed representation to smaller parties. Although Portugal has remained a multi-party system, with at least five different parties assuring representation in parliament at any given moment, two elements contributed to mitigate the proportionality of the system. First, among the formulas that could have conceivably been selected, the *d'Hondt* formula—the one ultimately chosen—

was also the one that, among the PR formulas, produces a stronger bias in favor of larger parties. Second, and most importantly, the conversion of votes into seats is made not in a single national electoral district, but rather in each of the twenty-two electoral districts in which the country is divided, including two districts for expatriates (one for the Portuguese citizens resident in European countries and another for those living outside of Europe).

These districts were designed to match a previously existing and stable administrative division of the country into provinces (*distritos*). Furthermore, the number of deputies elected has been kept roughly proportional to the population eligible to vote in each district: the ratio between number of registered voters and MPs elected per district ranges today between 54:316 (in the small district of Portalegre) and 39:508 (in the large district of Lisbon). Both of these features have prevented the kind of gerrymandering problems that have been frequent in countries such as the United States, Australia, France, Japan, and Spain.[38] However, there are huge differences between these districts in terms of their magnitude. Albeit some districts are quite large in terms of the number of candidates to be elected—with forty-seven MPs elected by Lisbon and thirty-nine MPs elected by Oporto—others are extremely small, such as Bragança in the North (three MPs), Évora and Portalegre in the South (three and two MPs, respectively) and the two districts for expatriates (two MPs each). In fact, no less than ten of the twenty-two districts in Portugal elect five MPs or less. Deviations in relation to proportionality have been reinforced, through time, both by demographic changes, which have led to the diminution of the population registered in the interior of the country, and by a 1989 constitutional amendment that reduced the overall number of MPs from 250 to 230.

As a consequence, the average district magnitude decreased from 11.4 to 10.5 MPs in 1989, and the "effective threshold of representation"—the share of the popular vote that a party needs to obtain in the average district in order to win one seat[39]—has increased from 6.2 to 6.8 percent. This is above those legally imposed, for example, in countries such as Germany or New Zealand (post-1996), and also above the effective thresholds found in many other PR systems, including Austria, Belgium, Finland, Sweden, Norway, Luxembourg, Israel, the Netherlands, and, for that matter, most of the new Eastern European democracies.[40] On the other hand, the average electoral disproportionality in Portuguese elections from 1975 to 2009, as measured by the Gallagher index,[41] has been 4.7 percent. Among Western European countries with PR systems, only Iceland, Norway, Greece, and Spain have exhibited, on average, higher levels of disproportionality. This has contributed—although it is certainly not the only explanation—to produce a relatively low level of fractionalization of the Portuguese Parliament, as will be explained below.

The consequences of the closed-list system have also been clearly visible in Portuguese political life, particularly in the patterns of candidate selection and the overall level of internal democratization of political parties. As predicted by most of the comparative literature,[42] the closed-list system has contributed to increase the control of party leaderships over individual candidates. Although there is some variation between the major Portuguese parties in this respect, there is no single case in which rank-and-file members play any institutionalized role in legislative recruitment, which has typically remained a centralized process in which national party organs have complete control over list composition, or at least the power to make final decisions.[43] As a result, the occurrence of "parachuting" in national leaders as candidates into districts with which they have no visible political ties is relatively frequent and party discipline remains very strong.[44]

In the first legislative elections, held in 1976, four parties emerged, which to date, constitute the core of the Portuguese party system. With the exception of the Communist Party (PCP: *Partido Comunista Português*),[45] founded in 1922, these parties were formed shortly before or after the coup. Thus, the Socialist Party (PS: *Partido Socialista*), was founded in Germany in 1973, while the center-right Social-Democrats (PSD: *Partido Social Democrata*) and the conservative Centrist Democrats-Popular Party (CDS-PP: *Centro Democrático Social-Partido Popular*) were founded in mid-1974, as explained above.

Initially, the radicalized environment within which the parties operated conditioned them in ideological terms as well. In the revolutionary atmosphere of 1974 and 1975, the parties of the Right "tended to define themselves much more to the Left than their leadership and social bases would suggest,"[46] if only to be allowed to function by the MFA. One telling factor is that the only remaining legal, most right-wing, party in Portugal, the CDS, was called the Social Democratic Center party. The other center-right party, the Popular Democratic Party, PPD called itself social democratic when in fact the representative of West European social democracy in Portugal is the PS, which portrayed itself then as more radical than it fundamentally was for the same reasons.[47]

The conflict between the two major left-wing parties stemmed from the democratic transition, where a political issue dominated and encompassed most other issues, namely, the nature of the political regime. The Communist party was opposed to a liberal democracy on West European lines, and this separated it from the Socialist Party which emerged as the most vigorous defender of that model.[48] Electorally, the relative hegemony on the left of the PS was established in the first elections. However, due to their fundamental disagreements on the nature of the new regime and its foreign orientation, as well as the international "Cold War" context, the PS could not enter a coalition with the PCP for fear of losing much of its moderate electorate—gained precisely because in 1975 and 1976, it had been seen as the most effective barrier to PCP take-over. It could however, from time to time ally with the PSD, or even the CDS.

Figure 2.1 shows the degree of party system fragmentation from 1976 until 2009.[49] Until 1980, the number of effective parliamentary parties (ENPP) decreased from 3.47 to 2.46.[50] This decrease was essentially due to the pre-electoral coalition that was formed in mid-1979 on the right, between the centrist PSD, the conservative CDS and the monarchist PPM, forming the AD (*Aliança Democrática*). The AD coalition was undone before the 1983 elections, leading the ENPP to increase to 3.36. In the following legislative elections, the effective number of parliamentary parties reached its peak value in the period (of 4.23), thanks to the entry of the new center-left party of outgoing President General Eanes—the PRD (*Partido Renovador Democrático*)—which took left-wing votes, and was the main cause of this increased parliamentary fragmentation.

After that, the ENPP decreased to relatively low levels as the PSD won an absolute majority in parliament, a result repeated in 1991. In 1995, there was alternation in government, with the PS falling four seats short of an absolute majority in parliament. In 1999, the PS did not manage to win an absolute majority. Indeed, it improved its share of the vote, but only marginally, winning exactly half of the seats in parliament (115 seats). Following two years of governing difficulties, Prime Minister Guterres resigned in December 2001. President Sampaio opted for the dissolution of parliament, and new elections were held, where the center-right PSD won, albeit without an absolute majority. The new prime minister, Durão Barroso, opted for a right-wing coalition with the conservative CDS, which did not last long. In June 2004, Barroso was designated president of the European Commission, thus becoming the second prime minister to abandon his functions in under two years. Rather than holding elections, President Sampaio opted to nominate Barroso's chosen successor, Santana Lopes, the mayor of Lisbon. His mandate did not last long though: Sampaio dissolved the Assembly four months after nominating Santana Lopes as prime minister.[51] In March 2005, the Socialists returned to power, with an absolute majority—the first ever in that party's history.

The government instability which occurred between 2002 and 2005 did not, by and large, have an impact on the number of effective parliamentary parties, with the two major parties managing to gather more than 70 percent of the vote (see Figure 2.1).

Figure 2.1 Effective number of parliamentary parties in Portugal and sum of percentage electoral share of two major parties, PS and PSD, 1976-2005

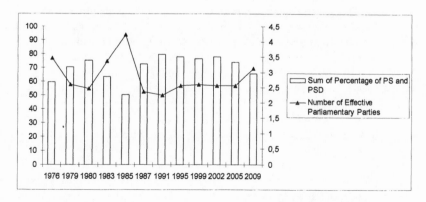

Indeed, between 1987 and 2005 levels of ENPP have been relatively low, thanks to the domination of the Assembly by two large parties alternatively in government or opposition—the left-center PS and the center-right PSD. This domination was mirrored by a long-term decline of the smaller parties on the flanks of the party system, namely, the conservative CDS-PP and the Communist PCP. Despite what appeared to be shrinking ground for smaller parties, a new party emerged in 1999 on the extreme-left, which has experienced both relative growth and consolidation—the Left-Block (BE: *Bloco de Esquerda*). The BE is a party that derived from the association of extreme-left parties and movements. It contested its first elections in 1999 and defends left-libertarian ideological principles. Since 1999 it has been increasing its share of the vote, from 2.4 percent to 6.4 percent in 2005 and has seen its number of MPs rise from two to eight in the same period.

In that respect, 2009 constitutes an important election year. As can be seen from Figure 2.1, in this election, for the first time since 1985, the PS and PSD together polled less than 70 percent of the vote: the Socialist party lost approximately half a million votes, and Prime Minister Sócrates decided to form a minority government.

The ENPP serves to both mirror and explain changes in the composition and durability of Portuguese Cabinets. During the first decade of democracy (1974-1987), governments proved quite vulnerable: none survived a full term, each lasting on average eleven months. In contrast, since 1987—with the exception of the period between 2002 and 2004—the two center parties (the PSD and the PS) have alternated in government, and the duration of government mandates has improved. However, they did not do so in equal conditions. As explained above, the PS won both the 1995 and the 1999 elections, but fell short of obtaining an absolute majority, which it only managed to obtain in 2005.

Even taking this two-year period (2002-2004) into account, the decrease in the number of relevant parties in the party system and the increase in government stability before and after 1987 is quite dramatic.[52] What may lie behind this realignment? Firstly, the lack of anchoring that political parties have within Portuguese society—as evidenced repeatedly by the high levels of electoral volatility in several elections—was fundamental to permit the concentration of votes.[53] Despite the fact that social cleavages are quite profound in Portugal, they are not important predictors of the vote. This is largely due to the political context within which the initial voting mobilization (1974-1975) occurred. As seen above, another conflict dimension (the type of regime to be established) had a major impact on political mobilization. Once democracy became consolidated, this conflict lost importance, leaving a centrist electorate which is quite sensitive to short-term political factors.[54] Secondly, successive presidential elections, where electors of smaller parties tend to vote strategically, may have then facilitated vote-switching to the larger center parties during the legislative elections.[55]

It remains to be seen whether 2009 marked the beginning of a new party system realignment in Portuguese politics. Observing the patterns of voting in previous presidential as well as European Parliament elections, it does seem that the centrist parties' hold on election behavior is waning.

The increase in government stability from 1987 onwards had important consequences for legislative activity and for the government's control of parliament. According to research by Leston-Bandeira and Freire, for the period between 1976 and 2002 the Portuguese Parliament has remained quite active: a substantial number of laws are presented per year by parliamentary groups and the percentage of those laws approved in the final vote averages 20 percent, even under absolute majorities. This sets the Portuguese apart from the majority of western parliaments where only about 10 percent of parliamentary laws are approved.[56] Notwithstanding these figures, the data concerning the government diplomas do show that since 1987 until 2002, the number of government diplomas approved in the final vote has also increased dramatically. With the onset of single-party governments in 1987, the "90 percent" law became applicable to the Portuguese *Assembleia da República*.

Not only have stable majority governments been able to approve almost all its legislation through parliament, but it is also important to note that often parliamentary laws presented are mere legislative authorizations giving the government the power to legislate on matters which normally had to be legislated by parliament.[57] Further, the government has traditionally also used decree-laws extensively and increasingly, which do not require parliamentary approval. Finally, the government also underwent a number of organizational changes to ensure greater efficacy and coordination from the late 1980s onwards.[58] Thus, constitutional, party system, and organizational changes have contributed to a strengthening of the government and the prime minister as the locus of executive power in the Portuguese political system. Next we discuss the existence of counterweights to that power.

Counterweights to Governmental Action

The extent to which electoral choices makes a difference for public policy depends on a range of factors, including international constraints on policymaking, policies' path-dependency, and economic and social contexts of policymaking.[59] Beyond these factors, the political system can also serve to reduce or magnify the impact of electoral choices on public policy, depending on the way in which power is disseminated among political institutions independent of the executive branch: a greater dissemination of power will lead to a weaker government, with less capacity to effect public policy change, and vice-versa. There have been three major approaches developed in the literature which attempt to measure the way in which democracies disseminate power.[60] These approaches are largely congruent and complement each other.

According to Lijphart, political institutions can be based on a majoritarian or consensus logic. A political system based on the majoritarian logic is characterized by (among other things) a strong executive which controls the legislature, a centralized state, single-party majority governments, a bipartisan party system, and a majoritarian electoral system. On the contrary, a political system based on consensus exhibits a relative balance of power between the legislative and the executive branches of government, a non-unitary state (federal, regional or simply decentralized), coalition governments, a multi party-system, and a proportional electoral system. In a majoritarian political system, the executive branch is the locus of power (which may or may not be collegial); by contrast in a consensus political system, power is disseminated across several institutions which are independent from the executive branch.

Tsebelis has developed a parallel line of inquiry through "veto players" analysis.[61] According to this author, a veto player is a political actor (individual or collective) whose agreement is necessary for a change of policy. The number of veto players, their cohesion, and their ideological proximity condition the ease with which it is possible to change the policy status quo. Using Tsebelis approach, we can characterize Lijphart's consensus democracy as one where there are multiple veto points, whereas majoritarian democracies have few veto points.

In a similar vein, Manfred Schmidt's index of counter-majoritarian constraints consists of an additive scale composed of six dummy variables: 1) EU membership; 2) degree of decentralization of administrative structure; 3) difficulty of amending constitutions; 4) a strong bicameralism; 5) central bank autonomy; 6) and frequent use of referendum.[62] Countries with a score between one and two on this scale are those where the executive has the potential to dominate the entire political system. Conversely, countries with a score between four and six on this scale have constitutional structures which severely circumscribe the government's course of action. Considering the Portuguese case, the Lijphart tipology, the Tsebelis veto-player analysis, and Schmidt's counter-majoritarian index (computed in the late 1990s/2000), place Portugal firmly in the majoritarian camp (Lijphart, 1999), in the low number of veto player's group (n=2), and as a political system where few counter-majoritarian constraints exist (n=1).[63] Portugal is thus placed alongside countries such as Iceland, Norway, Sweden, and the UK.

In this context, it is important to discuss once again the role of president of the Republic. The president's role in the Portuguese political system is never irrelevant.[64] However, it is the case that it can be influenced by the type of government the president faces. Whenever the head of state faces a government which enjoys an absolute majority in parliament, his effective veto powers are reduced. Although a president's veto of government decrees is supposedly definitive and cannot be overridden, a cabinet supported by a cohesive majority can simply reintroduce the previously vetoed decrees as parliament bills, and have them approved by an absolute majority—a situation which also occurs with most parliament bills. There are only few types of legislation in which a president facing an absolute majority has an effective veto. In bills concerning elections and referenda, national defense, state of emergency and the Constitutional Court, a two-thirds majority in parliament is required to override a presidential veto.[65]

Still, it is crucial not to underestimate a popular president's ability to shape public perceptions about the government, and thus government policy, through recourse to political vetoes and also by referring legislation to the Constitutional Court, even if these are not definitive per se. Also, going beyond these constitutional instruments, under Mário Soares, the presidency developed a special relationship with the media by holding "open presidencies." In these events, a region or a policy would be the focus of the president's attention, highlighting governmental failures.[66] These initiatives, which have been continued by successive presidents, reinforced the resident's role as an agenda setter for public policy and forced the government to respond to the issues that were periodically raised. This example serves to illustrate that the presidential role can become larger than the Constitution would suggest, especially in their second (and final) mandates, when presidents are free of reelection calculations, they have emerged as a de facto counterweight to governmental action, although perhaps not a de jure veto player.

Naturally, a president facing a minority government of a different party does have the possibility of being an effective veto player. Since the presidency became civilianized and partified in 1986, this situation has occurred very briefly at the beginning of Mário Soares' first presidential mandate, during the first Cavaco Silva minority government between 1986 and 1987, as well as since the legislative elections of 2009 (with Cavaco Silva now holding the presidency and Sócrates the prime minister of a minority socialist government) at the beginning of its mandate. Indeed, the possibility that the 2009 elections constitute a realignment of the party system becomes even more significant when we consider that not only the government's durability, but also the president's powers are influenced by such party system changes.

Considering Schmidt's counter-majoritarian index it is clear that the constitutional structures were designed to constrain the *demos*: the 1976 Constitution instituted a unitary state (with the important exceptions of the autonomous regions of Madeira and Azores), a unicameral legislature, and held no provisions for holding referendums.

Concerning the difficulty of amending Constitutions, Portugal belongs to the group of countries where there is legislative supremacy,[67] i.e., where a legislative vote suffices for a constitutional amendment.[68] A constitutional amendment (*revisão constitucional*) requires an initiative by MPs and is successful if two-thirds of MPs approve it, with the president having no option but to promulgate the law (Arts. 284-287 of the Constitution).

Portugal remains one of the most centralized countries in Western Europe, given that there is no intermediate locus of power between local and national government, with the local government having very little power or resources. Also, the inherited administrative tradition, characterized by a considerable weight of the state in society and a tradition of centralization in the state administration, was substantially reinforced since democratization. These thirty years of democracy witnessed the growth of the state both in the economy as well as in its welfare capacity.[69] Not only that, the role of the state in expenditure terms has increased substantially, almost doubling as a proportion of GDP in the last twenty years.[70] Part of this increase is explained by the large increase in the role of the state as a provider of social services, including education, health, and social security.

Referendums have been very infrequent in the Portuguese democratic experience. There were no provisions for referendums in the 1976 constitution. Only with the third revision of the constitution held in 1989 was a national referendum allowed under special circumstances, namely by government and parliamentary initiative, not by popular will and on specific topics. Referendums were initially created in Portugal, in effect, as another instrument at the government's disposal—more than an open channel for the *demos* to intervene in public policy-making. The 1997 revision of the Constitution extended the right of referendum initiative to citizen groups, and also allowed them to be held on issues purporting to international treaties. This latter option opened the door for having referendums on EU treaties adopted in parliament.[71] In practice, there have been three referendums in Portugal, on decriminalization of abortion (1998 and 2007), and on the creation of regional authorities (1999). The latest referendum on abortion was the only one which succeeded.

According to Schmidt's counter-majoritarian index, Portugal scores on only one count, namely its EU membership, which occurred in 1986. In public policy terms, EU membership has meant that the Portuguese government has less room for making autonomous policy decisions. This is due to the fact that, whenever a public policy is Europeanized, decision-making on that policy occurs at a supranational level, within EU institutions. The great advances in European integration which have occurred in the decades since Portuguese membership have meant that the number of public policies which have become Europeanized has increased significantly, with the creation of the single currency in 1999 epitomizing this trend. The impact on the Portuguese government has been complex. Although it is correct to state that EU membership decreases the autonomy and power of the government in terms of public policy initiative, and it is true that opposition parties, especially those with slight chances of entering government do criticize the EU for decreasing national sovereignty; de facto things are not so clear cut, for two reasons.

Portugal, being a net beneficiary of EU funds, has seen some policy areas benefit greatly from Europeanization, namely, infrastructure, education and sectoral transformation, to name but a few.[72] Indeed, Europeanization has been perceived as being fundamental to improve the outputs of democracy, measured in terms of economic and social indicators. The effect is that the state and the government, as its highest representative in the EU, have been strengthened through this process and not weakened, because its overall effectiveness is perceived as having increased since the first decade of democracy. Also, the Portuguese government is present in the EU Council of Ministers, which provides it with a role in the decision-making process at the supranational level. This presence then works to its advantage in the interinstitutional relationships at the national level, particularly with the Portuguese Parliament that remains poorly equipped to intervene effectively on developments in the EU. Perhaps paradoxically, the Portuguese government's ascendancy over other national institutions is overall *strengthened* vis-à-vis other institutions due to the existence of the EU as an external constraint.

Taking all indicators into consideration, it becomes clear that the Portuguese political system, until recently, evolved in a clearly majoritarian fashion due to constitutional and party system changes which occurred from the mid-1980s onwards. It is too early to say whether 2009 constitutes a realignment of the party system, towards a more consensual model and a more fragmented parliament.

Institutional Reform

The issue of institutional reform has been virtually omnipresent in Portuguese political life ever since the demise of authoritarian rule. Proposals for changes in the institutions regulating executive-legislative relations, the electoral system, judicial independence, and judicial review of legislation have been recurrently made by political, social, and institutional actors; and their discussion has assumed a large—some might even say excessive—role in public debate in Portugal. However, the extent to which these discussions have indeed led to actual reforms has varied significantly.

The rules regulating both the role of the president of the Republic and judicial review of legislation are the ones that were more extensively changed throughout the life of Portuguese democracy. This is largely a consequence of the particular settlement reached between party leaders and the factions of the military that, at different points in time during the 1974 to 1976 period, had control of the regime transition process and permitted a prominent role for the military in the democratic political system.

As was discussed above, a new change in both the role of the president and in the system of constitutional review of legislation was operated in 1982, following considerable political strife between President Eanes and the main political parties. This change was operated by the PS and the PSD, who enjoyed the necessary two-thirds majority in parliament and was aimed directly at curtailing presidential and military powers. Not only was the Council of the Revolution eliminated, but presidents lost, since 1982, their ability to dismiss the cabinet at will, albeit preserving the ability of both nominating the prime minister and dissolving parliament (constrained only, in the latter case, by time limits).

This outcome of the 1982 constitutional revision—which, for all purposes, completed the full transition to democracy by ending the military reserve powers over policy-making—was not enough, however, to put an end to the debates about the entwined issues of constitutional review and the role of the president. In what concerns the former, a new constitutional revision, in 1997, ended up extending the terms of Constitutional Court's justices to nine years and made them non-renewable (they were previously six years long and renewable), following a protracted debate about the extent to which the previous rules of appointment and retention favored a lack of independence vis-à-vis parliament in general and parties in particular. In this case, it can be said that it took almost twenty years for the Portuguese institutions of constitutional review to become fully aligned with what takes place in most comparable cases sharing the "European" or "Kelsenian" model of judicial review. This has not prevented, however, the recurrent criticisms made by the career judiciary about the "politicization" of the Court, accompanied by proposals ranging from more changes in the rules for the appointment of justices—which allow parliament the election of most justices by a qualified majority, with the predictable result that appointments are negotiated between parties—to its downright extinction, to be followed by the absorption of its competencies by the Supreme Court of Justice.

In what concerns the role of the president, almost every single constitutional revision process initiated since 1982—and there have been no less than six of them (1989, 1992, 1997, 2001, 2004, and 2005)—has not dispensed with proposals for changes in presidential powers, ranging from their curtailment to the full presidentialization of the regime, a debate that has been constantly reinvented either on the eve of presidential elections or following controversial decisions by the president.[73] In this case, however, the changes operated in 1982 have proved resilient, allowing the system to converge on a "premier-presidentialism" model: a system where, although the president is also elected by popular vote and preserves considerable powers, the premier and the cabinet are accountable only before parliament.[74]

Another area of almost permanent contention around institutional rules has been the organization of the judicial system itself. During the Portuguese democratic transition, although the basic hierarchical-bureaucratic organization of the Portuguese judiciary remained unchanged, important reforms have been introduced in order to ensure that governments would be devoid of mechanisms with which to limit the independence of courts and judges. In 1976, a Supreme Judicial Council, composed entirely of judges elected by and among themselves, was entrusted with all decisions pertaining to the promotions, transfers, evaluation of and disciplinary action vis-à-vis judges. Six years later, however, the 1982 constitutional revision changed the composition of this Council in order to combine judges and political appointees, making sure that albeit career judges would be in the majority, those elected by their peers would be in the minority. This change resulted from the diagnosis that "judicial independence," as operationalized in the "judicial council" model, had produced several negative unintended consequences, including the insulation of judges from any kind of accountability for performance and the closure of the profession in relation to lateral entries from qualified lawyers outside the career.[75] These changes—and yet another constitutional amendment in 1997 that guaranteed that career judges would be a minority across the board in the Council—were accompanied by a steady increase in the powers, independence vis-à-vis the executive and competencies in the penal process of public prosecutors, further and further away from the initial post-transition model—once shared with countries like Spain or Greece—of a prosecution accountable to the executive, and closer and closer to the Italian model of full prosecutorial independence.[76]

In any case, the issue remains profoundly controversial in public and political debates. A "crisis of justice"—manifested in the rising number of pending processes, the decline in judicial productivity, the bias of the system's performance in favor of "repeat players," and the inability to effectively obtain condemnations in many cases of corruption and "white-collar crime" uncovered by the press—is detected by all political and judicial protagonists, and the insufficiency of the previous "macro-level" institutional changes to address these problems is also becoming evident. Today, the lack of human and material resources, the typically "corporatist" reaction to any proposed reforms that the judicial professions tend to adopt, and the successive governments' temptation to politicize the judicial system have, however, led to what appears to be a deadlock in the process of judicial reform that, from the point of view of citizens, has played no small role in breeding a growing mistrust vis-à-vis the judicial branch and the overall performance of courts.[77]

The last institutional dimension of the Portuguese political system that has been the object of recurrent political debate is the electoral system. The presentation by several of the major parties of proposals for changing electoral rules began in the early 1980s. By the end of the decade, a broad, albeit vague, consensus had formed about the need to reform the electoral system. This is particularly the case in what concerns the consequences of the use of the closed list system; it is blamed for providing little to no incentive towards the establishment of strong representation and accountability links between individual MPs and their constituents and for neutralizing the role of the former in parliament. On a different note, calls for the further reduction of the number of MPs, often of a blatantly populist nature, are also a more or less permanent fixture of Portuguese institutional debate.

Proposals for changes in electoral rules have ranged from splitting up the largest electoral districts and introducing some sort of preferential voting—potentially allowing voters a better knowledge of which MPs they are actually electing—to the adoption of a mixed-member proportional system, where single-member districts could be combined with low levels of disproportionality in the conversion of votes into seats.[78] These proposals have emanated from the largest parties themselves, although they have remained unable to agree on any major reform. In other words, although it would be far too extreme to say that electoral institutions are delegitimized in Portugal, it is clear that their present shape remains a fundamentally contested issue in the political realm. The ability to effect changes, however, has been limited by four factors: partisan fears about the unintended consequences of electoral reform for the allocation of seats; the constant overloading of the electoral reform agenda with many other unrelated issues; the potential disturbances in the organization of parties at the local level that a redrafting of districts might cause; and, perhaps more importantly, the lack of incentives for the leaderships of the main parties to abandon a closed list system that, after all, has brought them obvious advantages.[79]

Conclusion

This overview of the Portuguese political system has shown that a consolidated political regime has emerged within difficult historical circumstances. The first section, dedicated to explaining the historical circumstances in which the political institutions were conceived and embodied in the Constitution, illustrated the problems that political actors—and especially pluralist political parties—faced in building a liberal democratic regime. Despite these difficulties, the transition led to consolidation in 1982; and since 1987, the concentration of votes has led to a functional political system, which while preserving a multi-party system, has been able to produce stable government. However, the degree to which institutional reform has been an issue in Portuguese politics is an important indicator of the underlying tensions which subsist regarding the suitability, the efficacy and perhaps even the support for the political system as it exists. Future research on political institutions should accommodate its impact on political attitudes, thus to better understand the full consequences of the workings of the political system.

Notes

1. This chapter updates and develops an earlier overview of Portuguese Democracy published in French: "Le Portugal," in J.M. De Waele and P. Magnette (eds.), *Les démocraties européenes*, Paris: Armand Colin, 2008: 330-346.

2. Refer to A. C. Pinto, *Contemporary Portugal* (Boulder: Social Science Monographs, 2003).

3. Juan J. Lintz and Alfred Stepan, *Problems of Democratic Transition and Consolidation: Southern Europe, South America and Post-Communist Europe* (Baltimore: Johns Hopkins University Press, 1997) 117.

4. Katherine Hite and L. Morlino, "Problematizing the Links Between Authoritarian Legacies and 'Good' Democracy," in *Authoritarian Legacies and Democracy in Latin America and Southern Europe*, ed. Katherine Hite and Paola Cesarini (Notre Dame: University of Notre Dame Press, 2004), 47.

5. Refer to Juan J. Lintz, *Totalitarian and Authoritarian Regimes* (Boulder: Lynne Rienner, 2000).

6. T. Fernandes, *Nem Ditadura nem Revolução: A Ala Liberal no Marcelismo (1968-1974)* (Lisbon: D. Quixote, 2006).

7. See D. P. Cerezales, *O Poder Caiu na Rua: Crise de Estado e Acções Colectivas na Revolução Portugesa, 1974-1975* (Lisbon: Imprensa de Ciências Socais, 2003).

8. A. C. Pinto, "Authoritarian Legacies, Transitional Justice and State Crisis in Portugal's Democratization," *Democratization* 13, no. 2 (April 2006): 173-204.

9. L. Morlino, *Democracy Between Consolidation and Crisis: Parties, Groups and Citizens in Southern Europe* (Oxford: Oxford University Press, 1998), 19.

10. Phillipe C. Schmitter, "The Democratization of Portugal in its Comparative Perspective," in *Portugal e a Transicao para a Democracia*, ed. Fernando Rosas (Lisbon: Colibri, 1999), 360.

11. A. G. Pereira, *O Semipresidencialismo em Portugal*, (Lisboa: Ática, 1984).

12. N. S. Teixerira, "Between Africa and Europe: Portuguese Foreign Policy," in *Contemporary Portugal*, ed. António Costa Pinto (Boulder: Social Science Monographs, 2003): 84-118.

13. K. Maxwell, *The Making of Portuguese Democracy*, (Cambridge: Cambridge University Press, 1995).

14. G. Pridham, "European Integration and Democratic Consolidation in Southern Europe," in *Southern Europe and the Making of the European Union*, ed. António Costa Pinto and Nuno Severiano Texeira (Boulder: Social Science Monographs, 2003).

15. M. Duverger, "A New Political System Model: Semi-presidential Government," European Journal of Political Research 8, no. 2 (1980): 165-187.

16. See G. Sartori, *Comparative Constitutional Engineering* (London: MacMillan, 1994); R. Elgie, *Semi-Presidentialism in Europe* (Oxford: Oxford University Press, 1999); and A. Freire and António Costa Pinto, *O Poder dos Presidentes* (Lisbon: Campo da Comunicação, 2005).

17. Elgie, *Semi-Presidentialism*, 280-299.

18. L. Graham, "The Portuguese Transition to Democracy," in *Elite Settlements and Democratic Consolidation in Latin America and Southern Europe*, ed. F. Gunther and J. Higley (Cambridge: Cambridge University Press, 1992), 287.

19. A. Moreira, *O Novíssimo Principe*, (Braga: Editorial Intervenção, 1977), 76-83.

20. See M. B. Cruz, "O Presidente da Républica na Génese e Evolução do Sistema de Governo Português," *Análise Social* 4a, 29 no. 125-126 (1994): 237-267; and M. Lucena, "Semi-presidencialismo: o Caso Português," mimeo, 17.

21. Art. 148—1976 version.

22. Lintz and Stephan, *Problems of Democratic Transition*, (1997).

23. Until 1982 it was the Council of the Revolution which verified the constitutionality of the laws, whereas thereafter it was the Constitutional Court.

24. Art.185—1976 version.

25. Pires, (1989), 293.

26. Canotilho and Moreira, *Fundamentos da Constituição* (Coibra ed., 1991), 27.

27. Pasquino (1995), 277.

28. Sousa (1992), 63.

29. Art.195—1982 version.

30. Art. 136—1982 version.

31. Art. 17—1982 version.

32. A. Siaroff, "Comparative Presidencies: the Inadequacy of the Presidential, Semi-presidential, and Parliamentay Distinction," *European Journal of Political Research* 42, (2003): 287-312.

33. O. Amorim Neto and Marina Costa Lobo, "Portugal's Semi-Presidentialism (Re)considered: An assessment of the Role of the President in the Policy-making Process (1976-2006)" *European Journal of Political Research* 48, no. 2 (2009): 234-255.

34. See Marina Costa Lobo, "The *Presidentialisation* of Portuguese Democracy?" in *The Presidentialisation of Parliamentary Democracies?*, ed. P. Webb and T Poguntke (Oxford: Oxford University Press, 2005a), 269-289; and Marina Costa Lobo, *Governar em Democracia,* (Lisboa: ICS, 2005b).

35. O. Amorim Neto and Marina Costa Lobo, "Portugal's Semi-Presidentialism," (2009).

36. Pedro C. Magalhães, "Elections, Parties and Policy-making Institutions in Democratic Portugal," in *Contemporary Portugal*, ed. A. C. Pinto (Boulder: Social Science Monographs, 2003).

37. See J. Montabés and C. Ortega, "Candidate Selection in Two Rigid List Systems: Spain and Portugal," (paper prepared for presentation at the European Consortium for Political Research Joint Sessions, Mannhem, 1999); and Magalhães, "Elections, Parties," (2003).

38. A. Freire, "Elecciones y Comportamiento electoral en Portugal," in *Portugal: Democracia y Sistema Politico*, ed. A. Barreto, B. Gómez, and Pedro C. Magalhães (Madrid: Siglo XXI, 2003).

39. Arend Lijphart's measure of effective threshold is used. It is calculated by summing the two quotients derived from dividing 0.5 by constituency magnitude plus one and dividing 0.5 by twice the constituency magnitude. See Arendt Lijphart, *Electoral Systems and Party Systems: A Study of 27 Democracies, 1945-1990* (Oxford: Oxford University Press, 1994), 27.

40. S. Birch, "Electoral Systems and Party Systems in Europe, East and West," (paper presented at the first conference of the European Consortium for Political Research, Canterbury, 2001).

41. Disproportionality is the difference between party seat shares and their share of the vote, and it is measured here by the Gallagher least squares index. See M. Gallagher, "Proportionality, Disproportionality, and Electoral Systems," *Electoral Studies* 10, (1991): 33-51.

42. See M. Gallagher and M. Marsh, *Candidate Selection in Comparative Perspective: the Secret Garden of Politics* (London: Sage, 1988); J. M. Carey and M. S. Shugart, "Incentives to Cultivate a Personal Vote: A Rank Ordering of Electoral Formulas," *Electoral Studies* 14, (1995): 417-439; and P. Norris, "Legislative Recruitment," in *Comparing Democracies: Elections and Voting in Global Perspective*, ed. L. LeDuc, R. G. Niemi, and P. Norris (London: Sage, 1996), 184-215.

43. See M. B. Cruz, *Instituições Politicas e Processos Sociais* (Venda Nova: Bertrand, 1995); and A. Freire, *Recrutamento Parlamentar: os Deputadoes Portugueses da Constituinte á VIII Legislatura* (Lisbon: STAPE, 2001).

44. Refer to W. C. Opello, "Portugal's Parliament: an Organizational Analysis of Legislative Performance," *Legislative Studies Quarterly*, 11 (1986); Montabes and Ortega, "Candidate Selection" (1999); and C. Leston-Bandeira, *Da Legislação á Legitimação: o Papel do Parlamento Português* (Lisbon: ICS, 2002).

45. In the 2002 election, the PCP ran in a coalition with the Green Party, the PEV (*Partido Ecologista- Os Verdes*), which is entitled CDU (*Coligação Democrática Unitária*). The Green Party is a micro-party which exists essentially due to Communist organizational and political support.

46. T. Bruneau and A. Macleod, *Politics in Contemporary Portugal* (Colorado: Lynne Rienner, 1986), 87.

47. T Bruneau, *Political Parties in Portugal* (Oxford: Westview, 1997).

48. A. Bosco, "Four Actors in Search of a Role: The Southern European Communist Parties," in *Parties, Politics, and Democracy in the New Southern Europe*, ed. P. N. Diamandouros and Richard Gunther (Baltimore: Johns Hopkins University Press, 2001).

49. See also Annex 2 for legislative election results between 1976 and 2005.

50. The effective number of parliamentary parties is derived from the following formula: $N = 1/\Sigma\ s_i^{\ 2}$ In which s_i is the proportion of Assembly seats won by the ith party. This formula was developed by M. Laakso and R. Taagepera, (1979), op. cit.

51. A. Freire and Maria Costa Lobo, "The Portuguese 2005 Legislative Election: Return to the Left," *West European Politics* 29, no. 3 (2006): 581-588.

52. See Marina Costa Lobo, (1996); and Pedro C. Magalhães, "Elections, Parties and Policy," (2003).

53. Gunther and Montero, "The Anchors of Partisanship: A Comparative Analysis of Voting Behaviour in Four Southern European Democracies," in *Parties, Politics, and Democracy in the New Southern Europe* (Baltimore: Johns Hopkins University Press, 2001).

54. A. Freire et al., *O Parlamento Português: Uma Reforma Necessária* (Lisbon: ICS, 2002).

55. See Maria Costa Lobo, "The Role of Parties in Portuguese Democratic Consolidation," *Party Politics* 7, no. 5 (2001); and Freire and Pinto, *O Poder dos Presidentes* (2005).

56. Freire et al., *O Parlamento*, (2002), 66.

57. Freire et al., *O Parlamento*, (2002).

58. Marina Costa Lobo (2005a, 2005b).

59. M. Schmidt, "The Impact of Political Parties, Constitutional Structures and Veto Players on Public Policy," in *Comparative Democratic Politics*, ed. H Keman (London: Sage, 2002), 174.

60. Refer to Arendt Lijphart, *Comparing Democracies* (New Haven: Yale University Press, 1999); George Tsebelis, *Veto Players: How Political Institutions Work* (New York: Princeton University Press, 2002); and Manfred Schmidt, "When Parties Matter: A Review of Possibilities and Limits of Partisan Influence on Public Policy," *European Journal of Political Research* 30 (1996): 155-183.

61. Tsebelis, *Veto Players.*

62. See the original work in 1996— Schmidt, "When Parties Matter"; and also Schmidt, "The Impact of Political Parties," 178.

63. Schmidt, "The Impact," 174.

64. Amorim Neto and Costa Lobo, "Portugal's Semi-Presidentialism."

65. Pedro C. Magalhães, "Elections, Parties and Policy…" 199-200.

66. Refer to E. Serrano, *As Presidências Bertas de Mário Soares: As Estratégias e o Aparelho do Comunicação do Presidente da República* (Coimbra: Minerva, 2002); A. Araujo, "El Presidente de la República en la Evolución del Sistema Político de Portugal," in *Portugal: Democracia y Sistema Político*, ed. A Barreto, Gomez Fortes, and Pedro C. Magalhães (Madrid: Siglo Veintiuno, 2003): 145-175; and Maria Lobo (2005a, 2005b).

67. D. S. Lutz, "Toward a Theory of Constitutional Amendment," *American Political Science Review* 88 (1994): 363.

68. The other countries which form part of the same group as Portugal include: Austria, Botswana, Brazil, Germany, India, Kenya, Malaysia, New Zealand, Papua New Guinea and Samoa. According to the same author, the size of the majority needed does not have an impact on the amendment rate of constitutions in his sample (thirty-two democracies with a written constitution).

48   Marina Costa Lobo, António Costa Pinto, and Pedro Magalhães

69. See G. Esping-Andersen, "Budgets and Democracy," *Developing Democracy—Essays in Honour of Jean Blondel*, ed. I. Budge and D. McKay (London: Sage, 1994); J. S. Lopes, "A Economia Portuguesa desde 1960," in *A Situação Social em Portugal*, ed. A. Barreto and C. V. e Preto (Lisboa: ICS, 1996); and Maria Costa Lobo, (2005a and 2005b).

70. Of course, the role of the state in market intervention changed radically in 1974 with the nationalizations undertaken at the time, which have been partially undone since 1989. Here however, we refer only to the direct state expenditure in public bodies not in public companies.

71. M. R. Sousa, *História (Política) da Revisão Constitucional de 1997 e do Referendo da Regionalização* (Lisboa: Bertrand, 1999), 36.

72. See J. S. Lopes, *Portugal and EC Membership Evaluated* (London: Pinter, 1991); and P. Lains and Maria Costa Lobo, *Em Nome da Europa: Portugal e Mudanca 1986-2006* (Cascais: Principa, forthcoming).

73. Pedro C. Magalhães, "The Institutional Framework of the Transition to Democracy in Portugal," in *The Transition to Democracy in Spain, Portugal, and Greece Thirty Years After*, ed. M. Minotos (Athens: Konstantinos G. Karamanlis Foundation, 2006).

74. See Shugart and Carey, *Presidents and Assemblies* (Cambridge: Cambridge University Press,1992), 24.

75. Pedro C. Magalhães (1995).

76. Pedro C. Magalhães, C. Guarnieri, and Y Kaminis, "Democratic Consolidation, Judicial Reform, and the Judicialization of Politics in Southern Europe," in *Democracy and the State in the New Southern Europe* (Oxford: Oxford University Press, 2006)

77. Magalhães, "Elections, Parties and Policy-making."

78. See Cruz (1998); Freire et al., *O Parlamento Português*; and Freire et al., (2008).

79. Magalhães, "Elections, Parties and Policy-making"; and N. Sampaio, *O Sistema Eleitoral Português: Crónica de Uma Reforma Adiada* (Lisbon: Alethea, 2009).

3 Portugal's Semi-Presidentialism (Re)Considered: An Assessment of the President's Role in the Policy Process, 1976-2006

Octavio Amorim Neto and Marina Costa Lobo[1]

This chapter investigates the policy-making role of Portugal's heads of state in the country's semi-presidential regime from 1976 to 2006. This is significant not only because Portugal is one of the world's oldest and most successful semi-presidential democracies, but also because there is an unresolved academic controversy regarding the most appropriate definition of its system of government. Moreover, there is a glaring gap in the comparative politics literature on Portugal in today's scientific *lingua franca*—that is, English. For example, the wide-ranging volume *Semi-Presidentialism in Europe*, edited by Elgie (1999), conspicuously does not feature a chapter on Portugal. This is ultimately due to this nation's small size and small political science community (including foreign experts on the country). Here we set out to fill this gap.

In the wake of the Third Wave of democratization, which began with Portugal's Revolution of the Carnations in 1974,[2] semi-presidentialism has become the most prevalent political regime in Europe, the continent historically associated with parliamentarism.[3] Thus, there is now an acute need to understand how semi-presidentialism works. When the Portuguese president is considered, some influential studies have tended to downplay his role within the political system.[4]

These studies contend that Portugal should not be placed alongside semi-presidential regimes, but should rather be considered a parliamentary system.[5] The rationale for this classification is that party system changes in the mid-1980s gave rise to single-party parliamentary majorities and cabinets, which in turn considerably strengthened the prime minister (henceforth PM or premier) within the executive branch to the detriment of the president, whose constitutional prerogatives had also been curtailed in 1982.

We consider this rationale to be inaccurate. Based on the work of Lobo, we argue that the growing power of the premier has derived largely from the reorganization of the executive branch and the "governamentalization" of parties—not from any major decrease in presidential powers.[6] These developments have certainly contributed to solidify the position of the PM. However, the president has retained some key constitutional powers that render him politically relevant at all times, despite the curtailing of some of his prerogatives in 1982. Moreover, government instability in 1999 to 2005 showed how politically important he can still be. Indeed, in 2004, socialist president Jorge Sampaio announced that he would dissolve parliament and call fresh elections, regardless of the fact that the Assembly of the Republic had a working majority of two right-wing parties. The last time a Portuguese president had taken such an initiative had occurred under a similar cohabitation in 1982.

There are two plausible reasons why some scholars have inaccurately classified Portugal as a parliamentary system: lack of precise information on the extent and details of presidential powers and overemphasis on the aggrandizement of the premiership within the political system from 1982 onwards. The first reason is particularly compelling regarding comparativists. For example, in the updated Portuguese edition of his classic *Democracies*, Lijphart devotes only one paragraph to Portugal's system of government, and states that, although the 1976 Constitution had been modeled on the French one, in 1982 the president's powers were "severely" reduced, and the country "returned" to a parliamentary system.[7] Note that this paragraph does not cite any book or article to support its contention. Interestingly enough, Sartori, also without citing any scholarly work, writes that "turning to Portugal, this is a case that can be dealt with quickly, for its semi-presidential experience was short lived: six years between 1976 and 1982."[8] Then, in a footnote, he mistakenly asserts that "the 1982 Portuguese constitution eliminates the presidential power to dismiss cabinets or ministers . . . and all his legislative powers; and restricts the president's power to dissolve parliament as well as his pocket veto on legislation. By and large, the Portuguese president is thus left, from 1982 onward, with little more than the normal powers of normal parliamentary presidents."[9]

The paragraph above makes it crystal clear that more scholarly work (in English) on the evolution of presidential power in Portugal is urgently needed. In this chapter, we propose to contribute to this agenda. Initially, we survey the existing literature on the role of the Portuguese president in the policy process, and provide an overview of the constitutional articles that underpin presidential power and how they have evolved. Then new data on the Portuguese chief of state's role in the policy process will be presented and discussed. We will focus on the president's role in cabinet appointment and dismissal; his powers to dissolve parliament; his influence over ministerial appointments; his prerogatives to refer legislative bills to prior judicial review; his veto powers; and his influence over agenda-setting through going-public tactics. Our conclusion stresses that Portugal remains solidly semi-presidential because the president still plays a relevant role in the policy process.

Portugal's Semi-Presidentialism in the Comparative Politics Literature

In Duverger's pioneering article, Portugal, together with the Weimar Republic and Finland, was characterized as a regime in which there was a balance between the presidency and the cabinet. In these three regimes, the constitution approximated political practice to the greatest extent, that is, with an effective power-sharing between the two organs of the executive branch.[10]

Subsequent studies have shown that dispositional differences regarding presidential powers and separation of assembly and cabinet survival are crucial for the characterization of sub-types within the semi-presidential family.[11] Let us delve into Shugart and Carey's influential treatise (1992). Initially, they quantitatively assess presidents' formal powers through ordinal scales. Presidential powers are divided in two categories: legislative powers and non-legislative powers. The overall measure of presidential power is the sum of the scores on six legislative powers and four non-legislative powers. Then Shugart and Carey distinguish between two types of semi-presidential systems: *premier*-presidential and president-parliamentary.

Premier-presidential regimes grant a popularly elected chief of state narrow powers over the cabinet and are also characterized by the separation of assembly and cabinet survival. The president has the power to appoint the PM, who, in turn, appoints the rest of the cabinet. The assembly, however, retains the power to dismiss the PM and the cabinet through a no-confidence vote. The French Fifth Republic is the prototypical *premier*-presidential regime.

President-parliamentary systems provide the chief of state with extensive powers over the cabinet (appointment and dismissal), but there is no separation of assembly and cabinet survival, for the assembly can also dismiss the cabinet. This is the only executive type under which the cabinet can be dismissed by both the head of state and the assembly. The Weimar Republic is the classic case of a president-parliamentary regime.

As regards Portugal, Shugart and Carey distinguish between the period before and after the 1982 constitutional revision, a key moment that will be discussed in detail below. Between 1976 and 1982, the powers of the president add up to nine, whereas since the 1982 constitutional reform the authors consider them to have decreased to six. Therefore, in the first period Portugal is characterized as belonging to the president-parliamentary type, and since 1982, to the *premier*-presidential category.[12]

More recently, Alan Siaroff (2003) analyzed nine key presidential powers in a host of countries where presidents are directly elected. Whereas Shugart and Carey had counted only constitutional powers, Siaroff included both constitutional and de facto powers. According to his scale, Portugal scores six in 1976-1982, and three since 1982. While in the former period the country's score is among the highest within the semi-presidential group of countries, in the latter the Portuguese president falls into an intermediate range. Thus, Siaroff and Shugart and Carey agree on the decrease in presidential powers since 1982. Overall, this finding has been widely corroborated by case studies, although there are a few exceptions (for example, Matos 1983).[13]

Despite this fundamental agreement on the decline of presidential powers after 1982, there are differences as to how to classify the post-1982 regime. As mentioned in the first section, in 1994 Sartori subtracted Portugal from the original list put forward by Duverger (because of the constitutional changes effected in 1982) on the ground that in practice the country worked like a parliamentary democracy.[14] Others have partly concurred with Sartori, arguing that the 1982 constitutional reforms made the regime "more semi-parliamentary and less semi-presidential:"[15] or that the country had a "parliamentary government conditioned by a presidential element."[16] Most authors, however, do contend that the regime remains semi-presidential.[17]

We strongly argue in favor of a constitutional reading of the semi-presidential nature of the regime, for Portuguese presidents have remained active and influential even at times of stable majority cabinets and are crucial players in times of government instability, as occurred between 2002 and 2004. This is what we will show below.

The President's Constitutional Powers

The choice of a semi-presidential system in 1976 arose from the need to reward the military for their role in the transition period, also reflecting recent political history and political culture.[18] The toppling of the authoritarian regime in 1974 was staged not by political parties but by a group of military officers, the *Movimento das Forças Armadas* (Armed Forces Movement, MFA for short).[19] Between 1974 and the promulgation of the Constitution in 1976, the MFA, allied with various left-wing groups, was the most important political actor amid great institutional uncertainty and fledgling parties.[20] Indeed, the Constituent Assembly, elected in April 1975, worked in tandem with a committee composed of the political parties and the MFA. Both agreed to a so-called Second Pact. All key items contained in this pact, signed in February 1976, were then incorporated into the final constitutional agreement, which the Constituent Assembly ratified.

As regards the presidency, the Second Pact stipulated that the chief of state should be directly elected. There was also a so-called "implicit" clause that emerged from the discussions about the Second Pact whereby the first president would be a military officer,[21] thus granting the head of state the possibility of embodying both revolutionary and electoral legitimacy. Not only would that military officer be elected, he would also be Supreme Commander of the Armed Forces (art. 137) and preside over the Council of Revolution (art. 136). This sovereign body, composed solely of military officers, had exclusive legislative powers over military issues (art. 149) and acted as a *sui generis* Constitutional Council (art. 146). By presiding over the Council of the Revolution, the chief of state became the ultimate guarantor of the Constitution.

Beyond these important powers, the president could withdraw political confidence from the cabinet and thus force its resignation, given that the cabinet was politically accountable to both the president and the Assembly (art. 194). Also, the president nominated the PM, after "taking into account election results" (arts. 136 and 190). According to the 1976 Constitution, a newly formed cabinet did not have to receive a motion of confidence from the Assembly, a passive non-rejection by the Assembly sufficing for investing the cabinet.

To dismiss the government, two motions of censure had to be approved by an absolute majority of the MPs within a thirty-day period (art. 198). The cabinet had to resign if its program was rejected by a simple majority in the Assembly, or a motion of confidence was not approved. However, the Assembly would be dissolved by the president if the former rejected the governmental program three consecutive times, or, alternatively, if the Assembly unseated a third cabinet (art. 196). Coupled with the chief of state's revolutionary legitimacy, these provisions contributed decisively to strengthen presidential powers and restrict the government's accountability to the Assembly.

The president's legislative powers were rather wide-ranging. Beyond the legislative powers that presiding over the Council of the Revolution gave him— over military issues and the constitutionality of laws—the president had specific powers over foreign policy. Article 138 stipulated that the president ratified international treaties and had the power to declare war and make peace after approval by the Council of the Revolution. He could also declare a state of emergency. In addition, he was given veto power over Assembly-approved bills and decree-laws issued by the cabinet, under certain conditions (art. 278). A presidential veto could not be overturned if the vetoed bill had been initiated by the cabinet, although it could be re-proposed as an Assembly-initiated bill. When it came to Assembly-initiated bills, presidential vetoes could be overturned through a second roll-call vote by an absolute or a two-thirds majority of MPs, depending on the content of the bill. The president could also request that the constitutionality of either parliamentary or government bills be verified, either *ex ante* or *ex post*, by the Council of the Revolution.

Finally, under the 1976 Constitution, the president had other important powers. On the PM's proposal, he appointed all members of the cabinet, the president of the *Tribunal de Contas* (accounts tribunal), the *Procurador Geral da República* (attorney general), and the state representatives in the autonomous regions (Madeira and Azores archipelagos). The regional governments elected in Azores and Madeira could be unseated by the president in certain circumstances.

In 1982 the Constitution was reformed so as to curtail the powers of the president and the military's role in the political system.[22] The most important change effected by the reform was the dissolution of the Council of the Revolution, which meant the subordination of the armed forces to civilian control—the final step in the consolidation of democracy in Portugal.[23] In its place, a *tribunal constitucional* (constitutional court) was created, with its judges being appointed by parliamentary parties. This court was granted the power to verify the constitutionality of laws and epitomized the civilianization of the regime.

Concerning the relationship between cabinet and the president, the most important change was that while the cabinet was still accountable to both the Assembly and president, it was now *politically* responsible only to the former. This meant that, in stark contrast to the original draft, the president could no longer dismiss the cabinet by invoking a lack of confidence. Yet note that this presidential power was only circumscribed, not eliminated, unlike what Shugart and Carey suggest.[24] Indeed, the president could still dismiss the cabinet in exceptional political circumstances "to ensure the regular functioning of democratic institutions." The vagueness of this article suggests that under certain conditions—in times of political instability—the president retains the prerogative to unseat the cabinet.

The change in presidential powers was accompanied by an increase in parliament's powers vis-à-vis the cabinet. There was a simplification of the procedures to unseat a government. Now passing only one (instead of two in less than thirty days) motion of censure sufficed to bring the cabinet down (art. 198). It was also established that there would be a caretaker cabinet until the incoming cabinet's program was approved by parliament (art.189), thus enhancing the accountability of the cabinet to parliament. From 1982 onwards, it was no longer after the president's nomination of the PM and the rest of the ministers, but with the approval of the governmental program, that the cabinet constitutionally came into being.[25] Thus, a previously existing loophole—whereby it was sufficient for the Assembly *not* to reject the cabinet for the latter to be invested—was eliminated. From 1982 onwards the presentation of the program to the Assembly had to be followed by a vote of confidence on the new cabinet (art. 195). Finally, the exclusive lawmaking domains of the Assembly were extended (arts. 167 and 168), there also being a greater specification of the terms upon which parliament could delegate legislative power to the cabinet.

Thus, the president's veto power was strengthened, because it became harder to overturn vetoes in a host of policy areas.[26] However, the president's pocket veto over both Assembly-initiated bills and cabinet-issued decree-laws was eliminated. This type of veto consisted of the ability to delay the promulgation of bills and decrees. The president also kept his powers over international relations, states of emergency, the appointment of higher officials, and the Madeira and Azores governments. More recently, the 1989 reform gave the chief of state the prerogative to refuse referenda proposed either by MPs or the cabinet. A president's refusal kills the proposal, which cannot be tabled for the remainder of the legislative term, except if new elections are held or the cabinet is dismissed.

In short, the president's constitutional powers were indeed curtailed in 1982. The head of state's legislative powers were reduced through the elimination of the Council of Revolution as well as of his pocket veto. The president's influence over the policy process thus shrank, as he could no longer freely dismiss the cabinet, except in special circumstances. However, the president, who continued to be chief of the armed forces, retained considerable powers, including the appointment and dismissal (under special circumstances) of the cabinet, the dissolution of the Assembly, the power of referral of bills to the Constitutional Court, veto powers, and the power to appoint the holders of certain key offices in the public administration and in some political bodies, as specified above. It is the exercise of these powers from 1976 to 2006 to which we now turn.

The Power to Appoint and Dismiss the Cabinet and Dissolve Parliament

The Portuguese Constitution stipulates that the president nominates the PM while "taking into account elections results" (art. 136). This suggests that the head of state can become a decisive cabinet *formateur* if legislative elections do not produce a clear-cut outcome.

Since Portugal democratized in 1976, four parties have dominated the country's politics. With the exception of the Portuguese Communist Party (PCP), which was founded in 1921, all the others were created shortly before or after 1974. The Socialist Party (PS) was founded in 1973, the center-right Social Democratic Party (PSD) and the conservative Social Democratic Center/Popular Party (CDS/PP), shortly after the April 1974 Revolution. These four parties have averaged 90.6 percent of the vote over the past thirty years. However, the centrist parties, the PS and the PSD, have steadily controlled a larger percentage of parliamentary seats, while the communists and the conservative CDS-PP have been declining. The effective number of parliamentary parties has decreased from 3.2 between 1976 and 1987 to 2.4 since 1987 (see Table 3.1). This defragmentation of the Portuguese party system had a decisive impact on the duration of governments, which increased from the mid-1980s on.

During the first ten years of democracy there were ten constitutional cabinets, with none completing a full parliamentary term. After two short-lived governments fell due to lack of party support, in 1978, President Eanes decided to tinker with the so-called "presidentially-inspired" cabinets. These were administrations composed mostly of non-partisan figures. None of them lasted long, however, because they had no stable parliamentary support. Those cabinets were opposed by the major parliamentary groups, which saw them as overt attempts to undermine both party and parliamentary control of government. Not surprisingly, the 1978 to 1979 period witnessed the formation of a solid inter-party consensus on the need to curtail presidential powers.

The cabinets from 1979 to 1983 had a stable right-wing legislative majority. However, the death of the premier in 1980 led to the formation of a new government which was considerably weaker and ultimately led PM Balsemão to try to find a replacement in December 1982. President Eanes rejected this alternative, deciding instead to dissolve parliament and call elections for January 1983. Note that this rejection by Eanes took place just after the 1982 constitutional reform. It indicates the extent to which the power to appoint the PM was maintained despite the reform.

Yet Eanes did not wield such power again. The next president, Mário Soares (1986-1996), the first civilian elected to the office, mostly faced majority cabinets that completed full parliamentary terms (1987-1995). When in 1987 the minority PSD government fell on a successful motion of censure initiated by left-wing parties, Soares refused to appoint a socialist PM, preferring to dissolve parliament and call fresh elections. Thus, the president's reading of the Constitution, together with strong centripetal changes in electoral behaviour in the mid-1980s, seemed to suggest that the president's role as *formateur* had become redundant.

However, recent political developments under the Sampaio presidency (1996-2006) show that such a role can reemerge once governments prove to be weak, as they did between 2001 and 2005. After a mediocre result in local elections for the Socialist Party in 2001, premier Guterres resigned. President Sampaio decided to dissolve parliament and fresh legislative elections were held in 2002.[27]

Those elections were won by the center-right PSD, but without an absolute majority of seats, thus prompting the party to form a coalition with the CDS-PP. Against the background of a deepening economic crisis and divergence from the EU average, PM Durão Barroso announced in 2004 that he was resigning his office to become president of the European Union's Commission. Sampaio accepted Durão Barroso's chosen successor, Santana Lopes, then mayor of Lisbon, on the grounds that "as long as the government produced by the legislative elections continues to display consistency, political will and legitimacy, the resignation of the prime minister per se is not a sufficient reason to . . . hold snap elections."[28] Four months later, following the resignation of a minister, Sampaio decided to dissolve parliament on the claim that the government was ineffective.[29] Unlike the power to dismiss the government, which was to be used after 1982 only to "ensure the regular functioning of institutions," the power to dissolve parliament remained unconstrained since 1976, thus necessitating no formal justification. The president's two key decisions in 2004—to invite the mayor of Lisbon to form a government and then, to unseat him—were a strong reminder that, despite constitutional changes, the role of the president in the appointment and dismissal of cabinets and the dissolution of parliament remains crucial in times of government instability. President Sampaio's last term (2001-2006), in particular, illustrates the way whereby the chief of state can become pivotal once the government is perceived as weak.

The Strengthening of the Premier at the Expense of Cabinet Ministers

The 1982 constitutional reforms surely curtailed some presidential prerogatives. Moreover, the fifteen years following those reforms also witnessed the growing power of the premier. It was the undeniable aggrandizement of the premiership within the political system that led many analysts to declare semi-presidentialism dead in Portugal and proclaim the country a parliamentary system. This analytical step supposed a zero-sum game between the two heads of the executive branch. Based on the work of Lobo,[30] we argue that this is inaccurate.

Lobo shows that the growing power of the premier has derived largely from the reorganization of the executive branch and the "governamentalization" of parties, not from any major decrease in presidential powers. Thus, a proper assessment of the distribution of actual power in a semi-presidential democracy should take into account the relative policy influence of three distinct players within the political system; namely (a) the head of state, (b) the premier, and (c) cabinet ministers. Under such a scheme, if one assumes that total policy influence always adds up to a constant (say, one), it is therefore possible that an increase in b's influence does not necessarily lead to a decrease in a's. That is what happened in Portugal after 1982, as we shall show below.

Let it be stated again that political developments after 1982 have certainly contributed to solidify the premier's position. The growth of prime ministerial power in Portugal can be understood from an analysis of the policy-making instruments the head of government has at her disposal. In essence, the resources available to the premier have been strengthened—particularly since 1987—through the reorganization of the PM's office, the increase in support structures, and the appointment of ministers without portfolio to oversee other ministers' work.

Besides the resources at the disposal of the PM vis-à-vis other cabinet members, it is important to ask whether the working methods in government tend to be collective or individual. This is a relevant question for this section, because prime ministerial power is enhanced if the methods are individual.

Available research shows that the cabinet has generally not been the preferred venue for strategic political coordination. Instead, political decision-making takes place in an inner cabinet, formed around the premier, and including mostly senior party members. Note that most inner cabinet members are also senior party members. Thus, policymaking has remained collective in Portuguese cabinets, even if it is not open to all cabinet members. This also means that parties continue to be the key agents in the policy process, given that practically all members of inner cabinets are senior party members.

It is important to stress, however, that the main governing parties—the PS and the PSD—have become governmentalized. By governmentalization of parties, we refer to the process by which the party leadership bodies become increasingly composed of government members when the party holds executive offices.[31] This control of the party's executive bodies by the PM and her cabinet serves to minimize the party's independent input in governmental affairs.

Thus, it is clear that after 1985, there was a successful attempt to strengthen the core executive by solidifying the position of the premier, to the detriment of cabinet ministers. Nevertheless, the role of the president has remained important because he is the cabinet *formateur* at times of government instability, and has preserved important instruments to intervene in the policy process, as we shall see below.

Presidential Influence over Ministerial Appointments

Ministerial appointments are the core personnel decisions in systems in which the cabinet is accountable to the legislature.[32] Traditionally in Europe, such appointments have been virtually monopolized by the governing political parties. Under semi-presidentialism, however, as recently argued by Amorim Neto and Strøm (2006), ministerial appointments may instead become a tug-of-war between a premier and a president with different partisan preferences, depending on their political circumstances and bargaining power.[33] During times of unified government, cabinet formation bargaining between the president and the premier is made easier because both prefer to appoint co-partisans. However, during cohabitation, presidents prefer their co-partisans to the ones in the premier's party (or coalition), or favor non-partisan ministers as a second best option. Thus, Amorim Neto and Strøm (henceforth ANS) contend that the proportion of non-partisan cabinet ministers is a measure that well captures the actual influence of the head of state, be he either popularly elected or parliament-selected, over the policy process.

Based on a sample of 134 European cabinets representing twelve semi-presidential and twelve purely parliamentary regimes in the 1990s, ANS show that the incidence of non-partisan appointments rises with electoral volatility and is higher under minority than under majority governments. There is also support for the hypotheses that non-partisan cabinet members are more common under presidents who are popularly elected and possess more extensive legislative powers. Finally, the authors find significant evidence that the heightened efficiency concerns that might accompany an economic crisis consistently and surprisingly lower the incidence of non-partisan appointments. Evidence from Por-

Table 3.1 Key political and economic attributes of executives and parliaments in Portugal, 1976-2006

President and his Party	Cabinet (begin date)	Parties	Size of Legislative Support (1)	Electoral Volatility (1)	Legislative Fragmentation (2)	Type of Cabinet	Recession in the previous year? (3)	Share of Non-Partisan Ministers (4)
	Mário Soares (Jul 1976)	PS	40.7	11.3	3.4	Minority	yes	27.8
	Mário Soares (Jan 1978)	PS and CDS	56.7	11.3	3.4	Majority	no	12.5
Ramalho Eanes (Military Officer, Non-partisan)	Nobre da Costa (Aug 1978)	N.A.	0	11.3	3.4	Minority	no	100
	Mota Pinto (Nov 1978)	N.A.	0	11.3	3.4	Minority	no	100
	Lurdes Pintassilgo (Jul 1979)	N.A.	0	11.3	3.4	Minority	yes	100
	Sá Carneiro (Jan 1980)	PSD, CDS, PPM	51.2	10.5	3.9	Majority	no	7.1
	Pinto Balsemão (Jan 1981)	PSD, CDS, PPM	53.6	4.6	4.0	Majority	no	11.1
	Pinto Balsemão (Sep 1981)	PSD, CDS, PPM	53.6	4.6	4.0	Majority	no	6.7
	Mário Soares (Jun 1983)	PS and PSD	70.4	11.2	3.3	Majority	yes	5.9
Mário Soares (PS)	Cavaco Silva (Nov 1985)	PSD	35.2	22.5	4.2	Minority	no	20.0
	Cavaco Silva (Aug 1987)	PSD	59.2	23.2	2.4	Majority	no	5.9
	Cavaco Silva (Oct 1991)	PSD	58.7	9.5	2.2	Majority	yes	16.7
Jorge Sampaio (PS)	A. Guterres (Oct 1995)	PS	48.7	18.2	2.5	Minority	no	42.1
	A. Guterres (Oct 1999)	PS	50.0	3.9	2.6	Minority	no	22.7
	Durão Barroso (Apr 2002)	PSD and CDS/PP	51.8	8.8	2.6	Majority	yes	20.0
	Santana Lopes (Jul 2004-Mar 2005)	PSD and CDS/PP	51.8	8.8	2.6	Majority	yes	34.8

Sources: (1) Magalhães (2003), Gunther and Montero (2001); (2) Freire and Lobo (2006); (3) The measure of recession is based on Alesina and Perotti (1995). According to this measure, a country is in recession in year t if its growth rate in t is 1% below the average growth rate in the previous two years. Economic data was culled from OECD Factbook 2006; and (4) Lobo (2000) and Guedes (2004).

tugal in 1976 though 2004 fits nicely with most of the hypotheses put forward by ANS (see Table 3.1).

In 1976 to 1982, when the system of government was president-parliamentary, and the president was therefore very strong, we observe the highest shares of non-partisan cabinet members for the whole 1976 to 2004 period. After 1982, when the regime became *premier*-presidential, the type of cabinet (majority versus minority) became the overriding factor in determining the level of partisanship, with minority cabinets displaying a higher average of non-partisan cabinet members (28.3 percent) than majority administrations (16.7 percent), as expected by ANS. Interestingly, after 1982, cabinets appointed one year after a recession have on average a lower share of non-partisans than cabinets invested one year after an economic expansion, thus confirming ANS's non-intuitive hypothesis.

The President's Veto and Referral Powers

In this section we empirically assess how Portuguese presidents have been wielding what many analysts consider to be the touchstones of their constitutional prerogatives, namely their veto and referral powers. Recall that the president's veto power was actually enhanced by the 1982 revision. Since then the veto has been one of the hallmarks of presidential power and should be understood as a kind of *ex post* mechanism to control the cabinet and parliament.[34] For example, President Mário Soares, a socialist, vetoed key policy initiatives of the centrist cabinets led by PM Cavaco Silva, with whom Soares "cohabited" during his two terms in office.[35] By using his veto powers—which he did particularly frequently during his second term—Soares was able to push Cavaco Silva's policy initiatives closer to the preferences of the median voter in the presidential election, which leaned to the left. Such evidence makes it crystal-clear that Portuguese presidents must be seen as more than figureheads. They actually affect government policy by exercising their formal powers and political clout. In sum, despite the 1982 constitutional revision, presidents have managed to retain an important policy-making role, albeit a negative one, mainly due to their ability to block the governmental agenda through the use of the veto.

Table 3.2 displays the number of vetoes issued per president and legislature, along with the total number of laws passed. It is clear that Mário Soares, who had to endure cohabitation cabinets during all his ten years in office, was the president with the highest number of political vetoes and the highest average of vetoes per laws passed. This clearly shows that Portuguese presidents who are politically at odds with the premier have the wherewithal to make themselves heard in the policy process.

Table 3.2 Presidential vetoes per president and legislature

President	Legislature	Largest cabinet parties	N of laws passed	Political vetoes and constitutionality-related vetoes	Average vetoes per N of laws passed	Average by president
Eanes	1976-1980	PS*	341	10	2.9	
	1980-1983	PSD-CDS	119	5	4.2	2.1
	1983-1985	PS-PSD	303	1	0.3	
Soares	1985-1987	PSD	163	3	1.8	
	1987-1991	PSD	405	10	2.5	2.9
	1991-1995	PSD	305	12	3.9	
Sampaio	1995-1999	PS	479	5	1.0	
	1999-2002	PS	198	6	3.0	2.3
	2002-2005	PSD-CDS	250	10	4.0	

Source: Division of Legislative and Parliamentary Information at the Assembly of the Republic, Dossier decretos, vetos, mensagens do Presidente da República e Leis, Colecção Legislação, n° 35, 2005.
Notes: *Together with the CDS in the 2nd cabinet.

The other significant negative power Portuguese presidents have is their ability to refer parliament- and cabinet-initiated bills or cabinet-issued decrees for prior judicial review by the Constitutional Tribunal. As seen above, this prerogative was created in 1982. Upon a president's request, the Tribunal must, within twenty days, rule whether a bill passed by the Assembly or a cabinet decree is constitutional.

The president-activated Constitutional Tribunal has been active in Portugal's political life. According to Magone, the Tribunal has reviewed important pieces of legislation supported by sizeable legislative majorities, such as the anti-corruption law, the law on incompatibilities, and the Official Secrets Act, all passed in 1993 under the second majority single-party cabinet led by Cavaco Silva.[36] Thus, the president's referral power is a relevant check on parliamentary majorities in Portugal, thus providing further evidence on the president's key role in the policy process.

Table 3.3 Constitutional referral of laws per president*

	Parliament-Initiated Laws	Cabinet-Initiated Laws	Total per Mandate	Total per President
Soares I	11 (8)	5 (5)	16 (13)	43 (30)
Soares II	17 (14)	10 (3)	27 (17)	
Sampaio I	3 (2)	2 (1)	5 (3)	16 (11)
Sampaio II	8 (8)	3 (0)	11 (8)	
Total	39 (32)	20 (9)	59 (41)	59(41)

Source: Documentation provided by the Presidency of the Republic.
Note: * In brackets are the laws that were considered unconstitutional.

Table 3.3 reports the number of parliament- and cabinet-initiated bills referred to the Constitutional Tribunal by Mário Soares and Jorge Sampaio, along
with the number of laws that were actually deemed unconstitutional. Again,
Soares referred 250 percent more laws to the Tribunal than Sampaio (forty-three
versus sixteen), although the frequency with which referred laws were deemed
unconstitutional is basically the same for both (around 70 percent). In short, veto
and referral powers give Portuguese presidents a considerable say in policymaking.

Framing the Political Agenda through "Going Public Tactics"

Portuguese presidents have another relevant way to influence the policy process
in addition to the direct use of their constitutional prerogatives, namely going
public tactics. This aspect of presidential activism has been completely ignored
but for the work of Serrano (2002). Walking in this author's footsteps, this section delves into what in the Portuguese political jargon is called "open presidencies," originally conceived by President Soares and maintained both by Sampaio
and more recently by Cavaco Silva, under different designations. An "open presidency" would take place when the chief of state would spend a considerable
amount of time in a given region (usually two weeks) and quasi-officially turn
the latter into the seat of the presidency. This sort of political tour would then
attract a lot of media attention—regionally and nationally—thus enabling the
president to informally frame the country's political agenda.

In the vast literature on U.S. presidents, it is often argued that the latter "go
public" and use the pressure of popular opinion to prompt Congress to approve
their policy initiatives. Kernell (1993) offers one of the best accounts of why and
how U.S. presidents employ "going public strategies" to get more leverage with
an opposition Congress: U.S. presidents go public to overcome political fragmentation in Washington, DC. In a similar vein, Linz contends that Latin American presidents do roughly the same when they resort to plebiscitary appeals to
the masses against unbending legislatures.[37] We are not contending that Portuguese presidents behave like their counterparts in the Americas as far as political
communication is concerned. That is why we downgrade "going public strategies" to "going public tactics." Yet, there is a striking resemblance between the
motivation underlying Portugal's open presidencies and that of the more histri-
onic practices often observed on the other side of the Atlantic.

As much as recourses to the "bully pulpit" by American presidents and to
plebiscitary appeals by their Latin American colleagues often take place in the
context of divided governments in the U.S. and minority administrations south
of the Rio Grande, open presidencies in Portugal were devised precisely in the
context of cohabitation.

Open presidencies seem to have generated the consequences expected by
those who have masterminded them. In this respect, Soares once asserted that

"the mere suggestion that I was going to hold an open presidency made the government and parties to examine the local situation: the government would be prompted to act; the opposition to highlight delays and unfulfilled promises."[38] Another piece of evidence that such presidential initiatives were successful in framing the political agenda is that they clearly angered the cabinet. In the 1992 Convention of his party (the PSD), Premier Cavaco Silva avowed that "the forces blocking [governmental action] have a clear face," and sternly warned that he would not permit an influential presidency to turn into an interfering one.[39] Note that the premier of a cohabitation publicly acknowledged that the president was influential. In his turn, Jorge Sampaio, a president who shared power mostly with his socialist co-partisans, as well as Cavaco Silva, centered his open presidencies on social issues, such as social inclusion, citizenship, and health and education, thus helping to put pressure on the government to expedite action on these policy areas.[40]

All told, Portuguese presidents can use political communication tools that are certainly not available to parliament-selected or monarchical chief of states in Western Europe and allow the former to voice opinions that frame the country's political agenda and prompt governments to act. The comparative literature on semi-presidentialism would be well advised to take stock of the relevant consequences of such "going public tactics" when analyzing presidential power in Portugal.

Conclusion

To use Shugart and Carey's terminology, in 1976 Portugal began its experiment with semi-presidentialism by adopting its president-parliamentary variety. In 1982 the country shifted to *premier*-presidentialism, and has remained so since then. This unique interaction of the two different kinds of semi-presidentialism with a changing multiparty system has given rise to an ample range of governing formulas: presidential, single-party minority, majority coalition, near majority single-party, single-party majority cabinets, let alone periods of cohabitation and unified executives. This is an eloquent sign of a flexibility that has helped consolidate one of Western Europe's youngest democracies. Moreover, even under such diversity of governance patterns, the policy role of the president has never been rendered irrelevant to the point of justifying the classification of Portugal as a parliamentary system. While it is true that the 1982 constitutional reform eliminated the possibility of undisguised presidential government, presidents have remained important in policymaking, particularly due to their use of the presidential veto and dissolution powers.

Yet the extent of Portuguese presidents' policy influence depends crucially on the type of cabinet with which he shares power. On the one hand, whenever the president faces a majority cabinet, his influence is reduced. Although a president's veto over cabinet decrees is formally definitive since it cannot be overridden, a majority government can simply reintroduce a previously vetoed decree as a standard legislative bill, and have the latter passed by the Assembly, a situation that often occurs with such bills. On the other hand, a president facing a minority cabinet whose composing parties he opposes can be more influential. Since the presidency became civilianized and particized in 1986, however, this situation only took place very briefly at the beginning of Soares's first presidential term.

At any rate, the second cohabitation period between President Soares and Premier Cavaco Silva showed how important the veto power can be. Soares used it as an *ex post* mechanism to influence Cavaco Silva's policy initiatives. The head of state also strengthened his hand vis-à-vis the premier through "open presidencies."

In addition, it should also be stressed that the president's veto power was actually enhanced by the 1982 revision. Since then the veto has been the touchstone of presidential power in Portugal and should be understood as a kind of *ex post* mechanism to control the cabinet and parliament. No other popularly elected president in Western Europe has this kind of reactive power, not even the powerful French head of state. In addition, Portuguese presidents, unlike their Austrian and Icelandic counterparts, have not abdicated their powers. By using their veto powers and "going public tactics," presidents are able to push the premier's policy initiatives closer to the preferences of the median voter in the presidential election. Thus, Portuguese presidents must definitely be seen as more than figureheads.

Furthermore, heavy emphasis should be placed on the fact that the undeniable aggrandizement of the premier that took place after 1987 was carried out not at the expense of the president but to the detriment of cabinet ministers. Greater prime ministerial powers led many analysts to immediately equate it with a weaker, waning presidency and declare semi-presidentialism moribund. We hope to have demonstrated this is plainly inaccurate.

It is important not to underestimate the president's ability to shape public perceptions of the cabinet, and thus of government policy, through political vetoes but also by referring legislation to the Constitutional Court, even if the use of such prerogatives does not necessarily lead to the enactment of the policies preferred by the chief of state. Also, going beyond these constitutional instruments, under Mário Soares the presidency developed a special relationship with the media by holding "open presidencies." These initiatives, which have been continued by successive presidents, have given the head of state a say in agenda-setting. Moreover, the open presidencies demonstrate that the president's role in the policy process can become larger than the Constitution would suggest. This is especially true in the president's second (and final) term, when the president is free of reelection calculations and can thus more easily assert himself as a de facto counterweight to cabinet policies.

Finally, this chapter also contributes to the debate on whether politics in democratic societies have become presidentialized, as argued recently by

Poguntke and Webb (2005). According to these authors, democracies "are becoming more presidentialized in their actual practice, without changing their formal structure, that is, their regime type" (1), meaning that PMs have become more powerful through increasing executive resources, wider autonomy vis-à-vis the parties, and the growing personalization of election campaigns. Following Lobo (2005a), we have argued that in Portugal in 1987 to 1999, constitutional, party system, and organizational changes led to the growth of prime ministerial power. However, even at the height of the premier's power, the PM was never independent of the parties, as shown in the composition of inner cabinets within the executive (Lobo 2005a: 279). Moreover, the strengthening of the PM's role was overwhelmingly contingent on party system changes after 1987 and ultimately dependent on election results (Lobo 2005a: 271-284). Thus, the Portuguese experience suggests that it is safer to speak of changes in prime ministerial power as a result of party system changes rather than the presidentialization of democracy *tout court*.

Notes

1. We would like to thank Nuno Guedes for his excellent research assistance. Amorim Neto thanks the Institute of Social Sciences at the University of Lisbon for its generous support through the grant of a Luso-Afro-Brazilian Fellowship in 2006. We also wish to thank António de Araújo, David Samuels, and Matthew Shugart for their helpful comments on earlier versions of the chapter. All remaining faults are the authors' responsibility.

2. S. Huntington, *The third wave: Democratization in the late twentieth century* (Norman: University of Oklahoma Press, 1991).

3. Octavio Amorim Neto and K. Strøm, "Breaking the parliamentary chain of delegation: Presidents and nonpartisan cabinet members in European democracies," *British Journal of Political Science*, vol. 36, (2006): 619-643.

4. Henceforth we will refer to the president as he and to the prime minister or premier as she.

5. T. Bruneau et al., "Democracy, Southern European style," in *Parties, Politics and Democracy in the New Southern Europe*, ed. N. Diamandorous and R. Gunther (Baltimore: Johns Hopkins University Press, 2001). J.G. Canotilho and V. Moreira, *Fundamentos da Constituição* (Coimbra: Coimbra Editora, 1991). A. Lijphart, *As democracias contemporâneas* (Lisbon: Gradiva, 1989). Pereira, A. G. *O Semipresidencialismo em Portugal* (Lisbon: Ática, 1984). G. Sartori, *Comparative constitutional engineering* (London: MacMillan, 1994).

6. M.C. Lobo, "The presidentialisation of Portuguese democracy?" in *The Presidentialisation of Parliamentary Democracies?* ed. P. Webb and T. Poguntke (Oxford: OUP, 2005a). Lobo, *Governar em Democracia* (Lisbon: ICS, 2005b).

7. Lijphart, *As democracias contemporâneas*, 274. In fairness to Lijphart, it should be stressed that in *Patterns of Democracy*, he places Portugal alongside the semi-presidential systems (1999: 119).

8. Sartori, *Comparative constitutional engineering*, 129.

9. Sartori, *Comparative constitutional engineering*, 138.

10. M. Duverger, "A new political system model: Semi-presidential government," *European Journal of Political Research* vol. 8, (1980): 187.

11. M.S. Shugart and J. M. Carey, *Presidents and Assemblies* (NY: Cambridge University Press, 1992).

12. Shugart and Carey, *Presidents and Assemblies*, 156-60.

13. O. Amorim Neto, "Portugal: Changing patterns of delegation and accountability under the president's watchful eyes," in *Delegation and accountability in Western European parliamentary democracies*, ed. K. Strom, W.Mueller, and T. Bergman (Oxford: Oxford University Press, 2003). A. Araújo and C. Tsimaras, "Os poderes presidenciais nas constituições grega e portuguesa," in *O Direito* (Jul-Dec 2000), 381-413.A. Araújo, "El Presidente de la República en la evolución del sistema político de Portugal," in *Portugal: democracia y sistema Político*, ed. A. Barreto, B. Gomez Fortes, and P. Magalhães (Madrid: Siglo Veintiuno, 2003). M.B. Cruz, *Instituições políticas e processos sociais* (Venda Nova: Bertrand, 1995). A. Freire and A.C. Pinto, *O poder dos presidentes* (Lisbon: Campo da Comunicação, 2005). M. Lucena, "Semipresidencialismo: Teoria geral e práticas portuguesas (I)," *Análise Social*, vol. XXXI (1996): 831-892. J. Miranda, "A experiência portuguesa de sistema semipresidencial," *Direito e Cidadania*, vol. 1 (1996): 9-25. J.R. Novais, *Semipresidencialismo* (Coimbra: Almedina, 2007). M.R. Sousa, *O sistema de governo português antes e depois da Revisão Constitucional* (Lisbon: Cognitio, 1984). M.R. Sousa, *O sistema de governo português* (Lisbon: Assoc. Académica FDUL, 1992). Metcalf (2000) adds to the list of Shugart and Carey a seventh power, judicial review, whose scores also vary from 0 to 4. If we use the seventh power proposed by Metcalf, Portugal scores 13 in 1976-1982 and 10 in 1982 to present.

14. Sartori, *Comparative constitutional engineering*, 129.

15. T. Bruneau, et al., "Democracy," 42.

16. Canoltiho and Moreira, *Fundamentos da Constituição*. A.G. Pereira, *O Semipresidencialismo em Portugal* (Lisbon: Ática, 1984), 53.

17. Amorim Neto, "Changing patterns." Araújo, "El Presidente de la República Cruz." Freire and Pinto, *O poder dos presidentes*. J. Miranda, "A experiência portuguesa de sistema semipresidencial," *Direito e Cidadania*, vol. 1 (1997): 9-25. Novais, *Semipresidencialismo*. G. Pasquino, *Sistemas políticos comparados* (Cascais: Principia, 2005). M.S. Shugart, "Semi-presidential systems: dual executive and mixed authority patterns." *French Politics*, vol. 3 (2005): 323-351. Shugart and Carey, *Presidents and Assemblies*. Sousa, *O sistema de governo português*. For a complete list of studies contending that Portugal should be classified as semi-presidential, see Araújo and Tsimaras (2000: 399-402), and Novais (2007).

18. M.B. Cruz, *Instituições políticas e processos sociais* (Venda Nova: Bertrand, 1995), 223.

19. K. Maxwell, *The making of Portuguese democracy* (Cambridge: Cambridge University Press, 1995). I. Rezola, *Os militares na Revolução de Abril: O Conselho da Revolução e a transição para a democracia em Portugal* (Lisbon: Campo da Comunicação, 2006).

20. L. Graham and D. Wheeler, *In search of modern Portugal: The revolution and its consequences* (Madison: University of Wisconsin, 1983).

21. A.G. Pereira, *O Semipresidencialismo em Portugal* (Lisbon: Ática, 1984), 42-43.

22. For an account of the goals of the right-wing government which oversaw the constitutional revision, see Lopes and Barroso (1980).

23. J. Linz and A. Stepan, *Problems of democratic transition and consolidation* (New York: Johns Hopkins, 1996).

24. Shugart and Carey, *Presidents and Assemblies.*

25. D.F. Amaral, *Governos de gestão* (Lisbon: author's edition, 1983).

26. The 1982 reform increased the number of policy areas on which a two-thirds majority is needed to overturn a presidential veto, namely legislation regarding a state of siege or emergency, the organization of the Armed Forces, the organization of the Constitutional Court, and the regulation of elections (Magalhães, 1989:113). These new powers are better understood bearing in mind the previous version of the Constitution. In 1976-1982 the president held a say in these policy areas because he also presided the Council of the Revolution, which functioned as a *sui generis* Constitutional Court and also legislated on all matters regarding the Armed Forces.

27. J. Gabriel, *Confidencial—A década de Sampaio em Lisboa* (Lisbon: Prime Books, 2007). M.C. Lobo and P. Magalhães, "Election report: The local elections of 2001 and the legislative elections of 2002," *Southern European Politics and Society*, vol. 7 (2003): 72-89.

28. Jorge Sampaio's speech on occasion of the decision to nominate Pedro Santana Lopes as the next prime minister (downloaded in 2004 from www.presidencia.pt).

29. A. Freire and M.C. Lobo, "The Portuguese 2005 legislative election: Return to the Left," *West European Politics*, vol. 29 (2006): 581-588. Gabriel, *Confidencial*. P.S. Lopes, *Percepções e realidade* (Lisbon: Aletheia, 2006).

30. Lobo, "The presidentialisation of Portuguese democracy?" and Lobo, *Governar em Democracia.*

31. M.C. Lobo, "El incremento del poder del primer ministro en Portugal desde 1976," in *Portugal: Democracia y Sistema Político*, ed. A. Barreto, B. Gomez, and P. Magalhães (Madrid: Siglo XXI , 2003). Katz and Mair (1994) and Biezen (2003) show that seats on European parties' executive bodies have been increasingly held by the party-in-office.

32. K. Strøm, "Parties at the core of government," in *Parties without partisans: Political change in advanced industrial democracies*, ed. R.J. Dalton and M.P. Wattenberg (Oxford: Oxford University Press, 2000).

33. O. Amorim Neto and K. Strøm, "Breaking the parliamentary chain of delegation: Presidents and nonpartisan cabinet members in European democracies," *British Journal of Political Science*, vol. 36 (2006): 619-643.

34. Amorim Neto, "Portugal: Changing patterns." Araújo, "El Presidente de la República." Freire and Pinto, *O poder dos presidentes.* A. Magalhães, *As armas dos fracos: o veto político e a litigância constitucional do Presidente da República. Actas do I Encontro Nacional de Ciência Política* (Lisbon: Bizâncio, 2001). Novais, *Semipresidencialismo.*

35. J. Aguiar, "A história múltipla," *Análise Social*, vol. XXXI (1996): 1235-1281. M.B. Cruz, "O Presidente da Républica na génese e evolução do sistema de governo português," *Análise Social*, vol. XXIX (1994): 255-56. M. Frain, "As relações entre o presidente e o primeiro-ministro em Portugal: 1985-1995," *Análise Social*, vol. XXX, (1995): 668. Magalhães, *As armas dos fracos*, 496. J.M. Magone, *European Portugal: The difficult road to sustainable democracy* (New York: St. Martin's Press, 1997), 42.

36. Magone, *European Portugal*, 52.

37. J. Linz, "Presidential versus parliamentary democracy: Does it make a difference?" in *The Failure of Presidential Democracy: The Case of Latin America, vol. 2*, ed. J. Linz and A. Valenuela (Baltimore: Johns Hopkins University Press, 1994), 29.

38. Quoted in Avillez (1996: 75).

39. Quoted in Cruz (1995: 259).

40. Source: Documentation Services of the Presidency of the Republic.

References

Alesina, A. and Perotti, R. "Fiscal expansions and adjustments in OECD countries." *Economic Policy*, vol. 21 (1995): 205-48.

Avillez, M. J. *Soares – Presidência*. Lisbon: Público, 1996.

Biezen, I. *Political parties in new democracies: Party organization in Southern and East Central Europe*. Hampshire: Palgrave MacMillan, 2003.

Elgie, R. *Semi-Presidentialism in Europe*. Oxford: Oxford University Press, 1999.

Guedes, N. "Formação de governos e recrutamento ministerial em Portugal, 1976-2004." B. A. thesis, Institute of Social Sciences, University of Lisbon, 2004.

Katz, R., and Mair, P. *How parties organize*. London: Sage, 1994.

Kernell, S. *Going public: New strategies of presidential leadership*, 2nd ed. Washington, DC: CQ Press, 1993.

Lopes, P. S., and Barroso, J. M. D. *Sistema de governo e sistema partidário*. Lisbon: Bertrand, 1980.

Lopes, P. S. *Percepções e realidade*. Lisbon: Aletheia, 2006.

Magalhães, J. *Dicionário da Revisão Constitucional*. Lisbon: Publicações Europa América, 1989.

Matos, L. S. "A eleição por sufrágio universal do Presidente da Républica: Significado e consequências." *Análise Social*, vol. XIX (1983): 235-260.

Metcalf, L. K. "Measuring presidential power." *Comparative Political Studies*, vol. 33 (2000): 660-685.

Moreira, A. "O regime: Presidencialismo do primeiro-ministro." In *Portugal: O Sistema Político e Constitucional*, edited by M.B. Coelho. Lisbon: ICS, 1989.

Poguntke, T., and Webb, P. *The presidentialisation of parliamentary democracies*. Oxford: Oxford University Press, 2005.

Serrano, E. *As presidências abertas de Mário Soares: As estratégias e o aparelho de comunicação do Presidente da República*. Coimbra: Minerva, 2002.

Siaroff, A. "Comparative presidencies: The inadequacy of the presidential, semi-presidential and parliamentary distinction." *European Journal of Political Research*, vol. 42 (2003): 287-312.

4

The Adjustment of Portuguese Political Parties to the Challenges of Multilevel Governance: A Comparative Analysis of Political Affiliation in the European Parliament

Ana Maria Evans[1]

In this chapter, I analyze how Portuguese political parties have adapted to the changing institutional make-up and decision-making processes of the European Union (EU), focusing on their behavior in the European Parliament (EP). The goal is to make an assessment of the political alliances that parties build in the supranational sphere, of the extent to which such alliances are conditioned by the specific institutional character of the EU's multilevel governance, and of their effects upon the capability by party leaders to achieve their most desired goals. Based on a battery of interviews with EP staff and with former and current Members of the European Parliament (MEPs), I examine the reasoning that drives the choices by Portuguese political parties for group affiliation in the EP during the period between the entry of Portugal in the (then) EC in 1986 and the end of the fifth EP legislature in 2004.

The entry of Portugal in the EC in January 1986 coincided with, and was followed by, major institutional developments that dramatically expanded the scope of supranational legislative activity and enhanced the powers of the EP vis-à-vis the Council and the Commission.[2] As the process of European integration has deepened and the EU has expanded to include new member states, political scientists have dedicated increasing attention to examining how party politics has evolved and responded to those changes. One major line of research has concentrated on party behavior in the two institutions where party activity is most visible in the supranational sphere, i.e., in the EP and the Council.[3] A second line of research has focused on the effects of institutional developments in the EU system of governance upon the evolution of national political cleavages, voters' political preferences, and the internal organization of political parties.[4]

We find little in the literature towards a systematic explanation of the make-up of EP parliamentary groups and of the choices associated with it. And yet, this is a critical element for understanding the relations between multiple layers of party strategy and the links between parties' domestic and international activity. Examining the incentives that drive the choice of EP group affiliation reveals important aspects of the opportunities available to political parties at the supranational level of governance and allows us to test the institutional and political elements that influence the most effective use of those resources. The process driving choices of political identification at the supranational level also indicates whether the EU's system of multilevel governance affects party hierarchies by setting off divergences between the party players in different institutional layers, which may induce breaches in the command-and-control center of parties with a longstanding tradition of unitary governance.[5]

The choice of political group membership is the first critical decision that national party representatives elected to the EP make. Political groups steer the flow of legislative activity in the EP and perform a number of functions comparable to those of national parliamentary groups. Membership in a given group conditions multiple aspects of the work of members of the European Parliament (MEPs), namely, their access to key parliamentary office positions which may enhance visibility and policy influence in either or both international and national spheres. Usually, EP groups apply the proportional *d'Hondt* method to allocate internal leadership positions, such as the president, vice-president, and co-ordinators of committees. This method is also generally accounted for when groups propose names for committee chairmanships and other leadership posts in the Parliament.[6] Thus, scholars generally assume that the largest national party delegations in a given group tend to dominate the allocation of the most desired positions and tend to exert influence over the group's voting line in important matters.[7] In short, there is an oligarchy in the internal structure of EP groups.

One should note that EP groups differ significantly from national parliamentary parties because they are made of post-electoral coalitions between individuals and national party delegations who are elected in national contests and through national political organizations, rather than constituting the parliamentary arms of unified and effectively operating supranational political parties. The small set of parliamentary groups that form in each EP legislature represent a panoply of national and regional parties, citizens' movements, single-issue movements, alternative movements and a variety of geographical, cultural, historical, and political tendencies that are beyond any imaginable mix at the national level.[8] It happens frequently that a given national party's program does not clearly fit in any of the available groups because it may be closer to one group's dominant views on the regulation of the economy, for example, and yet locate closer to another group in the "integration versus euro-scepticism" axis and/or to another group with regard to social values, and/or to environmental concerns, and/or to other matters. Hence, MEPs and national party delegations are often confronted with different possibilities for political affiliation at the start of a legislature.

These elements, and the absence of penalties for changes in political group affiliation during any given legislative mandate, make EP groups noticeably more volatile in composition than national parliamentary groups are: there have been over one hundred switches of MEPs between groups in each of the third, fourth, and fifth legislatures, representing one-fifth to one-fourth of seats in those legislatures.[9] Such political inconstancy raises fundamental questions on democratic representation in the EU, which are all the more relevant amidst the intense debates on the democratic deficit of its governance system. Moreover, the unstable character of political groups in the EP questions political parties' capacity to aggregate and represent the preferences of European citizens, which is a key function of parties according to the comparative politics literature.[10] It is hence critical to examine whether the volatile character of political identification in the EP reflects institutional underdevelopment or, instead, if it reveals a learning process whereby national political parties adjust their strategy so as to make the most efficient use of the opportunities and resources associated with the institutional evolution of the EU.[11]

Examining the specific case of Portuguese parties makes an important contribution for our understanding of the development of a supranational party system and of the character of party politics in EU decision-making. Existing studies in this ambit tend to focus mostly on the largest and most influential member states and, more recently, on the incoming nations of Central Eastern Europe—they dedicate less attention to middle-sized and periphery countries like Portugal. Even in the literatures specialized on the Portuguese political system, which have made critical contributions to comparative studies on electoral systems and on party competition, we find little information on the behavior and choices of party representatives at the supranational level.[12] In other words, we still lack systematic knowledge on the make-up of international alliances by Portuguese political parties, most particularly in the context of EU politics. My work aims to address this analytical challenge.

The questions that have driven research can be summarized as follows: What are the factors that influence the choice by national political parties and MEPs to affiliate with a given political group and/or to switch groups within the EP? How do policy, information, office, and financial goals fit in the process of group formation, in the specific institutional context and political market of the EP? Do cultural and historical legacies interfere with coalition building at the supranational level? If so, how? The following sections will try to address these queries in a systematic way.

I will start by making a summarized report on the incentives that previous comparative research on party politics suggests as primary drivers of political affiliation in national legislatures. Based upon a battery of original, in-depth interviews conducted with MEPs and EP staff, I will then proceed to a condensed narrative account of the reasoning that motivated the leaders of each major Portuguese party delegation that entered the EP at the time of the country's adhesion in 1986 to choose a specific political group and why there have been some changes of political identification since then. The chapter will conclude by situating the Portuguese case in the comparative perspective and analyzing the contributions of the study for a more general understanding of party behavior and of the making of policy coalitions in the EU's system of multilevel governance.

The Topic of Political Affiliation in Comparative Studies on Party Politics

In recent decades, the literatures on party behavior have linked private ambition to the choice of political affiliation and to the competitive or cooperative strategies of party leaders through the basic assumption that politicians are driven by any, or a combination, of three essential goals: the search for electoral gain, the will to enjoy the spoils of office, and the attempt to secure policy.[13] There has been great debate among scholars over which of these elements ultimately dominates the mindset of politicians when those goals conflict. Nevertheless, if we apply the assumptions of the literature to the specific context of the EP, we will expect to find one or more of the following observations:

1. party leaders prefer to join and remain in the European Parliamentary Group (EPG) that is closest to their party's policy preferences;
2. party leaders prefer to join and remain in the EPG that offers more office perks to the members of their national delegation;
3. party leaders search for the EPG that allows them the most policy influence in the EP and, more generally, in supranational decision-making.

Previous studies on party competition also suggest that national historical legacies and political cultures, as well as long-standing party cleavages, influence the reasoning and strategies of political leaders when making alliances at both national and international levels.[14] Applying this reasoning to the formation of groups in the EP, one should thus expect that:

1. historical rivalries between the parties of a given nation may influence negatively the choice or ability to affiliate in a given EPG;

On the other hand,

2. historical connections between parties of different nations may influence positively political membership in a given EPG.

Research on party competition in the EP has called our attention to a particular element that conditions the choices of MEPs, namely the fact that they respond to two principals: on the one hand, MEPs depend on the national party leaders who control the process of selection of candidates for the next EP election; on the other hand, their political group in the EP controls private goods, such as leadership positions, committee assignments, speaking time, and the legislative agenda. Accordingly, when MEPs face conflicting goals between their different principals, they tend to align with their national party because renomination comes first in the hierarchy of preferences.[15] Thus, we should expect that:

1. individuals and national party delegations in the EP tend to follow the line of their leadership at home with regard to membership in a given political group.

The literature goes further to suggest that changes in national political cleavages should affect party behavior in the EP as well, as Kreppel found out in her study of the political role of Italian MEPs after the dramatic reforms that unfolded in the Italian political system during the 1990s.[16] On the other hand, comparative studies have found out too that dramatic external events at a global scale may topple existing party lines and alter national political leaders' beliefs and strategies and even lead to the formation of new political parties and to the dissolution of old ones, as happened after the breakdown of the Soviet Empire and the fall of the ideology associated with it.[17] Drawing upon these findings, one may assume that:

2. changes in national party leadership, programmatic goals, and the breakdown of national parties or of traditional political alliances at the domestic level (either induced by major external events or internal political shake-ups) will translate into scissions of national party delegations at the EP level and induce changes in the make-up of EPGs.

The next sections will analyze the play of these factors and investigate whether the literature may have overlooked explanatory elements in the analysis of political affiliation in the EP. This will be done through a condensed narrative account of the reasoning and processes that have driven the choices of group membership by Portuguese parties in the EP in a dynamic perspective. We will see how the major parties in the country positioned themselves vis-à-vis European political families before the country joined the (then) EC; the indecisions and debates that preceded their entry and participation in EP party life; and the factors that have influenced some changes in their EP political identity after 1986.

The in-depth analysis of the choices by the most representative party delegations of Portugal in the EP does not intend to test the weight of each of the basic explanatory factors referred to above, as the units under scrutiny are not sufficient in number. Yet, the account aims to provide a clear picture of how leaders calculated their choices for political grouping in the EP to unearth new theoretical insights which can be later tested by further comparative work. Ultimately, the goal is to assess how choices of parliamentary affiliation in the EP affect the capability of national parties to influence supranational policy and, more generally, how they reflect on the institutionalization of a competitive party system in the EU.

We will see how the loose ideological bonds and miscellaneous policy representation that characterize EP parliamentary groups provide a fertile ground to allow national political parties that do not pledge extremist political goals to manipulate their political identity so as to maximize resources and influence in the highly consensual context of inter-institutional decision-making in multilevel governance. To this adds the conspicuous lack of knowledge by the majority of European citizens on party and legislative activity at the supranational level and the fact that European elections are run at the national level and between national parties rather than European political organizations, thus stimulating little, if any, attachment by voters to European labels.[18]

Portuguese Parties in the Path to Europeanization: The Historical and Political Meaning of Group Membership in the EP

Portugal was a young democracy facing the challenge to consolidate strong and effective political and economic organizations when, in early 1977, the first elected government under the new democratic constitution submitted the application of the country for EC membership. Little less than three years had passed since military officers had put an abrupt end to forty years of authoritarianism through the April 1974 coup. The sudden transition to democracy unfolded in a political context where only the Communist Party was prepared to function with a truly operating apparatus: although the Portuguese Socialist Action (renamed in 1973 as the Portuguese Socialist Party) had been founded in Geneva ten years before the revolution (i.e., in 1964), its leaders were in exile and the party did not develop its cadres and organizational structure until after the fall of the authoritarian regime.[19] The Portuguese Communist Party (PCP), on the other hand, had been created much earlier, in 1921, and under the leadership of Álvaro Cunhal after 1941 developed an efficient underground organization, based on the Leninist model of small cells; tight discipline; hidden identity of members; and top-down, centralized decision-making.[20] Following the 1974 military coup, the PCP used its organizational advantage to quickly dominate trade unions and the public administration, and to capture strong influence over the Armed Forces Movement, which had been largely responsible for staging the coup and for drafting the program that aimed to set the institutional and political framework for the transition to democracy. Confronted with the hegemonic threat of the PCP, a group of democratic reformist politicians, who were well-known in the late stages of the old regime, hastily created two new political organizations which aimed to represent, respectively, centrist and conservative tendencies among the population—i.e., the Popular Democratic Party (later renamed Social Democratic Party, PPD/PSD) and the Party of the Democratic and Social Center (later renamed Popular Party, CDS/PP).

Since the early stages of the transition to democracy, all parties favored the movement of the country towards European integration, with the exception of the Communist Party. Both the PSD and the CDS were manifestly pro-European at the time of their foundation in 1974, arguing for the need to start negotiations with the view to integrate timely into the EC. The Socialist Party changed its positioning on integration after the fall of the authoritarian rightist regime: in its 1973 Declaration of Principles and Program, the party had asserted that the European Community represented the neo-capitalist and imperialist goals of multinational businesses and was a venue for the invasion of national economies by American capital.[21] However, after the military coup, and when confronted with the hegemonic attempts by the Communist Party to dominate the administrative, political, and economic institutions of governance in the country, Socialist leaders quickly moved the party's official discourse to support a model of integration that would favor external trade, and the economic interests and development of the nation, while at the same time pledging the defense of workers' interests.[22] Eventually, it was the founder and leader of the Socialist Party, Mário Soares—the prime minister in the follow-up of the first constitutional elections—who submitted the application for the country's membership in the EC on March 1977, and who led the first round of negotiations with European peers. The Socialist initiative was backed by all parliamentary groups except for the Communist Party.[23]

Before the negotiations for EC membership unfolded, Portuguese political parties had already developed privileged relations with sister parties in Europe. In fact, due to the prolonged absence of democratic politics and party organizations in the country and to the hasty nature of party building following the 1974 coup, all political parties had to rely on massive financial support from foreign organizations for the training of their cadres, the building of regional and local apparatuses, and the mobilization of masses.[24] As we will see next, this mattered for the choices of political group in the EP when the country joined the EC in

1986. The following sections will examine Portugal's domestic political parties with respect to their behavior in the European Parliament.

The Social Democratic Party (PPD/PSD)

It is very interesting to examine how José Barroso, former leader of the PSD—who is currently the president of the European Commission and has been foreign minister and prime minister of Portugal—viewed the international relations of the party in the early eighties, and how he predicted the PSD would position with regard to group affiliation in the EP when the country joined the EC. According to Barroso, the PSD's ideological principles and social bases were ambiguous, as were the personal and institutional relations its leaders developed in the international sphere. On the one hand, the party's official discourse placed it at the center-left of the European political spectrum and in line with Social Democratic parties in Europe. On the other hand, the PSD behaved as a liberal party in important aspects of its national and international strategy, Barroso claimed. More concretely, at the national level, the party acted as a center-right party by establishing alliances with the Portuguese Party of the Social Democratic Center (CDS), which represented Christian-Democratic values. And yet the PSD had applied for membership in the Socialist International, to which the mainstream Socialist and Social-Democratic (i.e., center-left) parties of Western Europe were affiliated.[25]

The international situation of the party was far from settled when Barroso wrote his 1983 study. The Socialist International had not accepted the PSD's membership. In the view of many, this resulted of the unwillingness by the Portuguese Socialist Party (PS)—which was a member of the Socialist International—and, more particularly, of the PS founder and leader Mário Soares, to have the PSD in the same international group. The Socialist leader was not too keen on sharing the political and financial backing associated with membership, and he was also preoccupied with safeguarding the ideological distinction between the two parties at home.[26] Faced with the veto from the Socialist International, the leaders of the PSD started to approach the European Liberal Democrats and some of the PSD's cadres were given internships with the Liberals in Strasbourg, as stated by Barroso. Accordingly, the party's leaders also nurtured good international relations in the Council of Europe, with a mix of parties that included the Spanish UCD, the French UDF, and the English Liberals. At the same time, the PSD was receiving strong financial support for the development of its internal organization and mobilization capability from the German SPD, via the Friedrich Ebert Foundation.[27]

Based on his analysis of the party's ambiguous international situation and on previous statements whereby PSD leaders had declared that the PSD should not join any of the existing political groups in the EP, Barroso expected the party to remain non-attached when the country joined the EC.[28] Yet, by 1986, it was clear the leaders of the PSD had changed their minds. During the negotiations that preceded the entry of the PSD's first national delegation in the EP, the party's leaders had understood that the PSD's capacity for intervention and influence would be very limited, and that the party would not benefit from significant office and financial perks if it did not become member of a political group in the EP.

The only viable alternative was the Liberal group. The PSD shared common views with the Liberals with regard to social values, and this was the only group located ideologically between the People's Party of Europe (EPP) group—which represented Christian-Democratic Parties and to which the CDS was expected to affiliate—and the Socialist Party of Europe (PES) group, which the Portuguese Socialist Party was undoubtedly joining and not willing to share. The Liberals convinced the leaders of the PSD that the party's national delegation would play a leading role in the group because it would be the only party with a prime minister in national government and therefore with direct access to a representative in the Council.[29] All these factors influenced the Social-Democratic Portuguese delegation's decision to enter the group in 1986.

In fact, the course of membership in the liberal group was not exactly as the party had expected. Its MEPs felt that having the premiership at home—and hence access to the Council via the prime minister—did not really amount to much with regard to political leverage in the EP. While Giscard d'Éstaing held the presidency of the Liberals, he asserted his vest of former president of the French republic and used his influence and international connections to pursue his interests without much need for consent from the Portuguese delegation.[30] When d'Éstaing left the Liberals for the EPP in late 1991, in the pursuit of presidential office in the EP, the PSD was the largest national delegation in the group, but its MEPs realized that standing on their own and without a strong southern European partner who shared the same concerns for critical issues (such as the defense of traditional agricultural produce and fisheries), they lacked voice and could do little to defend key national interests. The PSD's prime minister, Cavaco Silva became especially aware of this limitation when he assumed the first Portuguese presidency of the EC in January 1992. He realized the party did not have access to key information and bargaining in the inter-institutional dynamics of the European system of governance, because it was the member of a political group that did not have significant representation either in the Council or in the Commission.[31] It became increasingly evident that it was indispensable for MEPs from a relatively small and periphery country like Portugal to develop solid channels of communication via close and sustained contact with key elements of large national party delegations and with rapporteurs and group coordinators in important committees, of which only the EPP and the PES had in significant number. This was critical for coordinating a common position across supranational institutions and ultimately for securing concessions in the rounds of item examination and negotiations that preceded the approval of important legislative packages at the supranational level.[32]

The Portuguese Socialist Party continued to resist the entry of the PSD in the PES, and thus the EPP constituted the only alternative venue for thriving in the process of inter-institutional party networking at the supranational level. The EPP had the tradition of organizing a summit before meetings of the European Council, where the national party leaders and heads of government who were members of the family met with the chair of the group in the European Parliament and with either the president or vice-president of the European Commission (depending on which of them was a member of a national party belonging to the EPP). The purpose of the summits was to build common positions on key policy issues within the party family and across the Council, the EP, and the Commission before the heads of government met to negotiate those issues at the Council's inter-governmental forum.[33]

The entry of the UK Liberal Democrats in the liberal group following the 1994 EP elections, and the adhesion of Finnish and Swedish parties from the Liberal and Center parties on January 1995 accentuated the weight of northern parties in the group. When the PSD lost the elections in October 1995, Marcelo Rebelo de Sousa, who became the new national party leader, considered it was urgent to join the EPP as soon as possible, so as to regain the information resources and inter-institutional links which the party had lost when it was replaced by the Socialists in the Council.[34]

Lucas Pires, who ran as an independent candidate under the PSD's banner in the 1994 EP elections but had been a former vice-president of the European Union of Christian Democrats (EUCD) and a member of the EPP since 1989, helped to conduct the negotiations between the PSD and the EPP. The latter was interested in having the former join in, because this would increase the number of MEPs in the group and add Portuguese to the group's working languages, therefore expanding the financial and office resources it was entitled to.[35] In exchange for bringing in those benefits for the EPP, the PSD's leaders got the assurance that they would be entitled to nomination for a vice-presidency in the European Parliament. The PSD joined the EPP in November 1996.[36]

Social Democratic leaders who have been closely involved in conducting the party's strategy at the European level claim that the choice to move to the EPP had a much bigger impact for the party's international standing than one would immediately comprehend. Accordingly, this switch was crucial to make it possible for José Barroso—who later became the leader of the PSD in the opposition before his brief stint as Portugal's prime minister—to build a strong international network and the kind of inter-institutional consensus and support that would eventually pave his way for the presidency of the European Commission.[37] In short, changing political affiliation in the EP made it possible for a national party, which represented a relatively small numerical weight in the EP, to attain a highly desired European office and to secure disproportionate influence in EU politics.

The Portuguese Socialist Party (PS)

Unlike the Social Democrats, Socialist leaders faced no dilemmas or obstacles in the choice of political group affiliation when the country joined the (then) EC. The PS was affiliated to the Socialist International. The party's founder and leader, Mário Soares, was a very active member of the Socialist International and had developed strong ties with Social Democrats across Western Europe as well as with Swedish and British Socialists.[38] As happened with the other Portuguese parties during the process of transition to democracy, the PS received extensive international financial and political support, which was critical for building organizational strength, training its cadres, and undertaking massive mobilization endeavors. In this respect, the West German Social Democratic Party played a key role under the leadership of Willy Brandt, by contributing several million dollars to assist the Portuguese Socialists.[39] There were no doubts in the mind of observers that, considering the political and financial character of the party's international relations, the PS would join the Party of European Socialists (PES) group, where the mainstream West European Socialist and Social Democratic Parties were represented.

And indeed the national delegation of the Portuguese Socialist Party joined the PES in 1986. Its continuity in the same group throughout the following mandates and, until present, illustrates the usual pattern of EP affiliation among party delegations that are members of a mainstream international family: these national party delegations are automatically assumed into the political group that represents their political family in the EP. For them, the primary issue on the negotiating table is the distribution of EP internal posts. Usually the outgoing leader of the given national party delegation and/or the most experienced MEP which remains for the following mandate helps with organizing the transition between legislatures and with the process of negotiating office and financial perks with the group's largest national delegations.[40]

The Portuguese Socialists did experience a major incident in the EP, which bears important implications for the analysis of the bargaining processes that drive political group membership in the EP, even if that was not the issue directly at stake. In 1999, Mário Soares, founder of the PS and former prime minister and president of Portugal was elected to the EP and expected that his prestige amidst European Socialists and his long-nurtured international connections would bear enough weight within the PES to fulfill his ambition for presidential office in the EP. And indeed, Soares managed to be considered as the official candidate of the PES for the post. But Soares was not willing to submit fully to the details of a tacit agreement which had prevailed between the PES and the EPP since 1989.[41] In the process of choosing the EP president in the two elected legislatures before 1989, the two groups had learned that they could guarantee sufficient votes to monopolize the choice for the post if each agreed informally to vote for the candidate proposed by the other, with the candidate from the group with the largest number of MEPs holding office during the first half of the legislative term, and the one proposed by the second largest group taking the post at the mid-term of the legislative mandate. According to this tacit agreement, in the 1999 legislature, the candidate from the EPP should hold the presidency during the first half of the term, because the EPP had become the largest group in the follow-up of the EP elections. However, Soares insisted he wanted to hold the presidency first and was unwilling to compromise on that. His rigid attitude led to the failure of negotiations between the EPP and the PES and culminated in an unexpected way: both the PES and the EPP searched to build alternative majorities with other EP groups. Eventually the EPP was able to negotiate an agreement with the Liberals, according to which Nicole Fontaine would occupy the presidency of the EP in the first half of the legislature and Pat Cox from the Liberals would be supported by the EPP for the second half of the term.[42]

While the EPP and the PES went back to their former tacit agreement in the following mandate, the Portuguese Socialist Party lost the opportunity to reach an influential and hard-to-get office position in the supranational forum. The Socialist delegation overlooked the critical element of inter-party and inter-institutional consensus that has marked the style of politics at the supranational level and which has made it possible for relatively small party leaders at the European level, like José Barroso—and even for independent candidates like Pat Cox—to reach highly desirable top posts in Europe.

The Portuguese Communist Party (PCP)

The PCP leaders did not have much choice among the political groups which existed in the EP when its leaders confronted the inevitability of integration in Europe. The party's pro-Soviet ideology and the massive financial assistance it received from the Soviet Union and from Eastern European countries were not in line with the program and modus operandi of the euro-Communist parties that belonged to the Communist group in the EP.[43] The PCP's founder and leader, Álvaro Cunhal, had always opposed the integration of Portugal in the EC, which he viewed as a vehicle for Western imperialism. Yet, before Portugal joined the EC, the PCP was already participating actively in the Council of Europe and voting in tandem with the Communist group there, as part of its strategy to be involved in European spheres of decision-making and to prepare for operating with efficacy in the EC's multilevel structures. The party's leaders reasoned that by working inside European organizations and making alliances with other Communist and leftist parties in strategic policy issues, the PCP would have a voice and exert some policy influence. On the other hand, if it did not participate in those venues, as its radical stance against Europe might lead one to expect, the party would end up marginalized from important decision-making.[44] Hence, pragmatism had to prevail over radicalism.

In the EP's Communist group, the PCP's national delegation felt at ease with its French and Greek peers but had strong disagreements with Italian Communist leaders who were aligned to socialist reformism. According to Carlos Carvalhas, the former secretary general of the PCP and the former MEP of the party, the strong divergences between the two trends within the group—i.e., between party delegations favorable to European integration and closer to Western socialism, on the one hand, and pro-Soviet communist parties that were manifestly anti-Europe, on the other—were associated with historical and cultural legacies as well as geographic specificities. In his view, because Italy and Germany emerged as states relatively recently—i.e., when compared to France or Portugal—and were formatted as decentralized countries, their Communist leaders could comprehend the concept of federalism and of multilevel governance much better than could those leaders socialized in unitary administrative traditions as the French and Portuguese ones.[45] The inability of the national delegations in the Communist group to overcome their notorious ideological divergences culminated dramatically in 1989, with the scission of the group into the Group of the Unitarian European Left (GUE), where the Italian PCI and the Spanish Isquierda Unida (IU) assembled, and the Coalition of the Left (CG), which included the Portuguese and French Communist parties, as well as three members of the Greek SYN.[46]

The course of membership by the PCP in the EP is also interesting by suggesting that it does not always hold true that the institutional setting of the EP provides incentives for national party delegations to join all the MEPs elected under their electoral banner in the same group. As mentioned in the introductory section of the chapter, the application of the proportional *d'Hondt* procedure for the internal distribution of leadership posts within EPGs, and for the nomination of individuals for key parliamentary positions to which each group is entitled, suggests the importance of the relative numerical strength of national party delegations within each group. Yet, when the PCP included Green militants in its pre-electoral coalition for the 1989 EP elections, the party's leaders agreed from the start that the latter would join the Greens, rather than the Communist group, in the EP. The leaders of the PCP reasoned that, in exchange for making a Green candidate eligible and free to choose her affiliation in the EP, the PCP would gain "green" votes in the elections and would subsequently secure inside information on the political activities of the Greens in the EU as well as a friendly negotiating partner when voting for important policy issues in the EP.[47] In short, the party calculated between the different kinds of benefits it could draw from its affiliation strategy and chose to spread out so as to attain informational resources that would otherwise be out of its range.

The Party of the Social Democratic Center (CDS-PP)

As mentioned above, the party of the Social Democratic Center was created soon after the revolution, in July 1974, by reformist leaders who were involved in politics during the late stages of the authoritarian regime, and who pledged to defend Christian-Democratic values and to represent the traditionalist and conservative strata of the population who found no voice after the military coup.[48] Its founder and first president, Diogo Freitas do Amaral, was also the president of the European Union of Christian Democrats (EUCD) between 1981 and 1983 and the party was a member of the International Democratic Union.[49] Political leaders and analysts had no doubt that the CDS would join the European People's Party (EPP) group in the European Parliament, as the latter represented centrist parties of Christian-Democratic inspiration that defended European federalism as well.[50]

Yet, the entry of the CDS into the EPP Group was subject to debate within the national party. In the year that preceded the adhesion of Portugal to the EC, Lucas Pires—who was then president of the CDS—discussed the options that the party had, and analyzed with other party leaders whether the CDS should follow the Spanish example. Portugal and Spain were going to become members of the EC at the same time, and the president of the CDS knew that the leaders of the Spanish Alianza Popular, with whom the CDS had close relations, were planning to (and did) join the British Conservatives in the European Democrats group. Although the British Conservatives were neither members of the Christian-Democratic family, nor did they share the basic ideology and programmatic goals of the CDS, the latter maintained tight relations with them.[51]

In the end, the CDS did send its national delegation to the EPP when Portugal joined the EC. According to analysts, three major factors influenced this choice. First, the party's ideological closeness to the Christian-Democratic family and the important role of CDS leaders in the organizations that represented it at the international level did, without doubt, weigh heavily in the party's alignment with the parliamentary group that represented Christian Democrats in the EP. Secondly, the party's leaders reasoned that if the two Iberian parties joined different political groups in the EP, they would have more voice and more influence at the European level than if they assembled in the same group.[52] Thirdly, there were financial considerations too, as there were with the other Portuguese parties; according to observers, the CDS had received critical aid from the Adenauer Foundation, i.e., the financial arm of the German CDU, which was a member of the EPP, and this contributed to its alignment.[53]

Paradoxically, after having started as the most euro-centric party in Portugal at the time of its foundation in 1974, adamant of the urgency to speed up the process of integration, and deeply in tune with the federalist views of other European Christian Democrats, the discourse of CDS leaders evolved in the opposite direction at the onset of the nineties, under the leadership of Manuel Monteiro. With the aim to mark a clear ideological distinction vis-à-vis the PSD, which was becoming less popular in its leadership of the executive, Monteiro assumed a strong euro-sceptical posture and made vehement speeches against the Treaty of Maastricht (as the latter was to expand the scope of supranational authority). The party's official statements were so radically opposed to the federalist goals of the EPP that the latter ousted it in 1992. However, the three representatives of the party's delegation in the EP, led by Lucas Pires, a sound Europeanist who had been leader of the CDS between 1983 and 1986 and vice-president of the European Parliament, rebuffed the national leadership's positioning and remained in the EPP group as independent MEPs. Lucas Pires would run for the following mandate as an independent candidate under the PSD banner and, as seen above, would play a key role in bringing the PSD into the EPP in 1996.[54]

In 1994, the MEPs elected under the CDS joined the French Gaullists and the Irish Fianna Fáil in the European Democratic Alliance group (the RDE, renamed Union for Europe Group, UPE, in 1995). Ironically, ten years later, the party was brought back to the EPP by the hand of the PSD and as a result of a change in national political alignments. In 2004, the Social Democratic Party was governing in coalition with the CDS-PP as a junior partner. Paulo Portas, who had played an important role in the PP's switch towards radical anti-integration during the leadership of Monteiro (and thus contributed to the party's exit from the EPP), was minister of state in the ruling coalition. He agreed with the leaders of the PSD that it would be detrimental for both parties to run separately for the European elections at a time when they were partners in national government. The CDS-PP joined the PSD in the coalition *Força Portugal* for the 2004 EP elections and the PSD negotiated with the EPP to have the MEPs elected under its list join the Group as "European Democrats" (DE) but not with the status of full members.[55]

In the view of Social Democratic leaders, the change of posture of the CDS/PP leaders with regard to changing membership again in the EP was influenced not only by the political conveniences of being in government at the time, but was also the result of a learning process: the party's leaders had understood during their stint out of the EPP that the possibility to attend the pre-Council summits with governmental peers, and to sit together and talk to key players in European politics was a necessary condition to allow any real information on the negotiations that were being held at the highest levels of EU's decision-making. Without being able to do so, the party had been completely marginalized from European politics.[56]

The Party of Democratic Renewal (PRD)

The Party of Democratic Renewal was a short-lived party and represented limited change in the Portuguese political system. However, its posture in the EP is revealing because it illustrates how new and small political parties that emerge of domestic political realignments can acquire disproportionate gains when searching for political identity in the EP. The PRD was a very young party when the country joined the EC. It had been created by supporters of President Eanes

in the run-up to the 1985 national elections, with the goal to weaken the Socialist party and to undermine the presidential ambitions of Mário Soares. Its leaders
claimed to be located in the center-left of the political spectrum, but the party
had a rather heterogeneous support basis.[57]

The PRD was not a member of any international political family and its political programme could easily fit ideologically in more than one political group
in the EP. Furthermore, its national delegation had the potential to bring extra
resources for more than one EPG—either because it represented one extra working language for the given groups, and/or because the number of MEPs it would
add allowed such groups to get one more senior parliamentary post.[58] According
to party leaders, all these factors together created such a favorable negotiating
position for the delegation that they basically waited to be approached by different EP groups to see who among them would offer the best benefits package. As
stated, this was the basic reasoning and process that culminated in the choice to
join the Gaullists in the Group of the European Democratic Alliance (RDE)
when the PRD entered the EP.[59]

Analytical Remarks and the Generalizability of the Study

This chapter has examined an important and yet unfamiliar aspect of the response of national political parties to the accelerating pace of European integration and to the shifting nature of decision-making authority in the EU's system
of governance. I have explored how the Portuguese party delegations elected to
the EP have defined their political identity in the supranational sphere and the
factors that have influenced changes in the course of group membership. The
research has covered the period since the entry of the country in the EC in 1986
until the end of the fifth legislature in 2004. The goal was to contribute to a better understanding of how national parties adapt their coalitional strategy at the
supranational level, so as to make the most efficient use of the opportunities
associated with the system of multilevel governance in European politics.

The analysis of the Portuguese case suggests that national party delegations
in the EP are concerned with joining a parliamentary group that shares *some* of
their main policy goals. This qualified statement does not provide much of an
explanation for political identification though, particularly in a context where
most often there is not a clear ideological fit between a given national party and
any one specific political group in the EP. EPGs include national parties that
represent different tendencies within a broad set of programmatic goals which
can be loosely identified with a political family. Such wide "catch-all" context
brings out the weight of pragmatic interests in the choice of political group
membership in the EP.

Portuguese political leaders have learned that there is an oligarchy in the
EP, and that the most efficient strategy for their relatively small and periphery

party delegations to exert some policy influence in EU decision-making is to cultivate good political and personal relations with key leaders of the largest national delegations in either one of the two groups that represent the large majority of government parties in the EU, namely the EPP and/or the PES. Getting along well with the coordinators of these groups, for important policy committees as well as with their rapporteurs and MEPs in such committees, may make a great difference towards negotiating a favorable clause in the rounds of negotiations which precede the writing and voting of legislative reports.

Playing the membership cards well in either the EPP or the PES may mean the ability to align one's interests with those of fellow party leaders in the Council and with representatives from the same party family in the Commission when a party holds national government. The communications network provided by the EPP and the PES becomes even more critical when governmental parties lose national elections and move to the opposition. It provides indirect access to, and information on, negotiations that are secluded to the Council—something that cannot be matched by any of the other groups in the EP.

On the other hand, national delegations—even of parties in national government and with strong connections at the European level—lose heavily if they do not comply with the informal, but deeply ingrained, agreements that characterize the EP's consensual modus operandi, as the failure of Mário Soares to get to the top leadership of the EP suggests. If one had to point out the most powerful element determining the character of politics in the EP in the twenty-first century, it would be the constant search for consensus within political groups, within committees, and between political groups, which moves everything that goes on in parliament, including the allocation of key posts. The institutional strengthening of the EP in European politics has relied on this element, and anyone who forgets it is subject to quick rebuke.

Membership in either the EPP or the PES is not the best market option for everybody, though. Parties that do not have real expectations to hold national government and/or that spend a long stint in the opposition can find a better niche—more concretely to add visibility at home and make a point against the "establishment"—by affiliating with one of the smaller EPGs. Again, because of the loose ideological character of parliamentary groups in the EP and the possibility to opt for different ones according to pragmatic interests, small party delegations can gain disproportionate bargaining leverage and attain unexpected perks, as the case of the PRD shows.

In summary, this study suggests that politicians have learned to use political membership in the EP as a mechanism to increase competitiveness in multilevel governance. The complex norms on co-decision in the EU influence the making of alliances and, consequently, the composition and nature of political groups in the EP. At the same time, the dynamic character of national political cleavages, national party leadership, and ideology reflect at the supranational level and influence group membership. One cannot have an adequate understanding of the workings of EP party politics without examining the history, political culture, regime type, and evolution of party alliances within the member states. In other words, studying party politics in the European Parliament in isolation entails substantive and methodological flaws.

Ultimately, the findings of this study remind us of Putnam's (1988) assertion that national political leaders play a "two-level" game in international politics, whereby they are able to make one movement on one level so as to trigger realignments on the other level which secure otherwise unattainable objectives and change their relative power position. Notwithstanding the impact of Putnam's findings in studies of international relations, little systematic research has been done to investigate how politicians use the opportunities provided by their participation in the European Parliament to escape domestic constraints and to secure resources that they would not access otherwise.[60] My work hopefully contributes to fill this gap.

The political logic underlying the make-up of supranational parliamentary groups is the search by national party leaders to increase competitiveness, i.e. the access to privileged policy information, the capability to negotiate with key players, and the ability to attract financial resources and international political support. That might explain why, after thirty years of democratic practice and in the increasingly integrated politics of the twenty-first century, EPGs maintain the character of (un)structured coalitions of national party delegations, formed after elections and subject to the will of domestic actors, rather than evolving towards autonomous political organizations with their own set of political leaders and directly subject to the scrutiny of voters. National political leaders are not keen on the development of effective European party organizations directly competing for the EP elections because their party apparatuses would lose control over the kinds of payoffs that explain the dynamics of political group affiliation in the EP.

Notes

1. I gratefully acknowledge financial support for the research from the *Fundação para a Ciência e a Tecnologia* (project ID: POCI/CPO/61012/2004). Vera Henriques provided excellent research assistance in carrying out field work for this project. Peter A. Hall, Thomas Banchoff, Robert Fishman, Sebastian Royo, Andrés Malamud, Marina Costa Lobo, Catherine Moury, and Pedro Leal Rosa have provided key feedback at earlier stages of writing, for which I am very grateful.

2. One may point out three basic landmarks in the movement towards deeper integration since Portugal joined the EC: The Single European Act, which was signed in February 1986 and brought into effect in July 1987, introduced the cooperation procedure for specific legislative areas, enabling the European Parliament (EP) to directly amend legislation. The Treaty of Maastricht, officially ratified in 1992 and implemented as of November 1993, enforced deadlines for the European Monetary Union and introduced the co-decision procedure, which gave the EP veto power in the making of supranational acts on the freedom of circulation of workers, the right of establishment, the internal market, services, education, health, consumers, environment, culture and research. The

multiple readings of the co-decision procedure were simplified by the Treaty of Amsterdam (adopted in 1997 and ratified in 1999), further enforcing the equal standing of the EP and the Council in supranational legislative activity and widening the scope of supranational legislative powers. See "Gabinete em Portugal do Parlamento Europeu e Comissão Nacional de Eleições" in *Um Parlamento Diferente dos Outros,* (Lisboa, 2004), 13; and A. Kreppel, *The European Parliament and Supranational Political System: A Study in Institutional Development* (Cambridge and New York: Cambridge University Press, 2002) 77-90.

3. See, among others, F. Attina "The Voting Behaviour of the European Parliament Members and the Problem of Europearties" *European Journal of Political Research,* no.18, (1990): 557-579; L. Bardi, "Transnational Party Federations, European Parliamentary Groups, and the Building of Euro-Parties," in *How Parties Organize: Adaptation and Change in Party Organizations in Western Democracies* ed. R. S. Katz and Peter Mair (London: Sage, 1994), 357-72; S. Hix, "The Transnational Party Federations" in *Political Parties and the European Union,* ed. J. Gaffney (London: Routledge, 1996); M. Marsh and P. Norris "Political Representation in the European Parliament," *European Journal of Political Research* 32, no. 6, (1997): 153-164; S. Hix, A. Kreppel and A. Noury "The Party System in the European Parliament: Collusive or Competitive?" *Journal of Common Market Studies* 39, no. 4 (2001).

4. See, among others, L. Ray, "Measuring Party Orientations Towards Political Integration: Results from an Expert Survey" *European Journal of Political Research,* 36 no. 2, (1999): 283-306; P. Mair, "The Limited Impact of Europe on National Political Systems," in *Europeanized Politics? Special Issue of West European Politics,* 23 no. 4 (2000): 27-51; S. Bartolini "A Integração Europeia Provocará uma Reestruturação dos Sistemas de Clivagens Nacionais?" *Sociologia, Problemas e Práticas,* no. 37, (2001): 91-114; Klaus H. Goetz and Simon Hix, eds *Europeanised Politics? European Integration and National Political Systems.* (London, 2001); Frank Cass; R. Ladrech "Europeanization and Political Parties: Towards a Framework for Analysis" *Party Politics* 8, no. 4, (2002): 389-403; T. Raunio "Why European Integration Increases Leadership Autonomy within Political Parties," *Party Politics,* 8 no. 4, (2002): 405-422; Maria Costa Lobo, "Atitudes dos Portugueses Perante a UE: Perspectivas Sociais e Políticas " *Portugal, Espanha e a Integração Europeia: Um Balanço,* ed. Sebastian Royo (Lisboa: Imprensa de Ciências Sociais, Instituto de Ciências Sociais da Universidade de Lisboa, 2005); T. Poguntke et al., *The Europeanization of National Political Parties: Power and Organizational Adaptation* (Abindgdon: Routledge, 2007); F. Wendler "The Impact of European Integration on the Structure of Political Conflict within Domestic Political Systems of EU Member States," (paper presented to the ECPR Joint Sessions of Workshops, Lisbon, 14-19 April 2009); C. Moury and L. de Sousa, *Institutional Challenges in Post-Constitutional Europe: Governing Change* (Routledge, 2009).

5. This was observed when new layers of governance emerged in the process of political and administrative devolution in Britain. See J. Hopkin and J. Bradbury, "British Parties and Multi-Level Politics," (paper for Discussion at Seminar "Devolution in the United Kingdom: State and Citizenship in Transition," a seminar of the ESRC Devolution and Constitutional Change Programme, together with *Publius. The Journal of Federalism.* Edinburgh, U.K., May 20-21, 2005).

6. See R. Corbett, F. Jacobs and M. Shackleton, *The European Parliament* (London: John Harper Publishing, 2005).

7. See Corbett et al., *The European Parliament*; and author's interviews with Raúl Rosado Fernandes.

8. The institutional development of the EP has been marked by the attempt to restrict the number of EPGs through rules that have made it increasingly harder to meet all the necessary numeric and geographical requirements of representation. In essence, such evolution has been motivated by the will by supranational legislators to curb nationalistic and extremist tendencies, either via the formation of single-nation groups or of groups that concentrate euroskeptic parties. Also, it has favored the settlement of stable majorities. Author's interviews with Carlos Coelho and Carlos Pimenta. See also Corbett et al., *The European Parliament.*

9. See Anna Maria Evans, "Bringing Back a Larger Pie from Brussels: The Adjustment of National Party Strategy through Party Switching in the EP," CIES e-Working Paper no. 63 (Lisboa: CIES-ISCTE, 2009)

10. For the importance of the aggregating function of political parties for overcoming the democratic deficit in the EU, see Christopher J. Lord, "The Aggregating Function of Political Parties in EU Decision-Making," Living Rev. in Euro. Gov., Vol. 1, no. 2 (2006) [Online Article].

11. Scholars tend to assume the volatility of parliamentary groups is a mark of underdevelopment and democratic deficit, as it interferes with the capability of political parties and legislatures to organize regular patterns of decision-making, i.e. the majorities needed to pass legislation and the opposition which is necessary for deliberation and amendment. See S. Mainwaring, "Politicians, Electoral Systems, and Parties: Brazil in Comparative Perspective," *Comparative Politics* 24, no. 1, (October 1991): 21-43; S. Mainwaring and T. R. Scully, eds *Building Democratic Institutions in Latin America* (Stanford: Stanford University Press, 1995); G. Shabad and K. M. Slomczynski, "Inter-Party Mobility among Parliamentary Candidates in Post-Communist East Central Europe," *Party Politics* 10, no. 2, (2004): 151-76; J. Zielinski, K. M. Slomczynski, and G. Shabad, "Electoral Control in New Democracies: The Perverse Incentives of Fluid Party Systems," *World Politics* 57, no. 3, (April 2005): 365-395; S. Desposato, "Parties for Rent? Ambition, Ideology, and Party Switching in Brazil's Chamber of Deputies," *American Journal of Political Science* 50, no. 1, (January 2006): 62-80.

12. See, among others, T. Bruneau, *Political Parties and Democracy in Portugal* (Boulder: Westview Press, 1997); A. Freire, *Mudança Eleitoral em Portugal: Clivagens, Economia e Voto em Eleições Legislativas, 1983-1999* (Oeiras: Celta Editora, 2003); C. Jalali, *Partidos e Democracia em Portugal 1974-2005: Da Revolução ao Bipartidarismo* (Lisboa: Imprensa de Ciências Sociais, Instituto de Ciências Sociais da Universidade de Lisboa, 2007); Maria Costa. Lobo, *Governar em Democracia* (Lisboa: Imprensa de Ciências Sociais, Instituto de Ciências Sociais da Universidade de Lisboa, 2005a); M.C. Lobo, "The Presidentialization of Portuguese Democracy?" In *The Presidentialization of Politics: A Comparative Study of Modern Democracies,* ed. T. Poguntke and P. Webb (Oxford: Oxford University Press, 2005b); Sebastían Royo, ed. (2005) *Portugal, Espanha e a Integração Europeia: Um Balanço* (Lisboa: Imprensa de Ciências Sociais, Instituto de Ciências Sociais da Universidade de Lisboa, 2005); Pedro Magalhães, "Disaffected Democrats: Political Attitudes and Political Action in Portugal," *West European Politics* 28, no. 5, (2005): 973-991; A. C. Pinto and N. S. Teixeira, eds. *Southern Europe and the Making of the European Union* (NY: Columbia University Press, 2005); J.M.L. Viegas, H. Carreiras and A. Malamud, orgs. *Instituições e Política: Portugal no Contexto Europeu* (Lisboa, CIES-ISCTE: Celta Editora, 2007); P. Magalhães (2007) "Voting and Intermediation: Informational Biases and Electoral Choices in Comparative Perspective," in *Democracy, Intermediation and Voting in Four Continents,* ed. Richard Gunther et al.,

(Oxford: Oxford University Press, 2007); A. Freire, "Party Polarization and Citizens Left-Right Orientations," *Party Politics* 14, no. 2, (2008): 189-209.

13. For comprehensive reviews on these debates, see K. Strom and W. C. Muller, "Political Parties and Hard Choices," in *Policy, Office, or Votes? How Political Parties in Western Europe Make Hard Decisions*, ed. W. C. Muller and K. Strom (NY: Cambridge University Press, 1999); M. Laver and K. Benoit, "The Evolution of Party Systems Between Elections," *American Journal of Political Science* 47, no. 2, (April 2003): 215-33. For the weight of policy, office or votes in party behavior in the specific context of EP party politics, see G. McElroy, "Party Switching in the European Parliament: Why Bother Defect?" (paper Presented at the Annual Meeting of the American Political Science Association, Philadelphia, Pennsylvania, August 28-31, 2003); G. McElroy, "Legislative Party Switching in the European Parliament: The Trans-National Experience," (paper presented at the Annual Meeting of the American Political Science Association, Boston, MA, August 28-31, 2008); S. Hix, *The Political System of the European Union* (London: Palgrave Macmillan, 2005), 91; and R. Corbett, F. Jacobs and M. Shackleton, *The European Parliament* (London: John Harper Publishing, 2005), 122 and ff.

14. See K. Strom and W. C. Muller (1999) and W. B. Heller and C. Mershon (2005).

15. Based upon analysis of roll-call votes, Hix argues that when national party delegations deliver voting instructions to their MEPs which differ from the official position of the EPG, MEPs tend to vote with the former and against the latter. See S. Hix, "Parliamentary Behaviour with Two Principals: Preferences, Parties and Voting in the European Parliament," *American Journal of Political Science* 46, no. 3, (July 2002): 688-98. Scully and Farrell, on the other hand have found small differences in the score MEPs attribute to the different categories of principals. R. Scully and D. M. Farrell, "MEPs as Representatives: Individual and Institutional Roles," *Journal of Common Market Studies* 41, no. 2, (2003): 271. For other analyzes on the relationship between the degree of autonomy of candidates vis-à-vis party leaders and its relation with the stability (vs. volatility) of political affiliation, see S. Mainwaring (1991) and S. Mainwaring and T. R. Scully (1995). .

16. See A. Kreppel, "Moving in the other Direction? The Impact of Domestic Party System Change on Italian MEPs," *Journal of European Public Policy* 11, no. 6, (2004): 975.

17. See K. Strom and W. C. Muller (1999); and W. B. Heller and C. Mershon, "Party Switching in the Italian Chamber of Deputies 1996-2001," *The Journal of Politics* 67, no. 2, (May 2005): 536-559.

18. Author's interviews with Carlos Carvalhas.

19. See K. Maxwell, "Regime Overthrow and the Prospects for Democratic Transition in Portugal," in *Transitions from Authoritarian Rule: Southern Europe*, ed. G. O'Donnell, P. Schmitter and L. Whitehead (Baltimore and London: Johns Hopkins University Press, 1986), 117.

20. Maxwell, "Regime Overthrow," 116.

21. See "Partido Socialista, Declaração de Princípios e Programa do Partido Socialista," Textos "Portugal Socialista," 63, cit. in José Manuel Durão Barroso (1983) *Le Systeme Politique Portugais Face a l'Integration Europeenne: Parties Politiques et Opinion Publique* (Associação Portuguesa para o Estudo das Relações Internacionais, 1973), 129.

22. See Barroso *Le Systeme Politique Portugai*, 133-136. Also, see S. Royo and P. Christopher Manuel, "Introdução," in *Portugal, Espanha e a Integração Europeia: Um*

Balanço, ed. S. Royo (org.) (Lisboa: Instituto de Ciências Sociais da Universidade de Lisboa, 2005), 37.

23. See Barroso, *Le Systeme*, 133-136.

24. See W. Opello, "Portugal: A Case Study of International Determinants of Regime Transition," in *Encouraging Democracy: The International Context of Regime Transition in Southern Europe*, ed. G. Pridham (Leicester: Leicester University Press, 1991), 84-102.

25. See Barroso, *Le Systeme*, 103.

26. See Barroso, *Le Systeme*, 103. Also author's interviews with Carlos Carvalhas and José Luís Fernandes.

27. See Barroso, *Le Systeme*, 107. For thorough analyses of the international dimensions of the process of democratization and party building in Portugal, see Opello, "Portugal: A Case Study," and L. Whitehead, ed. *The International Dimensions of Democratization: Europe and the Americas* (Oxford: Oxford University Press, 1996)

28. See Barroso *Le Systeme*, 107.

29. Author's interviews with Carlos Coelho. The PSD was the most voted party in the 1985 national elections.

30. Author's interviews with Carlos Coelho.

31. This account is based on author's interviews with José Luís Fernandes, Eduardo Bugalho, Mário David, José Pacheco Pereira, Nunes Liberato, Arlindo Cunha, Manuel Machado, and Carlos Coelho.

32. Author's interviews with José Luís Fernandes, Eduardo Bugalho, Mário David, José Pacheco Pereira, Nunes Liberato, Arlindo Cunha, Manuel Machado, and Carlos Coelho.

33. See http://www.epp.eu/subsubpagina.php?hoofdmenuID=1&submenuID=1&sub submenuID=6 . See also Hix *The Political System* 192; Corbett et al, *The European Parliament*, 106-107. Also, author's interviews with Luís Fernandes, Eduardo Bugalho, Mário David, José Pacheco Pereira, Nunes Liberato, Arlindo Cunha, Carlos Coelho.

34. http://www.epp.eu/subsubpagina.php?hoofdmenuID=1&submenuID=1&subsub menuID=6.

35. As we will see below, the Portuguese Party of the Social Democratic Center (CDS/PP) had been affiliated with the EPP since 1986 but was ousted in 1992 because of its new leadership's strong disagreement with the pro-European character of the group and because there was no other Portuguese delegation in the EPP.

36. Author's interviews with Luís Fernandes, Eduardo Bugalho, Mário David, José Pacheco Pereira, Nunes Liberato, Arlindo Cunha, Carlos Coelho.

37. [Sources omitted here by request]. This claim agrees with Hix's remark that "party leaders' summits could potentially serve as vehicles for organizing the selection of candidates to the post of Commission president." See Hix, *The Political System*, 192.

38. In his public speeches and writings, Soares frequently referred to his close friendship with leaders like Brandt, Callaghan, Olof Palme, de Joergensen, de Kreisky and Mitterand. See Barroso, *Le Systeme*, 108-109.

39. See K. Maxwell "Regime Overthrow," 130. Accordingly, the Portuguese Socialists also received between $2 million and $10 million per month in 1975.

40. Author's interviews with Torres Couto, Eduardo Bugalho, Carlos Pimenta, Jorge Pegado Liz, and José Luís Fernandes.

41. See Corbett et al. *The European Parliament*, 116.

42. This tale is based in conversations with several interviewees. See also Corbett et al. (2005): 116.

43. Author's interviews with Carlos Coelho. According to Szule (1975), such financial backing came via the Portuguese trade union *CGTP-Intersindical*, as well as through the newspaper "O Diário." See T. Szule, "Lisbon and Washington: Behind the Portuguese Revolution," *Foreign Policy*, 21, (1975) cit. in Barroso, *Le Systeme*, 111. For more on the party's international backing, see K. Maxwell "Regime Overthrow," 130; and Opello "Portugal: A Case Study."

44. See Barroso *Le Systeme*, 113.

45. Author's interviews with Carlos Carvalhas.

46. Author's interviews with Torres Couto, Carlos Carvalhas, and Sérgio Ribeiro. Also data-sheet provided by the European Parliament on "PE-Constitutive-III Legislature (1989-1994): Deputes au Parlement Europeen au 25/07/89—Repartition par Etat Membre et Appartenances aux Groupes Politiques. "

47. Author's interviews with Carlos Carvalhas. The Green candidate elected in alliance with the PCP (Maria Santos) was subsequently elected to lead the Green group in the EP.

48. See Jalali, *Partidos e Democracia em Portugal 1974-2005*, 130.

49. See http://www.cds.pt/items.aspx?id_item=584, consulted in August 1, 2009.

50. See Corbett et al., *The European Parliament*, 77.

51. Author's interviews with Miguel Seabra.

52. Author's interviews with Miguel Seabra.

53. The money was sent to the *Instituto Democracia e Liberdade*, which was responsible for diffusing the Christian-Democratic ideology in Portugal and for training Christian-Democratic party cadres at the regional and local levels. See Barroso *Le Systeme*, 115-116. Also author's interviews with Carlos Coelho.

54. This account is based on author's interviews with Miguel Seabra and Manuel Machado.

55. Author's interviews with Carlos Coelho. In 1999, under pressure from the British Conservatives who had joined the EPP in 1992, the latter changed its official name to "Group of the European People's Party (Christian-Democrats) and European Democrats." See Corbett et al., *The European* Parliament, 79.

56. Author's interviews with Carlos Coelho.

57. See Jalali, *Partidos e Democracia em Portugal 1974-2005*, 208 and 250.

58. In the case of smaller EPGs, the entry or continuity of a national delegation in the Group may constitute a question of survival. For example, in the 1994 EP elections, the Group of the European Right disappeared because the Alleanza Nazionale (AN) did not want to remain affiliated and hence the group did not have sufficient members to pass the threshold of parliamentary representation. See Corbett et al., *The European Parliament*, 74.

59. Author's interviews with José Luís Fernandes, Jorge Pegado Liz and Pedro Canavarro.

60. S. Hix and K. Goetz, "Introduction: European Integration and National Political Systems," in *Europeanised Politics? European Integration and National Political Systems*, ed. Klaus H. Goetz and Simon Hix, (London: Frank Cass 2001), 1.

5 Incomplete Modernity or Typically Modern? Portuguese National Identity in an Era of Rapid Transition

Michael Baum and Miguel Glatzer

States build nations. They structure societies and shape identities. In this chapter we explore the successes and dilemmas of these twin projects of socio-structural transformation and national identity formation in the case of Portugal. We argue that the questions of Portugal's incomplete modernity[1] and its development model have been central to the transformative projects of the Portuguese state and Portuguese national identity.

The chapter proceeds in three parts. We start by providing a historical overview that embeds the question of national identity in the international and domestic challenges faced by the state in four distinctive periods: the late nineteenth century, the First Republic, the Salazar dictatorship, and the current democratic regime. The second part focuses on the Europeanizing project of a modern liberal state committed to a social model that balances economic growth with equity. In this section, we examine three dramatic changes in Portuguese society that have occurred in the wake of democratization and European integration: the welfare state, issues of gender equity, and the incorporation of immigrants. The third part examines questions of identity with the nation and with Europe using public opinion data.

Our conclusion is that on balance, the Portuguese Third Republic has managed this transition from a semi-peripheral empire to a small European state in the EU quite well, despite current concerns about the future of the country's economic status and the quality of its democracy. Some aspects of this success rely on fortuitous and unique features of Portuguese history and geography, but others are policy-oriented and therefore worthy of study and modeling by other states and policymakers.

Nineteenth- and Early Twentieth-Century National Identity in Portugal

Scholars[2] generally date the beginning of modern Portuguese nationalism with the Liberal Revolution of 1820 to 1834. This period included the loss of Portugal's most important colony, Brazil, in 1822. Although it continued to officially *possess* a colonial empire that stretched from West Africa to southeast Asia, the economic and financial significance of these territories was minimal at best.[3] Thus, by at least the mid-to-late nineteenth century, Portugal was something of a world power. It was a hybrid colonial regime—simultaneously colonizer and colonized—due to its subaltern position in the hierarchy of European imperialism, in particular its dependent relationship with Great Britain and the peculiarity of its relationship with Brazil.[4] Given such a scenario, it is not surprising that nineteenth-century Portuguese elites were preoccupied with their country's general decline and loss of global prestige, thereby leading to their calls for "national regeneration."

By at least the 1880s, as Europeans began what came to be known as the "Scramble for Africa,"[5] Portugal's subordinate relationship with the British Empire created especially strong anti-British and anti-monarchical sentiments within Portugal. These came to a head in 1890 with the British Ultimatum.[6] Britain's demand that the Portuguese crown relinquish its claims in what is now Zimbabwe actually served to create the conditions that marked modern Portuguese nationalism. The intransigent defense of Portugal's colonial empire became the country's primary foreign policy goal, and remained so until 1974. As Severiano Teixeira says, "The ultimatum was a highly symbolic moment in Portuguese history, in both foreign and domestic political terms. It signaled the end of the monarchy."[7]

Politically and institutionally, Portugal entered the twentieth century as a non-industrialized constitutional monarchy governed by a stable "oligarchic parliamentarism." This liberal-minded urban oligarchy presided over a primarily rural country using clientelistic networks of "*rotativismo*" that kept the overwhelming majority of the population effectively excluded from political life.[8] Despite its many weaknesses, the constitutional monarchy also began to develop all the tools of a modern centralized state, even including the extension of some important freedoms.[9] Nevertheless, in what would become something of a harbinger of the end of the authoritarian Salazar regime some sixty-odd years later, the monarchy reformed too little and too late to save itself. In 1910, a republican political movement overthrew Portugal's centuries-old monarchy. The Republicans' base of support were the nascent urban middle and lower-middle classes that had previously been excluded from political power, but the actual coup was carried out by a coalition of dissident republican military officers, secret republican groups linked to the Masons and *Carbonária*, and even a few Lisbon-based anarchists.[10]

In order to place Portugal's First Republic and the country's hybrid or semi-peripheral status in its proper context, one needs to keep in mind the extent of Portugal's backwardness in 1911, one year after it finally shed its decadent monarchy. Nearly 60 percent of the country's economically active population was still engaged in agriculture, 25 percent engaged in industry, and 17 percent in the service sector. By 1930 the picture was almost identical, with industrial employment remaining stable and agriculture occupying only 3 percent less of the working population.

Given the weight of agricultural employment in the economy, it is no surprise that the country remained deeply rural and illiterate, despite the cosmopolitanism of its urban elites.[11] The literacy rate of those over the age of ten at the turn of the century was around 30 percent[12] and its improvement was exceptionally slow from a comparative perspective, taking until 1964 to reach even the 70 percent literacy threshold.[13] In fact, the urban-rural cleavage remained one of the key socio-political cleavages in the country until much later than elsewhere in Western Europe, until at least the mid to late 1960s. In a pattern typical of elsewhere in Southern Europe,[14] scholars frequently referred to Portugal as a "dualist" society in the 1960s.[15] Although we do not have the space here to provide a full theoretical exploration of our position, we understand efforts to create a "national identity" in such "dualist" societies as primarily a top-down project of national integration lead by the State, that is, largely carried out by urban elites.[16] According to scholars like Diamandouros, what distinguishes this process in late industrializing countries like those of Southern Europe, is the fact that the power and resources of those groups favoring modernizing transformation in social structures were never great enough to fully displace those groups favoring a more traditional economy and social structure, leading to a sort of permanent stalemate in the direction of the country.[17] We can see the effects of this stalemate in Portugal's relatively late convergence toward European income norms, which mainly occurred during the period from 1950 to 1973.[18]

The weight of the more traditional rural sector made the national integration efforts of the First Republic all the more difficult. This was especially true insofar as that cleavage overlapped with the religious-secular divide that largely divided the country between north and south. Secularization was a major goal of the new Republican regime. As Costa Pinto notes, convents were closed down and religious orders, such as the Jesuits, were expelled from the country.[19] A new divorce law was decreed and marriages were made exclusively civil ceremonies. The regime radically simplified and changed the orthography in a more phonetic direction, with the goal of promoting literacy and education among the masses.[20] New national holidays were created to replace many of the country's previously Catholic celebrations, a new flag and national hymn were tacked onto the equally new national curriculum of the country's public schools, all in an effort to instill the republican and secular values the regime sought to develop.[21] Wheeler quotes a republican theorist from 1911 who argued that the goals of the First Republic were nothing less than "the formation of a modern people."[22]

In Lisbon and the rural South, where the power of the Church was already much less significant than elsewhere in the country, the First Republic's secular reforms were welcomed, though their impact was often fleeting and uneven.[23] Elsewhere in the country (in a harbinger of the north-south and rural-urban cleavages that again became pertinent during the revolutionary upheavals of 1975), there was stiff resistance to the ethos emanating from Lisbon. A new Catholic political movement emerged from this conflict, its roots primarily in the rural North, and over the course of the First Republic it increasingly became corporatist and authoritarian. This counter-revolutionary movement provided support to the fleeting Sidónio Pais dictatorship of 1917 and 1918 and then again to the military dictatorship that ended Portugal's first experiment with democracy in 1926, eventually ushering in the corporatist and deeply traditional Salazar regime that lasted until 1974.[24]

In terms of its contributions to Portuguese national identity, the ironies of the First Republic are many. First, besides endemic cabinet instability[25] and foreign policy forays that were viewed as disastrous by the military,[26] the First Republic's ultimate failure was that its propaganda and nationalist rhetoric did not really live up to their billing. While sufficiently radical to provoke the more traditional sectors of Portuguese society into defensive action, the reforms were nevertheless too half-hearted—for example, as regards the extension of the universal franchise and women's voting rights—to permit the incorporation of the masses as a base of support for the new regime. Trade union development during the First Republic, like Portuguese industrialization more generally, was also uneven, fitful, and regionally concentrated, and thus did not serve as a tool for building a powerful labor or social democratic party, as occurred elsewhere in Europe.[27] Despite these weaknesses, all the major symbols of contemporary Portuguese national identity—the national anthem, the flag, the new civil calendar, and a secularized national educational system—came out of this failed regime that lasted from 1910 to 1926, and are still intact today as the key tools used by the state for building Portugal's contemporary national identity.

Salazar's Vision of National Identity

Besides its status as the longest lasting authoritarian regime in Western Europe (1926-1974), Antonio Salazar's *Estado Novo* has arguably had the largest impact on contemporary Portuguese national identity, albeit one that is still hotly contested.[28] Much has been written on the creation and use by the Salazar dictatorship of a particular conception of national identity.[29] Central to this state-sponsored national identity was the role of Portugal as a nation with a maritime and in particular Atlantic destiny. The empire was crucial to this narrative. The incorporation of overseas territories as national territory and a complex mythologized system of race relations were ingenious defenses of the notion of empire in the face of international criticism of colonialism.[30] One need only see the frescoes that Salazar's *Estado Novo* (New State) regime painted on the walls of the National Assembly great room to understand how that regime conceived and propagated this aspect of its vision of Portuguese national identity. Piousness and family, a bedrock of solid rural values (akin in some ways to the view in France of a rural depository of values and authenticity in *la France profonde*), and national characteristics such as moderation and gentle manners (*brandos costumes*) constituted further building blocks of these official descriptions of the nation.

As Costa Pinto and others have stressed, the Salazar regime had a deep conservative bent. Unlike the Italian fascists, modernization and a whole scale transformation of society were suspect projects.[31] *Orgulhosamente sos* (standing proudly, even defiantly, alone against the winds of change blowing in from abroad) represents this attitude very well. Autarchy and tradition had limits, as membership in NATO (1949) and EFTA (1960) attest, or as can be seen in the modernist housing developments and infrastructure that accommodated economic growth in Lisbon, or the social policies that started to benefit the area's new inhabitants. In fact, as Lains[32] has demonstrated, no political regime in Portugal enjoyed higher average increases in per capita income than the Salazar regime of the 1960s, despite its ultimately fatal decision to spend a large chunk of that wealth on futile wars to retain its colonies in Africa.[33] But the larger point stands: after nearly fifty years of authoritarian rule and compared to other European countries, Portugal was still much more rural and its population much more likely to be illiterate or to have only a few years of schooling. It might have been called the *Estado Novo*; it is a lot less clear that its goal was a radically transformed society.

National Identity and Three Distinct Types of State Projects: Conservative, Radically Transformative, and European Integration

A state-promoted national identity based on Portugal's Atlantic vocation, imperial stability, and Catholic piety, standing strong against the winds of change, fit well with the conservative nature of the Salazar regime and its ambivalent relationship with modernity. On the opposite end of the spectrum, one can imagine a logic of fit between radically transformative projects which aim to rupture with the past and the state-promoted national identities that these projects produce. If in the conservative cases the goal of the state is to preserve a mythologized view of the past and the social virtues embedded in it, in the radically transformative projects, the goal is to create a new man, a new society. It is therefore no accident that the state-promoted national identities of these transformative political projects are easily recalled by any educated reader. Italian fascist architecture, Nazi banners and mass rallies, Soviet or Maoist posters loudly proclaimed the new national identity. This is true of all radically transformative political projects, including those that aim to be liberal and democratic.

Among such cases is the First Portuguese Republic. Although ultimately unsuccessful in ushering in a stable liberal democratic order, its aims were certainly transformative and involved deep—and at times, violent—breaks with the past, as seen in the attacks on the monarchy and the considerable anticlericalism associated with the republican forces. The First Portuguese Republic's attempts to produce a new national identity are clear and still with us today. A political project of social transformation called for new symbols and new means of delivering this new identity. This explains why the First Portuguese Republic redesigned the flag, re-wrote the national anthem, and developed a secular school system.

In contrast to conservative projects focused on preservation or radically transformative projects—each of which has clear logics of fit with particular forms of national identity construction—it is much less clear what kind of national identity the current democratic state in Portugal should try to foster. This is not because of a lack of agreement on how Portugal should change. Few in the political elite, from right to left, would argue that Portugal should rest on its laurels, preserve its society and economy, and retard change. Joining Europe was, and remains, a project of deep reshaping of the state, the economy, and society. The purpose of modernization and Europeanization is widely shared,[34] even if there is some variation across political parties, with some placing relatively more emphasis on economic growth, social justice, or administrative efficiency than others. This modernizing and Europeanizing project can be seen in the ubiquity of European comparisons, of benchmarking, ranking, and other forms of measurement used in so many Portuguese ministry reports.[35]

Nonetheless, two features of this Europeanizing project distinguish it from earlier transformative projects and make it less clear what national identity the state should foster. First, the current transformative project is a gradualist and evolutionary one that involves learning from Europe, identifying best practices, and adapting them to the Portuguese case.[36] This is particularly apt in the current European era of an open method of coordination, but earlier European projects, such as the Single Market and the Euro, also involved learning and policy adoption by the state.[37] Second, as a good liberal state, procedural rules and adherence to the rule of law are as important, if not more important, than the substantive outcome. Liberal values also mean that individuals should be allowed to determine their own version of the good life, with one not imposed on them. This then is the paradox for a state-sponsored national identity in the current transformative project: What form of national identity is compatible with a project of Europeanization, particularly when Portugal ranks low on so many of the well-known comparative indicators? In a liberal state, aren't the values imparted by the state those of respect for the rule of law, personal freedom, tolerance, and active citizenship, with individuals free to choose what kind of life or identity they want to have? If Schengen means open borders and if Portugal is now wealthy enough to attract immigrants from poorer countries, how should the state respond to increasing diversity and multiculturalism? How, then, to build a national identity on this kind of project?

Structural Transformations[38]

Having posed the questions above, we now turn to three areas which demonstrate the ways in which the Portuguese state has embraced Europe, its social model, and the transformation of society it entails. We examine the welfare state, gender issues, and the integration of immigrants and find considerable variation in the success of state interventions in these areas. Portugal's turn towards Europe is often dated to 1960, when Portugal joined EFTA. This also marked the beginning of mass tourism flows to the country and of considerable emigration flows to Europe. To highlight transformations in Portuguese society since then, we use 1960 as a benchmark at various points in the following analysis.

The Welfare State: Income and Inequality

Economic growth, social change, and the development of the welfare state have led to dramatic transformations in work and income. One of the most striking changes is that the state has become a crucial provider of non-work income. The number of beneficiaries of the social security system rose from a mere 56,000 in 1960 to 800,000 by 1975, 2 million by 1985, and 2.5 million by 2000. Starting in the late 1960s (during the Caetano years) the rapid rise in the 1970s and 1980s reflected decisions to extend the pension system to previously unprotected segments of the population, such as rural workers or domestics. As a result of the non-contributory pension scheme, Portugal provides universal access to old-age pensions. Through old-age and widowed persons' pensions, the elderly represent by far the largest group receiving cash transfers from the state, although the unemployed, the disabled, the sick, families, and the very poor are also eligible for transfers.

From a human development perspective, this decision had tremendously positive implications. However, the cost of providing these benefits is large. From 1995 to 2008, social transfers increased from 11.2 percent of GDP to 15.6 percent.[39] By contrast, the weight of social transfers in the Euro Area 12 declined during this period from 16.9 percent to 16.1 percent of GDP. Portugal, the poorest country in the Euro Area 12, devotes a comparable share of its wealth to social transfers. The role of the state in income support—either directly through government employment or through social transfers—thus amounted to 28.5 percent of GDP in 2008. By contrast, the Euro Area 12 average was 26.2 percent. Portugal therefore has exceeded many of its European counterparts in the degree to which personal income is provided through the state.

The growth in cash transfers was mirrored in the education and health sectors, the two principal services of the welfare state, and can again be seen through the lens of government accounts. In the EU-15 in 2008, public spending on health and education (including salaries) consumed 11.7 percent of GDP. In Portugal, this share was over 13.8 percent (calculated from Banco de Portugal, 2009). Again in this case, government effort in the provision of health and education services, at least as measured in expenditure data, exceeds many of its European counterparts.

It is thus fair to say that in these three areas of access to income—pensions, education, and health—the immense social structural transformations in Portuguese society are deeply influenced by profound changes in the role of the state. This very large government effort has had mixed results. While income inequality and poverty remain high, improvements in health have been dramatic. Although educational access has expanded greatly, serious concerns over quality and attainment remain.[40]

Despite a significant state effort in income support, high employment rates and, prior to the recent rise in unemployment, historically low unemployment, Portugal continues to have among the highest poverty rates and levels of inequality in Western Europe. In 2007, with an 80/20 income quintile ratio of 6.5 in Portugal, only Romania and Bulgaria had worse levels of income inequality.[41] Similarly, 19.1 percent of the Portuguese population lived in poverty (defined as below 60 percent of median income) in 2000.[42]

Several factors explain the apparent paradox of convergence to European norms in terms of substantial welfare state effort and a high level of direct state employment, but continued high poverty rates. The first set of factors has to do with the labor market, and with the problem of low wages and high wage inequality. The distribution of income is highly unequal and correlates closely with the high inequality in educational attainment. Income among agricultural workers is also low, contributing to significant regional differences in income and poverty rates. This can be seen in the high poverty rates of 50.4 percent for people working in agriculture and of 48.3 percent for people with less than a primary education.[43]

There is debate about the degree to which the Portuguese tax system and social spending reduces or helps replicate income inequality. Many analysts argue that evasion, tax shifting, deductions, reductions in the number of tax brackets, and the differential treatment of wage income from capital gains reduce the progressivity of the Portuguese tax system.[44] Writing in 2001, the OECD found that Portuguese "income taxation achieves little in the way of income redistribution."[45] Two years later, the OECD had become more pessimistic, writing that "the fiscal system probably exacerbates the inequality of income distribution."[46] The Portuguese welfare state, like many of the welfare states in Southern Europe, privileges pension spending. Although a social pension scheme covers individuals who did not contribute enough during their working lives to qualify for the regular state pension system, the bulk of spending occurs in the latter system and this system is Bismarckian, replicating differences in earned income.

However, other analysts find that state taxes and targeted transfers are indeed redistributive and became substantially more so during the 1990s.[47] Improvements in tax collection and the development of substantial anti-poverty programs such as the *Rendimento Minimo Garantido* (Minimum Guaranteed Income) were effective in compensating for widening market inequalities of income. It is this greater redistributive effort of the state, countervailing an ever wider wage inequality, which accounts for the relative stability of the Gini index.

Because the Portuguese welfare state is pension-heavy, it under-provides community social services such as day centers and long-term care for the elderly, the disabled or the chronically ill.[48] In response, the Portuguese state has developed tax incentives for charitable giving to social service non-profits and has also contracted out with these groups to provide services.[49] The relative paucity of services in this area led some analysts to argue that Portugal was not a welfare state, but a welfare society.[50] In the absence of state provision, society—either through the extended family or through the community—met needs. This concept has been challenged by findings that supportive social networks are richer and more prevalent at the higher end of the socio-economic and educational distribution. As a result, informally provided welfare seems to "reinforce existing social inequalities and to offer less support for those who most need support."[51]

Despite the growth of a very substantial welfare state, results have been mixed. Income support from the state has grown dramatically and health outcomes are greatly improved, but inequality, poverty, and educational achievement remain problem areas when compared to EU averages.

Gender

One of the most reliably predictable outcomes of socio-economic development is the decline in birth and infant mortality rates, in the average size of the family, and in mean life expectancy.[52] What is distinctive about the Portuguese story in this regard, is the speed with which it developed a more modern demographic profile. In 1950, Portugal had the youngest population in Europe, but today it has one of the fastest aging populations.[53] This was accomplished by drastically lowering women's birth and fertility rates, maternal and infant mortalities, and the size of the average family, and increasing the average age at which women opt to start a family.[54] For example, the average number of children per woman aged fifteen to forty-nine years dropped from 3.2 in 1960, to 1.4 in 1995, and 1.32 in 2009.

This places Portugal among those countries with the lowest fertility rates in the world. As a result of significant investments in health, infant mortality rates dropped precipitously. In 1960 Portugal lost eighty-one infants per one thousand born—significantly worse than Spain (forty-four) and Greece's (fifty-three) rates—but by 2009, Portugal had surpassed both of those countries, with only three deaths per one thousand born.[55] That is half the rate of infant mortality in the United States and ranks Portugal among the best performing countries in the world on this development indicator.

These changes were linked to fundamental transformations in women's roles in Portuguese society. In 1960, many women in Portugal still did not have basic citizenship rights. Women were prohibited from the diplomatic service and could not serve as judges,[56] and until 1969 they needed written permission to leave the country. In some parts of rural Portugal, women's positions in society were described as similar to the public roles of women in traditional societies.[57] However, today women's roles throughout the national territory have converged with European norms, and in some areas, even surpassed them. Take for example Portuguese family structures and the rapid secularization of society. Since 1960, marriage rates have plummeted and the percentage of civil (as opposed to Catholic) marriages surpassed the 50 percent threshold in 2007. Related to this is the increasing number of children being born out of wedlock and the percentage of unions that involve cohabitation rather than marriage (civil or religious). This is particularly common in Lisbon and the southern half of the country.[58] More recently, abortion up to the tenth week was made legal in 2007[59] and in 2010, gay couples were permitted to marry—developments that were simply unthinkable before Portugal joined the European Union.

Linked to these transformations in the family and gender roles was the dramatic entrance of women into the paid workforce. In 1960, only 13 percent of women were in the paid labor force, whereas by 1996 they represented nearly 47 percent.[60] In terms of activity rates, while women made up only between 20 to 25 percent of the labor force in 1960[61], they now constitute 56 percent of those who are economically active.[62] This profile is atypical for Southern European countries, putting Portugal closer to the rates achieved in Scandinavia and northern Europe. For example, in 1995 only Denmark had more young mothers in the active labor force (87 percent), as compared to Portugal (77 percent); for comparison, Spain's rate was 47 percent.[63] As Barreto argues, while industrialization and "tertiarization" were partially behind women's integration into the labor force, emigration and the colonial wars were the main factors spurring women to earn cash wages.[64] The low wages of both male and female workers in Portugal have made the traditional "breadwinner model" difficult there, except for the most well-off families. Moreover, the proximity of families who could be relied upon for daycare and the relative availability of cheap (female) domestic labor are other factors that explain the high rates of female activity.[65] From this perspective, Portugal's dramatic convergence with Europe is primarily a bottom-up process, based upon the micro-motives of individual Portuguese women and families, but that is hardly the whole story.

Such decisions take place in a political and historical context deeply shaped by state action—witness how the colonial wars and the creation of a more export-oriented economy (following EFTA membership in 1959) provided new incentives for women to enter the paid labor force. The same is true for women's education. Education rates for women have improved dramatically, to the point where females are now significantly less likely than males to leave secondary school before completing their compulsory education, and make up 65 percent of those receiving university diplomas.[66] The feminization of university researchers has outpaced most other European countries, such that EUROSTAT data from 2003 show Portugal in fourth place among the EU-25.

Remaining inequalities from a traditionally patriarchal society continue to be addressed by the state in response to pressures from both Portuguese civil society actors as well as the diffusion of European best practices. Two examples in the political realm include the creation of a Commission for Equality and the Rights of Women (CIDM) and the government's 2006 passage of a gender quota law mandating that women make up 33 percent of the candidate lists for European, local, and national parliamentary elections.[67] Women now make up 27.4 percent of the national parliament, which places Portugal thirty-third in the world on this indicator of gender parity, well ahead of countries like Greece (seventy-second) or the United States, which is tied for seventy-third place with Turkmenistan (Inter-Parliamentary Union, 2010). Evidence of the state's relative progress on the gender equality front is also provided by the United Nation's Gender Empowerment Measure (GEM) which, in 2009, ranked Portugal nineteenth in the world, significantly higher than its Human Development Index (HDI) rank of thirty-fourth.[68]

On the other hand, we do not wish to present an unrealistic picture of gender equality in Portugal, since the state has clearly been reticent to tackle egregious gender gaps in other critical areas of the economy and society. For example, in a 2006 report issued by the European Professional Women's Network, Portugal was the only country that did not have a single woman on the board of any of its public companies. By 2008 it was still dead last, with only 2.1 percent, against a mean of nearly 10 percent in the seventeen countries reported.[69] Sociologists have also consistently reported on the relatively unequal division of (household) labor which continues to characterize the typical Portuguese family.[70] According to that survey, women's "double duty" is actually about four times greater than men's. Women who work outside the home in Portugal spend nearly four hours per day on household chores while their working male partners only spend 1.3 hours.[71]

In this policy area, as in the others we cover, the convergence story is clearly a mixed one. However, our perspective argues that Portuguese society has been radically altered by the changes that have occurred in the family and gender roles over the past fifty years, even if we have only been able to highlight a few of the most important ones here. We argue that in this policy area, despite uneven progress, the state has effectively promoted policies that have moved the country's gender and family roles to be more in line with European norms, including the implementation of legislation requiring positive efforts to address gender discrimination.

Migration/Immigration

Barreto argues convincingly that of all the changes in Portuguese society since 1960, the reversal of Portugal's position as a net exporter of its human capital to one of the fastest growing recipients of foreign immigrants is perhaps the most dramatic.[72] Between 1960 and 1973, before the first oil shock put an end to Europe's *Trentes Glorieuses*, more than 1.5 million Portuguese left their country to find work. No other European country experienced a greater hemorrhage as a share of its population in the 1960s. Barreto also notes that Portugal occupies the extreme outlier on several other variables of interest here.[73] For example, as a share of the population, the return in the 1970s of the white settler population from Portugal's newly independent ex-colonies in Africa represented the most rapid (and we would argue successful) mass migration back to the country of origin ever in Europe. It reached 7 percent in just one year. Similarly, in the 1990s and early 2000s, no other European country experienced a faster growth rate of foreign immigrants, despite the fact that their share of the total resident population has never reached greater than 7.2 percent.[74]

Whatever their actual share of the resident population, the presence of foreigners—in particular the sharp increase in those without close linguistic or cultural ties to Portugal—has meant that the country's visible identity has become significantly more cosmopolitan, particularly in Lisbon and other coastal cities. Whereas immigration was previously dominated by citizens from the Portuguese-speaking African countries (PALOPs), the profile of immigrants is now much more diversified, with a dramatic increase in the presence of Brazilians. As Figure 5.1 illustrates with EUROSTAT data from 1998 to 2009, Brazilians are now the largest group of non-EU-27 nationals with a presence in Portugal, followed by the Ukrainians. Cape Verdeans are now only the third largest group of non-EU-27 nationals.

Figure 5.1 Largest groups of foreigners by country/regional group living in Portugal, 1998-2009

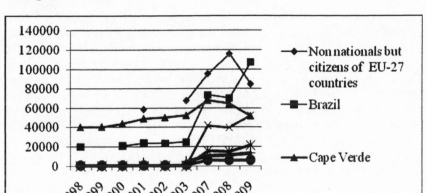

Source: EUROSTAT data explorer (migr_pop1ctz). Accessed 2/12/2011. Data last updated on 10/2/2011.
Note: Composition of "usually resident population" by country of citizenship does not include those with "permits of stay."

While this changeover in Portugal's status as a net "sender" of its people to a net "receiver" of other's country's citizens occurred in the 1970s and 1980s, the public perception of immigration as a hot-button political issue has only recently become more salient. The reasons for this are several. First, only recently has the total share of foreigners within the national population begun to reach significant levels. Second, just as immigration has gained visibility as a major social issue in the rest of (Western) Europe, its salience has grown in Portugal, particularly after 9/11.[75] Finally, it also gained visibility as a result of the controversies surrounding the 2008 ratification, by the Portuguese parliament, of the orthographic accords signed by the Community of Portuguese Language Countries (CPLP in its Portuguese acronym) in 1990.[76] Despite this increase, however, we would argue that compared to other EU states, the salience of the immigration issue remains low in Portugal.

As we argue in greater detail below, what is surprising about the rapid influx of foreigners in Portugal is the absence of any significant development of far-right or anti-foreigner political parties. They of course exist—the most prominent being the *Partido Nacional Renovador* (PNR)—but they have never gained enough public support to win any parliamentary or local council seats.[77] However, lest one assume that the Lusotropicalist thesis[78] explains the absence of virulent anti-immigrant or racist feelings in Portugal, or that the country's long history of emigration has somehow served as an empathetic vaccination against foreign immigrants; attitudinal surveys suggest a much more complicated reality.

Jorge Vala et al. have studied racism in Portugal and the different perceptions of threat using 2002 data from the European Social Survey (ESS).[79] Their comparative analysis came to the conclusion that among the four countries they studied closely—the UK, France, Germany and Portugal—Portugal was the country with the highest public expression of opposition to immigration. Even when compared against the full sample average of all EU-27 countries included in that module, the Portuguese were the least in favor of admitting "many or some" people coming from different types of countries—rich European, rich outside Europe, poor European, poor from outside Europe, etc.[80] For example, when considering immigrants that originate from European countries that are poorer than the receiving country, the variation between Portugal (the least supportive country), and Sweden (the most supportive) ranged from 39 percent to 87 respectively.[81] Curiously, unemployment rates are a poor predictor of these attitudinal differences, since Portugal had at the time of the survey, below average unemployment as it had throughout the 1980s and 1990s when immigration growth was booming in Portugal.

Moreover, we may also look at attitudes toward the integration of new migrants, with support for multiculturalism at one end of the spectrum versus support for assimilation at the other pole. Assimilation in this sense is defined as "the expectation that minorities adapt completely to the host society and its political system through a process of individual change, in which immigrants give up their different cultural backgrounds in order to adopt the hegemonic group culture."[82] Here again, Portuguese attitudes stand out as Europe's most *assimilationist*.[83]

The complicated nature of Portuguese attitudes toward immigrants is even more clearly underlined if we look at levels of support (in theory) for immigrants having equal rights with nationals. Two-thirds of Europeans (66 percent) agreed with the statement that "people who have come to live to their country ought to have the same rights as nationals." The rate is 80 percent in Portugal, the second-highest of all the countries surveyed. However, almost half of the Europeans (47 percent) also agreed with the sentiment that when immigrants experience a long period of unemployment, they should be expelled from the country. The citizens with the greatest support for expulsion were surprisingly the Portuguese (58 percent agree), as compared to the Spanish (24 percent) or the Swedes, where only 11 percent agreed with that sentiment.[84]

Now it could just be that the Portuguese are the least politically correct survey respondents in Europe and thus have no qualms about expressing less "politically correct" sentiments in public surveys, but this doesn't explain the inconsistencies we find in the Portuguese data as it relates to attitudes toward immigrants. Maritínez-Herrera and Moualhi suggest instead that it is more probably related to Portuguese respondents' lack of a thought out and real opinion on the themes of the study.[85] We agree with their suggestion that the limitations of sophisticated public debate on immigration issues in countries with a comparatively recent experience of immigration may well be what are behind the inconsistent attitudes. We should also keep in mind the low average levels of education and high levels of poverty in Portugal, which presumably are also related to ill-formed opinions on this and other complex policy issues.[86] These ambiguities in public opinion suggest that the state can play an especially influential role in shaping policy in this area.

By institutionalizing in 1996 a new government Commission on Immigrants and Ethnic Minorities (*Alto Commissariado para a Imigração e Minorías Étnicas*—ACIME) and using it to undertake outreach efforts and to commission studies, propose policy and legislative action, the state has recognized the need to pay attention to the issue of rising diversity and multiculturalism in Portugal. Pedro Zúqete for example, has argued that ACIME "displays a strong cultural and educational activism aimed at both enforcing a 'positive' public view of immigration and inoculating it against the message of the extreme right."[87] To this he also adds the influence of the Catholic subculture in Portugal—with an inclusive and ecumenical discourse—such that it also may serve as a brake on any political discourses of exclusion or intolerance on immigration. The Church, for example, has supported immigration reforms that are "sensitive" to the needs and demands of the immigrants and based on "solidarity," and rejects any nationalist leanings, because of Portugal's own historical status as a "country of emigrants."[88] While it is true that the power of the Church as a social actor has generally declined in Portugal since democratization, it is still a privileged civil society actor that has an impact on the political behavior of its members and sympathizers, particularly in certain regions of the country.[89]

External assessments of Portugal's relative success at integrating migrants have also been quite positive. For example, Peixoto and Sabino mention the fact that Portugal is ranked second out of 28 European countries in a recent comparative Migrant Integration Policy Index (MIPEX), which confirms the state's relatively successful policies in this area, at least in the European context.[90] The MIPEX overview for Portugal is worth quoting from directly:

> Proposed new immigration and nationality laws have aimed to simplify and facilitate access to family reunion, long-term residence, and nationality for legally-resident third-country-nationals (hereafter "migrants") and their children born in Portugal. A relatively new country of immigration, Portugal has put in place a legal framework on integration composed of favorable policies and best practice. Portugal does not have far to go to improve labor market access, family reunion, and anti-discrimination which all score 2nd out of the 28 MIPEX countries. Slightly favorable policies on long-term residence rank fourth in the EU-25, while access to nationality policies rank third (MIPEX, 2010).[91]

Moreover, despite the fact that some researchers and public officials consider the immigration process too complex, bureaucratic and ineffective,[92] the fact that no significant anti-immigration party has emerged in Portugal despite a dramatic uptick in new immigrants is, in our mind, yet another positive aspect to how the state has handled this challenge to "national identity." Of course, we in no way mean to paste over the fact that racism and prejudice are alive and well in Portugal, or that at times state representatives and the media have publicly associated criminality with the presence of immigrants, but thus far, a combination of deliberate state policy and a progressive stance on immigration by the Catholic Church have helped to defuse the "political opportunity structure" afforded by this structural change in Portuguese society. In this domain, we regard the Portuguese state as a relatively progressive policy maker, rather than a passive policy taker at the European level.

National and European Identity

As this chapter has shown, despite Salazar's professed desire to make the Portuguese "live by habit," socio-structural changes both during and since the Salazar period have been enormous. Portugal is no longer primarily rural, nor is its national identity tied to worldwide empire. Its primary institutional, political and economic links are to Europe, and its demographic and cultural shifts clearly conform to broadly European trends. It is now a net recipient of immigrants, many of whom have permanent residency permits and some of whom have acquired Portuguese citizenship. Portugal is thus becoming multicultural, multiracial, and better educated. Membership in the European Union is reflected not only in the material inflow of funds from Brussels or at the symbolic level of passports and currency but, crucially for our argument, at the level of identity.

What is especially instructive about the Portuguese case is the fact that the country's historically strong sense of national identity has been entirely compatible with high levels of support for EU membership. Take for example the public opinion results provided by the World Values (WVS) and International Social Survey Program (ISSP) series. As we can see in Figure 5.2, which compares the mean scores of citizens in each state who said they were "very proud" of their own nationality between 1990 and 1999 (as well as 2003 where available), the Portuguese exhibit comparatively high levels of national pride compared to the sample means.[93] Curiously, while volatility on this measure of national identity is not high for most countries, sentiments of national pride jumped a full 37 percentage points between 1990 and 1999 in Portugal—no doubt related to that country's successful hosting of the 1998 World's Fair, an extended period of macroeconomic growth with low inflation, and unexpected qualification as one of the first eleven states to meet the convergence criteria for Eurozone membership in 1999. Even in 2003, when signs of Portugal's post-honeymoon hangover with Euro membership were starting to become apparent, national pride remained high.

In terms of support for the EU within Portugal, trend analysis underlines the "instrumental"—some might say *contingent*—nature of this support. Despite relatively low levels of objective knowledge about the EU and its institutions, a broad permissive consensus has been maintained, despite the ups and downs we can broadly link to performance of the national economy[94] (see Figure 5.3).

Despite a severe economic downtown since 2000, one of the strongest arguments explaining the relatively sticky support for EU integration in Portugal comes from research conducted by Liesbet Hooghe and Gary Marks.[95] They effectively demonstrate that national identity is tricky; it both contributes to and diminishes support for European integration. What matters, they find, is the extent to which national identity is exclusive or inclusive.[96] Those respondents who say they think of themselves as "only British (or Portuguese, etc.)" have significantly lower levels of support for European integration compared to those with some form of multiple identity. However, these individuals are nested within countries, and their multi-level analysis finds that country-level variables matter, such that the impact of exclusive national identity is quite strong in a country like the UK (29.5 percent more Euroskeptical) while the Portuguese, with an exclusive national identification, are only 9.5 percent more Euroskeptic than their more multi-layered brethren. How do they explain this variation?

The answer, it seems, is the extent to which a country's elites are more or less divided about European integration. The more divided a country's elite, and the stronger the voice of anti-EU parties or movements, the stronger the causal power of exclusive national identity.[97] Political parties help to cue their publics; and the wider their disagreement, the more salient the EU issues become, and the stronger the causal connection between national identity and support for European integration.

What we know about Portugal is that elite consensus on the EU has remained high among all but the most left-wing parties. Radical right-wing or populist anti-EU parties are almost entirely absent from the Portuguese political scene, and as our analysis suggests, this is not just a happy accident. Portuguese elites have worked hard to maintain a consensus on Europe and to provide resources that mitigate some of the opportunity structures for more xenophobic and right-wing movements to get started. Whether they will remain successful in this regard as the economy continues to sputter and EU/Eurozone institutions demand ever greater levels of sacrifice from the Portuguese public remains an open question.

For now, being European, a member of the EU, is not an empty category but is a meaningful part of many people's identity. As the literature on supranational identity attests, identification with Europe does not necessitate a decline in national or sub-national identity.[98] Our main point here is that Portugal proves the rule that identities need not necessarily be a zero-sum game, where strength in one level comes at the expense of another.[99]

Figure 5.2 Percentage saying "very proud" of their nationality, 1990-1999 (mean) and 2003

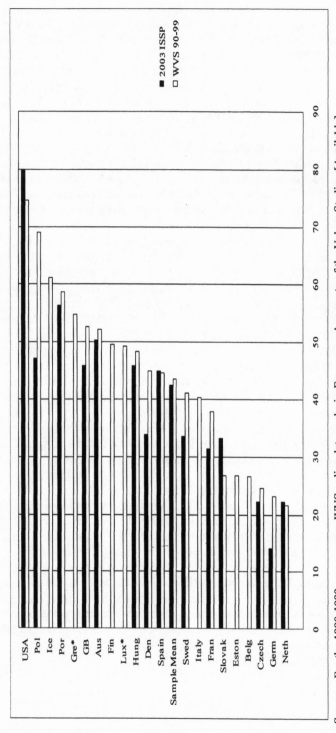

Sources: For the 1990-1999 mean scores: WVS online data analysis, Four-wave Aggregate of the Values Studies. [Available]
http://www.wvsevsdb.com/wvs/WVSAnalizeIndex.jsp Dataset/samples for 1990 and 1999/2000 in each country except Greece and Luxembourg
(*only 1999 available). Mean scores shown. For 2003, the International Social Survey Program "National Identity II" survey is available for online
data analysis at: http://www.gesis.org/en/services/data/survey-data/issp/modules-study-overview/national-identity/2003

Figure 5.3 GDP growth rate* support for EU membership by year, Portugal, 1985-2005

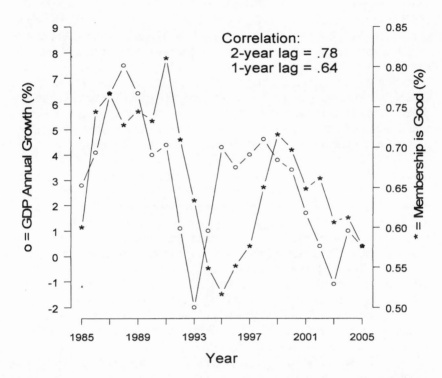

Sources: Mannheim Eurobarometer Trend File 1970-2002 + EB surveys from 2003-2005. GDP growth data 1985-2004 from OECD Factbook 2006: Economic, Environmental and Social Statistics [Available]
http://lysander.sourceoecd.org/vl=1044206/cl=32/nw=1/rpsv/factbook/02-02-01.htm
GDP growth in 2005 from OECD in Figures 2006/2007. [Available]
http://www.oecdobserver.org/news/fullstory.php/aid/1988/OECD_in_Figures_2006-2007.html

Conclusions

Socio-structural change that has "Europeanized" Portuguese society has been both broad and deep. In all three policy areas we analyzed—the welfare state (income and inequality) gender role transformation, and migration/multiculturalism—we see the transformative, developmental, and modernizing role of the state (both national and European), with varied though generally positive outcomes. In several of these areas we have argued that Portuguese progress compared to EU averages has actually been stronger and faster than one might predict based on its relative level of income.

Furthermore, these rapid and deep structural transformations do not appear to have affected the strong national identity of Portuguese citizens, and at least until the recent economic downtown, a strong national identity has proven quite compatible with high level of support for further European integration. The transition from a conservative, predominantly rural, poorly educated, and patriarchal society to a modern, open, service-sector-dominant economy marked by a large (if not always efficient) welfare state, and to a society that is increasingly multicultural and marked by large-scale changes in women's status, has been compatible with consistently high scores in strength of national identity.

That said, some important caveats are in order. One should distinguish between national identity and satisfaction with (or trust in) state institutions. Perceptions of corruption, widespread lack of faith in the judicial process and political parties, and gross power inequalities are frequent topics of public discourse in Portugal.[100] While the Portuguese may be proud of their nationality, they are also deeply critical of many of their political institutions and the way their democracy works, as has been amply demonstrated through comparative public opinion surveys.[101] Moreover, despite many scholars' generally positive reviews regarding the impact of European integration on the quality of Portuguese democracy,[102] Barreto has made a cogent argument for viewing the impact of the EU's democratic deficit on Portuguese democracy in largely negative terms.[103]

Seen from a purely resource transfer perspective, dark clouds clearly lie ahead. Economic growth and catching up to EU averages, transfers from Brussels in the form of social and structural funds, and Europe as an aspiration have frequently been cited as reasons for the long and consistent record of popular support for Europe. The largely instrumental nature of such support raises the possibility of a decline in identification with Europe should economic convergence continue to fail, as it has since 2000. Evidence from Figs. Y and Z suggest that this has in fact been occurring precisely since 2000, just as it did from 1991 to 1995, another period that coincided with economic recession and social contestation. The current situation is, however, even more dire than the early 1990s. Austerity packages, achingly slow growth, high unemployment and European conditionality for support might be accurate descriptions not just of the near but also medium future. Will there be a continued drop in support for Europe? We suspect so. This will be a good test of the instrumental support thesis.

Whether Portuguese elites will remain broadly pro-Europe also appears to have import as to whether a more exclusively national identity develops, particularly given the dangerously low levels of tolerance of foreigners and support for multiculturalism that we discussed in section two. The raw materials for a rightwing reaction are certainly visible in these attitudinal data, but thus far, political entrepreneurs ready to play on xenophobic fears have not gained the kind of electoral traction in Portugal that they have elsewhere in Europe.[104] However, our review of the research on national identity and support for European integration suggests that Portugal's relatively benign national identity can go either way when it comes to support for European integration. If elite consensus were to break down over some core aspects of Portugal's place in the EU, one could easily predict the rise of an exclusive nationalism that would lead to an intense Euroskepticism not seen in Portugal since the mid-1980s.

European identity and national identity are no zero-sum game: in Portugal, both have received high scores. So far at least, socio-structural transformation on a deep and broad level has been consistent with both a strong sense of belonging to Europe *and* national pride. No longer "orgulhosamente sos" (proudly alone), the Portuguese are still "orgulhosos" (proud). Fortunately, so far the Third Republic has avoided the confrontations of the First Republic. In comparison with that highly unstable attempt at a national makeover, the transformative European project has been much more successful. There has been much greater progress towards the goal of European convergence, higher levels of elite agreement on the goals and, despite popular distrust with particular state institutions, much lower levels of social contestation. Moreover the methods used to achieve these goals have been achieved through democratic means, unlike previous attempts at radical societal transformation in 1910 and the mid-1970s. Given current events surrounding the Euro crisis and doubts about Portugal's long-term fiscal health, we expect to see the strongest test yet of this model of societal transformation.

Notes

1. Antonio Firminio Da Costa and Fernando Luis Machado, "An Incomplete Modernity: Structural Change and Social Mobility," *Crossroads to Modernity: Contemporary Portuguese Society,* ed. Antonio Firminio Da Costa and José Manuel Leite Viegas (Oeiras: Celta, 2000), 15-40; Boaventura De Sousa Santos, "Estado e Sociedade na Semi-Periferia do Sistema Mundial: O Caso Português," *Análise Social* 87, no. 89 (1985); and *Portugal: Um Retrato Singular* (Porto: Edições Afrontamento, 1993).

2. António Costa Pinto, ed. *Contemporary Portugal: Politics, Society and Culture* (Boulder: Social Science Monographs, 2003), 50-55.

3. Jorge M. Pedreira, "From Growth to Collapse: Portugal, Brazil, and the Breakdown of the Old Colonial System (1760-1830)," *Hispanic American Historical Review* 80, no. 4 (2000): 839-864.

4. Boaventura De Sousa Santos, *Pelo mão de Alice: o social e o político na pós-modernidade* (Porto: Edições Afrontamento, 1994), 130-131.

5. Basil Davidson, *The Black Man's Burden: Africa and the Curse of the Nation-State* (New York: Times Books, 1992).

6. Nuno Severiano Teixeira,"Between Africa and Europe: Portuguese Foreign Policy, 1890-2000," *Contemporary Portugal: Politics, Society and Culture,* ed. António Costa Pinto (Boulder: Social Science Monographs, 2003), 85-118.

7. Severiano Teixeira, "Portuguese Foreign Policy," 86.

8. Pedro Tavares de Almeida, *Eleições e Caciquismo No Portugal Oitocentista (1868-1890)* (Lisbon: Difel, 1991).

9. António Costa Pinto and Xosé M. Núñez, "Portugal and Spain," *European Political Cultures: Conflict or Convergence?* ed. Roger Eatwell (New York: Rutledge, 1997), 176.

10. Douglas L. Wheeler, *Republican Portugal: A Political History, 1910-1926,* (Madison: University of Wisconsin Press, 1978). See also the exhibition and website (in Portuguese only) organized by the National Commission for the Commemoration of the Centenary of the First Republic (1910-2010): www.centenariorepublica.pt

11. Ramos, 1992 as cited in Costa Pinto, *Contemporary Portugal,* 52. For an analysis of how such developmental backwardness in the metropole played out in Portuguese Africa, see Gerald J. Bender, *Angola under the Portuguese: The Myth and the Reality* (Berkeley: University of California Press, 1978).

12. António Goucha Soares, "The Europeanization of Portugal," *European Societies* 12, no. 3 (2010): 328.

13. Rui Ramos, "Literacy and Illiteracy Cultures in Portugal: An Introduction to a History of Literacy in Contemporary Portugal; Culturas da alfabetizacao e culturas do analfabetismo em Portugal: uma introducao a Historia da Alfabetizacao no Portugal contemporaneo," *Análise Social* 24, nos. 4-5 (1988): 1067-1145.

14. Edward Malefakis, "The Political and Socioeconomic Contours of Southern European History," *The Politics of Democratic Consolidation: Southern Europe in Comparative Perspective,* ed. Richard Gunther, P. Nikofouros Diamandouros, and Hans-Jürgen Puhle (Baltimore: Johns Hopkins University Press, 1995), 33-76.

15. Mónica, 2000 as cited in António Barreto,"Social Change in Portugal: 1960-2000," *Contemporary Portugal: Politics, Society and Culture,* ed. António Costa Pinto (Boulder: Social Science Monographs, 2003), 165.

16. Ana Cristina Pereira, "Um projecto para aumentar a participação cívica das mulheres," *Público,* February 19, 2006; Fernanda Ribeiro, "Objecções do Presidente foram parcialmente atendidas," *Público,* August 8, 2006. For a fuller analysis of the vast literature on national identity as it pertains to the Portuguese and other Southern European cases, see Cabral (2009) and Eatwell (1998) respectively.

17. Nikiforos Diamandouros, "Cultural Dualism and Political Change in Postauthoritarian Greece," *Estúdio Working Paper* 1994, www.march.es/ceacs/ingles/publicaciones/working/archivos/1994_50.pdf (accessed July 12, 2010).

18. Pedro Lains, "The Portuguese Economy in the Twentieth Century: Growth and Structural Change," *Contemporary Portugal: Politics, Society and Culture,* ed. António Costa Pinto (Boulder: Social Science Monographs, 2003), 119-137.

19. Costa Pinto, *Contemporary Portugal,* 8-9.

20. José Pedro Zúqete, "Beyond Reform: The Orthographic Accord and the Future of the Portuguese Language," *South European Society and Politics* 13, no. 4 (December 2008): 496.

21. Wheeler, *Republican Portugal.*

22. Douglas L. Wheeler, "A Primeira República Portuguesa e a história," *Análise Social* XIV, no. 56 (1978): 878.

23. See, for example, Nancy Gina Bermeo, *The Revolution within the Revolution: Workers' Control in Rural Portugal* (Princeton: Princeton University Press, 1986); Manuel Villaverde Cabral, *Portugal na Alvorada do Século XX: Forças Sociais, Poder Político e Crescimento Económico de 1890 a 1914,* (Lisboa: Regra do Jogo, 1979).

24. António Costa Pinto, *Salazar's Dictatorship and European Fascism: Problems of Interpretation* (New York, Columbia University Press, 1995).

25. Costa Pinto, *Contemporary Portugal*, 7-8.

26. Severiano Teixeira, "Portuguese Foreign Policy."

27. Cabral, *Portugal na Alvorada do Século XX.*

28. Dan Bilefsky, "Nostalgia for António de Olieveira Salazar Divides the Portuguese," *New York Times* 2007, www.nytimes.com/2007/07/23/world/europe/23iht-salazar.4.6790015.html (accessed July 23, 2007).

29. Fernando Rosas, *Portugal e o Estado Novo (1930-1960* (Lisbon: Editorial Presença, 1992) and "O salazarismo e o homem novo: ensaio sobre o Estado Novo e a questão do totalitarismo," *Análise Social* XXXV, no. 157 (2001): 1031-1054; João Leal, *Etnografia Portuguesa (1870-1970): Cultural Popular e Identidade Nacional* (Lisbon: Dom Quixote, 2000).

30. Miguel Vale de Almeida, *An Earth-Colored Sea: Race, Culture, and the Politics of Identity in the Postcolonial Portuguese-Speaking World* (New York: Barghahn, 2004); Fernando Arenas, "(Post)colonialism, Globalization and Lusofonia or the 'Time-Space' of the Portuguese-Speaking World," *Institute of European Studies Working Paper Series* 2005. http://escholarship.org/uc/item/0vh0f7t9 (accessed July 5, 2010).

31. However, some scholars (such as, Rosas, 2001; R. Gomes, 2006-2007) have argued that despite their clear differences in terms of how they mobilized the masses, both regimes sought to indoctrinate, through their respective authoritarian apparatus, a "new man" that was revolutionary and totalitarian in its aims.

32. Pedro Lains, "Catching-Up to the European Core: Portuguese Economic Growth, 1910-1990," *Explorations in Economic History* 40, no. 4 (2003): 369-386.

33. Kenneth Maxwell, *The Making of Portuguese Democracy* (Cambridge: Cambridge University Press, 1995).

34. António Costa Pinto and Nuno Severiano Teixeira, "From Africa to Europe: Portugal and European Integration," *Southern Europe and the Making of the European Union* (Boulder: Social Science Monographs, 2002), 1-40; José Magone, "Attitudes of Southern European Citizens towards European Integration: Before and After Accession, 1974-2000," *Southern Europe and the Making of the European Union,* ed. Antonio Costa Pinto and Nuno Severiano Teixeira (Boulder: Social Science Monographs, 2002), 209-236; Marina Costa Lobo, "Portuguese Attitudes Towards EU Membership: Social and Political Perspectives," *Spain and Portugal in the European Union: The First Fifteen Years,* ed. Paul C. Manuel and Sebastian Royo (London: Frank Cass, 2003), 97-118; Diogo Moreira, António Costa Pinto, João Pedro Ruivo, and Pedro Tavares de Almeida, "Attitudes of the Portuguese Elites Towards the European Union," *South European Society and Politics* 15, no. 1 (2010): 57-77.

35. Stephen Syrett, ed. *Contemporary Portugal: Dimensions of Economic and Political Change* (Burlington, VT: Ashgate, 2002).

36. See Guillén et al., 2003; and José Magone, *The Politics of Southern Europe: Integration into the European Union* (Westport, CT: Praeger, 2003).

37. Royo, Sebastian and Paul C. Manuel, eds. *Spain and Portugal in the European Union: The First Fifteen Years* (London: Frank Cass, 2003).

38. This section draws upon our article "The Transformation of Portuguese Society: The Role of Europeanization" forthcoming in Laura C. Ferreira-Pereira (Ed.). *Portugal in the European Union: Assessing Twenty-Five Years of Integration Experience.* London: Routledge

116 Michael Baum and Miguel Glatzer

39. Banco De Portugal. "The Portuguese Economy in the Context of Economic, Financial and Monetary Integration," (Lisboa: Banco de Portugal Economics and Research Department, 2009), 350.

40. Goucha Soares, "The Europeanization of Portugal," 329-333.

41. Eurostat. "The Social Situation in the European Union: 2007." *European Union* (2009), 34.

42. Carlos Farinha Rodrigues, *Distribuicao do Rendimento, Desigualdade e Pobreza: Portugal nos Anos 90* (Coimbra: Almedina, 2007).

43. Rodrigues, *Distribuicao do Rendimento.*

44. Refer to José Da Silva Lopes, "Financas Publicas," in *História Económica de Portugal, Sec. XX*, ed. Alvaro Ferreira Da Silva and Pedro Lains (Lisboa: Imprensa de Ciencias Sociais, 2005), 265-305; and OECD. *Economic Survey: Portugal.* Paris: OECD, 2001; OECD. *Economic Survey: Portugal.* Paris: OECD, 2003.

45. OECD (2001), 77.

46. OECD (2003), 90.

47. Rodrigues, *Distribuicao do Rendimento.*

48. Chiara Bronchi, "The Effectiveness of Public Expenditure in Portugal." *OECD Working Papers No. 198/2003.* (2003). http://www-3.unipv.it/websiep/wp/198.pdf (accessed October 1, 2010).

49. Miguel Glatzer, "The Portuguese Welfare State and the Role of NGO's," in *Civil Society after Democratization: Reflections on Portugal 35 Years after the Revolution,* ed. Michael Baum (Lanham, MD: Lexington Books, forthcoming).

50. Boaventura De Sousa Santos, "O Estado, as relações salariais e o bem-estar social na semi-periferia: o caso português," in *Portugal: Um Retrato Singular,* ed. Boaventura De Sousa Santos (Porto: Edições Afrontamento, 1993), 17-58.

51. See Wall et al. (2003), 230.

52. Ronald Inglehart and Pippa Norris, *Rising Tide: Gender Equality and Cultural Change around the World* (New York: Cambridge University Press, 2003).

53. António Barreto, "Portugal: Democracy."

54. For more details, see Nunes de Almeida et al., (2000).

55. Gapminder. "Gapminder World Database." *Gapminder.* 2010. www.gapminder.org (accessed September 1, 2010).

56. Ana Vicente, "A Brief Look at Women in Portuguese History," *Ditos e Escritos,* no. 4 (1993).

57. José Cutileiro, *A Portuguese Rural Society* (Oxford: Clarendon Press, 1971).

58. Nunes de Almeida et al., (2000), 42

59. André Freire, *Sociedade Civil, Democracia Participativa e Poder Político. O Caso do Referendo do Aborto 2007* (Lisbon: Friedrich Ebert Stiftung, 2008).

60. Nunes de Almeida et al. (2000).

61. Barreto, "Portugal: Democracy," 167.

62. Pordata. "PORDATA- Base de Dados Portugal Contemporânea." *Pordata.* 2010. www.pordata.pt/azap_runtime (accessed July 29, 2010).

63. Nunes de Almeida et al., (2000), 50.

64. Barreto, "Portugal: Democracy," 167.

65. Wall et al., (2001).

66. Barreto, "Portugal: Democracy," 165.

67. Michael Baum and Ana Espírito-Santo, "The Causes of the Adoption of a Gender Quota Law in Portugal," *West European Politics* (Forthcoming).

68. United Nations Development Program. *2009 Human Development Report.* New York: UN, 2009.

69. European Professional Women's Network, "3rd European PWN Board Women Monitor 2008," *European Professional Women's Network.* (2008). www.europeanpwn.net/files/presentation_bwm_2008.pdf

70. Anália Torres, "Work and Family in Portugal," in *Reconciling Family and Work: New Challenges for Social Policies in Europe,* ed. Giovanna Rossi (Milan: Franco Agneli, 2006), 24.

71. ____, "Work and Family,"

72. Barreto, "Portugal: Democracy," 164-5.

73. ____, 313.

74. Refer to United Nations Development Program. "Human Movement: Snapshots and Trends," *2009 Human Development Report.* (New York: UN, 2009).

There are discrepancies in the reporting of immigrants as a share of the total population. Peixoto and Sabino (2009), for example, cite a figure of only 4 percent of the total population, based on official Portuguese government figures stating the total number of legal resident foreigners in 2007 as roughly 436,000. The 2009 UNDP study cites a figure of 764,000 resident foreigners in 2005, which equals 7.2 percent of the total resident population. Jorge Vala et al. (2006) cite a figure of 5 percent, but no date is given.

75. Isabel Ferin, Willy Filho, Ilda Fortes, and Clara Almeida Santos, "Media, Imigração e Minorias Étnicas – 2005-2006," *Alto-Comissariado Para a Imigração E Diálogo Intercultural* (2008). www.oi.acidi.gov.pt/docs/Col_EstudosOI/OI_28.pdf

76. see José Pedro Zúqete, "Beyond Reform,"

77. José Pedro Zúqete, "Portugal: A New Look at the Extreme Right," *Representation* 43, no. 3 (September 2007): 179-198. Though see Zúqete argues that the recent structural changes in Portuguese society: the sharp increase in immigration, a situation of economic crisis, above average unemployment rates and divergence from EU living standards, calls for the radical restructuring of the welfare state, etc., all provide a ripe "political opportunity structure" for the development of radical right discourse by new political entrepreneurs. To date, this has yet to materialize, but the opportunity for growth remains great.

78. The notion first advanced by the Brazilian sociologist/anthropologist Gilberto Freyre that purports to explain the multi-racial makeup of Brazil as a result of the supposedly unique characteristics of Portuguese colonialism. Specifically, that "due to a series of interrelated climatological, geographical, historical, cultural, and genetic factors, the Portuguese have been more inclined to racially intermix with peoples of the tropics." See Arenas, (2005).

79. Jorge Vala et al., (2006).

80. see also Enric Martínez-Herrera and Djaouida Moualhi, "Predispositions to Discriminatory Immigration Policies in Western Europe: An Exploration of Political Causes," *Portuguese Journal of Social Science* 5, no. 3 (2006): 215-233.

81. ____, "Predispositions to Discriminatory Immigration."

82. ____, "Predispositions to Discriminatory Immigration," 222.

83. ____, "Predispositions to Discriminatory Immigration," 222-223.

84. ____, "Predispositions to Discriminatory Immigration," 225.

85. ____, "Predispositions to Discriminatory Immigration."

86. Michael Baum and André Freire, "1998 Portuguese Referendums: Explaining the Results and Speculating on the Future of Direct Democracy in Portugal," *Portuguese*

118   Michael Baum and Miguel Glatzer

Journal of Social Science 2, no. 1 (September 2003): 5-19; and Baum and Espirito-Santo, "The Causes of Adoption."

87. Pedro Zúqete, "Portugal: A New Look," 193.

88. ____, "Portugal: A New Look," 193.

89. Paul C. Manuel, "Religion and Politics in Iberia: Clericalism, Anticlericalism, and Democratization in Portugal and Spain," in *Religion and Politics in Comparative Perspective: The One, the Few, and the Many*, ed. Ted G. Jelen and Clyde Wilcox (New York: Cambridge University Press, 2002), 71-96. Nowadays, Portuguese levels of religiosity, as measured by frequency of church attendance, are quite close to the European average (Economist, 2010).

90. João Peixoto and Catarina Sabino, "Immigration, Emigration and Policy Developments in Portugal," *ARI-Real Instituto Elcano* (July 2009), 5.

91. MIPEX. "Portugal-Overview." Migrant Integration Policy Index. (2010). www.integrationindex.eu/integrationindex/2509.html (accessed August 5, 2010).

92. Refer to sources listed in footnotes 90 and 91.

93. Caveats need to be made here. Using the same WVS data from 1999, one can find virtually no correlation between pride in one's nationality and *identification with one's country* as the first territorial identity of choice (compared to locality, region, continent, or world). Portugal has above average levels of identification with the country as the primordial first identity, but so does the Netherlands, which has the least amount of professed national pride. See: WVS online data analysis [Available] http://www.wvsevsdb.com/wvs/WVSAnalizeSample.jsp Chose 1999/2000 years and G001 "Geographical groups belonging to first."

94. See Antonio Costa Pinto and Marina Costa Lobo, "Forging a Positive but Instrumental View: Portuguese Attitudes Towards the EU, 1986-2002," in *Public Opinion and Europe: National Identity in European Perspective*, ed. Anne Dulphy and Christine Manigand (Paris: Peter Lang, 2004), 165-181; and Pedro Magalhães, "O Apoio à Integração Europeia em Portugal: Dimensões e Tendências," *IPRI Working Paper* 16, no. 30 (November 2006): 1-23.

95. Liesbet Hooghe and Gary Marks, "Calculation, Community and Cues: Public Opinion on European Integration," *European Union Politics* 6, no. 4 (2005): 419-443; and ———, "Does Identity or Economic Rationality Drive Public Opinion on European Integration?" *PS: Political Science & Politics* 37, no. 3 (July 2004): 415-420.

96. ____, "Does Identity or Economic Opinion," 3-4.

97. ____, "Does Identity or Economic Opinion," 3.

98. Refer to José R. Montero and Leonardo Morlino. "Legitimacy and Democracy in Southern Europe." In *The Politics of Democratic Consolidation: Southern Europe in Comparative Perspective*, ed. Richard P. Gunther, Nikofouros Diamandouros, and Hans-Jürgen Puhle (Baltimore: Johns Hopkins University Press, 1995), 231-260; and Moreira et al., "Attitudes of the Portuguese Elites."

99. Recent survey evidence from European elites confirms this point. Most of those surveyed who are strongly attached to Europe are also strongly attached to their country (Conti et al., 2010: 124).

100. Pedro Magalhães, "Democratas, descontentes e desafectos: as atitudes dos portugueses em relação ao sistema politico," in *Portugal a Votos: As eleições legislativas de 2002*, ed. André Freire, Marina Costa Lobo, and Pedro Magalhães (Lisboa: ICS, 2004), 333-357. Portugal News Online, "Perception of Corruption on the Rise in

Portugal," *Portugal News Online* (2010). www.theportugalnews.com/cgi-bin/article.pl?id=1092-11 (accessed December 18, 2010).

101. Pedro Magalhães, "A Qualidade da Democracia em Portugal: A Perspectiva dos Cidadãos," *Relatório inicial de um estudo promovido pela SEDES, com o apoio da Fundação Luso-Americana para o Desenvolvimento e da Intercampus* (2009).

102. See José Magone, *European Portugal.* New York: St. Martin's Press, 1997; Syrett, ed. *Contemporary Portugal;* and Royo and Manuel, *Spain and Portugal in the European Union.*

103. António Barreto, "Portugal: Democracy through Europe," In *Regional Integration and Democracy: Expanding on the European Experience,* ed. Jeffrey J. Anderson (Lanham, MD: Rowman & Littlefield, 1999), 95-122.

104. Herbert Kitschelt, *The Radical Right in Western Europe: A Comparative Analysis* (Ann Arbor: University of Michigan Press, 1996).

6

Portugal: An Incomplete Europeanization

António Goucha Soares[1]

With accession to the European Union, a member state is required to incorporate the *acquis communautaire* into its domestic law, open its frontiers to the free movement of persons, goods and capital, adopt the Euro as the single currency, and fully participate in the Union's political process, which extends from all areas of economic integration to some fields of justice and home affairs, as well as the making of a European foreign policy.

Despite the limits of EU jurisdiction and the consequences for the division of powers between the Union and the member states, there is an ongoing process of homogenization among European countries that is strictly related to the construction of Europe, but not confined by the EU boundaries of power. For instance, although education remains an area that is exclusive to each member state's competence, this did not prevent the creation of a European space of higher education, through the Bologna process, which aims to establish tertiary education systems where academic degrees and quality standards are closer and comparable throughout Europe. In fact, it is possible to refer to the process by which European countries tend to strengthen relationships through economic integration as well as greater homogeneity at the social and cultural levels as a "path of Europeanization."[2] This development is also derived from the common cultural heritage and the existence of shared political values, such as democracy, freedom, human rights, rule of law, and social state. Hence, we arrive at the idea of Europeanization as a concept that derives from the process of European construction, but has a larger scope than the EU because it is the outcome of a complex set of factors like economic interdependence, citizenship, cultural exchang-

121

es, civil society connections, fundamental rights protection, EU rules, or academic mobility.

In Portugal, there have been deep-seated political, economic, social, and cultural changes over the last decades, which were due to the processes of democratic consolidation and accession to the European Union. In particular, the latter allowed for a strong process of economic modernization and an important improvement in living conditions. However, there is a widespread feeling in Portuguese society that the country is facing a downshift when compared with other European states, with a Eurobarometer poll showing that 92 percent see the economic situation to be bad.[3] Indeed, regardless of the huge domestic transformations that have occurred since the advent of democracy, it must be remembered that European countries—in particular Eastern Europe—are also engaged in a continuous process of change and reform, and this tends to accentuate important Portuguese peculiarities within the European context.

This chapter aims to explore Portugal's performance in some crucial areas that can be included in a wide concept of Europeanization: the state of the economy, the rule of law, and education. These areas were selected because of their close relationship with the ongoing process of Europeanization. With regard to the economy, Portugal suffered from an historical backwardness when compared with other European countries.[4] Accession to the European Communities was seen as an opportunity for the catching-up of the Portuguese economy. In fact, in the fifteen years that followed the European accession Portuguese GDP was converging with the European Union average. Then, with the new century Portugal seemed to end its path of economic convergence with the Union to gradually become the big disappointment amongst the group of the catching-up states.[5]

There is a strong link between the rule of law and political democracy. The rule of law is based on the principles of legality of state action, equality of all citizens before the law and equal access to the courts. It should be noted that one of the main reasons that led the Portuguese government to apply to join the Union in the 1970s was to strengthen the democratic regime established in the aftermath of the 1974 revolution, which removed the political dictatorship.[6] Even if Portugal has a consolidated democracy, it is still important to question some critical dimensions of the rule of law that could affect the quality of Portuguese democracy—in particular, the principle of equality in the functioning of judicial institutions—and try to understand some of the reasons that prevent a better performance in this area.

The last area to be analyzed is education. Education plays a key role in the process of state modernization. A well-educated population is essential for the welfare of a country. Education plays a fundamental part in providing citizens with the knowledge and skills needed for an active participation in society and in the economy. The level of educational achievement of the population is used to measure the stock of human capital, that is, the skills available in the population and workforce.[7] For this reason, there is a firm relationship between the educational system and the level of economic and social development of each society. Hence, the Europeanization of Portugal is strictly related to the achievement of its educational policy.

The article starts with a brief reference to the evolution of the Portuguese economy since the European accession to find out that since the adoption of the single currency, Portugal entered into a phase of economic divergence, making it an exception within the Euro area. The second section is devoted to the rule of law. It highlights how a modern and updated legal system can have an outcome that threatens some basic foundations of the rule of law and can also contribute to increasing social inequality. The last section focuses on some problems affecting education. Particular attention is paid to the performance of the secondary education system and to issues related to the quality of higher education institutions.

Economic Divergence

Any global analysis of the national economy since the Portuguese accession to the European Communities has to be clearly positive. Indeed, it should be remembered that in 1986 Portugal's GDP was just 54 percent of the average European Community GDP of twelve member states. In 2008, the Portuguese GDP is 66 percent of the enlarged European Union GDP of twenty-seven member states. Greater than the progress in the relative income of the country is the perceived feeling of modernisation that swept across the country in the last two decades. This was mainly favored by European integration.[8]

However, it should be noted that in 2001 Portugal had reached 75 percent of the European Union GDP of fifteen member states.[9] Since then the relative income of the country has stalled at just 66 percent of the enlarged European Union. Hence, it seems that it is possible to divide Portugal's economic performance since the European accession in two periods: an initial phase starting with the accession in 1986 until the end of the century and then a second phase that has lasted till the present.

During the first phase, Portugal went through a remarkable improvement in its economic conditions, in part due to the effect of the financial transfers provided by the European Union structural funds. The European funds allowed for a deep-seated transformation of the physical infrastructures of the country. In particular, the motorway roads system grew from just a couple of hundreds of kilometres before accession to a huge motorway network, which has been reinforced by 2,500 km of recent roads. The modernisation of infrastructures also reached the educational system and the facilities available for the National Health Service. It contributed to an improvement in public transportation and a decrease in the housing deficit.[10] In general terms, it could be said that Portugal was very successful during the first phase of accession, with a noticeable increase in the quality of people's lives.[11]

The second phase saw a reversal of the catching-up trend towards the European Union average.[12] Indeed, during the first fifteen years of European accession, the Portuguese income came closer to that of the European Community, since the beginning of the new century Portugal has entered into a phase of clear divergence with the European Union. This divergence is even more troubling when the Eastern enlargement, which brought to the Union twelve new member states with worse economic situations, is considered.

What are the major reasons for this path of divergence with the European Union in the second period? It is considered that the main explanation for the Portuguese slowdown in economic growth was accession to the monetary union.[13] The adoption of the single currency could be considered the turning point regarding the Portuguese economic performance. Until the monetary union the Portuguese economy was doing well and was gradually narrowing the gap with the other Union member states. During the first half of the 1990s, Portugal was even held by the European Community institutions as a model for Eastern candidate countries, due to the success achieved in that period. But ten years later, Portugal had become a warning example to other European Union countries in the process of joining the euro.[14]

In its report on the successes and challenges after ten years of monetary union, the European Commission aims to demonstrate that the single currency has been a driver for real economic convergence. It notes that the so-called cohesion countries—Spain, Ireland, Greece, and Portugal—gained from the monetary union to benefit from a strong process of growth. Indeed, in 1999 the level of GDP per capita in Greece, Spain, and Portugal were, respectively, 71, 84, and 68 percent of the Euro area average. In 2008 Greece and Spain have further shortened the difference, with 90 and 94 percent of the Euro countries' average, respectively. By contrast, Portugal's level of GDP per capita has decreased to 64 percent. Hence, monetary union contributed to a strong pace of catching-up for the cohesion countries, not to speak of Ireland, with Portugal being the sole exception.[15]

The Portuguese downshift in economic terms is even more disturbing when it is compared with the countries that recently acceded to the monetary union. From 1999 to 2008 Slovenia's and Cyprus' per capita income level passed from 70 and 77 percent to 84 and 83 percent of the Euro area average, respectively. Moreover, it should be noted that over the last ten years, the GDP per capita level of the other EU new member states has grown in relative terms by about thirty points in the Baltic countries and by seventeen points in the Czech Republic and Slovakia.

One of the reasons that could help explain the poor performance of the Portuguese economy lies in the different behaviour of fiscal policy in the so-called cohesion countries in the last ten years. Ireland and Spain both had budget surpluses, and Greece reduced its public deficit to the monetary union red line of below 3 percent. During the period concerned Portugal was above 3 percent for most of the time, and it even peaked at 6 percent in 2005.[16] Since then the Portuguese public deficit has been drastically reduced to below 3 percent.[17]

As far as the public sector size is concerned, the total of expenditures in GDP was reduced in Spain and Greece during the last ten years, but it expanded in Portugal. Fiscal consolidation in Ireland and Greece took place on the expenditure side, and in Spain it was achieved through both expenditure restraint and higher revenues. Portugal was the only country that increased its expenditure in the same period. In fact, the Portuguese authorities took advantage of larger revenues coming from privatizations and from lower interest rates to increase public expenditures, instead of reducing the global weight of public administration in the national economy.[18] As a result of fiscal policy consolidation measures, public debt levels as a share of GDP have declined significantly in Ireland, Greece, and Spain in the last decade, but they have risen by about thirteen points in Portugal.[19]

However, it should be said that in the aftermath of the 2008 global financial crash Euro membership acted as a kind of a shield for the Portuguese economy. Indeed, and despite the road of divergence that has marked the Portuguese economy since the beginning of the single currency, the country has not suffered from the effects of the world economic and financial crisis in the same as other European Union member states, such as Hungary, the Baltic countries, or even Ireland. In fact, the Portugal economic slowdown is in line with the macroeconomic situation of the Euro area, and the European Union in general: Portuguese GDP stagnated in 2008 and is expected to fall 3.75 percent in 2009, compared with a timid 0.8 percent EU growth in 2008 and a contraction forecast of 4 percent in both the EU and the Euro area in 2009; the Portuguese unemployment rate was 7.7 percent in 2008 and is expected to reach 9.1 percent in 2009, against 7 percent in 2008 and a 2009 forecast of 9.4 percent at the EU level; the Portuguese government deficit represented 2.6 percent of the GDP in 2008 and is expected to increase to 6.5 percent in 2009, which compares with a budget deficit of 2.3 percent in 2008 at the EU level and a forecast of 6 percent in 2009; and finally, the Portuguese government debt was 66.4 percent in 2008 and is expected to reach 75.4 percent of the GDP in 2009, compared with an EU debt of 61.5 percent in 2008 and a forecast of 72.6 percent of the GDP in 2009.[20]

The divergent performance of the Portuguese economy in the period that followed the adoption of the euro can be further explained by a set of elements. Beyond fiscal policy grounds, where Portugal provides a striking contrast with the other cohesion countries, another reason that could help to understand the poor behaviour of the Portuguese economy in the last decade is the conversion rates, which had been fixed by the time of the monetary union entry: national currency rates were irrevocably converted at the end of 1998. The parity of Portuguese escudo with the euro was fixed at about 200; the parity of Spanish peseta was fixed at about 166. However, in the early 1990s, 128 Spanish pesetas were equivalent to one euro, while 179 Portuguese escudos were equivalent to one euro. This means that the Spanish currency underwent a devaluation of about 30 percent in the period concerned whereas the Portuguese currency devalued only 12 percent in the same period. Moreover, due to fast wage increases, the real effective exchange rate appreciated by about 15 percent in Portugal during the 1990s, while it depreciated by the same amount in Spain for the same period. The European Commission considers that the real effective exchange rate of Spain is now at the same level it was in the early 1990s, while that of Portugal is more than 20 percent higher. This helps to understand Portugal's stronger loss of economic competitiveness when compared to Spain.[21]

An additional explanation for the difficult situation of the Portuguese economy is to be found in its specialization model.[22] Portuguese exports are largely based on low-skill intensive industries such as textiles, footwear, and apparel. Those industries were particularly affected by the European Union Eastern enlargement, which favored the outsourcing of some multinational companies to the new member states, where they could obtain EU financial aid for their investments, benefit from cheap salaries, and be closer to the main European markets. Furthermore, some of those industries were especially exposed to the general effects of globalization, and to the entry of large low-wage countries in the world trade system, like India and China, as well as to the end of particular protectionist regimes such as the Multi-Fibres Agreement. EU commitments taken at the World Trade Organization level freed the access to European markets for textiles coming from emerging economies. The joint consequences of these European and global trade aspects eroded the competitiveness of core Portuguese export sectors.[23]

The situation of the Portuguese economy would recommend the adoption of measures aimed at achieving economic stabilization goals. The main tools available for stabilization policies are monetary policy, exchange rate policy, and fiscal policy. However, in the context of the single currency member states are deprived of the areas of monetary policy and exchange rate policy, to the benefit of the monetary union.[24] Moreover, even if fiscal policy is still formally part of member states' jurisdiction, this is an area where the adoption of national policy measures is strongly limited by the obligations coming from the Maastricht Treaty and the harder constraints deriving from the so-called Stability Pact.[25]

What remains to be seen is whether the crisis of the Portuguese economy—a crisis initiated in the beginning of the century, which is to be explained by reasons fully detached from the 2008 global economic and financial crash, even if it was aggravated by the latter—can pave the way for the kind of structural adjustments that most of the industrial export sectors must accomplish. In fact, the combined effect of the Eastern enlargement and globalization showed up the exhaustion of the old industrial pattern of the Portuguese economy based on cheap salaries and low-skilled workers. Furthermore, those industries were used to currency devaluations, which had worked for decades as the main tool to support their external competitiveness.[26] If Portugal wants to catch up with the European Union countries, it is crucial for the government and for the economic sectors to look for a new industrial reorganization based on innovation and an increase in economic productivity and to concentrate on areas where it could benefit from its comparative advantages.[27] Otherwise, the following situation will remain "the big disappointment amongst the group [of catching-up states] was undoubtedly the marked deterioration in the outturn for the Portuguese economy, especially over the last decade, with its potential rates now pointing to divergence, rather than convergence, relative to the living standards in the rest of the Euro area."[28]

Rule of Law

With the 1974 revolution and the transition to democracy that followed, Portugal moved to a pluralist political system inspired by the values of Western European democracies. With the adoption of the 1976 Constitution, Portugal took the route of a parliamentary democracy, which has since been consolidated. The democratic system of government is inspired by the principles of democratic elections, political freedom, human rights protection, and respect for the rule of law.

There is a direct relationship between the rule of law and liberal democracy. The rule of law is based on the principle that no one is above the law. Laws are for public knowledge and should apply equally to everyone. Public authorities accept that the law will be applied to their own action, and the government seeks to be law-abiding. Laws are to protect the political and civic rights and freedoms of the individuals, as they are understood as their basic fundamental rights. The main institutions of the political system should act within the limits of the law and respect the boundaries of their own powers. Courts are impartial and not subject to any form of political pressure. Moreover, anyone accused of a crime has the right to a fair trial and is presumed innocent until proven guilty.[29] Therefore, the rule of law is strictly related to the principles of legality of state action, equality of all citizens, human rights protection, separation of powers, judicial independence, as well as the presumption of innocence, no punishment without a previous penal law, and *habeas corpus*.

The 1976 Portuguese Constitution adopted a system of democratic power fully committed to the rule of law. This was particularly important given the fact that during the previous five decades the country had been ruled by an authoritarian regime that prevented the appearance of political parties and the organization of free elections, and denied citizens most of their basic political and civic rights. The Salazar government also organized the existence of a political police and practiced censorship of the press. In line with its repressive nature, it imposed political trials by the judiciary and it allowed for the existence of prisoners on political grounds, some of whom could be subjected to different forms of physical torture.[30]

The democratization process led to the adoption of an extensive bill of rights within the text of the national Constitution, as well as to the accession to the 1950 European Convention on Human Rights. As a consequence of the new democratic legal framework, Portugal also had to adopt important reforms in its legal system, mainly in those branches of law with a closer connection with the exercise of individual freedoms, such as criminal law and criminal law procedure.

Portugal also adopted a set of legal reforms in others branches of law, in line with the principles of the democratic Constitution, such as family law and gender equality rules. Moreover, with the accession to the European Communities in 1986, Portugal incorporated the *acquis communautaire* into its domestic law, which allowed for the adoption of a new economic law inspired by the principles of a market economy and free competition. Hence, the Portuguese legal order is, in formal terms, fully in line with the legal requisites that support the existence of a liberal democracy and respect for the rule of law.

However, there are some dimensions of the Portuguese democracy that clearly face a critical situation. The rule of law is, in all likelihood, the one where an idea of crisis is deeply entrenched in the common perception of the citizens.[31] Indeed, Portugal faces an emergency in the area of justice. The main dimensions of this crisis are related to the performance of the judicial power: on the one hand, courts are overburdened with legal proceedings and they very often extend the time used to deliver a legal decision beyond what would be reasonably acceptable for the achievement of justice; on the other hand, there is a widespread feeling throughout the country regarding the existence of a dual system of justice. It is the latter dimension of this crisis of the judicial system that critically affects the respect for the rule of law insofar as there is a public awareness that powerful people tend to benefit from a high level of immunity whenever they are taken to court within the scope of criminal legal proceedings.

Dual System of Justice

The crucial aspect of the crisis of justice concerns the idea that powerful people tend to receive different treatment within the scope of criminal legal proceedings. In fact, there is a prevalent feeling throughout the country that upper classes benefit from advantageous behaviour regarding legal decisions taken in the framework of criminal judgements. Indeed (and according to a recent study on the quality of Portuguese democracy), 82 percent of the people consider that wealthy citizens get a better treatment from the judicial system than poor people.[32]

In fact, there have been many public scandals concerning powerful people which have been the object of large media coverage. These scandals have included a wide range of corruption cases, illegal financing of political parties,[33] inside trading, corporate fraud, traffic of influences, financial abuses, illegal stock exchange practices, money laundering, tax evasion, sexual abuse, and other different types of crime that went on for years in the courts and ended with decisions where the defendants were usually declared not guilty. By contrast, most individuals who have been jailed as a consequence of criminal sanctions belong to lower social classes.[34] Hence, it seems that the so-called white collar class benefits more from the criminal legal order when compared with common people.

Bearing in mind that there could be different treatment in courts' decisions regarding criminal issues on the basis of social origins, it would be interesting to explore the reasons for such discrimination. At first glance, there is a seemingly natural explanation: rich and powerful persons can hire the best criminal lawyers, and as a consequence, they are able to get strategies of legal defence that common people cannot afford to pay for. This could be reasonable justification, and it also happens in other European countries. It is clearly true in the sense that it explains part of the difference concerning legal results, but it does not exhaust the issue of discrimination.

Indeed, another reason is to be found in the very nature of the legal system. It should be remembered that the Portuguese legal order is part of, and inspired by the continental law systems. Continental law has evolved in the last two centuries with the inspiration of strong schools of legal thought that favored a formalist approach to law and the legal system. With the democratic consolidation, Portugal adopted its domestic legal order in accordance with the new principles established by the 1976 Constitution and with the requirements stemming from the international conventions signed by the state. However, the transformation that marks the Portuguese law of the last decades—because of the new Constitution, the accession to the European Communities and other international commitments—has increased the complexity of its legal order.[35]

It must be said that criminal law and criminal law procedure were deeply reformed with a view to defending the legal status and the guarantees of the prosecuted, taking into consideration the principles established by the Constitution and other international agreements. Nor should the abuses that occurred in the area of criminal law during the long-lasting political dictatorship that ended with the 1974 Revolution be forgotten. Most of the reforms since then have been inspired by the so-called comparative law—mainly continental law. As a result of deep-seated transformations in the field of criminal law and criminal law procedure, the complexity of the penal law system increased substantially, especially when it comes to its implementation.[36] It is for judges to apply the law. In the case of criminal actions, the public ministry has the monopoly of legal accusation, which is exercised through a vast number of prosecutors.

It is the judges and prosecutors who have to deal with the complexity of the Portuguese legal system. It should be noted that the purpose of guaranteeing the legal position of those taken to court allows for a substantial number of appeals to be taken during the course of a trial. As a consequence of the appeals, as well as the decisions taken on the basis of those appeals, the conclusion of a case tends to be severely delayed.[37] Very often, appeals annul some written parts of the legal proceeding or the evidence produced during the court hearings on the grounds of formal aspects. Indeed, in the course of a case it is usual for the defendant lawyers to appeal against the evidence presented by prosecutors on the grounds of alleged unconstitutionality of, or illegality in, the way it was produced. Moreover, some of the intermediary appeals could be the object of further appeals to higher levels of the judicial system, with inconvenient effects for the due course of the legal proceeding. It should be noted that most of these legal incidents can also take place during the previous phases of the criminal inquiry conducted by a prosecutor or during the criminal instruction oriented by a judge. That is to say that it could be hard for prosecutors or judges of criminal instruction to take someone to court whenever those indicted of some kind of criminal act are wealthy persons.[38]

Therefore, the concern aimed at the protection of the legal status and the guarantees of the prosecuted goes well beyond what would be needed to ensure the right to a fair judgement of those taken to court. Indeed, the Portuguese criminal system has exacerbated the dimension of the guarantees up to a point where it is almost possible to block the due course of criminal investigations or the normal development of criminal legal proceedings for those who can afford to pay expensive lawyers. In reality, in the balance between the guarantees of the prosecuted and the regular course of criminal legal actions, lawmakers took their concern with the former further than the limits of what is necessary. That is the reason why the Portuguese criminal system can be considered as a "guarantistic" legal order, in the sense that it suffers from an excess of legal guarantees conferred on those indicted of a crime, and this jeopardises the achievement of justice.[39]

The legal incidents in the course of a trial due to formal aspects, the overcoming of legal delays caused by the statute of limitation, the various defendant strategies aimed to retard the path of legal proceedings, the multitude of intermediary appeals—all these aspects aggravate the complex task of the judges in the implementation of the law. It should be noted that the crisis of justice does not affect the criminal legal system only: because of the peculiar effects that it produces, it also affects one of the foundations of the rule of law—the principle of equality.[40] The crisis of justice is larger in scope; it extends to the areas of civil and administrative law. In reality, even if the social discrimination that marks the results produced within the criminal legal area are not so strongly perceived in civil or administrative jurisdictions, it does not mean that those branches of law remain unaffected by similar problems stemming from the complexity of the legal order.

One of the main reasons for the complexity of the legal system is the inflation of laws, decree-laws, regulations, and all sorts of normative acts that compose the national legal order. The intended rationality of the legal system, with its basis in the movement of legal codification, no longer guides the work of

Portuguese lawmakers or the agencies with rule-making power. Hence, there is an unstoppable number of legal acts whose aim is to regulate all forms of social behavior. It is for the courts to ensure the adequate implementation of the law.

Judges and prosecutors were trained at law schools and at the judiciary training center within the paradigm of the Law System—that is to say, coherence and compatibility of the legal norms emanating from public authorities. Yet, the coherence of the legal system is threatened every day by massive law production. As a result, judges and prosecutors look for ways of legal interpretation that conciliate the contradictory legal meanings stemming from a relentless law making power. Moreover, in the complexity of the legal system, the purpose of magistrates tends to be more oriented to the problem of legal interpretation than to the function of justice.[41] In reality, magistrates usually act more as managers of the legal system than as true actors of justice. In the legal arena the meaning of the justice function tends to be centered on law interpretation. The work of magistrates is seen by the other legal professions as a specialized job, which consists of finding the right norm or the right interpretation for different rules in the middle of the legal complexity. Hence, it deviates from the exercise of justice to the art of legal interpretation. On the work of managing law complexity, pressed by rampant lawyers permanently threatening with legal incidents, magistrates carry out the technocratic work of making the law disorder look coherent.[42] In reality, the essence of their jobs is actually closer to legal engineering than to achieving justice.

It must be said that magistrates are the product of the legal environment. And the Portuguese legal environment favors a reductive role for judges and prosecutors. Indeed, judges need to have more procedural autonomy to conduct the due course of legal proceedings than the positive law allows them to have.[43] However, it is not just the degree of procedural independence that magistrates need to acquire: they also need to take a different approach to the justice function. In reality, the dominant feature of their performance is the fact that they seem to be trapped by the legal system itself.[44] In searching for the rationality of the legal order, magistrates lose the goal of justice.

Hence, it is the whole legal culture that must be questioned. A legal system where public opinion is often confronted with cases showing clear evidence of corruption,[45] mismanagement of public goods, tax evasion, or illicit financing of political parties; and whose proceedings end, merely on the basis of legal technicalities, with no criminal sanction for those indicted after a long criminal investigation is a legal system that is unable to fulfil its mission. It is a sound legal principle of any democratic society that it is better to have a guilty person go free than to have an innocent one jailed. But when people about whom there was serious evidence of wrong doing are systematically acquitted on the basis of merely formal reasons, that is a legal order that creates a sentiment of legal impunity.

It should also be noted that there is some empirical evidence that common citizens fear the ability of the judicial system regarding conflict resolution due to technical issues. In fact, when asked whether judicial proceedings are so complicated that it is not worth taking a case to court, the majority of Portuguese people tend to give an affirmative answer.[46] Hence, at the present time the complexity of the legal system cannot be separated from the evaluation of the global outcome of justice across the country. This means a lack of trust in the capacity of judicial institutions to guarantee equal treatment for all citizens in the settlement of disputes.

Therefore, the problem of the Portuguese legal order is not one of lacking specific "rules on the books". Indeed, Portugal has a long legal thought tradition, with brilliant academics in several branches of law, famous law schools, a wide production of legal literature, a vast number of well remunerated magistrates and an advanced judiciary training center with a ratio of ten candidates for each available position of magistrate.[47] In addition, it has a modern and sophisticated legal order, inspired by the best examples of the law systems of leading European countries, like Germany, France, or Italy. Rather, the trouble seems to be the outcome of the legal order "on the ground."[48]

Indeed, the assessment of the legal system "on the ground" is a disappointment.[49] The system of justice works inefficiently in the sense that courts are overburdened with legal proceedings, despite some recent improvements concerning the extent of judicial caseload.[50] In some branches of law, the labyrinth of procedural rules and practices tend to jeopardize a reasonable level of substantive law enforcement, with the criminal system seeming to challenge a crucial foundation of the rule of law—the principle of equality of all citizens. In fact, given its discriminatory results on the basis of social reasons instead of conflict resolution, the legal order seems to increase the distance between powerful people and ordinary citizens. Therefore, it comes as no surprise that the above-mentioned study on the quality of democracy reveals that 79 percent of the Portuguese people consider that the judicial system does not provide the same treatment for politicians as for common citizens.[51] Additionally, the fundamental actors in the area of justice seem captured by the legal order itself and tend to work as simple public servants in the field of law with the mere goal of managing the legal system through a labyrinth composed of a huge array of different laws and procedures, often contradictory in meaning.

Education

It is well known that education plays a key role in the process of state modernization. A well-educated and trained population is essential for the social and economic wellbeing of countries and individuals. Education plays a fundamental part in providing individuals with the knowledge, skills, and competencies needed for an active participation in society and in the economy. Education also contributes to an expansion of scientific and technological knowledge. The level of educational achievement of the population is commonly used to measure the stock of human capital, that is, the skills available in the population and labor force.[52] Therefore, there is a strict relationship between the educational system and the level of economic and social development of each society.

Education is a field in which Portugal accumulated a historical retard when compared with other European countries. Indeed the general spread of a public education system had to wait until the rise of the Republic, in 1910. In the beginning of the twentieth century the country had an illiteracy rate of about 70 percent of the population. In 1974 the illiteracy rate was still above 30 percent, which is indicative of the low priority that the dictatorship gave to this issue. With the consolidation of democracy, there was huge progress in all sectors of the educational system; the illiteracy rate fell to around 8 percent of the population, which mainly corresponded to the elderly sectors of the society. In fact, there was a massive expansion at all levels of the educational system, from pre-primary schools to higher education, with the offer of state education reaching the whole country. An example of this educational growth is the number of students attending higher education, which increased from just 26,000 in 1960, to 380,000 in the year 2008.[53]

Indeed, in the last decades there was a strong public investment in the field of education, with the construction of hundreds of primary and secondary schools throughout the country as well as the establishment of a wide range of new higher education institutions.[54] Along with the building of new schools, there was also renovation of the older structures and widespread dissemination of equipment for the new technologies at all educational levels. There was also a vast increase in the appointment of school and university professors and significant enhancement of their salary conditions. The priority given to the field of education within the framework of public policies can be seen as evidence of the making of the Portuguese welfare state, which was one of the achievements of the twin processes of democratic consolidation and Europeanization.

Because Portugal privileged investment in the field of education, a growing amount of public money became devoted to education. In general terms, the amount of education expenditure as a percentage of GDP shows how a country prioritises education in relation to its overall allocation of resources. Taking into consideration 2005 data, Portugal allocated about 5.5 percent of its GDP to finance the global expenditures of the educational system—that is, all levels of education. It should be said that the OECD countries' average expenditure on education was 6.2 percent of the share of the national income, for the same year. But when compared to other European Union countries, Portugal ranked among the top ten positions of states' expenditure on education, ahead of countries like Germany, the Netherlands, Spain, Italy, or Ireland.[55] Hence, education can be considered a main area of public policy for the Portuguese government, not just at the level of political rhetoric, but also in the allocation of public money.

Despite the proportion of national income being invested in education, Portugal remains among the lower ranks of the European Union countries as far as the age group of people normally completing upper-secondary programs is concerned.[56] Indeed, the EU average of young people completing upper-secondary education was about 85 percent in 2005, up from 80 percent in 1995. In Portugal the rate of completion of the upper-secondary level for the same age group was just 53 percent in 2004.[57] But what seems really disturbing is the fact that ten years before, the rate of completion of upper-secondary education in Portugal was 67 percent.[58] It should be noted that in the same period of time the proportion of students who graduated from upper-secondary programs progressed by 7 percentage points on average in OECD states, and in countries such as Finland, Germany, Greece, Ireland, graduation rates equalled or exceeded 90 percent.[59]

Hence, it looks as if there is a problem of performance at the level of secondary education in Portugal: although the state made a strong investment in human and physical resources regarding education in the last decades, and the global expenditure on education in percentage of the GDP is above the EU level, the completion rate of upper secondary programs is much lower than the European average.[60] Therefore, there is a paradoxical situation regarding the efficiency of the educational system in the sense that the government spends more money on the educational sector than the EU average, but that does not prevent the country from having the worst results amongst the twenty-seven member states, as far as the completion of upper secondary is concerned.[61] Even when compared to OECD countries, Portugal ranks at the bottom of the scale, just above Turkey and Mexico.

Some of the reasons that could help to understand the low performance of the Portuguese system of secondary education are the huge rates of repetition, failure, and early school leavers.[62] These rates could also explain the fact while the percentage of people of the age that normally frequent upper-secondary education in Portugal is similar to that of other EU countries, Portugal has a lower performance when it comes to the completion rate for secondary education.[63] Moreover, Portugal is the EU member state with the highest rates regarding the global percentage of people in all age groups who do not have at least an upper-secondary education qualification,[64] which is a sign of the comparative disadvantages that the country faces with regard to the goals to develop a European Union knowledge economy.[65]

Higher Education

As far as higher education is concerned, Portugal is in a better situation in comparative terms. Indeed, the country has almost reached the EU average regarding tertiary graduate output, that is, the percentage of the population in the typical age cohort for higher education that follows and successfully completes tertiary programmes. From 1995 to 2005, Portugal went from a percentage of less than 20 percent of the age group of people normally completing tertiary programs to a rate of above 30 percent for the same age group,[66] which was a remarkable evolution. This evolution was due to strong state investment in enlarging the network of public universities and community colleges, as well as to the dissemination of private universities and other types of higher education institutions. In the 2008 academic year there were almost 380,000 students enrolled in undergraduate programmes, with 75 percent in the public sector and the remaining part in private establishments.[67]

Despite the quantitative progress of higher education reached during the last decade, tertiary education faces some major problems. It is well known that the economic growth of a country is closely linked to the state of innovation and the system of higher education. It is not by chance that the world's best universities tend to be located in the most advanced countries, such as the United States or in some European countries.

The main problem affecting the Portuguese system of higher education relates to quality of the institutions. Given that the universities of excellence are research universities, the quality of universities is to be measured by their research performance. One of the most recent devices to evaluate the quality of universities is the Shanghai ranking, which measures university performance across the world, based on different indicators of research success. The 2008 version of the academic ranking of the top five hundred world universities, organized by the Institute of Higher Education of Shanghai, includes just two Portuguese universities, which are placed in the group of the last 20 percent of universities considered (between 402 and 503).[68] Similarly, no Portuguese institutions are included in the top one hundred list of European best universities.[69] Hence, the Portuguese research universities need to increase their performance in order to make a stronger contribution to the economic growth of the country and to achieve a better position in international rankings of universities.

Several reasons could explain the low performance of the Portuguese higher education system. Most of the problems are not exclusive to the national system, but also affect other European countries, although on a different scale. However, there are some aspects where the Portuguese case has extreme features. One of these relates to faculty and career development.

It is well known that inbreeding is a serious problem in many higher education systems. Inbreeding is considered to be an obstacle to academic mobility because it enables the worst practices of university endogamy. In some European states, in particular in small and medium-sized countries, there is a long tradition of higher education institutions hiring from within the ranks of the same university.[70] However, in Portugal inbreeding is more than an academic practice; it has an absolute legal cover, in the sense that is expressly promoted by the statute of the university's teaching profession. Indeed, the law that regulates academic careers confers teaching assistants the right to become faculty members once they obtain their PhD degree. Hence, the law establishes an automatic link between achievement of the doctorate and promotion to the position of assistant professor.

Because most teaching assistants used to do their doctorates at the same university where they worked, they were immediately promoted to a position of assistant professor the moment they completed their PhD.[71] In reality, the large majority of faculty members of Portuguese universities entered as students in a certain academic institution for undergraduate studies, moved to the graduate program and became teaching assistants, and when they obtained their PhD degrees, directly initiated an academic career at the same university. Furthermore, the majority of them remained as professors at the same institution until the end of their academic life. In this context it should come as no surprise that the OECD considered that academic inbreeding in Portugal reaches the highest level among the European countries.[72]

Problems affecting faculty careers are not just confined to inbreeding. In an academic career that tends to develop from the beginning to the very end within the same institution, tenure procedure is the only moment where the university is allowed to assess the merit of assistant professors who have been promoted to the academic career by the effect of the law. Hence, tenure should be seen as an opportunity to select those with an acceptable research performance and a suitable teaching achievement. However, a brief look at data regarding tenure refusal shows that in the period between 1989 and 2004 there were surprisingly few cases of tenure rejection, with fifty denial decisions in the entire group of fifteen public universities.[73] In fact tenure, as well as other procedures of merit evaluation, is normally done by inside professors in an academic atmosphere that has not been oriented to promote professional merit or favor mobility.

The academic career is still very influenced by a civil servant mentality. Indeed, there is also a strict egalitarian policy in salary matters. Academic wages in public universities are determined by the government, and this does not allow any flexibility for the universities to compete for the best academics. In fact, professors throughout the country receive equal pay for the same academic position, regardless of whether they belong to a teaching institution with a negative assessment and located in a remote area, or whether they are leading academics in their field of studies and members of the best national research university.

A further weakness that marks the Portuguese higher education system has to do with governance. Even if public academic institutions do not benefit from much autonomy in the sense that they are not financially independent, they cannot select their own students, they do not freely choose fee levels, and they cannot decide on remuneration issues. During the last decades university boards have been fully dominated by internal members, with faculty, teaching assistants, students, and administrative personnel having complete control over the management of each institution. There is no room on the boards for any external members like alumni representatives, local authorities or independent counsellors.[74]

Moreover, a large number of internal bodies absorb the best energies of faculty members, but in the end they are unable to take decisions and implement them due to the overlapping functions of these bodies. The lack of clear leadership, the need to accommodate extensive consensus to carry out any reform, the inexistence of external representatives on the bodies, together with a strong endogamy that characterizes the academic career allowed the different structures of governance a high degree of capture from the constituent's interests. In fact, in a framework of self-government rule, without any form of professional management, universities remained trapped by the multitude of interests associated with the election of an entire set of bodies. Therefore, the question of governance is a central issue for the modernization of the academic institutions. Portuguese higher education needs a system of governance that ensures more accountability and is able to define the achievement of strategic goals for the management of each university.[75]

It should be noted that problems affecting Portuguese higher education are not limited to career development and governance issues. Indeed, there is a basic concern regarding the funding of higher education. Portugal is one of the EU countries that spends less on tertiary education, and expenditure on higher education has remained frozen in recent years. There is little hope that government will substantially increase financial transfers to public universities and community colleges in the medium term, due to the fiscal constraints stemming from the European monetary union.[76] Moreover, recent increases to university fees seem to have reached the critical balance between the fundamental right to accede to tertiary education and the price to pay for what is to be considered an investment in professional development. However, Portuguese higher education has a large margin to improve its teaching and research performances. If the academic career is to be deeply reformed, in order to prevent inbreeding and all forms of endogamy and to promote research merit and professional mobility, there must be a serious renewal of faculty, which will pave the way for hiring young researchers with PhDs from world-class universities. In the same way, with a new governance structure, universities would be able to define strategic development plans that would not be conditioned by corporatist and other types of protected interests.

Conclusion

For a country that had spent the previous five centuries mainly focused on its colonial possessions, the accession to the European Union was a major challenge for Portugal's external policy and economic relations. The decision to join the Union was preceded by a long route of democratic consolidation that is firmly linked with the course of Europeanization. However, the process of closing the gap with the EU member states had a different starting point when compared with other European countries. Indeed, the education skills of the Portuguese people lagged behind the European average—including those of the Eastern countries—and Portugal had always been one of the continent's poorest countries.

In spite of the difficulties represented by the nature of the European accession, the Portuguese economy had a brilliant performance during the initial years of EU membership. However, the early golden period seemed to end with the adoption of the single currency, and since then Portugal has embarked on a clear process of economic divergence within the Euro area. Unlike the other cohesion countries that were able to fill the gap with the European Union average over the last decade—benefiting from a strong process of economic growth—Portugal is referred by the European Commission as the disappointing exception among the so-called catching-up countries. The situation tends to be even more disturbing when a comparison is made with the Eastern countries' economic performance, as well as with the perspective of Portugal being continuously surpassed by those states in the Union's GDP ranking.

The problems affecting the Europeanization of the country go well beyond the economy. In fact, in fundamental areas of state action such as justice or the educational system, Portugal is also diverging from the other EU countries, despite devoting an identical percentage of the national income to those areas. Education is a foundation of economic growth and development. The country needs to find a new industrial pattern based on innovation. For that its educational system must improve. Among the twenty-seven member states, Portugal has the lowest rate of people completing upper-secondary education. In addition, the quality of higher education poses a serious threat to the ability of the country to face the challenges posed by the EU's new paradigm to create a European knowledge economy.

In the case of justice, the performance of the judicial branch of power also raises fears regarding the appropriate functioning of a democratic and fair society. In fact, it seems that there is a dual system of justice in Portugal, with powerful people being able to take advantage of redundant legal guarantees established by criminal law and criminal law procedure. The fact that in the framework of legal proceedings important people tend to escape from criminal sanctions could be understood as a violation of a basic dimension of the rule of law, insofar as it prevents the successful operation of the principle that laws should apply equally to every person and that no one is above the law. Moreover, it enables some fringes of the established elite to behave as if they benefit from a sort of legal impunity. This is truly damaging for the quality of democracy.

Notes

1. I am indebted to Professor Ann Henshall for very helpful linguistic revision of the article. The usual disclaimer applies.

2. Brigid Laffan and Alexander Stubb, "Member States," in *The European Union: How Does it Work?, 2nd ed.,* ed. Elizabeth Bomberg et al. (Oxford: Oxford University Press, 2008): 71-91.

3. "The overwhelming majority of the Portuguese (92 percent) considered the economic situation of the country to be bad, and an even higher proportion (95 percent) expressed an identical opinion with regard to the domestic employment situation. In comparative terms, the Portuguese stand out considerably from the European average – both with regard to the economic situation and to the employment situation, the proportion of negative evaluations in the EU was of 69 percent. Indeed, Portugal is the EU country with the largest percentage of negative assessments of the domestic employment situation and presents the third-highest proportion of negative evaluations of the country's economic situation. The pessimism of the Portuguese is also evident in their expectations for the coming year: 60 percent of respondents believe that the employment situation in Portugal will worsen over the next twelve months, and 58 percent have an equal expectation vis-à-vis the national economy. In both cases, the Portuguese exhibit a greater pessimism than their European counterparts, with the EU average being of 53 and 51 percent, respectively." Eurobarometer 70 (2008), *Public opinion in the European Union. National Report, Executive Summary, Portugal,* 2. Available at: http://ec.eduopa.eu/public_opinio n/archives/eb/eb70/eb70_pt_exec.pdf.

4. Jaime Reis, "Causas Históricas do Atraso Económico Português," in *História de Portugal,* ed. José Tengarrinha (São Paulo: UNESP, 2000): 245.

5. European Commission, "EMU@10. Successes and challenges after 10 years of Economic and Monetary Union," *European Economy 2* (2008): 115.

6. António Costa Pinto, "Twentieth-Century Portugal: An Introduction," in *Contemporary Portugal: Politics, society and culture,* ed, António C. Pinto (New York: Boulder, 2003), 46.

7. OECD, "Education at a Glance 2007," *OECD indicators,* 2007a: 28 http://213.253.134.43/oecd/pdfs/browseit/9607051E.PDF.

8. Sebastián Royo, "The Challenges of EU Integration: Iberian Lessons for Eastern Europe," in *Towards the Completion of Europe: Analysis and Perspectives of the New European Union Enlargement,* ed. Joaquin Roy and Roberto Domínguez (Miami: Imprimatur, 2006), 109.

9. European Commission, *European Economy 73* (2001): 309.

10. António G. Soares, "Portugal and the European Union: The Ups and Downs in 20 Years of Membership," *Perspectives on European Politics and Society* 8 (2007): 467.

11. António Barreto, "Social Change in Portugal: 1960-2000," in *Contemporary Portugal: Politics, society and culture,* ed. António C. Pinto (New York: Boulder, 2003), 175.

12. OECD, "Economic Survey of Portugal, 2008" *Policy Brief,* 2008a: 3 http://www.oecd.org/dataoecd/57/16/40857626.pdf.

13. It is interesting to note that when asked whether your country would have been better protected in face of the current financial and economic crisis if it had kept the former currency Portuguese were those that clearly delivered the highest positive answer within the Euro area, with 62 percent (Eurozone average, 45 percent). See Eurobarometer

(2009), "The Economic and Financial Crisis," *Eurobametre Special* 311, 37, available at: http://ec.europa.eu/public_opinion/archives/ebs/ebs_311_data.pdf

14. Orlando Abreu, "Portugal's boom and bust: lessons for euro newcomers," *ECFin Country Focus* 16 (2006): 5. http://ec.europa.eu/economy_finance/publications/country_focus/2006/cf16_2006en.pdf

15. European Commission, 2008: 106.

16. OECD, 2008a: 4.

17. European Commission, 2008: 110.

18. João F. Amaral,"A Economia Portuguesa na União Europeia," *Revista de Estudos Europeus* 1 (2007): 219.

19. European Commission, 2008: 111.

20. European Commission, "Economic Forecast—Spring 2009," *European Economy* 3 (2009a): 97. http://ec.europa.eu/economy_finance/publications/publication 15048_en.pdf. European Commission, 2009a: 3-4.

21. According to Mauro and Forster, Portugal is considered to be at the bottom of the ranking of competitiveness indicators within the Euro area because of its geographical situation, technological disadvantages and the high entry costs in new economic sectors (2008: 37-38). European Commission, 2008: 113.

22. OECD, 2008a: 6.

23. Soares, "Portugal and the European Union," 472.

24. European Commission, 2008: 52.

25. Amaral, "A Economia Portuguesa," 218.

26. Paula Fontoura, "Efeitos no comércio da integração económica," in *Economia Europeia* ed. António Romão (Oeiras: Celta, 2004), 79.

27. Álvaro S. Pereira, *Os Mitos da Economia Portuguesa, 2 ed.,* (Lisboa: Guerra & Paz, 2008), 81.

28. European Comimission, 2008: 115.

29. Thomas Carothers, "The Rule of Law Revival," *Foreign Affairs* 77 (1998), 96.

30. On political courts and political trials during the dictatorship, see Rosas (2009), *Tribunais Políticos. Tribunais Militares Especiais e Tribunais Plenários durante a Ditadura e o Estado Novo,* Lisboa: Temas e Debates.

31. Boaventura de Sousa Santos, Conceição Gomes, and João Pedroso, "Portugal" in *L'Administration de la Justice en Europe et L'Évaluation de sa Qualité* ed. Noëlle Rivero-Cabouat (Paris: Montchrestien, 2005), 334.

32. Pedro Magalhães, "A Qualidade da Democracia em Portugal: A Perspectiva dos Cidadãos," Lisboa: SEDES (2009), 17. http://www.sedes.pt/Multimedia/File/A percent20Qualidade percent20da percent20Democracia percent20em percent20Portugal.pdf

33. Luís D. Sousa, "Political Parties and Corruption in Portugal," *West European Politics* 24 (2001), 159.

34. As it is referred by Santos and Gomes, the vast majority of cases brought to court come from the so-called mass criminality, i.e., lower and medium criminal acts such as driving without license or drunk driving (2002: 189).

35. Jacques Ziller, "Europeização do Direito—Do Alargamento dos Domínios do Direito da União Europeia à Transformação dos Direitos dos Estados-membros," in *Novos Territórios do Direito. Europeização, Globalização e Transformação da Regulação Jurídica,* ed. Maria E. Gonçalves and Pierre Guibentif (Estoril: Principia, 2008), 29-31.

36. Transparency International, *Progress Report 2009 OECD Anti-Bribery Conven-*

-*tion*, http://www.transparency.org/news_room/in_focus/2009/oecd_pr_2009, 2009: 42.

37. Conceição Gomes, *O tempo dos Tribunais: Um estudo sobre a morosidade da Justiça*, (Coimbra: Coimbra Editora, 2003), 63.

38. Boaventura de Sousa Santos and Conceição Gomes, *As Reformas Processuais e a Criminalidade na Década de 90: As formas especiais de processo e a suspensão provisória do processo: problemas e bloqueios* (Coimbra: Observatório Permanente da Justiça Portuguesa/Centro de Estudos Sociais, 2002), 83.

39. Gomes, *O tempo dos Tribunais*, 15-16.

40. Magalhães, "A Qualidade da Democracia em Portugal," 3.

41. Santos and Gomes, *As Reformas Processuais e a Criminalidade,* 170.

42. A comparative analysis on judges' productivity can be found on: Santos and Gomes, *Os actos e os tempos dos juízes: contributos para a construção de indicadores da distribuição processual nos juízos cíveis* (Coimbra: Observatório Permanente da Justiça Portuguesa/Centro de Estudos Sociais, 2005), 509-521.

43. Nuno Garoupa, "Reforma da Justiça e Reformas na Justiça," *Iprisverbis* 3, http://www.iprisverbis.eu/files/IPRIS_Verbis_032008.pdf, 2008: 6.

44. Santos and Gomes, *As Reformas Processuais e a Criminalidade,* 178.

45. Luís D. Sousa, "I Don't Bribe, I Just Pull Strings: Assessing the Fluidity of Social Representations of Corruption in Portuguese Society," *Perspectives on European Politics and Society* 9 (2008): 10.

46. Magalhães, "A Qualidade da Democracia em Portugal," 3.

47. On judges and prosecutors' recruitment and training systems, see: Santos, Gomes and Pedroso, *O Recrutamento e a Formação de Magistrados: Uma Proposta de Renovação. Análise Comparada de Sistemas e do Discurso Judiciário em Portugal*, Volume I, (Coimbra: Observatório Permanente da Justiça Portuguesa/Centro de Estudos Sociais, 2001), 48-61.

48. Daniel Kaufmann and Aart Kraay, "Governance Indicators: Where Are We, Where Should We Be Going?" *The World Bank Research Observer* 23 (2008): 2.

49. For instance, as far as the OECD Anti-Bribery Convention is concerned, Portugal was included in the group of countries that provided little or no enforcement of the same Convention. See: Transparency International, *Progress Report 2009 OECD Anti-Bribery Convention*, (2009): 10-13. http://www.transparency.org/news_room/in_focus/2009/oecd_pr_2009.

50. Ministry of Justice, "Movimento de Processos nos Tribunais Judiciais de 1ª Instância, segundo a espécie, por tribunal (2006)," http://www.dgpj.mj.pt/sections/estatisticas-da-justica/informacao-estatistica/anexos/processos-segundo-a-area/downloadFile/file/TotalProcessos_AreaProcessual_2006.pdf?nocache=1207559837.08.

51. Magalhães, "A Qualidade da Democracia em Portugal," 16.

52. OECD, 2007a: 28.

53. Barreto, "Social Change in Portugal," 171. Gabinete de Planeamento, Estratégia, Avaliação e Relações Internacionais do Ministério da Ciência, Tecnologia e Ensino Superior. http://www.estatisticas.gpeari.mctes.pt/archive/doc/AlunosVagasDiplomados020708_capinscritosvf.pdf

54. Public expenditure on education, as a percentage of total public expenditure, rose from 11.7 in 1995 to 12.6 in the year 2000. As a percentage of the GDP, public expenditure on education represented 5.1 percent in 1995, and 5.4 percent in the year 2000 (OECD, 2008, 262).

55. OECD, 2007a: 196.

56. The typical age group corresponds to the most common age at the end of the last school/academic year of the corresponding level and the program in which the degree is obtained (OECD, 2008b: 66).

57. OECD, *Education at a Glance 2008. OECD indicators*, 2008b: 66. http://www.oecd.org/dataoecd/23/46/41284038.pdf.

58. OECD, 2007a: 51.

59. OECD, 2007a: 42.

60. In the EU over 78 percent of young people aged twenty to twenty-four have successfully completed upper secondary education. In the Czech Republic, Poland, Slovenia, and Slovakia this proportion rises to more than 90 percent. Only Malta (54.7 percent) and Portugal (53.4 percent) have a qualification rate of less than 60 percent (European Commission, 2009 b: 243).

61. European Commission, *Key Data on Education in Europe 2009*, Luxembourg: Official Publications of the European Communities. http://eacea.ec.europa.eu/education/eurydice/documents/key_data_series/105EN.pdf, 2009b: 243.

62. Barreto, "Social Change in Portugal," 171.

63. However, it should be referred the recent government's strategy to upgrade competences, the so-called *Novas Oportunidades* program. The initiative includes two main pillars: providing new opportunities to young people at risk of dropping out of school and offering learning opportunities to adults with low educational attainment, based on the recognition of acquired skills. The first results are encouraging with an increase of young people enrolled in technical and professional courses at the secondary level, and strong demand of adults for the recognition of competences and for lifelong learning (OECD, 2008a: 11).

64. OECD, 2008b: 43.

65. European Commission, 2005: 307.

66. OECD, 2007a: 54.

67. Gabinete de Planeamento, Estratégia, Avaliação e Relações Internacionais do Ministério da Ciência, Tecnologia e Ensino Superior. Available at: http://www.estatisticas.gpeari.mctes.pt/archive/doc/AlunosVagasDiplomados020708_cap inscritosvf.pdf

68. Available at: http://www.arwu.org/rank2008/ARWU2008_E(EN).htm

69. Lisbon University and the University of Porto, the only ones mentioned by the Shanghai ranking, are in the position 169-210 of the regional rank (Europe). See: http://www.arwu.org/rank2008/ARWU2008_E(EN).htm

70. Philippe Aghion, Mathias Dewatripont, Caroline Hoxby, Andreu Mas-Colell, and André Sapir, *Higher aspirations: An agenda for reforming European Universities* (Brussels: Bruegel Blueprint Series, 2008), 39.

71. The Statute of the University's teaching profession was approved in 1980. Since then there were several attempts to amend the law in order to remove some irrational features, like inbreeding. In 2009, one of the last decree-laws adopted by the government at the end of its mandate was the revision of the statute. Although the new law foresees that an academic career starts at the level of assistant professor, it allows current teaching assistants to be automatically promoted to the position of assistant professor if they obtain a PhD in the next five years.

72. OECD, *Reviews of National Policies for Education. Tertiary Education in Portugal*. http://www.oecd.org/document/14/0,3343,en_33873108_33873764_39713934_1_1_1_1,00.html, 2009b, 12.

73. See Gabinete de Planeamento, Estratégia, Avaliação e Relações Internacionais do Ministério da Ciência, Tecnologia e Ensino Superior. http://www.estatisticas.gpeari. mctes.pt/archive/doc/RecProvimento.xls. It is also interesting to note that in 2004 there were 6,945 PhD professors in those fifteen public universities, but in 1993 there were just 3,232 PhD professors in those universities. http://www.estatisticas.gpeari.mctes.pt/ archive/doc/Evol93_04Univ.xls

74. Aghion et al., *Higher aspirations*, 38.

75. A new law on university governance was adopted in 2007, and it has gradually been implemented in the universities' and schools' statutes. It establishes the presence of external members, along with a majority of members representing professors, students and workers, on the supervisory boards that elect university rectors and school presidents. The law also strengthens the powers of rectors and school presidents. This is a step forward for good governance in higher education. Nevertheless, it should be noted that even if the law foresees that the selection procedure for rectors and deans should be open to external candidates, these posts have, for the time being, been filled by their former rectors.

76. OECD, 2007b: 12.

References

Eurobarometer (2008) "Public Opinion in the European Union. National Report, Executive Summary, Portugal," *Eurobarometer 70*, Available at: http://ec.europa.eu/public _opinion/archives/eb/eb70/eb70_pt_exec.pdf.

Eurobarometer (2009) "The Economic and Financial Crisis," *Eurobametre Special* 311. Available at: http://ec.europa.eu/public_opinion/archives/ebs/ebs_311_data.pdf

European Commission (2005) *Key Data on Education in Europe 2005*, Luxembourg: Official Publications of the European Communities. Available at: http://www.eury dice.org/ressources/eurydice/pdf/0_integral/052EN.pdf.

Mauro, Filippo and Forster, Katrin (2008) "Globalisation and the Competitiveness of the Euro Area," *Occasional Paper Series*, No. 97, European Central Bank.

Rosas, Fernando (2009) (ed.) *Tribunais Políticos. Tribunais Militares Especiais e Tribunais Plenários durante a Ditadura e o Estado Novo*, Lisboa: Temas e Debates.

Santos, Boaventura de Sousa, Gomes, Conceição and Pedroso, João (2001) *O Recrutamento e a Formação de Magistrados: Uma Proposta de Renovação. Análise Comparada de Sistemas e do Discurso Judiciário em Portugal*, Vol. I, Coimbra: Observatório Permanente da Justiça Portuguesa/Centro de Estudos Sociais.

Santos, Boaventura de Sousa and Gomes, Conceição (2005) *Os Actos e os Tempos dos Juízes: Contributos para a Construção de Indicadores da Distribuição Processual nos Juízos Cíveis*, Coimbra: Observatório Permanente da Justiça Portuguesa/Centro de Estudos Sociais.

7 The Portuguese Migratory Experience: A New Migratory Cycle?

Sebastián Royo

Historically, Portugal has been known as a country of emigration. Over the last five centuries Portuguese citizens have emigrated all over the world as Portuguese colonization extended to South America, Africa, and Asia. The last major migratory movement took place following World War II, when the Portuguese emigrated mostly to West European countries, in search of economic opportunities. However, most of the political, economic, and social factors that led to this exodus have disappeared, and over the last two decades the transformation of Portugal has decreased dramatically the outflow of Portuguese citizens emigrating abroad.

Indeed, since the second half of the 1970s, there have been two main developments. First, the process of decolonization and the subsequent independence of the Portuguese colonies in the 1970s led to the return of Portuguese citizens that were still living in the former colonies. This development also led to an inflow of foreigners of African origin from the colonies, which has continued until today and has had an important impact on the makeup of Portuguese population. As a result Africa has surpassed Europe as the region of origin for the largest contingent of legalized foreigners living in Portugal.[1]

At the same time, the combined processes of democratization and European integration in the 1970s and 1980s transformed political, social, and economic conditions in Portugal. This development provided incentives for the return of Portuguese emigrants to the country and stemmed the outflow of Portuguese citizens abroad. Between 1974 and 1975 approximately six hundred thousand Portuguese citizens returned to the country largely as a result of the change to a democratic regime and decolonization. In addition, the increasing restrictions on entries that followed the establishment of a democratic regime and the incorporation to the European Community also influenced the immigration patterns of non-Portuguese citizens.

Historically Portugal has been a uniform country with centralized power enforced over the whole territory. Consequently, although there are differences among the country's regions, the language, law, currency, and culture has remained homogenous. Factors such as the mobilization of conscripts to fight the colonial wars, the broadening of television coverage, and the establishment of educational and social networks that cover all the country have contributed to the national integration. However, the social, cultural, demographic, and economic impact of immigration has grown exponentially over the last decade.

The purpose of this chapter will be to examine the evolution of migration flows in Portugal, and explore the reasons that have converted Portugal into a recipient of immigrations and the consequences of this development. The main sources of data are the Immigration and Border Department (SEF) and the Portuguese National Statistical Institute (INE).[2] The chapter will be divided into two main sections. The first one presents an overview of the Portuguese emigration experience over the last five decades. The second section outlines the evolution of migration flows over the last two decades. The chapter concludes with an examination of the impact of the European Union enlargement for Portugal.

Patterns of Portuguese Emigration after WWII

Portugal has a strong tradition as a country of emigrants. It is estimated that between 1886 and 1966, Portugal lost to emigration more than any West European country except Ireland. As a result, migration has been an important component of Portugal's history, and it has had a significant impact on the economic, social, and cultural landscape of the country. Emigration has been largely determined by economic, social, and political conditions within Portugal and abroad. The perception about the potential for opportunities as well as the strength of the network of emigrants in Portugal and other countries have also played a significant role in the evolution of migration patterns. Portuguese people have migrated to the Americas (United States, Venezuela, and Brazil); Europe (France, Luxembourg, and Germany); Africa; and Asia. Up to the 1950s, more than 80 percent of the Portuguese migration was directed to Brazil. After WWII, France replaced Brazil, as the main destination of Portuguese emigrants.

Until the second half of the 1970s, emigration policies in Portugal were highly regulated and conditioned by the economic needs of the state and the imperatives of colonialism. The 1933 Constitution established that the state has the "right and obligation" to "discipline emigration" (art. 31). A government agency, the *Junta da Emigração*, was charged with the role to supervise emigration and implement a quota system (a maximum of thirty thousand departures a year). Henceforth, emigration policies were determined by three complementary objectives: to satisfy the demands for labor of the domestic economy, to meet the interests of the colonies, and finally, to benefit from the remittances of emigrants.[3] These policies were highly interventionist (for instance, they prevented the departure of individuals who had jobs in Portugal). These restrictive regulations, however, did not prevent people from departing the country. Indeed, at least 36 percent of Portuguese emigrants left the country illegally between 1950 and 1976.[4] After the *Carnations Revolution* of April 25, 1974, the democratic government liberalized emigration policies and enshrined the freedom to emigrate and return in the 1976 Constitution.

Following World War II, Portuguese emigration grew constantly, from 22,000 departures in 1950 to 183,000 in 1980. The peak years were from 1964 to 1975. After 1971, it decreased. Overall, between 1950 and 1988 emigration totaled at least 2,152,000. The decade of the 1960s and the first half of the 1970s were years of an explosion of emigration. Emigration was influenced to a large extend—as we will see below—by the relative backwardness of the Portuguese economy (particularly in the countryside), the war in Africa, and the policies of the authoritarian regime.

After WWII, the main destination of Portuguese emigrants would become Western Europe. Between 1950 and 1988, the principal destinations of Portuguese emigrants were France (48 percent), Brazil (15 percent), Germany (11 percent), the United States (9 percent), and Canada (6 percent). Portugal was included in the Marshall Plan and became one of the founding members of the European Free Trade Association (EFTA). However, the country was left out of the Schuman Plan and the European Coal and Steel Community (ECSC) in the 1950s. This development was based on Salazar's skepticism regarding European integration, and his decision to maintain a preferential trade relationship with the colonies.[5] At the same time, the original founders of the European Economic Community (EEC) (France, Germany, Italy, and the Benelux countries) made it clear from the outset that the Community would only be open to democracies, and therefore the authoritarian nature of the Portuguese regime prevented EC membership.

European Community exclusion, however, did not impede emigration to the EEC. On the contrary, in order to cover for the labor shortages that resulted from World War II, the six founding members of the EEC issued eight million work-permits to facilitate the migration of labor from Southern Europe to work in the industrial plants of Northern Europe. In the case of Portugal, this led to an explosion of migration to Europe. Overall emigration increased from 245,000 between 1960 and 1964, to 542,000 between 1965 and 1969, and 630,000 between 1970 and 1974 (or 40 percent of the Portuguese labor force).[6] France was the preferred destination of Portuguese workers. Starting in 1961, Portuguese migration to France began to exceed ten thousand per year, and eventually this increasing flow made Portugal the main supplier of foreign labor for France in the second half of the 1960s. This migratory outflow peaked in 1970 with 255,000 emigrants. Most Portuguese workers took low-skilled, low-wage jobs in sectors such as construction, public works, and services. The subsequent crisis of the 1970s provoked by the oil shock—led to increasing unemployment in Western Europe and the imposition of migration controls by European countries to steam this flow—contributed to a sharp decline of departures from Portugal (i.e., they declined from 158,000 to 13,000 between 1971 and 1988). Altogether, as of 1989, some four million Portuguese were living abroad.

Portuguese emigration can be divided into three main phases: it increased between 1941 and 1964, stabilized during the following decade, and decreased after 1975. Based on the destination preferences, there were four main periods:[7]

a. Between 1950 and 1959, the preferred destinations of Portuguese migrants were countries overseas. Brazil accounted for most of the flow: 80 percent in the 1940s and 68 percent in the 1950s.

b. After 1960, Europe attracted most Portuguese migrants: 75 percent of the total, of which 59 percent went to France.

c. While Europe dominated up to 1977, starting in 1977 overseas destinations flourished again and the European share fell from 56 percent in 1977 to 39 percent in 1979. In the 1970s, emigration slowed down as a result of the recession and the oil crisis in receiving countries.

d. Between 1980 and 1988 overseas destinations attracted 51 percent of departures, led now by the United States and Canada.

These destination shifts were motivated by changes within Portugal and the receiving countries. For instance, migration restrictions following the first oil shock in the 1970s help explain the decrease of migration to Europe, and the passing of legislation in the United States in 1965 that fostered family reunifications and revised the quota system led to a sharp increase of Portuguese immigration to that country after that year (i.e., it grew from 1,852 Portuguese migrants in 1965 to 13,357 the following year).

In addition, over the period examined, the migration patterns were also quite different. Migration to Europe (mostly to France) was characterized by three main factors: it was clandestine through Spain, 37 percent of the workers were individuals and did not travel with their families, and most of them proceeded from the interior regions of Portugal.[8] Furthermore, the regional contribution to the migration flow was also differentiated: Most overseas migration proceeded from the rural areas, while immigrants to Europe came from urban and industrial areas. Between 1950 and 1959, migration from the mainland represented almost 79 percent of the total, with Lisbon and Aveiro contributing the highest percentage of emigrants. Most of them came from the coastal regions. However, the percentage of Portuguese that emigrated from the Azores increased sharply between 1950 and 1988—from 6.14 percent to 21.21 percent.[9]

Emigration continued in the 1990s and remained relatively stable throughout the decade. In 1996 around 29,000 Portuguese migrated to other countries (an increase of 28.7 percent from 1995). In the new century, these flows have continued: in 2002, the number of Portuguese emigrants totaled 27,359 people, and in 2003, 27,008. The main destination of Portuguese emigrants throughout the 1990s and 2000s has been European countries: Germany, France, and Switzerland received around 79 percent of total emigrants in 1996. In the last decade, European destinations have gained relative importance. Europe has received 93.5 percent of the total emigrants (in 2002, it was 81.3 percent). On the contrary, the Americas (mainly the United State and Canada)—which constituted the destination of 10.4 percent of the Portuguese emigrants in 2002—have lost relative importance, and in 2003 only accounted for 4.5 percent of the total. In 2003 France (7,399), Switzerland (4,785) and the United Kingdom (3,893) received 59 percent of the total emigrants (followed by Germany, Spain, and Luxembourg). During the last decade the Northern and Center regions—Lisbon and the Vale do Tejo—have been the main origin of Portuguese emigrants.

What Explains the Shift Toward European Destinations?

This development can be partly explained by a significant change in emigration patterns. First, as we have seen starting in the 1960s, there were significant changes in the composition of migration flows with emigrants originating not only from the rural areas, but from the most urban and industrial areas. Historically, while most emigrants from the rural areas have migrated overseas, those from urban and industrial ones have preferred European destinations.

The increase in clandestine emigration starting in the 1960s also contributed to this shift towards Europe. It was much easier and cheaper to enter France, or any other European country for that matter, than to be on a transatlantic voyage. Another important factor that contributed to the growth of emigration to Europe was the increase of temporary emigration. Since 1993 emigration figures show a sharp increase of temporary emigrants (i.e., individuals who leave the country with the intention to stay abroad for no more than one year) vis-à-vis permanent ones (those who seek to stay abroad for over a year).

Starting in 1976, the statistical information on Portuguese emigration becomes divided into permanent and temporary categories. From that year onwards we can observe a substantial decrease in permanent emigration and an increase in temporary one. The majority of temporary emigrants have migrated to Europe. Only during the stagflation years of the second half of the 1970s and 1980s, when European countries became less receptive to Portuguese emigrants, they considered other countries such as the United States, Canada and even Australia. This transoceanic emigration, however, was almost exclusively permanent.

During the decade of the 1990s (with the exception of 1992), temporary emigration has exceeded permanent emigration. Not surprisingly, European countries have become, once again, the preferred choice of Portuguese emigrants.
Indeed, the main destination of permanent emigrants over the last decade has
been Germany, France (63.6 percent of the total in 1996 and over 70 percent in
2003), and Switzerland.

As late as 2005, the stock of emigrants was still very significant: 1,950,486
people (or 18.6 percent of the population). The top ten destination countries are:
Angola, France, Mozambique, Brazil, Cape Verde, Germany, Venezuela, Guinea-Bissau, Spain, and Switzerland.[10]

Reasons for Portuguese Emigration

While it is widely assumed that emigration was a consequence of Portugal's
economic conditions and its high levels of poverty, the reasons for Portuguese
emigration after World War II had to do both with developments in Portugal and
in the receiving countries.

There is an extensive literature that seeks to explain the reasons that influence people to emigrate. Migratory flow can have its source not just in economic
factors but also in political, cultural, social, religious, and ethnical ones. Indeed,
there are multiple factors that come into play in people's decision to emigrate,
including: age, culture, language, education levels, immigration networks, geographical distance, sex, or income levels.

From an economic standpoint, international migratory flows are a response
to differences in economic conditions between the host and the home countries,
measured by unemployment levels and income. Economic explanations refer to
the expected economic opportunities for the emigrant:[11]

1. *Macroeconomic*: These explanations take into account *push* and *pull*
    factors to explain why some countries supply emigrants and other
    countries receive them.
    a.   From a *push* perspective, according to Mundel's neoclassic
    theory, migratory movements can be explained based on the differ-
    ences in factor allocation among countries. The countries that have
    an abundance of labor relative to capital (i.e., developing countries
    with high fertility rates and high youth mortality rates, which result
    in a saturated labor market and depressed wages), will supply
    workers to those countries that have abundance of capital and
    shortages of labor (i.e., rich countries with low fertility rates and
    high life expectancy).[12]

b. Piore's theory about the dual labor market explains the *pull* factors that attract emigrants to the host country. According to this explanation, the key factor that triggers international migration is the high demand for low skilled workers in developed countries.[13] Since developed countries are characterized by a dual economy in which a primary sector—based on intensive use of capital—coexists with a secondary one—based on the intensive use of labor—qualified workers work in the primary sector and low-skilled ones in the secondary. However, there are labor shortages for low skilled jobs because people do not want to work in low paid jobs with little social prestige. This generates an excess demand for these jobs that is fulfilled by immigrants.

2. *Microeconomic*: This explanation is based on the *human capital model*, which looks at the individual's decision to emigrate.[14] According to this account, the decision to emigrate is based on the emigrant's expectation that she/he will receive higher earnings in the host country than in the home one. In other words, emigrants seek to maximize individual earnings. They view emigration as an "investment" in which they calculate the net present value of future earnings. They emigrate when they decide that the benefits surpass the costs (including not just the economic ones but also the psychological, cultural, social, and assimilation ones) and uncertainties. They will also consider the existence of networks that may ease the transition and assimilation process. This decision is personal and each person views this trade-off differently based on his or her own personal characteristics, including: age, sex, education, and financial resources. Finally, the *new economy of immigration* model looks not just at individual earnings, but also at the diversification of the sources of family income. From this perspective people emigrate to minimize the fluctuations of family earnings and they send back part of their earnings.[15]

To account for Portuguese emigration, scholars have stressed *push* factors such as the duality of the Portuguese economy or the imbalances in the country's economic structure, as well as *pull* factors such as wage differentials.[16] Moreover, domestic conditions exerted considerable pressure on Portuguese citizens, and other factors, such as political sanctions of the recipient nations and the strength of migrant networks, also played an important role.

From an economic standpoint, several factors have contributed to Portuguese emigration:[17]

1. Uneven economic growth. Following WWII the Portuguese economy remained virtually stagnant. Only after 1950, did the economy consistently grow (until 1973).[18]

2. Income inequality. The *International Labour Organization* estimates that the *Gini* ratio, which measures income concentration, for Portugal changed little between 1967 and 1968 (0.423) and 1973 and 1974 (0.431). By comparison, in the early 1970s, France's Gini ratio was 0.416, Germany's 0.376, and Sweden's 0.346.

3. The underdevelopment of certain parts of the country. As we have seen, the most developed regions of the country (Lisbon interior and the Algarve) were not major sources of emigration, whereas the coastal regions (particularly in the north), have contributed historically most of the emigrants.

4. The imbalances in the country's economic structure. This accounts for differences in migration patterns between the more developed industrial areas around Lisbon and Porto and the less-developed rural ones of the coast.

5. Changes in the economic structure, particularly the shift of labor out of agriculture and into the industry and service sector. The number of people working in the agricultural sector declined by about 550,000 workers between 1960—when Portugal became a founding member of EFTA—and 1973. During this period the share of the civilian labor force engaged in agriculture, forestry, and fishing fell from nearly 44 percent to just around 28 percent. The share of labor engaged in industry and construction increased from less than 29 percent to almost 36 percent, and in the services sector (including transport and communications) from nearly 28 percent to more than 36 percent. However, the reduction in the number of workers in the agricultural sector was not accompanied by a similar increase in the industrial and services sectors. Indeed, nearly two out of every three Portuguese taking up nonagricultural employment during this period did so in another European country.[19]

6. Wage differentials between Portugal and the receiving countries. As late as 1980, Portuguese wages were 45 percent of the European average and 41 percent of that of France. Even in the 1990s, using Purchasing Power Parity, wages remain far lower than in the richest European countries and even lower than in Spain and Greece; that is, in 1998 Portuguese wages stood at 63 percent of the European average, 57 percent of France's, 71 percent of Spain's, and 91 percent of Greece's. Average hourly rates of pay are still one-half (or even one-third) of other European countries, and average disposable monthly earnings of a couple with two manual workers are 48 percent of those in Greece, 40 percent of those in Spain, and 34 percent of those in France.

7. Labor shortages and economic growth in the receiving countries following WWII.

8. Changes in the productive structure in the 1960s, which resulted in higher unemployment in the industrial sector and underemployment in

the rural areas, thus forcing thousands of Portuguese to emigrate looking for new opportunities.[20]

From a domestic standpoint, the policies of the Salazar and Caetano administration were also important factors.[21] Repression and political prosecution forced thousands of Portuguese out of their country. In addition, as we have seen, the establishment of the fascist *Estado Novo* resulted in a highly regulated and interventionist framework informed by the corporatist regime's decision to subdue individual rights to the collective interest. Emigration controls also sought to satisfy the economic and political demands of the country and colonial empire. Consequently, the fascist government, starting in the 1940s, imposed legislation limiting the number of departures and banning the legal departure of certain strategic occupations. At the same time, the government negotiated and signed bilateral agreements with third party countries to tightly regulate the flow of migration. Only Portugal's industrialization (1950s) and the internationalization of the economy (1960s and 1970s) led to a gradual process of emigration liberalization, which was viewed as a development that could absorb part of the rural exodus of population and contribute to modernization. Population growth and the development of labor-intensive industries in northern Portugal and Lisbon in the 1950s led to a further liberalization of emigration policies in the 1960s and 1970s. These policies influenced the composition of migratory flows.

Characteristics of Portuguese Emigration

Between 1933 and 1974 almost two million Portuguese left the country (32 percent clandestinely). The key characteristics of Portuguese departing the country were:[22]

1. Before 1960, Portuguese emigrants tended to be male, aged fifteen to thirty-five, and originated from a rural area. In the 1960s, however, the process of family reunification changed the character of emigration.
2. The secondary economic sector has been consistently the main source of emigrants. Departures from people engaged in this sector increased from 20,245 in the 1955 and 1959 period to 105,908 between 1960 and 1969. In the 1980s, 64 percent of the Portuguese who migrated and were active came from this sector.
3. The marital status of emigrants has also changed overtime: while 58 percent of the people departing between 1955 and 1959 were single, this lessened to about 46 percent during the 1980 to 1988 period.
4. While males have tended to migrate more than females, the proportion of females departing has increased: from 39.65 percent in 1955 through 1959 to 43.89 percent in the 1980s.

5. In the 1970s there was an increase of family reunification flows as suggested by the growth in the number of married migrants and in the number of children under fifteen.
6. The dominant age group was consistently between fifteen to sixty-four years old.
7. A large proportion of emigrants were not active (from 40 percent in the 1950s to up to 59 percent in the 1980s).
8. In the 1990s, the profile of a typical emigrant changed from a relatively unskilled to a semi-skilled professional one. This was possible due to the higher standards of education and linguistic skills attained by Portuguese workers, who were now able to respond to the increasing demand for specialized workers from other European countries.[23]

Impact of Emigration

Emigration had an impact on demographic growth, the Portuguese economy, and its labor market.

From a demographic perspective emigration was a significant factor because a large number of Portuguese of childbearing age left the country permanently. Indeed, between 1960 and 1973 more than 1.5 million Portuguese emigrated to work abroad a figure larger than the natural increase in the Portuguese population. Because of heavy emigration, the working population shrank from more than 3.1 million in 1960 to just 2.9 million in 1973, and employment fell by an annual rate averaging 0.5 percent. The unprecedented increase of emigration during the mid-1960s canceled out the natural population increase, which meant in absolute terms, a population decrease.[24]

From an economic standpoint, one of the most notable effects of emigration has to do with remittances.[25] In the 1950s the ratio of remittances to exports was about 13 percent; in the 1960s, 25 percent; and in the 1960s, it reached 56 percent. In other words, given the consistent and reliable flow of remittances, emigration was the "single most valuable export." Vis-à-vis GDP, remittances also had a growing importance: 2 percent in the 1950s, 4 percent in the 1960s, and 8 percent in the 1970s.[26] They are still very important today (see Table 7.2).

Emigration and the military draft (from 1961 to 1974, 1.5 million Portuguese served in Africa) were also important factors that contributed to keeping unemployment levels very low. Between 1961 and 1974, unemployment was kept down to about 4 percent (and to less than 3 percent in the early 1970s). However, according to Baganha's analysis, emigration's impact on the Portuguese labor market and economy has been less important than was anticipated.[27] Each year thousands of Portuguese, who could have been part of the active population, migrated to other countries. From an economic standpoint this could have had a significant cost in terms of human capital.

Table 7.1 Characteristics of Portuguese legal migrants, 1955-1988

	1955-59		1960-69		1970-79		1980-88	
Gender	No.	%	No.	%	No.	%	No.	%
Male	96,357	60.35	378,080	58.44	210,347	58.79	50,253	56.11
Female	63,300	39.65	268,882	41.56	147,455	41.21	39,309	43.89
Age	No.	%	No.	%	No.	%	No.	%
-15	37,376	23.41	171,434	26.50	99,757	27.88	21,695	24.22
15-64	120,104	75.23	468,994	72.49	254,163	71.03	66,165	73.88
65+	2,177	1.36	6,534	1.01	3,882	1.08	1,702	1.90
Marital Status	No.	%	No.	%	No.	%	No.	%
Single	93,066	58.29	307,161	47.48	166,593	46.56	39,545	44.15
Married	63,608	39.84	329,594	50.94	185,894	51.95	47,789	53.36
Other	2,983	1.87	10,207	1.58	5,315	1.49	2,228	2.49
Economic Sector*	No.	%	No.	%	No.	%	No.	%
1ary	43,634	56.43	140,730	50.05	54,175	32.39	6,157	16.86
2ary	20,245	26.18	105,908	37.67	84,101	50.29	23,421	64.15
3ary	13,448	17.39	34,539	12.28	28,969	17.32	6,932	18.99
Total Active	77,327	100.00	281,177	100.00	167,245	100.00	36,510	100.00
Inactive	52,425	40.40	240,399	46.09	163,155	49.38	53,052	59.23
Total	129,752		521,576		330,400		89,562	
Total	159,657	100.00	646,962	100.00	357,802	100.00	89,562	100.00

Source: Baganha. Data: SECP, Boletim Anual, 1980-81, 1988.
Note: * Emigrants aged ten or older.

However, in Portugal, the share of scientific and technical personnel was lower than in other countries with similar per capita income levels (in the 1960s Portugal had a per capita income of less than six hundred dollars).[28] In addition, the overwhelming majority of Portuguese emigrants were not professionals or technical workers, and although some of these skilled workers left the country in opposition to the authoritarian regime, the number was not high enough to impact the economy.[29] Indeed, of the 88,634 Portuguese that migrated to France in 1970 only thirty-one people belonged to that group. In addition, 93 percent of the returning migrants had no more than primary education, and only 1 percent had gone to the university.[30] In the end, since the relative number of scientific and technical people in the active population restricted the level of industrial employment in the economy, the migration of poorly skilled or unskilled workers did not have much of an economic impact either, because had they stayed in the country, they would have most likely remained unemployed or underemployed and their production potential would not have been utilized. In other words, Portugal would not have been able to cope with a larger industrial force, and migrants presented "zero marginal productivity for the domestic economy."[31]

Table 7.2 Remittances, 1975-2007

Year	Workers' Remittances (Million $)	Compensation of Employees (Million $)	Total (Million $)
1975	1,103	24	1,127
1976	907	17	924
1977	1,173	24	1,197
1978	1,673	24	1,697
1979	2,454	32	2,486
1980	2,982	41	3,023
1981	2,831	45	2,876
1982	2,601	34	2,635
1983	2,150	37	2,187
1984	2,152	48	2,200
1985	2,091	73	2,164
1986	2,580	74	2,654
1987	3,254	118	3,372
1988	3,378	147	3,525
1989	3,562	144	3,706
1990	4,263	216	4,479
1991	4,517	200	4,717
1992	4,650	2,112	6,762
1993	4,179	136	4,315
1994	3,669	137	3,806
1995	3,793	160	3,953
1996	3,560	148	3,708
1997	3,344	144	3,488
1998	3,361	170	3,531
1999	3,343	138	3,481
2000	3,171	241	3,406
2001	3,340	221	3,566
2002	2,664	201	2,858
2003	2,752	237	3,042
2004	3,032	230	3,305
2005	2,826	235	3,102
2006	3,045	260	3,329
2007	-	-	3,750

Source: IMF, *Balance of Payment Statistics Yearbook*. Annual.

In sum, for decades Portugal exchanged a productive factor—labor—for another one—capital—in the form of remittances: in other words, it substituted labor for capital. This means that the growth of the labor force was not such an important factor in Portugal's economic growth as it was in other countries, because of higher level of emigration and lower demographic growth. Therefore, it is not surprising to find that the main source of economic growth in Portugal between 1910 and 1990 was capital. In the periods between 1947 and 1973 and 1973 and 1990, capital growth accounted for 49.9 percent and 44.3 percent, respectively, of domestic output growth. Human capital growth's contribution was smaller: only 15.9 percent between 1947 and 1973, but it increased to 41 percent between 1973 and 1990.[32]

The End of a Migratory Cycle?

As we have seen in the previous section, Portugal has been historically a country of emigrants. As late as the mid-1980s, an estimated 3.5 to 4 million Portuguese citizens were still living in foreign lands—the equivalent of over a third of the population residing in Portugal. This started to change, however, in the 1970s and 1980s when the flows reversed, and eventually the country became a net recipient of immigrants in the 1990s. This is perhaps one of the most dramatic developments that took place in Portugal over the last few decades.[33] Within a few years, there was an inversion of migration movements in Portugal. While the net migratory balance fluctuated in the 1990s, Portugal has moved from a country historically associated with large-scale emigration to one characterized by a new cycle of immigration that throughout the 1990s, has changed towards a net inward movement. In 2006, according to official records of the Services for Foreigners and Border Control (SEF), 435,000 legal immigrants were officially registered in Portugal. Yet, according to immigrant support organizations, the total number of foreign nationals in the country is 620,000—which makes Portugal one of the European countries with the largest number of immigrants, in proportional terms.[34]

Indeed, the development of the domestic economy and international conditions gradually reversed the migratory process, and Portugal started to become a receiving country. The consolidation of the flow of immigrants from Brazil in the 1980s, combined with the stabilization in the number of emigrants (around ten thousand permanent and fifteen thousand temporary per year) and the growing number of Europeans who were choosing Portugal for their home solidified this trend. By 1994 the number of immigrants overtook that of emigrants and in the mid-1990s the legal resident population represented close to 2 percent of the total population.

Over the last few years, the increasing number of immigrants, particularly from Eastern and Central European countries (Ukraine, Russia, Romania, the former Yugoslavia, and Moldova) has intensified this trend. By the year 2002, the legal resident population had reached 4 percent of the total, and by 2007 it reached 5 percent of the resident population (approximately five hundred thousand legal immigrants) or 8 percent of the working population, increasing 400 percent in fifteen years.[35]

Table 7.3 Inflows of foreign population into Portugal (thousands)

1998	1999	2000	2001	2002	2003	2004	2005	2006	2007
6.5	10.5	15.9	151.4	72.0	31.8	34.1	28.1	22.5	32.6

Source: OECD, International Migration Outlook, 2009

Between 1974 and 2004 we can distinguish three main immigration periods.[36] First, between 1975 and 1982, the return of Portuguese citizens and foreigners from the colonies and Western European countries led to a positive migratory balance, an outcome that had last happened in 1943. Second, the diminishing return of Portuguese emigrants in the 1980s, new restrictions to immigrants, and the recovery of Portuguese emigration led once again to a negative migratory balance between 1982 and 1992. Finally, after that year, the decrease in Portuguese emigration, fueled by economic recovery and the continuing inflow of returning emigrants and foreigners, led to a positive migration balance.

In the 1990s and 2000s there has been an explosion in the number of individuals of foreign origin living in Portugal. In 1975 there were 31,000 foreigners registered (or 0.3 percent of the population); by 1989, this number had increased to 101,011, and it has grown to 191,143 in 1999 (or 2 percent of the population), to 434,548 in 2003 (or 4.19 percent of the population), and to 440,277 in 2008.

As this table shows, the stock of legal residents in Portugal increased marginally after 2003. This was linked to the fact that many immigrants from Brazil and Eastern Europe—who migrated to the country at the beginning of the century looking for employment—have left the country due to the economic crisis, as seen in chapter 8. In recent years, the nature of immigration flows has shifted from labor migration to a family reunion one, and the increase in 2006 was driven by changes in the migration regulatory framework, which became more liberal.

The "new immigrants" differed from previous ones in terms of their nationalities and occupations. They reflect a mix of cultures, ethnicities, and peoples from different countries and regions of the world including Americans, Europeans, Asians, Luso-Africans, and South Americans. Many come from Cape Verde and Brazil, countries with a long association with Portugal that have provided workers since the 1960s, when Portugal faced labor shortages as a result of the colonial wars and the expansion of the economy.[37] In most recent years, the proportion of immigrants from former colonies such as Angola and Ginea-Bissau has also grown significantly. There are three main groups. First, there are low-skilled workers from sub-Saharan Africa and Eastern and Central Europe who mainly take jobs in construction (men) and domestic/industrial cleaning (women). Second, there are professionals coming from Western Europe, and to a lesser extent the United States. Finally, there are Brazilians, a group that includes high-skilled professionals but also low-skilled workers. In 2007, the three largest foreign communities in Portugal were from Brazil, Cape Verde, and the Ukraine (in that order).

Table 7.4 Foreign residents in Portugal by nationality of origin, 2004-2007

Year	2004	2005	2006	2007
Number of Residence Permits				
Total	263,322	274,631	332,137	401,612
Cape Verde	54,788	55,608	57,349	61,110
Brazil	28,730	31,500	41,737	55,665
Ukraine	1,551	2,120	21,953	34,240
Angola	26,517	27,533	28,854	30,431
United Kingdom	17,976	19,005	19,758	23,608
Guinea-Bissau	20,511	20,935	21,425	22,174
Spain	15,874	16,398	16,613	18,030
Romania	1,219	1,564	5,278	17,200
Germany	13,097	13,622	13,874	15,498
Moldavia	1,048	1,390	6,992	11,414
Residence Permits (%)				
Cape Verde	20.8	20.2	17.3	15.2
Brazil	10.9	11.5	12.6	13.9
Ukraine	0.6	0.8	6.6	8.5
Angola	10.1	10.0	8.7	7.6
United Kingdom	6.8	6.9	5.9	5.9
Guinea-Bissau	7.8	7.6	6.5	5.5
Spain	6.0	6.0	5.0	4.5
Romania	0.5	0.6	1.6	4.3
Germany	5.0	5.0	4.2	3.9
Moldavia	0.4	0.5	2.1	2.8

Source: SEF

The global economic crisis of 2008 and 2009 has also had a significant impact on migration patterns, but this time it has prompted an increase in immigration into Portugal. As the recession spread to other European countries (notably to Spain, in which the construction sector has been severely hit but the crisis), immigrants from the newest members of the European Union (particularly Romania), and other countries (particularly Brazil) have started to flock back to Portugal. This return has been driven by the public works program that has been developed by the Sócrates administration (between 2008 and 2017, a total of 41 billion dollars will be invested in major public works around the country), which include construction of the new Lisbon and *Beja* airports, the high-speed train lines, the expansion of the *Sines* port and refinery, and the irrigation system supplied by the *Alqueva* dam.

Table 7.5 The twenty largest legal immigrant communities, 1999-2007

Legal foreign residents	Number in 1999	Number in 2007	Growth in percentage
Brazilians	20,851	66,354	+ 218%
Capeverdeans	43,951	63,925	+ 45%
Ukrainians	123	39,480	+ 31,998%
Angolans	17,721	32,728	+ 85%
Guineans	14,217	23,733	+ 67%
British*	13,335	23,608	+ 77%
Romanians*	224	19,155	+ 8,451%
Spanish*	11,122	18,030	+ 62%
Germans*	9,605	15,498	+ 61%
Moldovans	3	14,053	+ 468,333%
Santomeans	4,809	10,627	+ 121%
French*	6,499	10,556	+ 62%
Chinese	2,762	10,448	+ 278%
US-Americans	7,975	8,264	+ 4%
Dutch*	3,675	6,589	+ 79%
Italians*	2,700	5,985	+ 122%
Mozambicans	4,502	5,681	+ 26%
Russians	448	5,114	+ 1,042%
Bulgarians*	347	5,028	+ 1,349%
Indians	1,211	4,104	+ 239%

Source: Instituto Nacional de Estatística, December 13, 2007

Illegal immigration has also emerged as an important development. Some reports have suggested that the number of illegal immigrants in Portugal in the 1990s reached between 25,000 and 75,000.[38] People from African and Eastern European countries view Portugal as an attractive destination to work in the informal economy (civil construction, tourism, or the service sector). Most illegal immigrants originate from Luso-African countries, South and North America,

Eastern and Central Europe, as well as Asia and Oceania.[39] Most have settled in shantytowns (*bairros de lata*) in Lisbon's suburbs and around transportation arteries (see Table 7.5).[40]

Reasons for the Inversion of Migration Patterns

As we have seen, starting in the 1970s the migration flows reversed and eventually Portugal became a net recipient of immigrants. Annual average departures decreased from 122,000 per year between 1968 and 1975, to 22,000 per year between 1976 and 1988. During the 1990s this figure has been relatively stable. In 1996 only 29,000 Portuguese emigrated, and in 2003 there were 27,008 departures. *How can we account for this shift?* A combination of push factors, such as improvements in Portugal's economic conditions, as well as pull factors (i.e., the reduction of wage differentials), have contributed to the shift in migration patterns over the last two decades. In addition, the political restrictions adopted by the host countries and the political changes taking place within the country have also played a role.

First, starting in the mid-1970s, the first oil shock provoked a recession in the Organization for Economic Cooperation and Development (OECD) countries, which had a significant impact on migration patterns. The receiving countries halted and/or imposed restrictions on immigration to cope with the surge in unemployment. In the following decades, some of the recipient countries have imposed further restrictive migratory policies, which have also hindered migration and reduced the range of destinations.

In addition, the process of decolonization in Portugal prompted a return to the country of thousands of people who had been residing in the colonies. The beginning of the end of the Portuguese empire started in 1961, when independence movements started an armed struggle in Angola, and when the troops of the Indian Union invaded the Portuguese possessions in India (Goa, Damáo, and Diu) defeating the Portuguese.[41] The uprising in Angola triggered a colonial war when the Portuguese government sent the armed forces. The conflict—which subsequently extended to Mozambique and Guinea—lasted over thirteen years, involved around two hundred thousand soldiers from the armed forces, and represented almost 50 percent of public spending. Politically, the war also influenced events in the metropolis. It led to the hardening of the authoritarian regime and also acted as a barrier against political liberalization. The military coup of 1974 brought an end of the authoritarian regime and the colonial war.

The subsequent revolutionary period of 1974 to 1976 led to a process of rapid decolonization. Consequently, around 650,000 European settlers (*retornados*) returned from the African colonies (mainly Mozambique and Angola), along with one hundred thousand troops, as the armed forces demobilized 95,000 soldiers in 1974 and sixty thousand in 1975. The end of the colonial empire also meant the reduction of overseas economic links and diminished the prospects of emigration from Portugal to the African colonies, which has been a constant in Portuguese history and a major destination of Portuguese emigrants.

Another contributory factor to the migration shift was the generalization of the welfare system to cover the whole population. Between 1960 and 2000, the number of pensioners rose from 56,000 to 2.5 million. The expansion of the system of social protection had started in the late 1960s when Caetano's government increased the number of contributors and beneficiaries to the system, including, for the first time, many rural, elderly, and domestic workers. Successive democratic governments increased the coverage of the system and developed new mechanisms of support, including a new "minimum income guarantee" that covered around 430,000 people.[42] Since the 1970s, Portugal has strengthened further the welfare state with significant increases in social expenditures. While the overall architecture of the system has been maintained, there was a significant growth of benefits. Indeed, the Portuguese welfare state has undergone an important transformation with the introduction of new universal polices and the extension of tax-funded non-contributory benefits and services. As a result Portugal, has successfully reduced the differential with the EU average expenditure on social protection by 50 percent.[43]

The beginning of mass tourism towards Portugal was also an important factor in the migration shift. European citizens, attracted by the social, cultural, and geographic conditions of the country, as well as the climate and the life style headed toward Portugal (the Algarve in the south became a particularly attractive location). As we have seen, in a few years the annual number of people (from countries like Britain, Germany, France, or Spain) migrating and visiting the country increased significantly.

An additional reason for the inflow of immigrants was the government's decision to regularize illegal immigrants in the 1990s (in 1992, 1993, and 1996). Over fifty thousand foreigners were legalized as a result of the implementation of these measures. Increasing concerns about the growth of illegal immigrants, particularly from Eastern European countries, led to the approval of a Decree-Law 4 in 2001, which created a new judicial framework for the entry, stay, and departure of foreigners from Portugal. The decree created also a new legal figure, the so-called "stay permit," which allows immigrants to stay in the country if they have a valid work contract. Immigrants who are granted the "stay permit" can apply for permanent residency after five years of consecutive residence.[44]

The most important factor, however, has been the dramatic improvement of economic conditions in Portugal that followed the transition to democracy and the incorporation of the country to the European Community on 1986.[45] By the late 1950s and early 1960s, Portugal had started to tentatively liberalize its economy. Portugal was a founding member of the European Free Trade Association (EFTA) and joined the General Agreement of Trade and tariffs (GATT) in 1962. EFTA membership had very important consequences for the Portuguese economy. It prevented the adoption of protectionist policies and excluded economic strategies based on import substitution, thus forcing the opening of the

Portuguese economy and providing the basis for an export oriented strategy of industrialization. From 1960 through 1973, Portuguese exports to EFTA countries increased an average per year of 16 percent, which was one of the factors that contributed to rapid economic growth (around 7 percent) in the same period, making Portugal increasingly prosperous over the two decades prior to EC accession.[46] Throughout the 1960s, the process of industrialization accelerated, shifting the composition of GDP (the industrial sector increased from 37 to 44 percent of GDP between 1961 and 1973). When Caetano became president of the Council of Ministers in 1968, he continued with the liberalization process. This coincided with the implementation of the Third Development Plan (1968-1973), which strengthened the role of the private sector and established better conditions for FDI.

The turbulent period that followed the events of April 25, 1974 threw the Portuguese economy into a tailspin. The nationalization of the main economic and financial groups, and the agrarian reform had negative economic consequences. Unemployment, inflation (25 percent in 1977), and the public deficit spiraled out of control. The revolutionary policies however, did not last long. In 1977, Portugal negotiated the first agreement with the International Monetary Fund (IMF) to implement an economic stabilization program, which coincided with the country's formal application to the EC.[47]

As noted in chapter 8, it was the perspective of EC integration that gave a final push to the modernization and liberalization of the Portuguese economy. The Preferential Trade Agreement (PTA) between the EC and Portugal (1972) resulted in the further opening of European markets to the country. In addition, the perspective of EU membership acted as an essential motivational factor that influenced the actions of policymakers and economic actors, thus acting as a catalyst for change. The economic crisis of 1981 and 1982 caused by a new oil shock, and the dramatic surge in international interest rates forced the Portuguese government to negotiate a new agreement with the IMF that led to the implementation of another stabilization program. In addition, Portugal took unilateral measures in preparation for EC accession, including increasing economic flexibility, industrial restructuring, the adoption of the VAT, and intensifying trade liberalization. Through the European Investment Bank, the country also received European aid to mitigate some of the expected adjustment costs (for instance, on fisheries).

At the same time, in a context in which most citizens supported integration, this perspective facilitated the implementation of (in many cases quite painful) micro and macro economic reforms. In the 1990s the desire to participate in European Monetary Union led to the implementation of policies that resulted in fiscal consolidation, and the independence of the Portugal's Central Bank.

Portugal, with relatively good infrastructure, an educated and cheap labor force, and a market of millions of potential consumers has become an attractive production base. FDI has also been fostered by factors such as the deeper economic integration with other European countries, larger potential growth, lower exchange rate risk, lower economic uncertainty, and institutional reforms.

In the 1980s and 1990s, Portugal has ranked among the four European Union countries with the lowest rates of unemployment (together with Austria, the Netherlands, and Luxembourg), never reaching close to the over 10 percent unemployment European average. As we have seen, while wages are still lower than the European average, Portuguese wages—using Purchasing Power Parity— have increased from 45 percent of the European average in 1980 to 63 percent in 1998.

In the end, the combined impetuses of economic modernization and European integration transformed the Portuguese economy and allowed thousands of workers—who for decades had not had this opportunity—to stay at home and prosper, while making the country an attractive destination for emigrants from other countries. Indeed, the last four decades have represented a period of almost unprecedented improvement in collective and individual well-being. In the 1960s, only half of all households had access to basic infrastructure: electricity, water, sewers, etc. Today virtually all the country has access. According to the census, in 1960, water was available only to 28 percent of the population, 19 percent of inhabitants had a shower or bath, and 42 percent had a domestic toilet. Today 87 percent of Portuguese have access to water, 82 percent have a shower or bath, and 89 percent have a domestic toilet. In 1960, only 41 percent of Portuguese had electricity mains, and 38 percent benefited from sewage mains. Today, 98 percent have electricity and 91 percent sewage. Almost 100 percent of the households have television and telephone and 60 percent have a car. Finally, 65 percent of households are homeowners—levels that are very high even for European standards. Additionally, since 1970 the Portuguese have experienced increases in the national product and income per inhabitant: national income increased 4.5 times between 1960 and 1999, earnings increased at almost the same rate. Disposable income increased from 47 percent in 1960 to 60.1 percent in 1974, and the national minimum wage for industry and services, introduced in 1974, increased from 3,300 escudos that year to around sixty thousand in 1999.[48]

Lastly, a final factor that has influenced the migration flow has been changes in the legal and institutional framework of migration. The 2007 law on the "Entry, Stay, Departure and Expulsion of Foreigners" transposed EU directives into Portuguese legislation. This reform has facilitated family reunions, as well as a simplified the visa system and replaced the former quota system with a new called "global contingent"—one based on annual estimates of labor market needs that cannot be filled by the domestic labor market. A new, comprehensive *Plan for the Integration of Immigrants* was introduced in 2007, which seeks to coordinate the actions of all ministries involved in integration. Finally, the High Commissariat for Integration and Ethnic Minorities (ACIME) has now become the High Commissariat for Immigration and Intercultural Dialogue (ACIDI), a public institute with additional financial and administrative autonomy.[49]

Consequences of Immigration

The new migratory flow towards Portugal is having significant socioeconomic consequences for the country, and is influencing a new configuration of citizenship. The insertion of immigrants into the country has been a parallel process with decolonization, democratization, and Europeanization. The days of a closed, traditional, and homogeneous society are long gone. The affirmation of individual rights and the establishment of political rights after the April 25 Revolution opened up opportunities for political and civic participation. New liberties, immigration, and the increasing opening of the country to the outside world have made Portuguese society more permissive and secular.

The integration of most immigrants into the active population has resulted in the acceleration of socioeconomic change in Portugal. A dual labor market (with a formal and informal sector) has emerged, fuelled by the employment of foreign immigrants. Legal and illegal immigrants are becoming a significant component in the formal and informal economies. Occupational rates among immigrants (55 percent) are higher than the average (45 percent). Most of them are manual workers (48 percent) or professional employees (245), but illegal immigrants do not have redress to trade union protection, social security, basic minimum wage or insurance; and their wages are much lower. In other words, they are second-class workers. Most immigrants work low paid jobs in civil construction, transport, hygiene, domestic services, and the manufacturing industry. The origin of the immigrants influences their position in the country's socioeconomic structure: while northern Europeans are well paid and occupy (with the expatriate retirees) the top of the socioeconomic pyramid, the immigrants from Angola and Cabo Verde with their menial jobs, occupy the lowest end. In between are the Lusophones from Brazil, and Guinea-Bissau, who have started to join the country's professional ranks.[50]

Furthermore, most immigrants have settled around the more modern, urbanized, and industrialized western part of the country along the line that cuts through Porto, Coimbra, Lisbon, Setúbal, and Faro where most of the jobs are. Lisbon hosts around 55 percent of all the country's immigrants (5 percent of the population).[51] Faro, in the Algarve, has emerged as a main destination for foreigners settling in Portugal (i.e., from Germany, Holland, or Britain) by virtue of its attraction as a retirement destination for expatriates.[52] This, in turn, has attracted expatriate residents to work in the sectors (services, tourism, and construction) that have emerged to serve this community. Since economic growth over the last decade has centered in the Metropolitan Area of Lisbon—where the major public works programs (such as the World Expo 98, or the Vasco de Gama bridge) have taken place—this spatial clustering has contributed to reinforce the existing economic divide within the country.[53]

Socioeconomic change is being accompanied by transformations in other areas: politics, culture, labor market, legislation, etc. Portugal is no longer a country with a traditional culture and single ethnicity. New immigrants are contributing to the cultural, linguistic, ethnic, and religious diversification of the country.[54] Several religious groups and denominations (Christian, Islamic, or Hindu) are challenging the historical dominance of the Catholic Church and attracting thousands of followers. A random walk through Portugal these days will allow a visitor to hear a wide variety of languages (Creole, African, Latin languages, Slavic, etc.) even in rural areas. This is a novelty, reinforced daily through global media.[55]

Conclusion

The analysis of the previous sections can lead one to conclude that the era of Portuguese emigration may be over. Some scholars, however, warn that it may be too early to write the "obituary" of Portuguese emigration, and point out to the increase of Portuguese emigration to Europe in the 1990s.[56] It is likely that in the short and medium term emigration will continue as one of Portugal's constant features. The pattern of migration will continue to influence the country's socioeconomic structure, demography, and culture. For the reasons that we have examined, the expatriate community is likely to expand in the near future, and the growing number of immigrants—although still relatively small at 4 percent of the population—will become more and more important transcending their number.

What are the prospects for the future? As we have seen, migration patterns are influenced by domestic as well as external factors. With this in mind, we can distinguish three types of migratory flows as we look to the short term:

1. Inter-EU flows
2. Flows from the new member states
3. Flows from the South.

Inter-EU Flows

Inter-EU migratory flows are relatively small nowadays. As we have seen, Portugal, who sent hundreds of thousands of emigrants to European countries since WWII, has become a recipient of immigration from the EU. This is true also of other EU countries like Spain, Greece, Italy, Ireland, and Finland, that sent thousands of emigrants to EC countries like Belgium, Luxembourg, Germany, France, Sweden, and the United Kingdom. While there is a still a significant group of immigrants in the latter countries from the groups that emigrated decades ago, their tendency has been to return to the home country.

This development is worrisome because it will hinder the creation of a true unified labor market within the EU. Low labor mobility in the EU has been explained based on factors such as the improvement of economic conditions in the home country that reduces the perspectives for higher returns in other countries; the development of the welfare state and the extension of benefits like unemployment; the difficulties finding jobs in the host country; and last but not least, cultural differences that make the transition very difficult.

In the context of the Monetary Union, in which competitive devaluations are no longer possible, low labor mobility will make it more difficult to confront asymmetric shocks within the EMU.

Flows from New Member States

One of the most significant developments that has taken place in Europe has been the European Union enlargement to incorporate Central and Eastern European countries. Enlargement is having a large impact in Portugal, and raises a number of policy and research issues regarding immigration.

The population stock in the EU from the new member states in 2000 was 0.2 percent—most of them originating from Poland (almost 50 percent) followed by Hungary (9 percent). However, the main concern is that, given the existing network of immigrants from the new member states, there will be a significant inflow of immigrants from these countries into Portugal. Yet, these fears may be misplaced. As I have indicated elsewhere, the Iberian enlargement of 1986 illustrates that patterns of migration can be reversed.[57] Both Spain and Portugal had to wait for accession in the 1980s, partly over immigration fears that did never materialize. Like in 1986, the new treaty of accession has established a period of seven years for the new member states of Central and Eastern Europe.

As we have seen, over the last decade there has been an increase of immigration to Portugal from these countries—some of it illegal—largely motivated by income and unemployment differentials. The opening of the borders to the citizens of these countries has raised concerns about massive inflows, yet most EU-15 countries have imposed transition rules governing the right of access to their labor markets from citizens from the ten new member states.

However, fears of uncontrolled migration were not substantiated after 1986, or even after the seven years transition period. On the contrary, as a consequence of improved economic conditions in Iberia, one of the key results of EU access was that by 1995, there were one hundred thousand fewer Spaniards and 110,000 Portuguese living in other EU member states than before enlargement. Furthermore, the reverse process took place when thousands of Europeans (particularly from Germany and Britain) migrated to Portugal and Spain. Such concerns are likely to be unfounded again with the new member states. Both countries lifted restrictions in May 2006.

Some reports have estimated that over thirty years between three and five million people from the new member states will emigrate to other EU countries (the equivalent of 1.3 percent of the current population).[58] The European Commission estimates that seventy thousand to 150,000 workers (out of a population of 350 million people) could migrate from Eastern Europe to the current EU states per year. This is hardly a large number. The continuing existence of language, cultural, and structural barriers will most likely continue hindering labor mobility in an enlarged Europe. In addition, the rapid economic growth of Eastern European countries (particularly compared to some of the sclerotic EU members, like Germany) is likely to have the same effect than it had on migration patterns in Spain and Portugal after 1986. This is already happening in the Czech Republic, Slovakia, and Slovenia, in which emigrants are returning home. In addition, although some of the new members, like Poland, have a strong migratory tradition, some of the main factors that influence this pattern are the geographical distance, as well as cultural and historical links. Therefore, it is far more likely that people from Central and Eastern Europe will migrate to countries with sharing borders, such as Austria, Germany, or Finland, than to Portugal.

Finally, although it is likely that migration will cause difficulties in some regions (particularly on the eastern borders zones of Austria and Germany) and industries, the problem may not be too much migration from the east but instead too little. Given the aging of EU population and the low levels of fertility rates, it will be important to facilitate the migration of more young people from eastern European countries. Since 1989, immigration has been the main contributor to population growth in the EU-15 countries. According to some reports, in order to keep its population young, the EU would need seven hundred million immigrants by 2050—an impossible goal.[59] In the end, instead of displacing local people from the labor market or lowering wages, immigrants from the new member states will contribute to the host economy by adding value, creating jobs, and pushing up wages because these workers will now be able to work legally (before May, several hundred thousand worked illegally in the EU).[60]

North-South Flows

As we have seen, immigration flows from Luso-African and other countries from the South have increased significantly over the last decade. Political and economic factors (such as poverty, unemployment, or income inequalities), as well as cultural and historical links with the former colonies help explain this development. Furthermore, the consolidation of a dual economy in Portugal over the last two decades has facilitated their insertion into the labor market. Since income differentials between these countries and Portugal are likely to remain and even widen, it is realistic to expect that the migratory flows from the South will intensify in the short and medium term.

To sum up, the intensification of the processes described is likely to consolidate the migratory trends that we have observed over the last few years. While emigration will stabilize, immigration (particularly from the South, but also from other European countries) will continue to expand. The deepening of globalization will contribute to this development, as people from the South seek to improve their living conditions. However, the increasing threat of terrorism is already affecting migratory policies and access to the EU countries. In this uneasy context Portugal, as well as the EU, has to develop new mechanisms to regulate migration and coordinate further migration policies. The main challenge, however, will remain the development and intensification of policies that address the existing disequilibria that motivates migration flows from the South, and the promotion of mechanisms that improve and accelerate the integration of immigrants into the host country. Portugal, with a long tradition of emigration, is ideally positioned to set the pace. In the end, the debate about migration is not simply one about economics, but about the sort of country that Portugal desires to be.

Notes

1. Raul M. C. Branco, "Portuguese Immigration: An Approach to the Mortality Patterns." Paper presented at the European Population Conference, Helsinki, June 7-9, 2000, 2-4.

2. The INE published the statistics for official Portuguese emigration from 1941-88. However, the abolition of the emigrant passport in November of 1988 to adopt a uniform model of passport and follow EC rules changed the legal landscape and the INE ceased to be able to produce this data. To overcome this shortcoming the INE created a Working Group chaired with International Migration. The new methodology for obtaining statistical data on emigration is now based on survey of a sampler of families, the *Survey of Departing Migratory Movements*. See INE, "Statistical information on Emigration: methods and results," *Working Paper No. 8*, Statistical Commission and Economic Commission for Europe. Presented at the Conference of European Statisticians, ECE Work Sessions on Migration Statistics, Geneva, March 25-27, 1998.

3. Maria Ioannis B. Baganha, "Portuguese Emigration After WWII," in António Costa Pinto, Ed., *Modern Portugal* (Palo Alto, CA: SPOSS, 1998), 191.

4. Baganha, "Portuguese Emigration," 192. See also, J.C. Ferreira de Almeida, "A Emigração Portuguesa para a França: Alguns Aspectos Quantitativos," in *Análise Social*, Vol. 2, No. 7-8 (1964), 599-622; and M.L. Marinho Antunes, "Migrações, Mobilidade Social e Identidade Cultural: Factos e Hipóteses Sobre o Caso Portugués," in *Análise Social*, Vol. 19, No. 65 (1981), 17-37.

5. António Costa Pinto and Nuno Severiano Teixeira, "From Africa to Europe: Portugal and European Integration," in António Costa Pinto and Nuno Severiano Teixeira, eds., *Southern Europe and the Making of the European Union* (New York: Columbia University Press, 2002); 10-11. José da Silva Lopes, "Introduction," in José da

Silva Lopes, ed. *Portugal and EC Membership Evaluated* (New York: St. Martin's Press, 1993), 1-4.

6. João Ferreira do Amaral, "Portugal and the Free Movement of Labour," in Silva Lopes, 240-41.

7. Baganha, 190-91.

8. Ferreira do Amaral, 241.

9. Baganha, 196-97.

10. *Migration and Remittances Factbook*, World Bank, 2007.

11. From Encarnación Cereijo and Francisco J. Velázquez, "Los Determinantes de las Migraciones de la Unión Europea," in *Economistas*, No. 99, 2004-Año XXII, 38-40.

12. R. A. Mundell, "International Trade and Factor Mobility," in *American Economic Review*, Vol. 47 (1957): 321-35.

13. Michael Piore, *Birds of Passage: Migrant Labor and Industrial Societies* (Cambridge: Cambridge University Press, 1979).

14. L. A. Sjaastad, "The Costs and Returns of Human Migration," in *Journal of Political Economy*, No. 70, 1962, 80-93.

15. O. Stark, *The Migration of Labor*. Cambridge: Basil Blackwell, 1991.

16. Baganha, 201-3.

17. See M., Fonseca, M.J. Caldeira, and A. Esteves, "New forms of Migration into the European South: Challenges for Citizenship and Governance—the Portuguese Case." *International Journal of Population Geography*, Vol. 8, No. 2, 2002, 135-52. Sedas A. Nunes, "Portugal: Sociedada Dualista em Evolução," in *Análise Social* Vol. 2, No 7-8, (1964): 407-62; Carlos Almeida and António Barreto, *Capitalismo e Emigração em Portugal* (Lisbon: Prelo, 1976); Joel Serrão, *A Emigração Portuguesa: Sondagem Histórica* (Lisbon: Livros Horizonte, 1977); Eduardo S. Ferreira, *Origens e Formas da Emigracão*, (Lisbon: Iniciativas Editoriais, 1976); Thomas Bruneau *et al.*, *Portugal in Development: Emigration, Industrialization, The European Community* (Canada: University of Ottawa Press, 1984).

18. Pedro Lains "The Portuguese Economy in the Twentieth Century," in *Contemporary Portugal* ed. António Costa Pinto (New York: Social Science Monographs-CUP, 2003).

19. See, Portugal: "Human Resources and Income Distribution," in www.country-studies.com/portugal/human-resources-and-income-distribution.html.

20. See José P. Barosa and Pedro T. Pereira, "Economic Integration and Labour Flows: The European Single Act and its Consequences," *FE-UNL Working Paper*, 123, (1988): 8.

21. See Maria Ioannis B. Baganha, "From Closed to Open Doors: Portuguese Emigration under the Corporatist Regime," Brown University, *e-JPH*, Vol. 1., No. 1. (Summer 2003).

22. Baganha, 1998, 197-98; and Baganha 2003, 6-7.

23. F.L. Machado, "Contornos e Especificidades da Immigração em Portugal," *Sociologia: Problemas e Práticas*, No. 16 (1994): 111-34.

24. António Barreto, "Social Change in Portugal," in Costa Pinto, 2003, 160.

25. Remittances are the monies that migrants return to their country of origin. Since labor is considered an export remittances are that part of the payment for exporting labor services, which returns to the country of origin.

26. Baganha 2003, 6.

27. This analysis draws from Baganha 2003, 7-8.

28. According to Baganha (2003) with the economic structure of the 1960s and 70s, the proportion of scientific and technical workers should have been roughly twice of that of Portugal.

29. These workers did not have incentives to leave the country because they had similar standards of living and wages than their European counterparts. See Xavier Pintado. "Nives e Estructuras de Salaries Comparados: os Salarios Portugueses e os Europeos," in *Análise Social*, Vol. V, No. 17 (1967): 57-89.

30. Eduardo S. Ferreira, *Origens e Formas da Emigração* (Lisbon: Iniciativas Editoriais, 1976); and Manuela Silva, et al., *Retorno, Emigração e Desenvolvimiento Regional em Portugal* (Lisbon: Instituto de Estudos para o Desemvolvimento, 1982).

31. From Baganha 2003, 7-8.

32. Lains, 131.

33. Barreto, 164-65. See also, S.L. Engerman and J.C. das Neves, "The Bricks of an Empire 1415-1999: 585 Years of Portuguese Emigration," *Journal of European Economic History*, Vol. 26, No. 3 (1997): 471-510; M. Do C. Esteves, *Portugal: Pais de Imigração* (Lisbon: IEDP, 1991); R. King and K. Rybaczuk, eds., "Southern Europe and the International Division of Labour: From Emigration to Immigration," in *The New Geography of European Migration*, ed. R. King (London: Belhaven, 1993), 175-206.

34. Mario Queiroz, "Migration-Portugal. The promised South," in http://ipsnews.net/news.asp?idnews=44719

35. Data from *Alto Comissariado para a Imigração e Minorias Étnicas*.

36. Branco, 3.

37. J.L. Filho, "Immigrantes Caboverdianos en Portugal," *Arbor*, Vol. 154, No. 607, (1996): 151-70; and L. França et al., *A Comunidadde Cabo Verdiana em Portugal*. (Lisbon: IED, 1992).

38. Martin Eaton, "International Population Mobility, Immigration and Labour Market Change in Portugal," in *Contemporary Portugal*, ed. Stephen Syrett (Burlington: Ashgate, 2002). He includes an extensive References of this subject from which this article draws. See also, R. King, "Post-Oil Crisis, Post Communism: New geographies of International Migration," in *The New Europe: Economy, Society and Environment*, ed. D. Pinder (Chichester: Wiley, 1998), 281-304; and R. King, and R. Black, *Southern Europe and the New Immigrations* (Brighton: Sussex Academic Press, 1997).

39. David Corkill and Martin Eaton, "Multicultural Insertion in a Small Economy: Portugal's Immigration Communities," *South European Society & Politics*, Vol. 3., No. 3, 149-68.

40. F. Miguelez-Lobo, "Irregular Work in Portugal," in Commission of the European Communities, *Underground Economy and irregular Forms of Employment*. (Luxembourg: Commission of the European Communities, 1990); Maria Ioannis B. Baganha, "Immigrant Involvement in the Informal Economy: The Portuguese Case," *Journal of Ethnic and Migration Studies*, Vol. 24, No. 2 (1998): 367-85; Martin Eaton, "Foreign Residents and Illegal immigrants: Os Negros em Portugal," *Ethnic and Racial Studies*, Vo. 16, No. 3 (1998): 284-90; Martin Eaton, "Foreign Residents and Illegal Immigrants in Portugal," *International Journal of Intercultural Relations*, Vol. 22, No. 1, 49-66.

41. See Valentim Alexandre, "The Colonial Empire," in Costa Pinto, 41-59.

42. Barreto, 170.

43. See Ana Guillén et al. "Redesigning the Spanish and Portuguese Welfare States: the Impact of Accession into the European Union," in *Spain and Portugal in the European Union: The First Fifteen Years*, ed. Sebastián Royo and Paul Manuel (London: Frank Cass, 2003), 231-68.

44. Branco, 4.

45. This section draws from Sebastián Royo, "From Authoritarianism to the European Union: The Europeanization of Portugal," *Mediterranean Quarterly* Vol. 15, No. 3 (2004). See also David Corkill, *The development of the Portuguese Economy: A case of Europeanization* (London: Routledge, 1999).

46. Silva Lopes, 2-3.

47. José Maria Brandão de Brito, "The Portuguese Economy: From Salazarism to the European Community," in Costa Pinto 1998, 109-11.

48. Barreto, 173-77. See also António Barreto, ed., *A Situação Social em Portugal, 1990-1995* (Lisbon: ICS, 1996).

49. OECD, *International Migration Outlook: 2008*. Paris: OECD, 2008

50. Eaton 2002, 122-25. See also, R. Rowland, "La Migración a Grandes Distancias y sus Contextos: Portugal y Brasil," *Estudios Migratorios Latinoamericanos*, Vol. 7, No. 21, 225-74.

51. J. M. Malheiros, *Imigrantes na Região de Lisboa: Os Anos da Mudança* (Lisbon: Ed. Colobri, 1996); and J. M. Malheiros "Immigration, Clandestine Work and Labour Market Strategies: The Construction Sector in the Metropolitan Region of Lisbon," *South European Society & Politics*, Vo. 3, No. 3 (1999): 169-85.

52. A.M. Williams, R. King, and T. Warnes, "A Place in the Sun: International Retirement Migration from Northern to Southern Europe," *European Urban and Regional Studies*, Vol. 4, No. 2 (1997): 115-34; A.M. Williams abd G. Patterson, "An Empire Lost but a Province Gained: A Cohort Analysis of British International Retirement in the Algarve," *International Journal of Population Geography*, Vol. 4, No. 2, 135-55.

53. Eaton 2002, 118-120. See also, M.L. Fonseca and C. Cavaco, "Portugal in the 1980s and 1990s: Economic Restructuring and Population Mobility," in *People, Jobs and Mobility in the New Europe,* ed. H.H. Blotevogel and A.J. Fielding (Chichester: Wiley, 1997); J. Peixoto, "Recent Trends in regional Migration and Urban Dynamics in Portugal," in *Population Migration in the European Union,* ed. P. Rees et al. (Chichester: Wiley, 1996), 261-74.

54. David Corkill, "Multiple National Identities, Immigration and Racism in Spain and Portugal," in *Nation and Identity in Contemporary Europe*, ed. B. Jenkins and S.A. Sofos (London: Routledge, 1996), 155-71.

55. Barreto 2003, 177-82.

56. Baganha 1998, and 2003; Ioannis B. Baganha and João Peixoto, "Trends in the '90s: The Portuguese Migratory Experience" (paper presented at the Cost A2 Workshop Immigration in Southern Europe, Coimbra, 1994).

57. Royo, 306.

58. Cereijo and Velázquez, 42.

59. See "An endangered species: fewer births make old Europe fear for its future," *Financial Times*, June 11, 2004, 11.

60. See "UK leads way on opening borders to new workers," *Financial Times*, December 13, 2002, 2; and "Fears of big move west may be unfounded," *Financial Times*, December 2, 2002, 4.

8

Portugal and Spain in the EU: The Paradox of Economic Divergence, 2000-2007

Sebastián Royo

After decades of relative isolation under authoritarian regimes, the success of democratic transition in Portugal and Spain in the second half of the 1970s paved the way for full membership in the European Community. For Spain, Portugal, and their European Community (EC) partners, this momentous and long-awaited development had profound consequences and set in motion complex processes of adjustment.[1]

There was no dispute that the Iberian countries belonged to Europe. This was not just a geographical fact; Spain and Portugal shared their traditions, their culture, their religion, and their intellectual values with the rest of Europe. Moreover, both countries had historically contributed to the Christian occidental conceptions of mankind and society dominant in Europe. Without Portugal and Spain the European identity would only be a reflection of an incomplete body. Iberian countries belonged to Europe. Their entry into the European Community was a reaffirmation of that fact, and it would enable both countries to recover their own cultural identity, lost since the Treaty of Utrecht, if not before.

This chapter will identify the basic changes in the economies of Portugal and Spain that occurred as a result of European integration and will focus in particular on their economic performance during the 2000 to 2007 period. Indeed, one of the central paradoxes of the integration of both countries into the

European Union and the European Monetary Union (EMU) has been the divergence of their economic performance since 2000. While Spain has experienced some of the fastest rates of growth in the EU between 2000 and 2007 and has already reached the EU per capita average, Portugal, on the contrary, has experienced much lower rates of growth and both nominal and real convergence with the EU have diverged. This paradox has to be explained.

The examination of these two cases will shed new light on the challenges (and opportunities) that countries face when trying to integrate regionally or into the global economy. It will show that countries do respond differently to similar challenges and pressures, and that there is still room for policy choices within a monetary union. These policy choices will affect economic performance.

The chapter proceeds in three steps. As historical background information, I analyze briefly in the first section the overall economic consequences of the EU integration for the Iberian countries. In the second section, I examine the economic performance of Portugal, and then Spain. The chapter closes with an analysis of the reasons for the performance differences between the two countries during the 2000 to 2007 period.

Historical Background: Economic Consequences of EC/EU Integration[2]

Economic conditions in Spain and Portugal in the second half of the 1970s and first half of the 1980s were not buoyant. The world crisis caused by the second oil shock in the late 1970s and the lack of adequate response from the collapsing authoritarian regimes in both countries intensified the structural problems of these economies. Portugal had been a founding member of EFTA and had lowered its trade barriers earlier and was theoretically in a better position than Spain. However, Salazar did even less than Franco to encourage entrepreneurship and competition. This factor, combined with the costs of the colonial wars and the disruptions caused by the revolution and near decade of political upheaval dramatically worsened the economic situation. For instance, in the 1960s Portugal's income per capita was about three quarters that of Spain and in the late 1980s it was only one-half. By the time of accession, Spain was the EC's fifth-largest economy, and Portugal its tenth.[3]

The economic crisis of the late 1970s and the first half of the 1980s had devastating consequences in both countries and made any additional adjustments caused by the accession to the EC a daunting prospect. The response to the crisis was also influenced by the return to democracy in both countries. The transition period led to a surge in wage demands, industrial unrest, and indecisive macroeconomic policies often driven by workers. These were demands that led to expansionary fiscal policies, as well as intense conflict (particularly in Portugal) over the role of the state in the economy.

In Spain, the high unemployment levels—which reached 22 percent in 1986—suggested that any additional adjustment cost would have painful consequences.[4] In addition, the country was unprepared for accession; i.e., Spanish custom duties remained on the average five times higher than the EC's, and EC products faced a major disadvantage in the Spanish market because the country had a compensatory tax system and restrictive administrative practices that more greatly penalized imported products.[5] Slow license delivery was common, and constructors who sold vehicles in the country did not have import quotas to introduce cars into Spain from abroad. Finally, when Spain and Portugal called at the door of the EC for accession in 1977, protectionist institutions—which were incompatible with EC rules—were still fully operative in both countries. For instance, the Spanish government controlled, through the INI (National Institute of Industry), a considerable size of the economy and subsidized public enterprises such as the auto making companies (SEAT, ENASA), as well as the metallurgic, chemical, ship construction, and electronic sectors. This situation provided a considerable advantage for Spanish manufacturers, which were highly protected from foreign competition.

In this context, EC integration was a catalyst for the final conversion of the Iberian countries into modern Western-type economies. Indeed, one of the key consequences of their entry into Europe has been that membership has facilitated the modernization of the two economies.[6] This is not to say, however, that membership was the only reason for this development. The economic liberalization, trade integration, and modernization of these economies started in the 1950s and 1960s and both countries became increasingly prosperous over the two decades prior to EC accession.

Indeed, the economic impact of the EC started long before accession. The Preferential Trade Agreements (PTAs) between the EC and Spain (1970) and the EC and Portugal (1972), resulted in the further opening of European markets to the latter countries, which paved the way for a model of development and industrialization that could also be based on exports. The prospect of EC membership acted as an essential motivational factor that influenced the actions of policymakers and businesses in both countries. Henceforth, both countries took unilateral measures in preparation for accession, including increasing economic flexibility, industrial restructuring, the adoption of the VAT, and intensifying trade liberalization. Through the European Investment Bank they also received European aid (Spain since 1981) to mitigate some of the expected adjustment costs (for instance on fisheries).

The actual accession of both countries after 1986 had a substantive impact because it forced the political and economic actors to adopt economic policies and business strategies consistent with membership and the *acquis communautaire* (which included the custom union, the VAT, the Common Agriculture and Fisheries Polices, and the external trade agreements; and later the Single Market, the ERM, and the European Monetary Union). At the same time, EC membership also facilitated the micro- and macroeconomic reforms that successive Iberian governments undertook throughout the 1980s and 1990s. In a context of strong support among Iberian citizens for integration, membership became a facilitating mechanism that allowed the Iberian governments to prioritize economic rather than social modernization and, hence, to pursue difficult economic and social policies (i.e., to reform their labor and financial markets), with short-term painful effects. Finally, the decision to comply with the EMU Maastricht Treaty criteria led to the implementation of macro- and microeconomic policies that resulted in fiscal consolidation, central bank independence, and wage moderation.

Nevertheless, the process of EC integration also brought significant costs in terms of economic adjustment and loss of sovereignty. Under the terms of the accession agreement signed in 1985, both countries had to undertake significant steps to align their legislation on industrial, agricultural, economic, and financial polices to that of the European Community. These accession agreements also established significant transition periods to cushion the negative effects of integration. This meant that both countries had to phase in tariffs and prices, and approve tax changes (including the establishment of a VAT) that the rest of the Community had already put in place. This process also involved, in a second phase, the removal of technical barriers to trade. These requirements brought significant adjustment costs to both economies.

As opposed to the Spanish economy, the Portuguese one was highly open when it joined the EEC (exports and imports represented 75 percent of GDP). As one of the founding members of EFTA, Portugal had liberalized trade in the 1950s and 1960s. Therefore, the effects of accession were different: there was trade creation with an increase in bilateral flows with the other member states, as well as a shift effect caused by the diversion of EC exports away from Portugal and toward the EEC countries. At the same time, accession also had an impact on the export structure of the country because the share of labor intensive sectors such as textiles and footwear decreased, while the share of machinery and vehicle supplies increased (by 2000 the latter outweighed the former by ten percentage points).[7] Finally, it is important to note that EU accession also had different impacts on the economic structures of both countries. For instance, in Portugal it contributed to the devastation of the primary sector and the deindustrialization of the country, while in Spain those effects were somewhat more mitigated. Indeed, new studies have shown how patterns of trade have fundamentally different effects on patterns of production and employment.[8]

Since 1986, the Portuguese and Spanish economies have undergone profound economic changes. EU membership has led to policy and institutional reforms in the following economic areas: monetary and exchange rate policies (first independent coordination, followed by accession to the ERM, and finally EMU membership); reform of the tax system (i.e., the introduction of the VAT, and reduction of import duties); and a fiscal consolidation process. These changes have led to deep processes of structural reforms aimed at macroeconomic stability and the strengthening of competitiveness of the productive sector. On the supply side, these reforms sought the development of well-functioning capital markets, the promotion of efficiency in public services, and the enhancement of flexibility in the labor market. As a result of subsequent reforms, markets and prices have been deregulated and liberalized; the labor market has been the subject of limited deregulatory reforms; a privatization program was started in the early 1980s to roll back the presence of the government in the economy and to increase the overall efficiency of the system; and competition policy was adapted to EU regulations.[9] In sum, from an economic standpoint, the combined impetuses of European integration and economic modernization have resulted in the following outcomes:

Figure 8.1: The Iberian economic transformation

• The end of economic isolation	• Increasing competition
• Institutional reforms	• Industrial restructuring
• Tax harmonization	• Capital flow liberalization
• Openness of the Iberian economies	• Deregulation
• Nominal convergence	• Lower inflation
• Capital infrastructure effort	• Fiscal consolidation
• Financial liberalization	• Cohesion policies
• Central Bank independence	• Lower nominal interest rates
• Privatization	• Internationalization
• FDI in Iberia	• Higher efficiency
• Labor market reform	• Deregulation
• Reduction in government subsidies	• Economic growth

At the same time, however, for the Iberian manufacturers, accession to the Community has also resulted in more competition. Since Portuguese and Spanish nominal tariffs averaged 10 to 20 percent before EC entry, and generally speaking, manufacturing EC products was cheaper and more competitive, membership resulted in an increase of imports from the EC and therefore, in a worsening in the balance of current account (and the closure of many industrial enterprises in Iberia). The intensity of the adjustment, however, was mitigated by the behavior of exchange rates and by the dramatic increase in the levels of investment in these two countries. Spain and Portugal have been attractive production bases since they both offered access to a large market of 48 million people, and a well educated and cheap—compared with the EC standards—labor base. In the end, the transitional periods adopted in the treaty to alleviate these adjustment problems and the financial support received from the EC played an important role minimizing the costs for the sectors involved.

At the time of accession, it was considered that a critical factor determining the final outcome of integration would be the pattern of investment, which would bring about important *dynamics effects*. Spain and Portugal had a number of attractive features as a production base, including good infrastructure, an educated and cheap labor force, and access to markets with a growing potential. In addition, EC entry would add the incentive of further access to the EC countries for non-EC Iberian investors—i.e., Japan or the United States. As expected, one of the key outcomes of integration was a dramatic increase in foreign direct investment, from less than 2 percent to more than 6 percent of GDP over the last decade. This development was the result of the following processes: economic integration, larger potential growth, lower exchange rate risk, lower economic uncertainty, and institutional reforms. EC membership has also resulted in more tourism (which has become one of the main sources of income for Spain).

Another significant dynamic effect has been the strengthening of Iberian firms' competitive position. As a result of enlargement, Iberian producers gained access to the European market, which provided additional incentives for investment and allowed for the development of economies of scale, resulting in increasing competitiveness. By the 1980s, Spain and Portugal were already facing increasing competition for their main exports—clothing, textiles, leather—from countries in the Far East and Latin America, which produced all these goods at cheaper costs by exploiting their low wages. As a result of this development, the latter countries were attracting foreign investment in sectors where traditionally Portugal and Spain had been favored. This situation convinced the Iberian leaders that their countries had to shift toward more capital-intensive industries requiring greater skills in the labor force but relying on standard technology—e.g., chemicals, vehicles, steel and metal manufacturers. In this regard, Portugal and Spain's entry to the EC facilitated this shift. Both countries gained access to the EC market, thus attracting investment that would help build these new industries. Finally, Portugal and Spain also benefited from the EC's financial assistance programs—i.e., the European Regional Development Fund, the Social Fund, the Agriculture Guidance and Guarantee Fund, and the newly created Integrated Mediterranean Program for agriculture (and later on from the Cohesion Funds).

EC integration has also allowed both economies to become integrated internationally and to modernize, thus securing convergence in nominal terms with Europe. One of the major gains of financial liberalization, the significant decline in real interest rates, permitted Portugal and Spain to meet the Maastricht convergence criteria. Indeed, on January 1, 1999, Spain and Portugal became founding members of the European Monetary Union. In the end, both countries—which as late as 1997 were considered outside candidates for joining the Eurozone—fulfilled the inflation, interest rates, debt, exchange rate, and public deficit requirements established by the Maastricht Treaty. This development confirmed the nominal convergence of both countries with the rest of the EU.

The EU contributed significantly to this development. Article Two of the Treaty of Rome established that the common market would "promote throughout the Community a harmonious development of economic activities" and therefore lower disparities among regions. While regional disparities among the original EC members were not striking (with the exception of Southern Italy),

Table 8.1: Compliance of the EMU convergence criteria, 1996-2006

		Spain			Portugal		
		1986	1996	2006	1986	1996	2006
Inflation	%	9.3	3.6	3.5	13.1	2.9	3.1
General Government Deficit	% GDP	5.1	4.6	-1.8	6.4	3.2	4.6
General Government Gross Debt	% GDP	42.3	70.1	40.0	68.0	65.0	72.8
Long-term Interest rates	%	12.2	8.7	3.82	19.5	8.6	3.96

Source: OECD, IMF, ECB and EMU Reports.

successive enlargements increased regional disparities with regard to per capita income, employment, education, productivity, and infrastructure. Regional differences led to a north-south divide, which motivated the development of EC structural policies. The election of Jacques Delors in 1985 as president of the Commission led to renewed efforts to address these imbalances. They culminated in the establishment of new cohesion policies that were embodied in the 1986 Single European Act, which introduced new provisions making economic and social cohesion a new EU common policy. In this regard, the regional development policy emerged as an instrument of solidarity between some Europeans and others. Since the late 1980s, the structural funds have become the second largest EU budgetary item. These funds have had a significant impact in relationship to the investment needs of poorer EU countries and have made an impressive contribution to growth in aggregate demand in these countries.

Indeed, the structural and cohesion funds have been the instruments designed by the EU to develop social and cohesion policy within the European Union, in order to compensate for the efforts that countries with the lowest per capita income relative to the EU (Ireland, Greece, Portugal, and Spain) would need to make in order to comply with the nominal convergence criteria. These funds, which amount to just over one-third of the EU budget, have contributed significantly to reducing regional disparities and fostering convergence within the EU. As a result, major infrastructure shortcomings have been addressed, and road and telecommunication networks have improved dramatically both in quantity and quality. In addition, increased spending on education and training has contributed to the upgrading of the labor force. In sum, these funds have played a prominent role in developing the factors that improve the competitiveness and determine the potential growth of the least developed regions of both countries.[10]

During the 1994 to 1999 period, EU aid accounted for 1.5 percent of GDP in Spain and 3.3 percent in Portugal. EU funding has allowed rates of public investment to remain relatively stable since the mid-1980s. The percentage of public investment financed by EU funds has been rising, since 1985, to reach average values of 42 percent for Portugal and 15 percent for Spain. Moreover, the European Commission has estimated that the impact of EU structural funds on GDP growth and employment has been significant. Indeed, Spain has benefited extensively from European funds: approximately 150 billion euros from agricultural and regional development, training, and cohesion programs. In the absence of these funds public investment would have been greatly affected.

The combined impetuses of lowered trade barriers, the introduction of the VAT, the suppression of import tariffs, the adoption of economic policy rules (such as quality standards or the harmonization of indirect taxes), and the increasing mobility of goods and factors of production that comes with greater economic integration have boosted trade and enhanced the openness of the Portuguese and Spanish economies. Since 1999, this development has been nurtured by the lower transaction cost and greater exchange rate stability associated with the single currency. For instance, imports of goods and services in real terms as a proportion of GDP rose sharply in Spain (to 13.6 percent in 1987 from 9.6 percent in 1984), while the share of exports shrank slightly (to 15.8 percent of GDP from 16.6 percent in 1984, and from 17.1 percent of real GDP in 1992 to 27 percent in 1997). As a result, the degree of openness of the Portuguese and Spanish economies has increased sharply over the last two decades. Henceforth, changes to the production structure and in the structure of exports—indicators of the degree of competitiveness of the Portuguese and Spanish economies (i.e., in terms of human capital skills, stock of capital, technological capital)—show important improvements, although significant differences remain in comparison to the leading developed economies (which confirms the need to press ahead with the structural reforms). These achievements verify that in terms of economic stability, Spain and Portugal are part of Europe's "rich club."

The Paradox of Divergence

Real Convergence

Yet, while nominal convergence has largely taken place, the income levels of Portugal and Spain have increased at a much slower pace, and for Portugal in particular, they remain far behind the EU average.

The data from Tables 8.1 and 8.2 show that nominal convergence has advanced at a faster pace than real convergence. Indeed, twenty-four years have not been long enough. Portugal and Spain's European integration has revealed both convergence and divergence, nominal and real. Since 1997 inflation in Spain has exceeded the EU average every year. In Portugal real convergence has been slowing down each year since 1998, actually turning negative in 2000 and with both real and nominal divergence decreasing until 2006.

Table 8.2 GDP per capita performance, 1980-2006

	1980	1985	1990	2000	2006
EU Totals	100.0%	100.0%	100.0%	100.0%	100.0%
Spain	74.2	72.5	77.8	81.0	98.0
Portugal	55.0	52.0	55.7	74.0	70.0

Source: European Union.

While there is significant controversy over the definition of real convergence, most scholars agree that a per capita GDP is a valid reference to measure the living standards of a country. This variable, however, has experienced a cyclical evolution in the Iberian countries, with significant increases during periods of economic expansion and sharp decreases during economic recessions. For instance, in the first fifteen years from the adhesion of Spain to the EU in 1986, per capita income increased "only" 11.5 percent and Portugal's 14.2 percent. Ireland's, in contrast, increased 38 percent. Only Greece, with an increase of 6.8 percent, had a lower real convergence than Spain and Portugal.

A possible explanation for this development is the fact that while Spain grew between 1990 and 1998 an average of 2.1 percent, Portugal grew 2.5 percent, and Ireland 7.3 percent over the same period. This growth differential explains the divergences in real convergence. Other explanations include: the higher level of unemployment (15.4 percent in Spain in the mid-1990s); the low rate of labor participation (i.e., active population over total population, standing at 50 percent, which means that expanding the Spanish labor participation rate to the EU average would increase per capita income to 98.2 percent of the EU average); the inadequate education of the labor force (i.e., only 28 percent of the Spanish potential labor force has at least a high school diploma, in contrast with the EU average of 56 percent); low investment in R&D and information technology (the lowest in the EU, with Spain ranked 61, spending even less proportionally than many developing countries, including Vietnam);[11] and inadequate infrastructures (i.e., road mile per one thousand inhabitants in Spain is 47 percent of the EU average and railroads 73 percent). The inadequate structure of the labor market with high dismissal costs, a relatively centralized collective bargaining system, and a system of unemployment benefits that guarantees income instead of encouraging job search, have also hindered the convergence process.[12]

More remarkable in light of this more recent divergence is the fact that the performance of both economies was quite similar during the first thirteen years that followed their accession to the EU. Indeed, between 1994 and 2000 the growth in income per capita was 3.1 percent in Spain and 3.1 percent in Portugal. Yet since then, instead of catching up, Portugal has been falling behind with GDP per capita decreasing from 80 percent of the EU-25 average (without Bulgaria and Romania) in 1999, to just over 70 percent in 2006; and labor productivity, still at 40 percent of the EU average, has shown no growth since 2000. Portugal's per capita GDP has fallen far behind Spain, and since 2000, the Czech Republic, Greece, Malta, and Slovenia have all surpassed Portugal. Moreover, Portugal was the first member of the European Monetary Union to be threatened with sanctions by the European Commission under the Growth and Stability pact (GSA) for violating the excessive deficit provisions. The country became, in the words of *The Economist*, "the new sick man of Europe." We will examine next the performance of both countries during the 1999 to 2008 period.

Spain

Before the global crisis, which has had devastating consequences for the Spanish economy, hit Spain in the spring of 2008, the country had become one of Europe's (until then) most successful economies.[13] While other European countries had been stuck in the mud, Spain performed much better at reforming its welfare systems and labor markets, as well as at improving flexibility and lowering unemployment. Indeed, over the last decade and a half the Spanish economy has been able to break with the historical pattern of boom and bust, and the country's economic performance was nothing short of remarkable. Propped by low interest rates and immigration, Spain was (in 2008) in its fourteenth year of uninterrupted growth and it was benefiting from the longest cycle of continuing expansion of the Spanish economy in modern history (only Ireland in the Eurozone has a better record), which contributed to the narrowing of per capita GDP with the EU.[14] Indeed, in twenty years per capita income grew twenty points, one point per year, to reach close to 90 percent of the EU-15 average. With the EU-25 Spain has already reached the average. The country has grown on average 1.4 percentage points more than the EU since 1996.

Unemployment fell from 20 percent in the mid-1990s to 7.95 percent in the first half of 2007 (the lowest level since 1978), as Spain became the second country in the EU (after Germany with a much larger economy) creating the most jobs (an average of six hundred thousand per year over the last decade).[15] In 2006 the Spanish economy grew a spectacular 3.9 percent and then 3.8 percent in 2007. As we have seen, economic growth contributed to per capita income growth and employment. Indeed, the performance of the labor market was spectacular: between 1997 and 2007, 33 percent of all the total employment created in the EU-15 was created in Spain. In 2006, the active population increased by 3.5 percent, the highest in the EU (led by new immigrants and the incorporation of women in the labor market, which increased from 59 percent in 1995 to 72 percent in 2006), and 772,000 new jobs were created. The public deficit was also eliminated (the country had a *superavit* between 2005 and 2006, which reached 1.8 percent of GDP, or 18 billion euros in 2006), and the public debt was reduced to 39.8 percent of GDP, the lowest in the last two decades.[16] The construction boom has also been remarkable: more than four hundred thousand new homes have been built in and around Madrid between 2002 and 2007.

The overall effects of EMU integration were also very positive for the country: it contributed to macroeconomic stability, it imposed fiscal discipline and central bank independence, and it dramatically lowered the cost of capital. One of the key benefits was the dramatic reduction in short-term and long-term nominal interest rates: from 13.3 percent and 11.7 percent in 1992, to 3.0 percent and 4.7 percent in 1999, and 2.2 percent and 3.4 percent in 2005.[17] The lower costs of capital led to an important surge in investment from families (in housing and consumer goods) and businesses (in employment and capital goods). Without the euro the huge trade deficit that exploded in the second half of the 2000s would have forced a devaluation of the peseta and the implementation of more restrictive fiscal policies.

The economic success extended to Spanish companies, which now expanded beyond their traditional frontiers.[18] In 2006 they spent a total of 140 billion euros ($184 billion) on domestic and overseas acquisitions, putting the country third behind the United Kingdom and France.[19] Of this, 80 billion euros were to buy companies abroad (compared with the 65 billion euros spent by German companies).[20] In 2006 Spanish FDI abroad increased 113 percent, reaching 71,487 billion euros (or the equivalent of 7.3 percent of GDP, compared with 3.7 percent in 2005).[21] In 2006 *Iberdrola*, an electricity supplier purchased *Scottish Power* for 22.5 billion dollars to create Europe's third largest utility; *Banco Santander*, Spain's largest bank, purchased Britain's *Abbey National Bank* for 24 billion dollars, *Ferrovial*, a family construction group, concluded a takeover of the *British BAA* (which operates the three main airports of the United Kingdom) for 10 billion pounds; and *Telefónica* bought *O2*, the U.K. mobile phone company.[22] Indeed, 2006 was a banner year for Spanish firms: 72 percent of them increased their production and 75.1 percent their profits, 55.4 percent hired new employees, and 77.6 percent increased their investments.[23]

The country's transformation was not only economic but also social. The Spanish had become more optimistic and self-confident (i.e., a Harris poll showed that they were more confident of their economic future than their European and American counterparts, and a poll by the Center for Sociological Analysis showed that 80 percent were satisfied or very satisfied with their economic situation).[24] Spain is "different" again, and according to a recent poll, it has become the most popular country in which to work for Europeans.[25] Between 2000 and 2007, some five million immigrants (645,000 in 2004 and five hundred thousand in 2006) settled in Spain (8.7 percent of the population compared with 3.7 percent in the EU-15), making the country the biggest recipient of immigrants in the EU. This is a radical departure for a country that used to be a net exporter of people, and more so because it has been able to absorb these immigrants without falling prey (at least so far) to the social tensions that have plagued other European countries (although there have been isolated incidents of racial violence).[26] Several factors have contributed to this development:[27] first, economic growth, with its accompanying job creation, provided jobs for the newcomers while pushing down overall unemployment; second, cultural factors: about one-third of the immigrants come from Latin America, and they share the same language and part of the culture, which facilitates their integration; third, demographics: an aging population and low birthrates. Finally, the national temperament characterized by a generally tolerant attitude, marked by the memory of a history of emigration, which make the Spanish more sympathetic to immigrants (according to a recent poll, no fewer than 42 percent state that migration has had a positive effect on the economy). The proportion of children from mixed marriages increased from 1.8 percent in 1995 to 11.5 percent in 2005.[28]

These immigrants contributed significantly to the economic success of the country in that decade because they boosted the aggregate performance of the economy: they raised the supply of labor, increased demand as they spent money, moderated wages, put downward pressure on inflation, boosted output, allowed the labor market to avoid labor shortages, contributed to consumption, and increased more flexibility in the economy with their mobility and willingness to take on low-paid jobs in sectors such as construction and agriculture, in which the Spanish were no longer interested.[29]

Indeed, an important factor in the per capita convergence surge after 2000 was the substantive revision of the Spanish GDP data as a result of changes in the National Accounts from 1995 to 2000. These changes represented an increase in GPD per capita of 4 percent in real terms (the equivalent of Slovakia's GDP). This dramatic change was the result of the significant growth of the Spanish population since 1998, as a result of the surge in immigration (for instance in 2003 population grew 2.1 percent). The key factor in this acceleration of convergence, given the negative behavior of productivity (if productivity had grown at the EU average, Spain would have surpassed in 2007 the EU per capita average by three points), was the important increase in the participation rate, which was the result of the reduction in unemployment, immigration growth, and the increase in the activity rate that followed the incorporation of female workers into the labor market. Indeed between 2000 and 2004 the immigrant population has multiplied threefold.

As a matter of fact, most of the 772,000 new jobs created in Spain in 2006 went to immigrants (about 60 percent).[30] Their motivation to work hard also opened the way for productivity improvements (which in 2006 resulted in the largest increase since 1997, with a 0.8 percent hike). It is estimated that the contribution of immigrants to GDP in the last four years has been of 0.8 percentage points.[31] Immigration has represented more than 50 percent of employment growth, and 78.6 percent of the demographic growth. As a result, Spain has led the demographic growth of the European countries between 1995 and 2005 with a demographic advance of 10.7 percent compared with the EU-15 average of 4.8 percent.[32] Immigration has also contributed to the huge increase in employment, which has been one of the key reasons for the impressive economic expansion. Indeed, between 1988 and 2006, employment contributed 3 percentage points to the 3.5 percent annual rise in Spain's potential GDP (see Table 8.3).[33]

However, this economic success was marred by some glaring deficiencies that came to the fore in 2008 when the global financial crisis hit the country, because it was largely a "miracle" based on bricks and mortar.[34] The foundations of economic growth were fragile because the country has low productivity growth (productivity contributed only 0.5 percentage points to potential GDP between 1998 and 2006) and deteriorating external competitiveness.[35] Over the last decade Spain did not address its fundamental challenge: its declining productivity, which has only grown an average of 0.3 percent in the last ten years (0.7 percent in 2006), one whole point below the EU average, placing Spain at the bottom of the EU and ahead of only Italy and Greece (the productivity of a Spanish worker is the equivalent of 75 percent of a U.S. one). The most productive activities (energy, industry, and financial services) contribute only 11 percent of GDP growth.[36]

Moreover, growth was largely based on low-intensity economic sectors, such as services and construction, which are not exposed to international competition. In 2006, most of the new jobs were created in low-productivity sectors such as construction (33 percent); services associated with housing such as sales and rentals (15 percent); and tourism and domestic service (30 percent). These sectors represent 75 percent of all the new jobs created in Spain in 2006 (new manufacturing jobs, in contrast, represented only 5 percent). Furthermore, the labor temporary rate reached 33.3 percent in 2007, and inflation is a recurrent problem: Spain closed 2006 with a 2.7 percent increase, but the average for that year was 3.6 percent. Thus, the inflation differential with the EU (almost 1 point) has not decreased, which reduces the competitiveness of Spanish products abroad (and consequently makes Spanish companies lose market share abroad).[37]

In addition, family indebtedness reached a record 115 percent of disposable income in 2006, and the construction and housing sectors accounted for 18.5 percent of GDP (twice the Eurozone average). House prices have risen by 150 percent since 1998, and the average price of a square meter of residential property went up from 700 euros in 1997 to 2,000 at the end of 2006, even though the housing stock had doubled. Many wonder whether this bubble is sustainable.[38] The crisis that started in 2008 confirmed the worst fears.

Between 40 and 60 percent of the benefits of the largest Spanish companies came from abroad. Yet, in the last few years this figure has decreased by approximately 10 percentage points, and there has been a decline in direct foreign investment of all types in the country, falling from a peak of 38.3 billion euros in 2000 to 16.6 billion euros in 2005.[39] The current account deficit reached 8.9 percent of GDP in 2006 and over 10 percent in 2007, which makes Spain the country with the largest deficit in absolute terms (86,026 million euros), behind

Table 8.3 Economic summary, Spain, 2000-2008

SPAIN	Units	Scale	2000	2001	2002	2003	2004	2005	2006	2007	2008
GDP constant prices	National currency	Billions	546.886	566.82	582.146	600.179	619.784	642.192	667.991	691.807	697.727
GDP constant prices	Annual percent change		5.053	3.645	2.704	3.098	3.267	3.615	4.017	3.565	0.856
GDP per capita, constant prices	National currency	Units	13,582	13,919	14,090	14,288	14,517	14,797	15,149	15,415	15,294
Output gap in percent of potential GDP	Percent of potential GDP		1.898	1.474	0.293	0.132	0.501	1.403	2.876	3.937	3.106
GDP based on purchasing-power-parity (PPP) share of world total	Percent		2.146	2.178	2.177	2.168	2.128	2.109	2.087	2.062	2.017
Inflation, average consumer prices	Annual percent change		3.484	2.827	3.589	3.102	3.053	3.382	3.562	2.844	4.13
Unemployment rate	Percent of total labor force		13.873	10.553	11.475	11.48	10.97	9.16	8.513	8.263	11.327
Employment	Persons	Millions	16.412	16.931	17.338	17.878	18.51	19.267	20.024	20.626	20.532
General government balance	National currency	Billions	-6.161	-4.361	-3.312	-1.622	-2.862	8.759	19.847	23.259	-41.874
General government balance	Percent of GDP		-0.978	-0.641	-0.454	-0.207	-0.34	0.964	2.016	2.209	-3.847
Current account balance	Percent of GDP		-3.959	-3.941	-3.259	-3.509	-5.251	-7.357	-8.972	-10.01	-9.592

Source: International Monetary Fund, World Economic Outlook Database, October 2009.

only the United States. And the prospects are not very bright: the trade deficit reached 9.5 percent in 2008.[40]

While there is overall consensus that the country needs to improve its education system and invest in research and development to lift productivity, as well as modernize the public sector, and make the labor market more stable (i.e., reduce the temporary rate) and flexible, the government has not taken the necessary actions to address these problems. Spain spends only half of what the Organization of European Cooperation and Development (OECD) spends on average on education; it lags behind most of Europe on investment in Research and Development (R&D); and it is ranked twenty-ninth by the UNCTAD as an attractive location for research and development. Finally, other observers note that Spain is failing to do more to integrate its immigrant population, as social divisions are beginning to emerge (see Calavita 2005).[41]

By the summer of 2008, the effects of the crisis were very evident, and since then the country has suffered one of the worst recessions in history, with unemployment reaching over 18 percent at the end of 2009, and more than 4.2 million people unemployed. This collapse was not fully unexpected. The global liquidity crisis caused by the subprime and the surge in commodities, food, and energy prices brought to the fore the imbalances in the Spanish economy: the record current account deficit, unabating inflation, low productivity growth, dwindling competitiveness, increasing unitary labor costs, excess consumption, and low savings had all set the ground for the current devastating economic crisis.[42]

Portugal

Portugal's economic performance was also remarkable in the 1990s. Between 1994 and 2000, real GDP growth (export-led but also boosted by private consumption and fixed investment) averaged more than 3 percent annually and economic expansion continued for seven years. In 1996, the fifth year of expansion, GDP growth reached almost 4 percent, and in 2000, 3.25 percent. The unemployment rate also fell, reaching a record low of around 4 percent in 2000 (one of the lowest in Europe), and inflation was brought down to just over 2 percent in 1999. Portugal was also able to meet the Maastricht criteria for fiscal deficit following the consolidation efforts prior to 1997, which brought the deficit down to 2.5 percent of GDP. One of the important factors that contributed to this performance was the transformation of the financial sector—largely spurred by EU directives in interest rate deregulation—liberalization of the regulatory framework, privatization, and the freeing of international capital movements.[43] The privatization program, one of the most ambitious in Europe at the time (more than one hundred firms were sold), was also a contributing factor because it

Table 8.4 Macroeconomic performance, Portugal and Spain, 1994-1999

		PORTUGAL					
Subject Descriptor	Units	1994	1995	1996	1997	1998	1999
Gross domestic product, constant prices	Annual percent change	1.489	2.307	3.619	4.186	4.852	3.841
Gross domestic product per capita, constant prices	National currency	9,792	9,991	10,326	10,727	11,207	11,592
Output gap in percent of potential GDP	Percent of potential GDP	-2.374	-3.213	-2.729	-1.598	0.34	1.545
Gross domestic product based on purchasing-power-parity (PPP) share of world total	Percent	0.425	0.422	0.422	0.422	0.432	0.434
Inflation, average consumer prices	Annual percent change	4.971	3.969	2.934	1.892	2.214	2.168
Unemployment rate	Percent of total labor force	6.34	7.2	7.2	6.7	4.95	4.4
General government balance	Percent of GDP	-7.478	-5.153	-4.592	-3.538	-3.379	-2.769
General government structural balance	Percent of potential GDP	-6.373	-3.743	-3.405	-2.898	-3.266	-3.571
Current account balance	Percent of GDP	-2.303	-0.117	-3.476	-5.833	-7.053	-8.464

		SPAIN					
Subject Descriptor	Units	1994	1995	1996	1997	1998	1999
Gross domestic product, constant prices	Annual percent change	2.335	4.122	2.421	3.865	4.469	4.745
Gross domestic product per capita, constant prices	National currency	10,930	11,354	11,602	12,018	12,512	13,038
Output gap in percent of potential GDP	Percent of potential GDP	-1.905	-0.45	-2.521	-1.595	-0.31	0.741
Gross domestic product based on purchasing-power-parity (PPP) share of world total	Percent	2.079	2.099	2.074	2.069	2.111	2.138

Continued on next page

Table 8.4—Continued

Inflation, average consumer prices	Annual percent change	4.718	4.674	3.599	1.877	1.764	2.235
Unemployment rate	Percent of total labor force	24.118	22.9	22.08	20.61	18.605	15.64
General government balance	Percent of GDP	-5.989	-6.886	-4.848	-3.371	-3.216	-1.423
General government structural balance	Percent of potential GDP	-5.115	-5.104	-0.066	0.941	0.337	0.933
Current account balance	Percent of GDP	-1.238	-0.307	-0.228	-0.089	-1.176	-2.926

Source: International Monetary Fund, World Economic Outlook Database, October 2009.

increased competition, enhanced productivity gains, and generated revenues that averaged more than 2 percent of GDP per year.

The performance of the labor market was also very satisfactory, particularly compared with Spain (see Table 8.4). Real wage flexibility facilitated labor market adjustments, and access to atypical forms of employment, such as self-employment, made it possible to circumvent rigid regulations. In addition, regulatory reforms and new policy initiatives contributed to: improve education and training; modify the legal regime governing redundancies; reduce the compensations that companies had to pay to dismiss workers; change the unemployment benefit system to avoid the unemployment "trap"; and the social security contributions for self-employed were brought into line with those for employees.[44] A high degree of wage flexibility, active employment policies, and the increasing use of more flexible forms of employment, such as fixed-term contracts, were all credited for the low unemployment (4.0 percent in 2000, down from 7.3 percent in 1996) and relatively high employment rates (the participation rate was 71.3 percent by 2000). Moreover, the concertation policies of the 1990s contributed to social peace and wage moderation. For instance, in the Social Pact of 1996, management and labor reached binding commitments that facilitated reforms and wage restraint.[45] Yet, the economic boom pushed wages up, and since 1999, there was increasing wage drift, which hindered competitiveness.

However, starting in 1998, this performance started to deteriorate. The disinflation process was halted, and inflation increased 2.8 percent by the end of that year fueled by inflation and the Expo 98; and the trade deficit deteriorated from 5.4 percent of GDP in 1997 to 6.6 percent in 1999. The harmonized CPI reached over 4 percent in early 2001 (above the EU average), pushed by higher oil prices and a weaker euro. Furthermore, economic growth also started to slow, dragged down by the ending of major infrastructure projects and Expo 98. The outset of EMU membership led to a progressive easing of monetary conditions and a sharp decline of interest rates. This happened, however, at a time of high consumer demand, in which domestic credit was also booming and the current account deficit was widening (it remained at around 10 percent of GDP up to 2002). Access to EMU in 1999 did not alleviate the situation because Portugal was in a more advanced position in the cycle than the other EMU member states (the country was experiencing a credit boom and signs of overheating were starting to emerge), but now monetary policy was in the hands of the European central bank, and it was making decisions based on developments in the entire EMU area—hence the cut in interest rates in April of 1999.[46] Indeed, there was a change of conditions as the tightening of monetary conditions after the ECB started to gradually raise rates from November 1999 on.

Furthermore, the end of the decade—which coincided with the country's accession to EMU (e.g., the pressure to fulfill the Maastricht criteria was no longer a powerful incentive)—also witnessed a slowdown in the fiscal consolidation efforts, which had led to the successful reduction of the fiscal deficit between 1994 and 1997 (there was an annual reduction of almost 1.2 percentage points, and the deficit was reduced to 2.5 percent by 1997). Yet, about half of this fiscal adjustment was the result of the reduction of the public debt burden facilitated by the lower interest rates and non-recurring receipts (such as the sale of mobile concessions in 2000). As a matter of fact, the primary surplus increased half a point per year between 1994 and 1997. On the contrary, there was no increase of taxes or increases in revenues as the result of improvements in the collection of taxes or social security contributions. Moreover, current expenditures on education, health, and social protection increased steadily.[47] This procyclical policy stance did not bode well for the subsequent slowdown of the economy because Portugal was left with little fiscal leeway to apply countercyclical measures once the crisis hit. In order to improve the margin of maneuver, Portugal should have reduced the weight of the public sector and also implemented structural reforms to check the growth of current expenditures, which would have allowed for a reduction in tax pressure. The country would have needed a significant surplus to ensure balance for the budget over the cycle, but unfortunately this did not happen.

Indeed, in the context of EMU, fiscal policy was the main instrument available to the government to dampen demand pressures and bring the current account deficit (8 percent of GDP in 2002) and inflation (over 3.8 percent) down. Yet, while the general government deficit continued to decline in accordance with the Stability and Growth pact (SGP) and fall below 3 percent of GDP in 2000, the pace of fiscal consolidation was slow and the gains from lower debt payments and higher revenues were used to increase primary current spending. Given the inflationary pressures and the advanced stage of the economic cycle, fiscal consolidation would have helped to control demand pressures. Increasing taxes was not an attractive option because, although the overall tax burden (at 34 percent in 2000) was comparatively low, it would have been difficult politically, and also it risked eroding the export-oriented growth and harming the country's competitive position. Therefore, in order to meet budget deficit targets, the

Table 8.5 Economic summary, Portugal, 2000–2008

PORTUGAL	Units	Scale	2000	2001	2002	2003	2004	2005	2006	2007	2008
GDP constant prices	National currency	Billions	122.27	124.735	125.682	124.67	126.56	127.711	129.458	131.882	131.823
GDP constant prices	Annual percent change		3.925	2.016	0.759	-0.805	1.516	0.91	1.368	1.872	-0.045
GDP per capita, constant prices	National currency	Units	11,993	12,161	12,167	11,978	12,082	12,129	12,248	12,442	12,415
Output gap in percent of potential GDP	Percent of potential GDP		3.114	3.081	2.071	-0.242	-0.011	-0.208	0.181	1.172	0.316
GDP based on purchasing-power-parity (PPP) share of world total	Percent		0.431	0.43	0.422	0.404	0.389	0.375	0.363	0.352	0.341
Inflation, average consumer prices	Annual percent change		2.804	4.41	3.678	3.258	2.509	2.127	3.043	2.423	2.651
Unemployment rate	Percent of total labor force		3.925	4	5	6.25	6.65	7.6	7.65	8	7.6
Employment	Persons	Millions	5.021	5.112	5.137	5.118	5.123	5.123	5.159	5.17	5.198
General government balance	National currency	Billions	-3.569	-5.519	-3.845	-3.994	-4.831	-9.133	-6.092	-4.218	-4.341
General government balance	Percent of GDP		-2.919	-4.268	-2.839	-2.882	-3.352	-6.124	-3.919	-2.585	-2.611
Current account balance	Percent of GDP		-10.241	-9.9	-8.093	-6.103	-7.578	-9.481	-10.029	-9.422	-12.13

Source: International Monetary Fund, World Economic Outlook Database, October 2009.

government became accustomed to implementing spending freezes. But it failed to address the structural causes of spending overruns: the public sector payroll bill (spending per employee had been growing rapidly due to high wage increases and pension benefits) and pressures in the social security system caused by population aging. On the contrary, it continued to rely on increases in current revenue—as opposed to significant progress in spending control—and when these did not materialize, it adopted contingency measures to reduce expenditures, which showed fundamental weaknesses in the budget process.[48] This would prove to be a major Achilles heel for the sustainability of economic growth.

In the end, economic performance started to deteriorate markedly after 2000. Real GDP growth averaged less than 1 percent between 2000 and 2005 (in 2003 the economy contracted 0.8 percent), and annual growth remained fragile until 2006. In 2005, the Portuguese economy grew a meager 0.91 percent of GDP, and in 2006, grew only 1.3 percent as a result of the depression of demand (consumption is one of Portugal's important pillars of economic growth but it grew only 2.3 percent in 2004, 2.1 percent in 2005, and 1.1 percent in 2006). In particular of private demand, given the few incentives on consumption (it grew 0.2 percent in 2004, decreased 3 percent in 2005, and grew only 0.8 percent in 2006), as well as investment, which was pushed down as a consequence of the restrictions on public spending and the increase of taxes to bring down the deficit. The accumulated output gap since the recession was one of the largest in the Euro area, and productivity growth in the business sector fell to around 1 percent between 2004 and 2005 (it was 3 percent in the 1990s). Unemployment also increased sharply, reaching 7.6 percent in 2005 and 8 percent in 2007—the highest rate in twenty years (it was only 3.8 percent in 2000).[49]

The recession was far longer and more intense than anyone anticipated, with a dramatic impact on the government accounts: the fiscal deficit reached unsustainably high levels (see Table 8.5), pushed by the bill from organizing the European Championship Cup in 2004, which left no room to stimulate demand and thereby contributed to the length of the crisis. The government attempted to reduce the fiscal deficit by raising indirect taxes and establishing emergency spending cuts or freezes and one-off decisions, such as measures to control the wage bill over the short-term. However, while these measures helped to reduce the deficit in the short-term (and it was brought down to 2.8 percent in 2003), they proved insufficient because of the lower revenues at a time of a depressed economic environment (it went up again to 6.1 percent in 2005). Portugal had violated the SGP during several years (see Table 8.5), as it had remained above the maximum 3 percent deficit established by the SGP, and therefore it was submitted to the excessive deficit procedure, which further hindered confidence and dampened expectations. Public debt also deteriorated: it grew from 53 percent of GDP in 2000, to 65.9 percent in 2005, and decreased to 60 percent in 2006; as well as capital fixed formation, which fell 2.9 percent in 2005, 0.7 percent in 2006 and grew 2.8 percent in 2007. The country also suffered a decline in investment and savings. The investment rate fell from a peak of 28.1 percent of GDP in 2000 to 20.6 percent in 2006, while the gross savings rate fell from 17 percent in 2000 to a pale 12.3 percent in 2006, bouncing back a bit in 2007 to 15.1 percent.[50]

In the end, the reliance on one-off measures, however, did not address the structural reasons for the deficit, and also reduced the necessary sense of urgency to tackle structural reforms. For instance, once the deficit was below 3 percent, the government decided to lower taxes rapidly, despite the fact that the situation had not improved much. Three fundamental challenges were, first, the reform of the civil servants pension system and the need to bring it into line with the general pension system;[51] second, the reform of the health system; and finally, the reform of the public administration to align legal condition of employment, and remuneration with the private sector, and restructure the central administration.[52]

The victory of the Socialist Party in the 2005 election brought in a new government committed to implementing the structural reforms needed to bring the deficit below 3 percent by 2008. Indeed, the new government pushed for important structural reforms and implemented tough decisions. Upon taking office in March 2005, Prime Minister Sócrates announced the immediate increase of the value added tax by 2 percent—breaking his electoral commitment not to increase taxes—in order to cope with the budget deficit. Moreover, in the face of strident opposition from labor unions and organized interests, his government pushed for the reform of the public sector and the civil servants, and an extensive restructuring of Portugal's state bureaucracy (increasing the retirement age to sixty-five years and eliminating traditional benefits such as vacations, automatic promotions, and corporative medical insurance). One of the main goals of this reform, according to Fernando Teixeira dos Santos, Finance Minister, was that "from now on, governments will be able to run the public administration in accordance with the demands of public management and not, as it has been in the past, the other way around."[53]

The government also approved a comprehensive pension reform plan in the summer of 2005, which sought to address the combined threat of a sharp decline in birth rates—which had fallen 35 percent over the last thirty years (from 2.6 to 1.5)—and increased longevity (people over sixty-five years old are forecast to comprise more than 32 percent of the population in 2050, compared to 17 percent in 2005). As a result, the pension system posed a serious structural challenge: Portugal has 1.7 million pensioners, 1.1 million of whom receive less than 375 euros per month, but pensions in Portugal were in 2006 among the most generous in the European Union, often reaching more than 100 percent of an employee's final salary, and the system was expected to face financial collapse by 2015. It was estimated that pension expenditures would grow from 5.5 percent of GDP in 2006 to 9.6 percent by 2050. Based on this reform, workers have the choice of working longer or increasing their pension contributions, and it includes a "sustainability co-efficient" that will be used to adjust pensions according to life expectancy during the working life of contributions (for instance, it would decrease pension about 5 percent if the life expectancy were to increase by one year over the next decade). At the same time, in order to increase Portugal's birth rate, the reform also establishes a new system under which pension contributions are calculated as a percentage of earnings according to the number of children employees have: contributions would remain unchanged for employees with two children, decrease if they have more than two, and increase if they have less. Finally, the system establishes a radical change in the way pensions are calculated: before the reform only the ten best years of the last fifteen years of an employee's working life were taken into account to calculate the pension; after the reform the pension would be calculated using the whole working life of the contributors. According to some estimates, as a result of these reforms, most pensions are expected to be reduced by at least 10 percent for people retiring over the next twenty years and will hit high earners the hardest. These reforms, which came into force in 2006, are expected to guarantee the sustainability of the system up to 2050 and beyond.[54]

The Sócrates government also carried through an ambitious privatization plan that sought to raise 2.4 billion euros from the sale of public enterprises between 2006 and 2009, including the three leading public energy groups (GALP, EDP, and REN) and the paper sector (Portucel Tejo, Portucel, and Inapa), as well as the Portuguese flag airline company (TAP) and the national airport company (ANA). This was quite exceptional coming from a Socialist government, especially in light of the long-standing opposition to the privatization of companies that have been declared "untouchable" for years. The aim of this decision was to reduce the public deficit and the role of the state in the economy, which in 2006, still had direct participation in 150 companies.

Education reform has also been high on the agenda. Education attainment is a huge problem in Portugal, and its low level has hindered competitiveness and productivity. The government decided that "it cannot wait for the next generation to replace the current workforce," in the words of Prime Minister Sócrates, and therefore it tried to provide education and training for people currently at work, with the aim "to have a million more employees with an educational level equivalent to full secondary schooling." In order to achieve this goal, the government introduced a new program called New Opportunities that seeks to encourage adults to complete their secondary education. It also provides vocational training for youngsters. The initial results were very encouraging: it attracted 250,000 applicants within three months of its launch in early 2007.[55]

The government also tried to counter the opposition to these reforms with an ambitious infrastructure plan that would have cost over 50 billion euros (only 8 percent from public funds—the rest will be from private funding and mixed concessions), and included the constructions of new airports (Lisbon, Alcochete); the building of new dams (one of the cornerstones of the government's energy policy to reduce oil dependency) and highways (there are eleven new tenders); new high speed trains (AVE Porto-Lisbon, and Lisbon-Madrid, which also involves a new bridge over the Tagus river); as well as other projects in the private sector, such as a new refinery in Sines (4 billion euros); a Volkswagen manufacturing plant in Palmela to produce the VW models Siroco and Eos (750 million); new tourist resorts in Melides (510 million) and Tróia (500 million); a new paper plant in Figueira da Foz (500 million); a new furniture plant and new Ikea shops (350 million); and a new Corte Inglés commercial center in Gaia (150 million), which is expected to generate billions of euros in investment and employment. The most ambitious proposal, however, is the Technological Plan to advance the EU-Lisbon Agenda in Knowledge, Technology, and Innovation. The government is committed to install broadband network connections in all Portuguese schools and has signed innovative agreements with MIT[56] and Bill Gates to facilitate the learning of computing to one million Portuguese.[57]

In the end, the combination of fiscal consolidation (the ratio of public spending to GDP fell from an excessive 47.7 percent of GDP in 2005 to 45 percent in 2008), structural reforms, and increasing revenues from stronger economic growth have all helped Portugal to bring the deficit back under control: the Sócrates government, which inherited a deficit of 6.8 percent of GDP from the previous administration, has been able to bring its budget deficit below the maximum limit allowed by the EU a year ahead of schedule, after achieving a larger cut than forecast in 2006. The deficit fell to 3.9 percent of GDP in 2006— 0.7 percentage points lower than the 4.6 percent target agreed with the European Commission as part of the plan to avoid the sanctions hanging over the country for breaching the SGP. In 2007, one year ahead of schedule, the deficit fell to 2.5 percent, below 3 percent (well down from the initial goal of 3.7 percent) and the lowest level since 2000. More importantly, this reduction was achieved not only through ad hoc cuts (although the government had to apply severe cuts in public spending and investment), but largely through structural reforms and a sharp increase in tax revenues (after the government recruited a private sector banker to spearhead the crackdown on tax evasion), which will make it easier to consolidate the gains.

The government was also relatively successful in its attempt to bring down inflation, which decreased from 4.41 percent in 2001, to 2.1 percent in 2005 (but it grew to 3 percent in 2006). Other economic indicators also improved markedly: exports (which represent 20 percent of GDP) increased 8.9 percent in 2006, 6.2 percent in 2007, and 5.6 percent in 2008; fixed capital formation also increased 2.5 percent in 2007 (it fell 1.6 percent in 2006); as well as consumption, which grew 1.5 percent in 2007. Unemployment, however, is still a challenge: despite the creation of more than one hundred thousand jobs since 2005, it rose from 6.25 percent in 2003 to 7.65 percent in 2006, and the unemployment rate more than doubled between 2000 and 2007 (from less than 3.9 percent to 8 percent). Finally, stronger economic growth resumed: in 2006, the economy grew 1.3 percent, and in 2007, 1.8 percent, the highest rate in six years. This sudden and unexpected turnaround since 2006 took many economists by surprise. Yet, growth was negative again in 2008 at -0.045 percent, led by the effects of the global economic crisis. This has forced the government to adopt new measures to address it, including the so-called Robin Hood Tax, an exceptional tax of 25 percent for the oil companies to fund social expenditures,[58] and the reduction of taxes (the IRS) for housing purposes for the population in the lower tax brackets, as well as a modification of the maximum rates of the municipal real estate taxes.[59]

Reasons for the Iberian Economic Divergence Between 2000-2007

Domestic Fiscal Policies

Lax monetary policies had played a significant role in the slowdown of the convergence process prior to EC accession.[60] However, since Spain and Portugal became founding members of EMU, monetary policies were no longer in the hands of their national governments and therefore cannot help to account for differences in performance between the two countries. However, different fiscal policies, within the constraints imposed by the Growth and Stability Pact, have played a central role. It is now widely accepted that increases in government consumption adversely affect long-term growth, and also, that while fiscal consolidation may have short-term costs in terms of activity, they can be minimized if consolidation is credible by implementing consistent decisions that deliver solid results.

Both the Portuguese and Spanish economies experienced a boom in the second half of the 1990s—boosted by the considerable fall in interest rates—when nominal short-term interest rates converged to those set by the ECB. In both countries, they fell more rapidly than did inflation, and the simultaneous processes of financial liberalization and increasing competition that took place at the same time—which contributed to increasing domestic demand, and in particular housing demand—further boosted their impact. The expansion in these years was driven largely by internal demand. This boom also coincided with a period of international expansion. The growth, however, would have required a concomitant prudent fiscal policy, which in the case of Portugal did not take place. On the contrary, the cyclically adjusted primary balance fell from 1.2 percent of GDP in 1994 to 1996 to -0.6 percent in 1999 to 2001. At the same time, the combination of expansionary fiscal policies and insufficient structural reforms did not prepare the country for the economic downturn.

Indeed, as we have seen in the previous section, one of the fundamental reasons for the poor performance of the Portuguese economy between 1999 and 2006 was the lack of fiscal discipline and the failure in the adoption of ad hoc measures to control the deficit. Spain, on the contrary, was one of the most disciplined countries in Europe (even in the world) and was able to maintain a margin of maneuver that allowed fiscal policy to be used in a counter-cyclical way (see Table 8.6).

Indeed, there is widespread consensus that Portugal's biggest mistake was its "chronic fiscal misbehavior."[61] Vítor Constancio, governor of the Bank of Portugal, has acknowledged that "in 2001, we had these big shocks to growth, tax revenues dropped and suddenly we were in a situation of an excessive deficit. . . . The sudden emergence of budget problems led to a big revision of expectations about the future."[62] As we have seen, largely as a result of this revision of expectations, the Portuguese economy contracted by 0.8 percent in 2003. The deficit reduction, on the contrary, is credited by Finance Minister Fernando Teixeira dos Santos, with restoring "Portugal's credibility in international markets and strengthen[ing] confidence in the economy."[63] The improvement in the financial position of the budget allowed the government to cut the value added tax from 21 to 20 percent in July 2008 to stimulate the economy. Fiscal consolidation and structural reforms were expected to allow more robust growth and place Portugal in a better position to face the current global crisis caused by the U.S. subprime crisis and international crunch, as well as the high prices of energy and commodities. As a result, the Portuguese experience shows that countries wishing to join the Eurozone need to have a "comfortable budget position because that will give for maneuver once inside."[64] Not surprisingly, of the cohesion countries, the ones that have done better in the last decade and a half have been those who have maintained fiscal discipline—Ireland and Spain—which have either maintained a budget surplus or reduced their budget deficits to comply with the SGP, while reducing their total expenditures vis-à-vis GDP. Portugal, as we have seen, was the exception.

EMU Accession

The experiences of Portugal and Spain within the EMU show that there have been lasting performance differences across countries. These differences can be explained at least in part by a lack of responsiveness to prices and wages, which have not adjusted smoothly across sectors; in the case of Portugal and Spain, this has led to accumulated competitiveness loses and large external imbalances.

The economic downturn coincided with Portugal's accession to the European Monetary Union and the adoption of the euro in 2002. The EMU, however, cannot be blamed for the poor performance of the Portuguese economy. If that was the culprit, it would be hard to explain how the other cohesion countries have performed much better. Yet, it is important to note that there was a significant difference in the conversion rate of the peseta and the escudo vis-à-vis the euro, which further hampered Portugal's competitiveness.[65] When the national currencies were fixed to the euro at the end of 1998, the Spanish peseta was converted at a rate of 166 pesetas to one euro, and the Portuguese euro

Table 8.6 General government balance, Portugal and Spain, 2000-2007

	Units	Scale	2000	2001	2002	2003	2004	2005	2006	2007	2008
SPAIN	General government balance	Percent of GDP	-0.978	-0.641	-0.454	-0.207	-0.34	0.964	2.016	2.209	-3.847
PORTUGAL	General government balance	Percent of GDP	-2.919	-4.268	-2.839	-2.882	-3.352	-6.124	-3.919	-2.585	-2.611

Source: International Monetary Fund, World Economic Outlook Database, October 2009.

was fixed at 200 escudos. Yet, in the years previous to the final conversion of exchange rates, there had been a significant devaluation of the peseta *vis-à-vis* the euro: it had devalued about 30 percent, while the escudo had devalued only 12 percent (in the early 1990s the exchange rate was 128 pesetas for one euro and 179 escudos to one Euro, respectively). In other words, the fixed exchange rate at which Spain joined the EMU was significantly more favorable than Portugal's. This problem was compounded by the appreciation of the real effective exchange rate in the 1990s due to wage increases: while it depreciated by approximately 15 percent in Spain, in Portugal it appreciated by the same amount. According to the European Commission, the Portuguese real effective exchange rate is approximately 20 percent higher than it was in the early 1990s (while Spain's is at the same level).[66] This is an important consideration when trying to account for the loss of competitiveness of Portugal vis-à-vis Spain.

Both countries provide interesting insights into the pitfalls of integration into a monetary union. As noted by Vítor Constancio, governor of the Bank of Portugal, one of the main lessons from Portugal's experience is that "countries used previously to high inflation and high interest rates are likely to experience an explosion in consumer spending and borrowing" upon joining the monetary union. This spurt will make a downturn inevitable, particularly in cases such as Portugal, who is vulnerable to higher oil prices and increasing competition from developing countries like India and China. In both Portugal and Spain, the strong demand stemmed from the sharp fall in interest rates, but in Portugal it was further fueled by expansive fiscal policies. Demand, however, was not followed in either country by a parallel increase in supply, as it was hindered by low productivity growth, which led to a significant increase in imports and high external deficits and debts. External indebtedness in turn has led to lower available income domestically.

This is a potential lesson for future EMU applicants: lower interest rates and the loosening of credit will likely lead to a credit boom that may increase housing demand and household indebtedness. This boom will lead to higher wage increases (caused by the tightening of the labor market) and losses in external competitiveness, together with a shift from the tradable to the non-tradable sector of the economy.[67] In Spain the tightening of fiscal policies prevented the consequent bust. Even so, in the end, the global crisis that started in 2008 also exposed the imbalances of the Spanish economy.

Labor Market Policies

While this chapter has emphasized the relative underperformance of Portugal's economy in terms of real convergence, it is important to highlight that Portugal has a much better employment record than Spain. Labor market rigidities are seen to have played an important role in accounting for the Spanish labor market performance throughout the 1980s and 1990s. On the contrary, Portugal has had a remarkably successful employment record, which has been the object of important work by scholars such as Robert Fishman, Oliver Blanchard, Juan F. Jimeno, Pedro Portugal, José da Silva Lopes, Gosta Esping-Andersen, David Cameron, and others. According to Fishman, there are three main reasons associated with the legacies of Portugal's democratic transition in the 1970s: the high level of female participation rate; the availability of credit to small companies; and finally, the "nature of the Portuguese welfare state which became increasingly 'employment-friendly' in the 1990s."[68]

As we have seen, Spain introduced far-reaching reforms in the 1990s which have contributed to bringing down the highest unemployment rate in the EU. Still, in Spain, a central concern has been the so-called "safeguard clauses" included in labor agreements, which allow for the indexation of wages if inflation increases over the government's forecast for the year (which is used as the basis for the agreement). A consequence of these clauses has been the increase in unitary labor costs, which has hindered Spain's competitiveness. The other main problem is job instability: as we have seen temporary rates standing at over 30 percent, the highest in the OECD, which also dampens competitiveness.[69]

Indeed, while Germany (and other EMU countries) implemented supply-side reforms to bring labor costs down (through wage restraint, payroll tax cuts, and productivity increases, making it the most competitive economy with labor costs 13 percent below the Eurozone average), Portugal and Spain continued with the tradition of indexing wage increases to domestic inflation rather than the European Central Bank target, and they became the most expensive ones: Portugal with labor costs 23.5 percent above average and Spain with 16 percent (followed by Greece with 14 percent and Italy with 5 percent).[70]

Policy Stability

One of the key differences between the two countries is that in Spain there has been remarkable economic policy stability following the crisis of 1992 and 1993. There were few economic policy shifts throughout the 1990s and first half of the 2000s, despite changes in government. Between 1993 and 2008, there were only two ministers of finance: Pedro Solbes (1993-1996 and 2004-2008) and Rodrigo Rato (1996-2004);[71] and the country had only two prime ministers (José María Aznar and José Luís Rodríguez Zapatero).[72] More importantly, each of the last three governments has completed its mandate and there have been no early elections. In addition, as a rare occurrence, Pedro Solbes, who was minister of finance under a Socialist government in the early 1990s— when the process of fiscal consolidation started—became minister of finance again in 2004 after the Socialist Party won the general election. He still holds this position. The power of the minister of finance was also reinforced vis-à-vis the other cabinet members, because both of them also served as deputies of the prime minister in the government under the Conservative and Socialist administrations. This pattern was further reinforced by the ideological cohesiveness of these parties and the strong control that party leaders exercise over all the members of the cabinet and parliament deputies.

In addition, this stability was bolstered by the shared (and rare) agreement among the Conservatives and Socialist leaders regarding fiscal consolidation (the balanced budget objective was established by law by the Popular Party), as well as the need to stand firm in the application of conservative fiscal policies and the achievement of budgetary fiscal surpluses. Indeed, this happened to such a degree that Spain became the paradigmatic model of a country applying the budget surplus policy mantra. The Aznar government repeatedly chastised other European governments that were far laxer in their fiscal policies, to the point that it created tensions with the richer EU countries, because although they were in fact running higher deficits, they were net contributors to the EU budget and provided Spain with cohesion and structural funds (i.e., Germany and France). Not surprisingly, it was hard for them to accept being called irresponsible and to have fingers pointed at them while they were subsidizing Spain through the European solidarity programs.

This dogmatism, however, worked well in the short-term and contributed to the credibility of the government policies. In the medium- and long-terms, however, there are disputes about whether a more accommodating policy would have made it possible to upgrade the productive base of the country with investments in necessary infrastructure and human capital. The maintenance of the balanced deficit paradigm as a goal on its own may have blinded the governments to the benefits of investing in new technology areas (in which Spain is still lagging behind). This may have contributed to a faster change in the model of growth and may have reduced the dependency on the construction sector, which is now in the midst of a sharp recession that is having devastating consequences for the Spanish economy.

In Portugal, however, there have been more changes at the prime minister level (there were four PMs between 1995 and 2005), as the previous three prime ministers resigned before their terms were over for different reasons. António Guterres was PM from October 28, 1995, to April 6, 2002. During his first term, Portugal enjoyed a solid economic expansion and very successfully staged the Expo 98. However, the beginning of the economic crisis and the Hintze Ribeiro disaster, in which seventy people died when the bridge collapsed, damaging his popularity, marred his second term. He resigned following the disastrous result for the Socialist party in the 2002 local elections stating that "I will resign to prevent the country from falling into a political swamp." Following a general election won by the opposition Social Democratic Party, the Social Democrat party leader José Manuel Durão Barroso became PM on April 6, 2002. He held the post through July 17, 2004, ruling in coalition with the People's Party. He resigned when he was named president of the European Commission (at a time when the Portuguese economy was entering one of the worst phases of the economic crisis, which was very criticized). Pedro Miguel Santana Lopes replaced him from his own party, and held the position between 29 June 2004 and 12 March 2005. His short tenure was marred by controversies over his unusual election (he was not elected by popular vote), the fact that he was not a member of parliament (he was mayor of Lisbon when he was selected PM), and continuous PR fiascos, which led President Sampaio to dissolve Parliament and call for early elections. Finally, the Socialist José Sócrates, who won the general election in a landslide victory with an overwhelming absolute majority (45 percent of the vote and 121 seats) for the first time since the democratic transition, became PM in 2005 and he is still in that position (re-elected in September 2009). These constant changes up to 2005 made economic policy continuity more problematic and more importantly and made the implementation of reforms in the face of popular opposition very difficult.

Furthermore, the minister of finance position became a revolving door, bringing instability to the economic policy portfolio, with ministers often resigning in protest for their inability to hold sway over their colleagues and control fiscal policies and expenditures. Between 1990 and 2005, there were ten ministers of finance, and on average they have been less than two years in the position. The problem was compounded—as opposed to Spain—by the finance minister's limited powers over the budget. Indeed, according to a recent study of all the EU-15 finance ministers the Portuguese one has the least amount of control over the formulation, approval, and implementation of the budget.[73]

Table 8.7 Minister of finance, Portugal, 1990-2008

21 July 2005	Fernando Teixeira dos Santos
12 March 2005	Luís Campos e Cunha
17 July 2004	António Bagão Félix
06 April 2002	Maria Manuela Ferreira Leite
03 July 2001	Guilherme d'Oliveira Martins
25 October 1999	Joaquim Augusto Nunes de Pina Moura
28 October 1995	António Luciano Pacheco de Sousa Franco
07 December 1993	Eduardo Almeida Catroga
31 October 1991	Jorge Braga de Macedo
04 January 1990	Luís Miguel Beleza

This problem extends to other critical areas, such as education: Maria Isabel Girão de Melo Veiga Vilar Alçada, the current minister of education (as of 2009), was the twenty-eighth education minister in thirty-three years.

In the end, the credibility of economic policies (and fiscal policies in particular) was undermined by the relative political instability that prevailed in Portugal in the first half of the decade. It is not surprising, therefore, that once some stability has been achieved in the position (Fernando Teixeira dos Santos has been in the position for over four years, the longest tenure in the past eighteen years), the government has been able to implement substantive reforms and pursue fiscal consolidation. The fact that the PS had an absolute majority in parliament has also been an important factor in facilitating the implementation of reforms.

Differences in Educational Attainment

EU funds have been used to co-finance projects improving infrastructure and human resources, and to help in areas such as technological innovation and investment. EU-funded investments in infrastructure have improved accessibility and from a supply-side effect have contributed to boost productivity. Yet the educational attainment performance of both countries has been disappointing. This performance has been particularly disappointing in Portugal, where a large share of young students leave school before completing upper secondary education, and the achievements of students in PISA are among the poorest in the OECD.

According to the OECD, the performance of Portuguese secondary school students was among the weakest in the developed world, and the dropout rate one of the highest.[74] In the last ten years, half of Portugal's youth left school at fifteen, before completing secondary education, and the current dropout rate is still 40 percent, more than double the EU average (at 16 percent). Furthermore, reading and math skills among fifteen year olds are among the weakest in Europe: Portuguese students number between 22 and 33 percent performing at or below the level of "very basic," while only about 5 percent achieve the highest international standards. The problem also affects higher education: in 2008, the percentage of the population with a university education was 12 percent (up from 2 percent in 1974 when democracy was restored), compared with an EU average of 24 percent. In order to increase this figure, students must stay in school longer and graduate from high school. According to the IMF, Portugal's low educational standards, job skills, research and development investment, and computer use were among the greatest challenges for regaining lost competitiveness.[75] Indeed, the educational level of the workforce has to reflect the shift from low-cost, unskilled manufacturing to more value-added sectors.

While illiteracy, which affected a fifth of the fifteen- to sixty-four-year olds in 1974, has been virtually eradicated, the education system had still failed to limit the repetition of underperformance from one generation to another within families and to foster the necessary inter-generational mobility. This problem is compounded by the low educational standards for many parents, who left school at the age of fifteen and still make education a low priority for their families. Poor schooling results have a ripple effect on productivity, research, and innovation, which helps account for Portugal's (and Spain's) weak competitiveness and slow growth. It is therefore critical for Portugal (and Spain) to narrow this "human capital gap" in order to improve productivity and resume "catching up." The problem, however, has been not so much insufficient funding, but the system's low efficiency. Public spending per student is close to the European average and the education budget has doubled over the past decade, but the number of students has fallen. Most East European countries spend much less but still achieve similar or better results.[76] One of the main problems is that teachers' salaries account for 93 percent of spending (compared with 75 percent in the OECD). Therefore, it is not lack of resources, but how to use them. Not surprisingly, the Portuguese PM, José Socrates, has recognized that "problems like the budget deficit can be solved in two or three years, [but] our structural deficit in education and training is a much bigger challenge."[77]

There are some positive signs, however. The number of students enrolling in Portuguese universities is growing faster than in any other EU country, increasing by almost 6 percent annually (compared with an average of 3 percent in the EU-15). More importantly, this growth has been particularly strong in the fields of science and technology, which are growing at 7 to 10 percent a year. The number of PhDs has also increased from fewer than one hundred per year in the 1970s to more than one thousand today; and Portuguese scholars produce more than four thousand scientific papers a year, compared with merely about two hundred in 1981. In 2001, Portugal was included in the list of "countries of excellence" that contribute to the top 1 percent of the world's most highly cited scientific publications. Despite all of this, Portugal still has significant ground to cover: for every one thousand workers, it has only about 3.6 researchers (in the EU the average is 5.4, and in the United States, eight). The government wants to increase the number of researchers to six per one thousand workers by 2010, and it is increasing public investment in research from 0.47 percent of GDP in 2003 to 1 percent by 2010, as well as pushing the private sector to increase its R&D spending (a meager 0.26 percent of GDP compared to 1.23 percent in the EU) to 0.75 percent by the end of the decade. Finally, the country is also committed to implementing an international dimension to its education and scientific programs to increase the credibility of Portugal's research. For instance, it has extended international assessment and accreditation to higher education as a whole, commissioning the OECD and the European Network of Quality Assurance in Higher Education to evaluate the performance of the country's universities. These initiatives and the availability of qualified scientists and technicians are making Portugal a very attractive destination for foreign investors.[78]

Finally, Research and Development (R&D) indicators also provide one possible measure to chart the level of development of firms and businesses. In 2007 Spain spent approximately 1.2 percent on R&D as a percentage of GDP and Portugal 0.8 percent (the average in the EU was 1.8 percent).

New Players in World Trade and the Erosion of Comparative Advantage

Low economic growth, combined with a huge current account deficit (averaging 8.6 percent of GDP from 2001 to 2007) and decreasing investment, suggests a serious competitiveness problem for Portugal. This, according to economists, also helps to account for the severity of the crises: although export performance was not too bad (exports of goods and services grew 31 percent between 2000 and 2007), and unitary labor costs remained fairly stable between 1998 and 2007 (much better than Spain's), Portugal was unable to generate enough external demand to compensate for the lack of a domestic one.[79]

Spain also has a serious competitiveness problem as reflected in the record trade deficit: Spain's current account deficit, which has been growing steadily over the last decade, is expected to reach 11 percent of GDP in 2008. The reasons, however, are somewhat different than Portugal's. First is the decoupling between production and domestic demand: increasing internal demand has led to a growth in imports, while exports have been hindered by the appreciation of the euro, the crisis in the larger European economies, and the growing competition from other countries. Second, the savings rate is insufficient to cover investment projects. The current account deficit shows the imbalance between savings and private investment. While the public sector is no longer in deficit, the private one shows a large deficit (particularly the one from nonfinancial enterprises). Third, Spanish exports are concentrated in a few markets. Seventy percent of Spanish exports go to the EU-15, but the average growth of Spanish markets in the last five years has been 4.5 percent, while global markets grew by 7 percent. The slow growth of European economies during the last few years has had a deleterious effect on Spanish exports. Finally, Spanish products' limited degree of technological sophistication has also been a problem because most Spanish exports are labor intensive, making them very vulnerable to cost-based competition. Indeed, high-technology exports represent only 8 percent of the total (less than half of the EU-15 average).

The problem for Portugal, on the other hand, was the dramatic erosion of its comparative advantage (as opposed to Spain, which relies a bit less on exports, represented by the 25.7 percent of GDP in 2004 and imports of 29.3 percent; and more importantly, did not lack for domestic demand). The emergence of major new players in world trade, like India and China, as well as the eastern enlargements of the European Union were particularly damaging to the Portuguese economy, because these countries have lower labor costs and they competed with Portugal's traditional exports (as an exporter of relatively unsophisticated labor-intensive products). This led to losses in export market shares (aggravated by the appreciation of the euro, and the increase of unit labor costs relative to those in its trading competitors). At the same time Portugal's attempt to specialize in medium- and higher-technology products was also hindered by the accession of the Eastern European countries into the EU, who were moving into those sectors and also specializing in those products. Finally, it is important to note that as opposed to Spanish privatized firms, which have focused on internationalization (i.e., Telefónica), many Portuguese economic groups adopted defensive growth strategies based on investments in non-tradable sectors.[80] Indeed, the success of Spanish multinationals has to be highlighted: there were eight firms in the *Financial Times* list of the world's largest multinationals in 2000, and fourteen in 2008.

In the end, the country's ability to keep the lid on unitary labor costs was insufficient to generate enough growth in exports to compensate for decreasing domestic demand. While easy access to cheap credit had boosted domestic demand for households, it also caused a shift of resources from tradables to non-tradables (services). This shift was further hastened by high wage increases (also in the public sector) caused by a tighter labor market in the second half of the 1990s, which further hampered external competitiveness and productivity. The result was an imbalanced economy sustained by strong domestic demand that translated into higher imports (and external deficit).

Until 2000, the impact of wage increases was offset by high productivity growth—it grew yearly at an average of 2.2 percent between 1996 and 2000—thus limiting the growth of unit labor costs. After 2000, however, the international expansionary cycle started to reverse, particularly in the EU, which is the leading market for Portuguese exports, where growth slowed to 1.4 percent between 2001 and 2003 (compared to 2.8 percent between 1995 and 2000). This deceleration of the international economic cycle hit Portugal severely, and affected expectations among consumers and businesses.

Furthermore, some Portuguese sectors of the economy did not prepare well for the WTO liberalization of sectors with major economic impact in the country, particularly footwear and textiles. The situation was compounded by the Asian crisis of the late 1990s, which led to the devaluation of these currencies, further eroding the competitiveness of Portuguese exports. As a result, Portuguese exports of footwear and textiles fell from almost two thirds of total exports of goods between 1995 and 1996, to a little more than one-third between 2004 and 2005, with the concurrent wave of dismissals and closures, which further dampened expectations and caused social problems, particularly in the north of the country, where these industries are based.[81]

Conclusions

This chapter has sought to shed light on the divergent economic performance of the Portuguese and Spanish economies between 2000 and 2007. While Spain's per capita income has reached the EU average, Portugal's has stagnated below that level. The chapter has argued that macroeconomic policy stability, consensus among the leading political parties, differences in educational attainment, fiscal consolidation, and differences in the erosion of their comparative advantage help account for economic divergence.

While the Spanish economy has performed significantly better since 2000, in the end, the reforms implemented by the Sócrates' government in Portugal may have placed that country in a better position to face the current international economic crisis. In Spain, the downturn in the construction sector is having dire consequences, as the country had already suffered a considerable loss of competitiveness. Moreover, the technological capacity of Spain's tradable good industries is weak, and much of Spain's recent investment effort has gone into the production of nontradables, particularly buildings. Furthermore, Spain's (like Portugal's) industries are relatively vulnerable to competition from cheaper wage producers in Central and Eastern Europe and Asia, and productivity growth has been low, which will make it harder to restore competitiveness. Finally, (unlike Portugal) wage bargaining is quite rigid and, above all, unresponsive to conditions in the Eurozone.[82] As we have seen, while unitary labor costs have remained fairly stable in Portugal, they have increased significantly in Spain, further eroding its competitiveness.

A competitiveness agenda in both countries will have to focus on productivity growth, which is even more important in Spain than nominal wage growth. Addressing this challenge will demand actions to improve policy across a wide front: higher investment in infrastructure, improvements in land-use planning, efforts to increase the quality of education, rigorous promotion of competition in all areas of the economy, tax simplification, and rationalization of existing regulations.[83] Furthermore, such an agenda will demand a shift from a low-cost, low-skill manufacturing base that relies on technical design and marketing skills from elsewhere, toward more capital-intensive industries that require greater skills in the labor force and rely on standard technology—for example, chemicals, vehicles, steel, and metal manufacturers. It also calls for a change in the existing growth model (based on relatively low production costs) in order to build a new framework based on innovation, quality, and productivity. Small companies must carve out market niches in the global market and develop the technical capacity for short production runs to be able to respond to shifting demand. They have to develop their own brands and distribution networks and create their own customer bases. This will require the development of technological know-how and marketing techniques.

For the Iberian economies, the goal must be to increase productivity by increasing the capital intensity of production. Innovation and higher productivity will require the following four main conditions:

1. Investment in capital technology (i.e., information systems and tele-communications);
2. A new culture of entrepreneurship, innovation, and risk, which is an historically rooted problem in both countries;
3. Human capital with strong skills and the flexibility to adapt to new technologies and processes, based on a model of continuous training; and
4. A flexible and adaptable industrial relations framework.

There are good reasons for optimism. Despite the challenging international economic environment, Iberian companies have been very successful at diversifying their export markets and investments, increasing the technology content of their exports, and adding value to their products. Still, to consolidate a new growth pattern based on value added and productivity, both countries will have to achieve a massive upgrade of their productive base that will allow them to move up the value chain. In order to do this they need to improve productivity, develop a more flexible economy with a better-educated labor force, achieve higher savings and investment, and develop a more efficient public sector.

Notes

1. References to the European Economic Community (EEC) or the European Union (EU) can be misleading if the historical period covered extends past the last two decades. This paper addresses themes in the European Economic Community prior to the introduction of the European Union label in the Maastricht Treaty of 1991. The terms "the European Community" (EC) or "the European Union" (EU) are used indistinctly to refer to the European integration process and institutions throughout the article. Similarly, "Europe" is here always used to refer to the countries that are members of the European Union, either before or after the Maastricht Treaty.

2. This sections draws from Royo 2006; Royo 2006a; Royo and Manuel, 2003.

3. From "Not quite kissing cousins," in *The Economist*, 5 May 1990, v. 315, n. 7653, 21.

4. Robert C. Hine,"Customs Union Enlargement and Adjustment: Spain's Accession to the European Community," *Journal of Common Market Studies*, Volume XXVIII, No. 1 (September 1989): 7.

5. For example, EC vehicles imported to Spain paid a custom duty of 27 percent to 30.4 percent plus a compensatory tax of 13 percent.

6. Alfred Tovias, "The Southern European Economies and European Integration," in *Southern Europe and the Making of the European Union*, ed. António Costa Pinto and Nuno Severiano Teixeira (New York: Columbia University Press, 2002).

7. Nuno Crespo, Maria Paula Fontoura, and Frank Barry, *EU Enlargement and the Portuguese economy* (London: Blackwell Publishing, 2004).

8. Steven Saeger, "Globalization and Deindustrialization: Myth and Reality in the OECD," in Globalization and Economic Structure in the OECD (Unpublished Ph.D. Dissertation, Harvard University, 1996).

9. Sebastián Royo, "The 2004 Enlargement: Iberian Lessons for Post-Communist Europe," in Royo and Manuel, 291-92.

10. Miguel Sebastián, "Spain in the EU: Fifteen Years May Not be Enough" (paper presented at the conference From Isolation to Europe: 15 Years of Spanish and Portuguese Membership in the European Union, Minda de Gunzburg Center for European Studies, Harvard University, November 2-3, 2001).

11. World Economic Forum, *Global Report of Information Technologies 2002-2003* (New York: Oxford University Press, 2003).

12. From "La Convergencia Real a Paso Lento," *El País*, February 14, 2000.

13. This section draws upon Royo, 2008

14. "Zapatero Accentuates Positives in Economy, but Spain Has Other Problems," in *Financial Times,* April 16, 2007, 4; and "Spanish Economy at Its Best for 29 years, Says Zapatero," *Financial Times*, April 2007, 3.

15. "El paro se sitúa en el 7.95 percent y alcanza su nivel más bajo desde 1978," *El País*, July 27, 2007.

16. "La economía española se hace fuerte," *El País*, March 25, 2007 and "La economía repuntó al 3.9 percent en 2006 tras el mayor avance de la productividad en nueve años," *El País*, February 22, 2007.

17. Guillermo de la Dehesa, "La Próxima Recesión," *El País*, January 21, 2007.

18. Mauro Guillén, *The Rise of Spanish Multinationals* (New York: CUP, 2005).

19. "Spain's Bold Investors to Offset 'Gentle Slowdown,'" *Financial Times*, February 22, 2007.

20. From "Modernised Nation Faces Uncharted Territory," *Financial Times: Special Report*, June 21, 2007, 1.

21. Emilio Ontiveros, "Redimensionamiento Transfronterizo," *El País*, July 15, 2007.

22. "Siesta's Over for Spain's Economy," *Los Angeles Times*, April 7, 2007.

23. Deloitte's "Barometro de Empresas," from "Un año de grandes resultados," *El País*, January 14, 2006.

24. "Spanish Bulls," *Financial Times,* February 20, 2007.

25. According to the *Financial Times*, 17 percent of those polled selected Spain as the country where they would prefer to work ahead of the United Kingdom (15 percent) and France (11 percent). See "España vuelve a ser diferente," in *El País*, 19 February 2007, and *Financial Times*, February 19, 2007.

26. Kitty Calativa, *Immigrants at the Margins* (New York: Cambridge University Press, 2005). Calativa provides a detailed analysis of the immigration experience in Spain and exposes the tensions associated with this development. She also highlights the shortcomings of governments' actions in regard to integration, and the impact of lack of integration on exclusion, criminalization, and radicalization.

27. "Tolerant Spain Is Booming as It Absorbs Flood of Foreign Workers," *Financial Times*, February 20, 2007, 3.

28. "Spanish Bulls," *Financial Times,* February 20, 2007. Still, 59 percent thought that there were "too many foreigners" in the country.

29. "Immigrants Boost British and Spanish Economies," *Financial Times*, February 20, 2007, 3.

30. "El paro baja hasta el 8.3 percent en 2006, la mejor tasa desde 1979," *El País*, January 26, 2007.

31. Guillermo de la Dehesa, "La Próxima Recesión," *El País*, January 21, 2007.

32. "La Economía española creció en la última década gracias a la aportación de los inmigrantes," *El País*, August 28, 2006.

33. See Martin Wolf, "Pain Will Follow Years of Economic Gain," *Financial Times*, March 29, 2007.

34. C. Martinez-Mongay, "Spain and Portugal in the Euro area: Lessons for Cyprus," *Cyprus Economic Policy Review*, Vol. 2, No. 1 (2008): 33-62; C. Martinez-Mongay and L.A. Maza Lasierra, "Competitiveness and growth in EMU: The role of the external sector in the adjustment of the Spanish economy," *Economic Papers* 355, Directorate-General for Economic and Financial Affairs (January 2009). According to Martinez-Mongay and Maza Lasierra, "The outstanding economic performance of Spain in EMU would be the result of a series of lucky shocks, including a large and persistent credit impulse and strong immigration, underpinned by some right policy choices. In the absence of new positive shocks, the resilience of the Spanish economy to the financial crisis might be weaker than that exhibited in the early 2000s. The credit impulse has ended, fiscal consolidation has stopped, and the competitiveness gains of the nineties have gone long ago."

35. "Fears of Recession as Spain Basks in Economic Bonanza," *Financial Times*, June 8, 2006.

36. "Los expertos piden cambios en la política de I+D," in *El País*, 18 December 2006.

37. Angel Laborda, "El comercio en 2006," *El País*, March 11, 2007, 20.

38. Wolfgang Munchau, "Spain, Ireland and Threats to the Property Boom," *Financial Times*, March 19, 2007; "Spain Shudders as Ill Winds Batter US Mortgages," *Financial Times*, March 21, 2007.

39. "Spanish Muscle Abroad Contrast with Weakling Status among Investors," *Financial Times*, December 11, 2006.

40. "La Comisión Europea advierte a España de los riesgos de su baja competitividad," *El País*, February 4, 2007.

41. "Zapatero Accentuates Positives in Economy, but Spain Has Other Problems," *Financial Times,* April 16, 2007, 4.

42. Sebastián Royo, "After the Fiesta: The Spanish Economy Meets the Global Financial Crisis," *South European Society & Politics*, Vol. 14, No.1 (March 2009): 19-34.

43. OECD, *OECD Economic Surveys: Portugal* (Paris: OECD, 1999): 13.

44. OECD, 1999: 16-17.

45. Sebastián Royo, *A New the Century of Corporatism?* (Westport, CT: Praeger, 2002).

46. OECD, 1999: 10-11.

47. OECD, 1999: 11.

48. OECD, 2001: 12.

49. IMF, *World Economic Outlook 2009* (Washington, DC: International Monetary Fund, 2009).

50. OECD, 2006.

51. The system was under strong pressure from the aging population, and also by the high replacement rates granted to pensioners: it was estimated that lack of action would bring the system into deficit by 2007.

52. OECD, 2006.

53. Interview in *Financial Times*, See "On the tipping point of transition," and "Tough cuts to strengthen confidence," in *Financial Times*, April 8, 2008, 1-2 (special section on *Investing in Portugal*).

54. See "Child-free to pay more under Lisbon pension reform," *Financial Times*, May 5, 2006; and "Portugal reducirá las pensiones para evitar la quiebra," *El País*, May 16, 2006.

55. From "Lisbon leads the Union while lagging in performance leagues," *Financial Times*, July 3, 2007, 4.

56. The agreement with MIT provides for long-term collaboration to expand research and education in Portugal in the fields of engineering systems, in areas such as energy, transportation, information systems, and telecommunications. In September of 1996, 160 students started Ph.D.s and other advanced degree programs, which have targeted bio-engineering systems, engineering design, advanced manufacturing, sustainable energy, and transportation systems. The government is investing 80 million Euros in the first five years of the MIT program. More than twenty companies have already signed up to the project's industrial affiliates program. This program illustrates the commitment of the Portuguese government to science and technology, and higher education: it has increased the budget of its ministry by more than 60 percent at a time in which it was cutting expenses in every other ministry. See "Strategic step with lasting impact," in *Financial Times*, 8 April 2008, 4 (special section on *Investing in Portugal*).

57. See "Portugal ingresara 2,4000 millones con la venta de empresas públicas," *El País*, February 20, 2006, and "La nueva cara de Portugal," *El País*, June 29, 2008. It is important to note, however, that some of these initiatives were real investments (Corte Ingles in Gaia, for instance), while others were previous investments (automobile plants in Palmela), and other mere plans (Ave, the new airports).

58. The tax would be applied at a rate of 25 percent on the oil stocks of oil producing and distributing companies. The oil tax was expected to raise 100 million Euros in revenues for the government in 2008. In the end, however, declining global oil prices, combined with the fact that Portugal imports most of the oil that it consumes and that it cannot tax producers in other countries, means that the long-term overall impact of this tax is likely to be more modest. In fact, Italian oil companies' profits have been declining, not rising.

59. "Liberando el lastre," *El País*, March 9, 2008, 20(N); "Portugal sufre mal de ojo," *El País*, May 4, 2008, 40(N); and "Un impuesto 'Robin Hood' en Portugal," *El País*, July 20, 2007.

60. Frank Barry, "Economic integration and convergence process in the EU cohesion countries," *Journal of Common Market Studies*. Vol. 41, No. 5 (2003): 1-25.

61. Martin Wolf, "Struggling to tackle bad fiscal behavior," *Financial Times*, April 8, 2008, 1-2 (special section on *Investing in Portugal*).

62. "Concerns about divergence 'overlook ability to change'," interview with Vítor Constancio. Gobernor of the Bank of Portugal in *Financial Times*, May 16, 2008, 2.

63. Interview in *Financial Times*, See "Tough cuts to strengthen confidence," in *Financial Times*, 8 April 2008, 2 (special section on *Investing in Portugal*).

64. "Concerns about divergence 'overlook ability to change'," interview with Vítor Constancio, Gobernor of the Bank of Portugal, *Financial Times*, May 16, 2008, 2.

65. António Goucha Soares, "Portugal: The Incomplete Europeanization" (paper presented at the 2008 Annual Meeting of the American Political Science Association, Boston, MA, August 29, 2008), 5.

66. European Commission, 2008: 111-13.

67. Orlando Abreu, "Portugal's boom and bust: lessons for euro newcomers," *ECFIN Country Focus*, Volume 3, Issue 16 (December 22, 2006): 5.

68. Robert Fishman, "Legacies of Democratizing Reform and Revolution: Portugal and Spain Compared" (paper prepared for presentation at the Annual Meeting of the American Political Science Association, Chicago, IL, September 2004).

69. Sebastián Royo, *Varieties of Capitalism in Spain*. (New York: Palgrave, 2008).

70. Stefan Collignon, "Germany Keeps dancing as the Iceberg Looms," *Financial Times*, January 20, 2009, 13.

71. And prior to them Carlos Solchaga had been in the position between 1995 and 2003.

72. Prior to them Felipe González was Prime Minister for almost fourteen years, between 1982 and 1996.

73. M. Halleberg, R. Strauch and J. von Hagen, "The Design of Fiscal Rules and Forms of Governance in European Union Countries," *ECB Working Paper*, No. 419 (December 2004).

74. OECD, 2006.

75. From "Lisbon leads the Union while lagging in performance leagues," *Financial Times*, July 3, 2007, 4.

76. OECD, 2006: 6.

77. From "Lisbon leads the Union while lagging in performance leagues," *Financial Times*, July 3, 2007, 4.

78. See "Bar raised for home trained talent," *Financial Times*, April 8, 2008, 4 (special section on *Investing in Portugal*).

79. Martin Wolf, "Struggling to tackle bad fiscal behavior," in *Financial Times*, 8 April 2008, 1-2 (special section on *Investing in Portugal*).

80. Guillén, *Rise of Spanish Multinationals*; Ana Teresa Tavares and Aurora Teixeira, eds., *Multinationals, Clusters and Innovation. Does Public Policy Matter?* (New York: Palgrave, 2008).

81. Abreu, "Portugal's boom and bust," 3-4. Other factors such as corruption, or the legal and regulatory frameworks on competition and FDI, may have played a role in explaining economic divergences between both countries. However, the evidence is not very solid. Indeed, according to the latest (2008) World Bank's Governance Indicators on *Control of Corruption*; Portugal was ranked 83 percent and Spain 85 percent; and on *Regulatory Quality* Portugal was ranked 84 percent and Spain 88 percent.

82. Martin Wolf, "Struggling to tackle bad fiscal behavior," *Financial Times*, April 8, 2008, 1-2 (special section on *Investing in Portugal*).

83. See Martin Wolf, "Britain Must Get to Grips with Lackluster Productivity Growth," *Financial Times*, November 8, 2005.

References

"Emu@10: Successes and challenges after 10 years of Economic and Monetary Union," *Mimeo*, Brussels, May 7, 2008.

Royo, Sebastián, "The Challenges of EU Integration: Iberian Lessons for Eastern Europe," in Joaquín Roy and Roberto Domínguez, eds., *Towards the Completion of Europe*, Miami: Jean Monnet EU Chair, University of Miami, 2006.

———. "Portugal, Espanha e a União Europeia" in *Relações Internacionais*. No. 9, 2006a.

Royo, Sebastián and Paul C. Manuel, eds. *Spain and Portugal in the European Union*. London: Frank Cass, 2003.

World Bank, *Governance Matters VIII: Governance Indicators for 1996-2008* (Washington, DC: World Bank, 2008).

9 Consolidating Partnerships: History and Geopolitics in Portugal's Twenty-First Century Foreign Policy

Teresa de Almeida Cravo[1]

Portuguese foreign policy in the twenty-first century flows directly from the major political opening that followed the end of the dictatorship in 1974. Post-Revolution governments have sought thereafter to reverse Portugal's legacy of isolationism and reengage with world affairs while redefining the country's national identity. Despite its status as a small and peripheral state, the country's historical role as a former European colonial power fueled pretentions to global influence. In rethinking Portugal's position and role in the international arena, the political elite have sought to increase the country's external standing beyond that expected of a small state with limited internal resources.

In pursuing a larger presence on the world stage, Portugal has been guided by two fundamental realist principles: managing partnerships to avoid overdependence and countering exclusion from centers of international decision-making. These two overarching concerns have served, on the one hand, to safeguard the state's sovereign independence and, on the other, to meet a perceived need to redefine itself as a Euro-Atlantic country. Imbued with a certain sense of "geopolitical fate,"[2] Portuguese external ambitions have steered the country toward pursuing, in particular, rapprochement with Europe, reinforcement of relations with the United States, and renewal of ties with the Portuguese-speaking world.

Admission to the European Community (EC)[3] rapidly became the country's primary foreign policy goal, displacing all others in terms of both human resources and financial priorities. After decades of rejection, Portugal was now finally ready to embrace its European identity. Membership in the Community would bolster the country's new-born democracy and provide a source of much needed financial aid to modernize the state. At the same time, relations with the United States received renewed impetus. Aligning with the superpower represented an indispensable security safeguard and would serve to enhance the country's international standing.

Portugal's former empire, a signal of weakness in the immediate aftermath of decolonization, has more recently been leveraged to strengthen the country's special ties beyond the North Atlantic. After years of indecision and discomfort, Portugal has "put history to good use" to rebuild broken relations and recover neglected ones. In this context, the Portuguese-speaking African Countries (PALOP)—Angola, Cape Verde, Guinea-Bissau, Mozambique, and São Tomé e Príncipe—receive special attention, as do Brazil and East Timor.

How does Portugal take advantage of these relationships in order to play a larger role in international affairs? This chapter seeks to analyze Lisbon's foreign policy toward the EU, the United States, and the Lusophone countries, in order to understand how these three dimensions interrelate and shape Portugal's profile in the world in its transition to a new century. It argues that, for a small state like Portugal, investing concomitantly in these three main foreign policy dimensions has promoted the expansion of the country's status in the international theater. This three-tiered strategy overcomes the inevitable vulnerability resulting from dependence on a single ally. Garnering more than one close partner on which the country can rely fulfills two goals simultaneously: where interests align, a symbiotic relationship is created, which buttresses Portugal's global weight and relevance; where interests conflict, multiple connections allow the country to juggle partners—goals otherwise foreclosed can thus be pursued. In short, a multiplicity of significant partners allows Portugal, as we shall see below, to both resist and bring to bear pressure in order to turn situations to its favor.

Viewed by many as "one of Western Europe's most introverted and unassuming countries," as the *New York Times* put it recently,[4] Portugal nonetheless has an unexpectedly active and wide-ranging foreign policy. And yet, a decade into the twenty-first century, cracks are appearing in the national consensus as policy choices are increasingly questioned. Moreover, the advantageous balance struck between the three pillars—Europe, the United States, and the Lusophone world—has been precarious at times, with Portugal's decision to side with one partner creating tensions with others. How these patterns will evolve in the coming years remains uncertain. For now, the political elite's perception of Portugal's national interest encourages a realist approach to international relations and discourages efforts to craft a more progressive foreign policy.

A Small State Yet a Former Empire

For a traditional outlook on international relations, size matters. A large territory and population, high GDP, natural resource wealth, or a strong military are perceived as advantages and the necessary basis for playing an influential role in world affairs. On this view, size reflects might. The quantitative measurement of individual states' attributes informs a qualitative assessment of their power within the interstate system. Physical characteristics are translated into power, which in turn underpins predictable state behavior. Powerful states thus garner sufficient means to achieve their goals and are capable of influencing the international arena to conform to their preferred outcomes.

Conversely, a small state,[5] given its limited resources, has a necessarily narrow international potential and is considered to be inexorably handicapped in acting in an "anarchical" system. Smallness therefore means powerlessness—hence the interchangeable use of "small" and "weak" states in much of the literature. Countries placed under these categories are depicted as less able to influence, much less determine, the international setting. As Keohane puts it, "for these small, 'system-ineffectual' states, foreign policy is adjustment to reality, not rearrangement of it."[6] They lack human and financial resources for foreign policy in terms of the country's administration and bureaucracy, and have consequently a low external profile. Small states thus tend to have a small impact on international affairs. They are assumed to have a limited functional and geographical range of interests—mostly local and regional, as opposed to universal, like great powers—and are also expected to have low levels of foreign activity.[7] They will generally also need assistance to survive and navigate the system and are thus externally dependent on other actors and vulnerable to the volatility of the international environment.

Size and power are, however, relative, not absolute; as concepts they depend on a comparison with the international arena as a whole. Both "small states and great powers are mutually constitutive"—without one the system could not have the other.[8] The smallness or greatness of a country is thus contestable and mutable. In reality, the appellation of the small can reflect a considerably arbitrary attempt to define the state.[9] The predominant realist view of an "anarchic world" has made small states look weaker than might actually be the case. There are, in fact, opportunities as well as constraints facing small states in the contemporary world, as we shall see in the example of Portugal below. On many occasions, small states' influence "turns out to be much greater than any inventory of its internal resources would suggest."[10]

What diverse strategies do small states have at their disposal to overcome their weaknesses? First, many advocate for the formal equality of states in order to restrain the arbitrariness of the international system. Their internal security is guaranteed through the promotion of a favorable international order—one which respects every state's formal sovereignty and independence, regardless of size or might. In addition, membership in international organizations is usually a route pursued by small states, representing a means to participate in global governance at low costs. A limited resource base demands that small states search for the least costly forms of interaction with the outside world in defense of what they perceive to be their national interests. This leads most to take part in multilateral diplomacy through international and regional organizations, as opposed to bilateral diplomacy. Multilateral fora and partnerships also provide a means to resist direct pressure from a larger power.[11]

A second approach for a state unable to guarantee its own security and survival is the creation of alliances. Alliances add to the political and material resources upon which the state can effectively rely by allowing it to summon a protecting power. Protection, however, can demand a high price in terms of autonomy or even sovereignty.[12] One way to cope with such costs of dependence is to pursue multiple allies which can balance one another, rather than relying on only one.

A third, more drastic option available to a small state is integration into a system attuned to its national interests. This allows it to mediate and attempt to shape what otherwise often amounts to foreign determination of its affairs. The small state can thus increase its leverage from the inside, albeit with varying degrees of success.

All these solutions are means through which small states seek to exercise influence over other states' decisions by which they will regardless be affected. Each state develops its own combination of techniques to turn less than ideal circumstances to its advantage. Success is by no means guaranteed, and from a realist perspective, the status of small states within the interstate system remains precarious, contingent on dynamics largely beyond their control.[13] However, despite limited room to maneuver in the international decision-making process, the position and behavior of a small state on the world stage are not static, and the style and substance of its foreign policy will vary depending on context. In fact, historically, a number of small states "provide examples of Lilliputian success."[14]

Portugal broadly fits the "small state" vulnerability scenario: it has a small territory and a small population, it is not particularly rich in terms of natural resources, and it is economically and militarily weak.[15] According to the small states literature, the prospects for a significant role in the international system are thus rather dim. And yet, at a time when it was marginalized by the European powers, Portugal defied its peripheral status: maritime enterprise in the fifteenth and sixteenth centuries granted it a permanent prominence in world history. Today, Portugal continues to draw on its historical role to leverage a global range of interests and options otherwise inaccessible to a country of its size and power. Thus, Portugal, in contrast to other small states, has a "universal foreign policy."[16] Of course, given a shortage of staff, expertise, and financial resources, Portugal is only proactive in those sectors it perceives to be of great importance, remaining reactive in all others; however, its geographical range extends beyond the merely local or regional.[17]

In addition, the country's strategic location—probably its main asset—has been instrumental in Portugal's quest for international status. Its geographical position as Europe's western-most country has encouraged it, for centuries, to diversify its range of interests. It was the base from which to launch expansion toward the African, Asian, and American continents, and it has traditionally provided the world's great powers with a key gateway into Europe.[18] Indeed, the strategic value of the mainland and the archipelagos in the Atlantic Ocean—Azores and Madeira—makes the country geopolitically relevant. With its Economic Exclusion Zone—the third largest in the EU and the eleventh in the world—Portugal controls a major transportation crossroads and refueling point, essential during peacetime and war alike. The Second World War and the 1973 Yom Kippur war illustrated the territory's importance for mounting a large-scale resupply operation for Europe, the Mediterranean, or the Gulf. Where maritime control of the Atlantic or management of shipping routes is necessary, Portugal's cooperation remains essential.[19] This has long assured the country a bargaining chip and a way to guarantee its interests are taken into account.

Overall, Portugal's participation in world politics is disproportionate to its size, population, and military and economic power. A quantitative assessment of its internal resources would not predict this active external policy. Although Portugal is not a strong international actor, it is nonetheless a relevant one in world affairs. Indeed, its international profile has expanded especially dramatically in the past three decades.

The relative success of its foreign policy is all the more striking when one considers the country's international standing on the eve of the Revolution. Seeking to preserve its colonial empire throughout the dictatorship, Portugal limited its closest ties to Spain, Britain, and the United States. Much of the rest of the world boycotted relations with Portugal, especially once the country became involved in a long and protracted colonial war, from 1961 until 1974, in Angola, Guinea-Bissau, and Mozambique. Significant isolation followed, deliberate as well as imposed,[20] with Portugal engaging only with the outside world to the extent needed for the regime's survival.

If the maintenance of the colonies had excluded Portugal from international decision-making, the post-dictatorial government used decolonization to open a range of diplomatic possibilities. Integration into the world community became the primary concern. Engagement with international organizations and reestablishment of contact with as many countries as possible was the first step and allowed Portugal to diversify its external relations. In particular, interaction within the context of major organizations, such as the UN, served to broaden horizons and connections and quickly enhance the country's international profile.

Nevertheless, doubts over the specific direction the country should take and which external ties it should pursue led to a moment of crisis and ambiguity. Indeed, the period immediately after the fall of the dictatorship was characterized by confrontation between the competing interests of different groups, which was reflected in the country's foreign policy. These groups espoused the common goal of rejecting the dictatorship's legacies of colonialism and isolation, but initially diverged on the strategic options to be pursued.[21] As Severiano Teixeira describes, "a silent battle over the objectives and strategic options of the country's foreign policy underlay the noisy struggles of the internal democratization process."[22]

The ideological split was soon resolved with the preponderance of the political elite identifying Portugal as a Euro-Atlantic nation with a global role.[23] Favored by the population and perceived as geopolitically inevitable, this identity as a "Western state" garnered sufficient support to dictate the country's future orientation and has hitherto guided Portuguese foreign policy.

In addition to favoring interaction with major multilateral organizations—a common strategy among small states—Portugal also directed its main efforts more narrowly. Integration with Europe, a strengthened alliance with the United States, and renewed ties with the Portuguese-speaking world were prioritized. As Portugal enters the twenty-first century, its challenge is to link these three main vectors. The following sections explain how Lisbon has pursued and balanced these pillars of foreign policy and sought to craft a coherent strategy to enhance the country's standing in the international arena.

The Return to Europe

The European Community lay an unreachable distance from Portugal through much of the dictatorship. The colonial empire, and the attendant rhetoric of an "Atlantic vocation," had justified turning the country's back to Europe for half a century. Moreover, international repudiation of Salazar's colonial policies prevented the country from acceptance by its European peers. Thus, the end of forty-eight years of autocratic rule ushered in a dramatic transition not only from authoritarianism to democracy and rejection of conformity with international norms, but also one from isolationism to integration.

Mário Soares of the Socialist Party (PS), who led the post-revolution foreign policy, had nurtured contacts with Europe since the late 1960s[24] and received financial and political support from fellow socialist parties. This cooperation strengthened the party's support for the renewed engagement with Europe.[25]

It also contributed to making European integration not only a viable but also a desired option, defeating those forces within the revolutionary elite which favored ties with the Soviet bloc or non-alignment. Power shifted toward the political center after 1976, bringing Portugal definitively into the European orbit. From that point, a European future became the indisputable priority for all subsequent Portuguese governments. Indeed, the end of the revolutionary period confirmed that Portugal was, and still is, geopolitically part of "the West."[26]

For the next three decades, Europe was to replace the colonial empire as the main force driving the country's foreign policy. Until its accession, the locus of decisions impacting Portugal lay outside the country and beyond its influence. Its capacity to exert pressure over policies which affected the country was minimal or even non-existent.[27] Lisbon wished, understandably, to take part in the decision-making process in Brussels and influence it in its favor: participation in the European decision-making process was an inherent benefit of accession. Moreover, the continent was appealing on a second front: engagement with Europe would assure full transition to democracy and help the country modernize. The post-1974 governance was thus eager to turn fully toward the European horizon; meeting requirements for EC membership and garnering the necessary popular support at home quickly became priorities.

In order to surmount the country's severe economic weaknesses, Lisbon needed access to funds that would allow it to modernize and catch up with Europe's most developed states. The turbulence which followed the revolutionary period had impacted the Portuguese economy, dramatically increasing inflation, public deficit, and unemployment. In light also of centuries of backwardness and underdevelopment relative to Europe's core, the benefits of integration, with its promise of economic development, provided valuable ammunition to Europhiles and acted as a "catalyst for change."[28]

Portugal's European accession, though, was not only driven by the need to improve its economic performance; it was also political. Approaching the EU would require overcoming the country's political fragilities as a young democracy but would also earn Europe's support during this inevitably volatile transitional phase. Portugal had, since 1960, been a founding member of EFTA, its membership motivated largely by economic advantages. Membership in the EC, by way of contrast, represented a qualitative step into the European political and cultural realms.[29]

Portugal's gravitation toward the Community also offered a means to compensate, at least partially, for the country's inevitable decline as an international actor following the loss of its empire in the midst of the Cold War. It was also a springboard for the redefinition of Portugal's ambitions on the world stage. Intending to increase the country's influence at a global scale, Lisbon sought to take advantage of its geography, which made relations with Europe, as well as with the United States, a "quasi-given."[30] The government thus began developing ties with other European countries. Against the discourse of autarky voiced

by the dictatorship, the new post-Revolution elite embraced a discourse of interdependence, pointing to Europe as the solution for (and the means to overcome)
the loss of the empire. The loss of national autonomy as a consequence of integration was minimized by recourse to the promised gains the country would
extract through membership. In this sense, Europe was interestingly both instrumentalized and, simultaneously, idealized. The Portuguese public, for its
part, was convinced.

Europe, on the other hand, was generally welcoming of Portugal's accession, in spite of difficulties encountered throughout the negotiation process. Existing members were interested in proving the Community's capacity to deal
with its "natural space," expanding its stability, peace, and economic prosperity
to other countries within its sphere of influence.

Negotiations started in 1977, when Portugal formally requested to join the
EC, and, surprisingly, lasted until 1985, when both Portugal and Spain finally
became members. The reason for such prolonged negotiations lay with Spain
and the resistance on the part of countries like France and Germany to its accession, for fear of resulting competition with their internal agricultural market.
Portugal attempted several times to have its application considered separately
from Spain but was unsuccessful. Europe was more inclined to deal with the
Peninsula as a whole and begin this new phase of membership with a dual accession. Confronted with hesitation from Member States, and seeking to demonstrate the country's other foreign policy options, the Portuguese government
declared, in 1983, that it had other alternatives to the Common Market, such as
Africa, the United States, and Latin America.[31] Nonetheless, Portugal, and
Spain, finally signed the Treaty of Accession on June 12,1985.

During the first decade of membership, the positive impact and the benefits
resulting from accession to the restricted EC club were visible and sustained
favorable public opinion toward Europe. Indeed, with integration, the Portuguese rapidly became "mainstream Europeans."[32] The economic impact of
membership in the first decade was remarkable. Qualification for Brussels'
structural funds allowed Portugal to receive between three and four percent of its
annual GDP and up to 42 percent of its public investment from European funding.[33] Trade with European countries increased significantly, as did foreign investment in the country. Portuguese per capita income rose from 56 percent to
74 percent of the EU average up until the late 1990s. As a result, Portuguese
opinion of European membership increased dramatically between 1980 and
1991, from 24 to 71 percent, respectively.[34] In 1999, Portugal gave a clear signal
of its successful "catching up" by meeting the requirements to enter the first
group of the European Monetary Union (EMU).[35]

At the decision-making level, Portugal was finally able to exert influence,
namely by voting, on European policies which affected the country. This represented Portugal's return to European high politics, after centuries of both deliberate and imposed absence. Portugal's foreign policy was refined as a result of

the integration process. As a member of a system deeply engaged in world affairs, Lisbon took the opportunity to expand its external objectives beyond traditional areas and both enlarge and deepen the scope of its foreign activities.[36] Portugal was a staunch advocate of a maximalist approach, which sought to enhance the Community's external profile and performance. Indeed, as Vasconcelos points out, "were the EU to revert to the stage of a mere market, albeit huge, Portugal would be little more than a poor relation."[37] On the contrary, in the context of a more proactive Europe, Lisbon has a better chance of meeting its own foreign policy goals and raising its profile in the world arena. Joining the EU represented thus an added value to Portugal's place in international life, allowing the country to build on synergies that were favorable to the pursuit of its perceived national interests. This was reflected, for instance, in the "Mediterraneazation" of Portugal's foreign affairs: once limited to close relations with Morocco at the time of its accession, Portuguese external relations were significantly expanded, within the European framework, to the rest of the Mediterranean.[38]

Another of Portugal's greatest strengths which benefited from the country's participation in the EC was its relation with the Lusophone world. Historical ties with its former colonies allowed it to assert a unique identity and enhance its influence in agenda-setting within the European framework. On the one hand, Portugal's traditional focus on "southern" countries shaped the Union's political orientation, which increased its scope to encompass in a more systematic way all Lusophone countries; on the other, Portugal "Europeanized" its Lusophone policies, bringing them into the European arena. Portugal found, after decades of international isolation, new possibilities to act and so did the EU, profiting from Portugal's historical ties.

Portugal's accession—with its potential and actual world connections—had a considerable impact on the EU's foreign policy, which significantly enhanced and deepened external relations with these countries. On their part, Lusophone states were pleased to have in Portugal their "special envoy" within the EU. These regions, Latin America and Africa, found a special place within the Union which had, thus far, remained unreachable for them. In what concerns the former, Portugal not only added an appendix to their accession treaties on developing the EC relationship with Latin America,[39] it took advantage of its EC Presidency in 1992 to make this sub-region a niche of Europe's foreign interests. Moreover, at the first ever EU-Brazil summit in 2007, organized during its third EC Presidency, Portugal presented itself as a "natural partner," essential to redress the absence of a regular and privileged dialogue between the EU and the largest country in Latin America. It further sponsored Brazil's entrance to the restricted club of EU's "strategic partners."[40]

During its two presidencies, Portugal also organized the only two EU-Africa summits, in Cairo in 2000 and in Lisbon in 2007. Despite poor results, "Portugal managed to fulfill its objective of focusing European attentions on a continent with which it has strategic historical connections and thus reinforce its vocation as a mediator between one and the other."[41] These summits, both considered top priorities of Portuguese presidencies, materialized one of the main goals of Lisbon's foreign policy: to affirm Portugal as a historical partner of Brazil and Africa, and as a privileged intermediary in the external relations between the Lusophone countries and the EU.

Portugal has also paid special attention to the compatibility between the promotion of a more active EU and the other anchors of its foreign policy, namely the country's special relationship with the U.S. Lisbon remains a vocal advocate of NATO and U.S. roles in European security. Portugal became a Western European Union (WEU) member in 1988—the European face of mutual defense—yet has always sought to prevent the development of a European defense identity at the expense of NATO's presence in the continent. Lisbon considers the Alliance the most important security arrangement in Europe, since it assures Portuguese-Atlantic ties with the superpower and prevents overdependence on the security interests of Europe's largest states.[42] As a result, it opposes the group led by France, which has pushed for a European defense more autonomous from the United States. As Ambassador José Cutileiro, who served as the Portuguese secretary general to the WEU (1994-1999) made clear, the organization is subsidiary to NATO, acting only in crises where North America does not wish to intervene.[43] Portugal therefore only supports the reinforcement of Europe's own defense capabilities when compatible with U.S. strategic interests and with the maintenance of the Atlantic Alliance dominance.[44]

Another cornerstone of Portugal's foreign relations within the European framework is its relationship with Spain. One of the most dramatic changes brought about by Portugal's accession to the European Community was indeed the rapport between the two Iberian countries; a relationship long based on mistrust and lack of knowledge.[45] Spain has historically represented the largest external threat to Portugal's security and independence. Simultaneous peninsular integration into Europe, though not planned, has helped improve interconnection and mutual understanding. In particular, joint involvement of Portugal and Spain in European institutions has allowed for the resolution, or at least "decompression," of delicate issues at the center of the two countries' relations, such as river management, fisheries, and regional cooperation. Indeed, relations between the two countries are no longer difficult, even if matters of disagreement—along with a certain anxiety on the part of Lisbon—still persist.

Despite the rapprochement of the last years, there is still nothing that would resemble an "Iberian identity."[46] Portugal's attachment to its sovereignty and national identity remains as vivid as before, notwithstanding the strong participation in the European institutions. Moreover, the obvious imbalance in size, population, and power between the two countries remains a source of inquietude. Portugal still perceives itself as vulnerable to Spanish economic penetration, although the counterbalancing game is now officially played inside institutions like the EU and NATO.

Portugal has sought to emphasize the distinction between the two countries.[47] Being clumped together with its big neighbor would only mean reducing its capacity to affirm the country's autonomy and have its voice heard when in disagreement with Spain. Portugal does not want the outside world to perceive "Iberia" as a single unit, since, given the considerable differences at every level of the states' capabilities, the center of decision would inevitably belong to Madrid, to Lisbon's detriment.

In several instances, however, both countries' goals within the Union converge, and it is possible to present a unified position to the remaining European partners. The EU's policies toward the Mediterranean, the Maghreb, and Latin America, for instance, have allowed for common demands and proposals to come from the Peninsula. Both countries also have a vested interest in preventing a shift of attention, policy, and funding from the South to the East. Nevertheless, notwithstanding significant converging positions on many issues, Portugal has made clear this convergence is the result of negotiations between peers, and not the reflection of a unity which surpasses the countries' differences.

This distinction is particularly visible at the institutional level, where Portugal struggles to defend small countries' positions and where Spain struggles to become one of the larger Member States.[48] Indeed, Lisbon's apprehension of European institutional reform directly concerns its relations with Spain. It was simultaneous integration into the EC and the equal standing both countries enjoy within its framework that has allowed the normalization and significant improvement of relations. "When the Portuguese government stresses that the current institutional balance should be preserved, one of its major concerns is the maintenance of an equilibrium of Portuguese and Spanish participation in the European process."[49]

Presently, two concerns remain paramount to the Portuguese strategy within the European context: ensuring that the institutional evolution is favorable to small states and preventing the enlargement to the East from diminishing Portugal's impact in the formulation of the Union's domestic and foreign agenda.

In regard to the first concern, Lisbon is worried it may lose influence in the Union's decision-making process if this is reformed to benefit large and populous countries and thus opposes a directory of powerful states from which it would inevitably be excluded. In this type of European politics, based on great power concert, Portugal has no space. It would be marginalized, as occurred previously in past centuries, after it declined as a world power into an underdeveloped country, when it ultimately chose to isolate itself and turn its back to the continent in which it felt it could not participate. Portugal feels "the clubbishness of the old guard keenly."[50] The country was long relegated to the "geographical and political 'corner' of Europe" and will resist a "two-speed Europe" which would most likely place Portugal in the rear group.[51]

Hence, Lisbon has repeatedly joined other small states in voicing demands and pressing for fair rules and democratic governance of the Union. This foreign policy goal toward the European framework manifests itself in two institutional designs: the voting system and evolution toward a supranational structure. Given the voting system's importance for the decision-making process in Brussels, Portugal is understandably in favor of unanimity, as opposed to majority rule. Lisbon insists that each country's profile in the international arena is not necessarily related to its size and power. The qualified majority voting system applied to community matters (which inevitably expresses the power differential within the Union) should not be expanded to the foreign policy pillar, thus allowing each country to retain its influence over decisions.[52] Portugal fought to keep the European Political Cooperation (created in 1970) and, its successor, the Common Foreign and Security Policy (created in 1993), which coordinates the Community's external relations, consensual in order to safeguard its national interests in the external domain.[53]

For similar reasons, Lisbon is also opposed to the development of a supranational structure. Fearing "the institutionalization of differences," it favors a Union which retains its intergovernmental nature whereby states, regardless of their size and might, retain veto power and control decisions that will affect them.[54]

The process finally culminating in the signing of the Lisbon Treaty—during a Portuguese presidency—illustrated the persistent divergence between Member States on the question of what a future European Union should look like. As President Sarkozy declared, this new treaty "solves Europe's institutional crisis, but not its moral and political crisis."[55] This period of uncertainty is bound to be compensated by the gradual affirmation of a directory composed of France, Germany and the United Kingdom, in terms of CFSP, and contrary to small states' ability to participate.[56] Facing the strengthening of Europe's "hard core," which inevitably reinforces the exclusion of those Member States at the margins, Portugal has tried hard to become part of the leading group. It did so successfully when it managed to be part of the first group entering the EMU, but has been far from successful since then and is today further from this goal than a decade ago.

In regard to the second concern, Portugal is afraid that the current geographical shift of interest to Central and Eastern European countries marginalizes the Western Mediterranean states and thus has argued in favor of striking a balance to ensure the eastward trend is not made at the expense of the South.[57]

The enlargement and institutional reform represent a difficult challenge for Portugal and will deeply impact the country's space of maneuver within the Union: the weight of its vote has already diminished with the increase to twenty-seven Member States. Moreover, bringing former Soviet satellite states into the EU's orbit risks a diversion of attention, funds, and human resources to these new countries undertaking a complex democratic and economic transition. As

Royo points out, in economic terms, these states compete for structural funds, from which Portugal has benefited for decades and on which it still relies deeply. Foreign investment is being diverted to the new members, given their lower labor costs and higher education levels. Finally, they compete for the same products which make up Portuguese exports, such as textiles and machinery, and have a negative effect on Portuguese competitiveness and export revenues.[58] Portugal's foreign policy has been directed toward negotiating the continuation of the Union's financial commitments throughout this difficult transition, especially at a time of severe economic crisis.

Indeed, when the international crisis of 2008 hit, Portugal was not in any way prepared and felt the blow severely. Yet, economic decadence had started long ago. The first signs that EC membership also had a negative impact were felt immediately after 1991. The country was not prepared for the pressure from opening its borders and Portuguese industry and agriculture suffered from competition from its European partners.[59] The beginning of an economic recession, increasingly visible, opened up political space for nationalist rhetoric against Europe and protectionist movements which "announced the end of the 'golden age' stemming from Portugal's admittance into the EC."[60]

From 1998 onwards, income convergence between Portugal and Europe started to lose pace.[61] This sign of difficult times has become a recurrent theme of opposition speeches against government performance. By 2009, there remained no doubts as to the graveness of Portuguese economic situation.[62] A sharp deterioration of the country's account balance, dramatic decrease of investment and exports, high budget deficits and foreign debt, unsustainable booms in internal demand, along with the country's lack of competitiveness and productivity, signaled a structural problem that had been left unaddressed during the first decade of integration. Economic stagnation from weak growth and unemployment of nearly 10 percent further undermined recovery. In ten years, "far from catching up, Portugal has fallen further behind."[63]

Initially enthusiastic about Portugal's successful integration, analysts are now disenchanted. Portugal went from "good student" to a disappointment, from a common example of "lessons learned" from its successes, to a common example of "lessons learned" from its mistakes. After making it into the vanguard group of the Euro, Portugal has now been labeled one of the so-called "PIGS"— an acronym which stands for the weakest Eurozone countries: Portugal, Ireland, Greece, and Spain. The world's economic crisis has only worsened what were already severe internal problems. Portugal is now particularly concerned with not lagging behind when the world and the European economies eventually recover. The fear that the current gap will widen has reawakened nightmares of castigation as a profligate and imposed distance from that "other Europe" it had so proudly joined.

Aligning with the Superpower

Portugal's "special relationship" with the United States dates from World War II. A first step was taken in 1943, when American and British forces were granted use of the Portuguese island of Terceira, a strategically valuable location for the conduct of air and naval operations in the European theater. This marked the start of a decisive shift in Lisbon's Atlantic relations. Great Britain, hitherto Portugal's primary and oldest ally, still figured prominently in the foreign policy calculus and, indeed, facilitated these early contacts with the United States. Yet there was also a growing recognition in Lisbon that significant political capital would derive from alliance with the rising superpower.

As British naval preeminence declined and post-war American dominance crystallized, Portugal was confronted with the need to reinforce relations with the new Atlantic power.[64] In February 1948, it renewed the *Lajes Agreement*, which extended U.S. rights over the military base in Terceira.[65] That same year, the country was included in the U.S. Marshall Plan to rebuild post-war Europe. Portugal's relationship with the United States has since grown stronger, and while at times waxing and waning, it remains today central to Portuguese foreign relations. It revolves around two central, intertwined pillars: the U.S. base in the Azores (thus ensuring American presence in national territory) and Portuguese membership in NATO.

In the context of the Cold War, the Azores proved a valuable asset. The Portuguese dictator Salazar, though wary of subservience to American demands, quickly sought to take advantage of the archipelago's relevance to Washington's grand scheme for overseas power projection. Concern over Soviet control of the Atlantic ensured Truman's backing for the right wing authoritarian regime. This patronage, in turn, was crucial to Portugal's invitation to be a founding member of NATO in 1949, and ultimately objections over the membership of a non-democratic state were muffled by Portugal's overriding strategic importance.

For Salazar and Portugal, NATO's membership represented an opportunity to legitimize the regime and its colonial policy.[66] The Portuguese leader even sought, unsuccessfully, to have the Portuguese colonies included within NATO's area of responsibility, as France had done with respect to Algeria. Moreover, as Severiano Teixeira rightly points out, "Portugal's inclusion and Spain's exclusion reinforced Lisbon's status on the peninsula and turned Portugal into a privileged interlocutor."[67] In 1951, a new bilateral defense agreement between Lisbon and Washington was signed; in exchange for base rights, Portugal would receive military and economic aid.[68]

Nevertheless, relations soon deteriorated with the start of the colonial wars and vocal criticism of the country's anachronistic colonial policy. Kennedy imposed an embargo on U.S. supplies to NATO that could be used in the colonies.

Salazar, though, could still play "the Azores card" in 1962, when the agreement was renegotiated. The archipelago's strategic value and Portugal's threat of voluntary withdrawal from NATO helped lessen pressure for decolonization. Fearing the impact of a split on alliance unity, Member States moderated criticism and, although NATO never *officially* intervened in the Portuguese colonial war, France and West Germany supplied materiel for Portuguese use in its colonial conflicts.[69]

A change of administration in the United States led to a new rapprochement in U.S.-Portuguese relations. Whereas the Kennedy and Johnson administrations were vocal in their criticism of Portuguese colonial policy, Nixon and Kissinger were more amicable toward the Iberian regime, now led by Caetano following Salazar's death. Less sympathetic to African liberation movements and aspirations for self-determination,[70] the Nixon administration was committed to a "pragmatic" interpretation of U.S. foreign policy in Africa.[71] Not only was Nixon willing to accept a permanent Portuguese presence in Africa, he also provided discreet support to Portugal's military operations.[72] In Nixon, Portugal found a receptive audience for claims for the need for a bulwark against Soviet expansionism in Africa. The Yom Kippur war in 1973—during which the United States used the Azores base to supply Israel—reinforced Portugal's strategic importance and Nixon's determination to support his ally in the face of hostile world opinion.

The Revolution in 1974 represented a moment of turbulence in Portuguese-American relations. The United States was initially reassured by the post-Revolution government's promise to renegotiate the Azores agreement. Portugal's commitment to NATO was not questioned at the time, not even by the Communist Party, since, as Vasconcelos observes, "membership in NATO was considered an unavoidable consequence of our geopolitical fate."[73] As Mário Soares, then Minister of Foreign Affairs, clearly stated, "we affirm our absolute loyalty to the Atlantic Alliance"; "it is not our intention to call it in question."[74]

Soon, however, Portugal's U.S.-centered orientation began to lose its appearance of immutability. The initial anti-fascist alliance proved ephemeral, and Portuguese domestic politics quickly took a leftward turn, highlighted by the performance of the Communist Party. "In a little over a year Portugal swung from being the oldest right-wing dictatorship in Europe to becoming the first European nation since the 1940s where a communist takeover seemed possible."[75] The threat of closer ties with the Soviet Union awoke Washington's fears and relations with the United States started to deteriorate. In Kissinger's eyes, Portugal suggested a new application of the "domino theory": Communist capture of the state would rapidly spread to other European countries, namely those with strong Communist parties, such as Italy, Spain and Greece.[76] Fearing Portugal would become a new Cuba in Europe, Kissinger worked to keep it isolated and contained, while entertaining more aggressive counterrevolutionary alternatives.[77] He also made Portugal an issue in détente conversations, warning of the risk of creating a setback to the process and stating that any interference on the part of the Soviets "in a country which is an old friend and ally of ours is inconsistent with any principle of European security."[78]

United States efforts to isolate post-Revolution Portugal were restrained and countered by Western European optimism in Portugal's democratic future. Western European countries argued that a policy of isolation would be counterproductive and self-defeating, inevitably pushing Portugal toward the Soviet bloc. They thus preferred economic enticement—carrots rather than sticks—to sway the Portuguese internal balance of power in favor of alignment with the West, a policy that was ultimately successful.

With the end of the Cold War and the solidification of American hegemony, Portugal's alignment with the superpower became even stronger. A consensus exists among the country's political and military elite which holds that the United States—and Portugal's alliance with the United States—is essential to Portuguese security. On this view, NATO is not so much a multilateral security arrangement, as essentially an instrument for allying with Washington: an extension of U.S. power in Europe, NATO materializes American security guarantees and institutionalizes Portugal's relations with the great power. In recent years, Portuguese foreign policy has become even more subservient to U.S. interests. Alignment with Washington is now instinctive, and Lisbon's elites have supported American policy quite consistently.

Portugal's determination to demonstrate its reliability was illustrated in 1999 during the Kosovo war. NATO's intervention in Kosovo was contentious: it was a military action undertaken without the UN Security Council's explicit approval (and, *prima facie*, a violation of international law), as well as an "out-of-area" operation. Portugal was nonetheless a vocal supporter of the action, strongly in favor of expanding NATO's sphere of concern beyond the territory of Member States.

There was of course a self-interested motive for Portuguese advocacy of "out-of-area" operations on NATO's perimeter. Such intervention carries with it a greater need for military bases such as the Azores. Increased demand for the Azores base, in turn, emphasizes Portugal's strategic importance to its allies, in particular the United States. Furthermore, Lisbon has a vested interest in using its standing troops abroad, not only in order to maintain their training at low costs, but also as a means to raise the country's international presence and recognition.

And yet, the country's political leaders did not appeal to geopolitical or realist imperatives while selling the intervention to the Portuguese electorate. Rather, NATO action was justified on the basis of moral principles, the war purportedly necessary to halt a humanitarian crisis in the face of UN paralysis. Invoking Western inaction in the Yugoslav wars in the early 1990s, Prime Minister Guterres explained that "We are an Alliance. Have we got an enemy? I think yes. No longer a country, a system, an ideology. . . . Our enemy is extreme nationalism, religious fundamentalism, racism, xenophobia, ethnic cleansing. That is why we are active in Kosovo."[79]

Many Portuguese were unconvinced and opposition to the war was significant; led by two important public figures in Portugal, former President Mário Soares and Freitas do Amaral, former President of the UN General Assembly. These figures noted the absence of a UN mandate and stressed the illegality of the intervention. Their influence on public opinion was palpable: according to polls in April 1999, as much as 63.7 percent of Portuguese opposed NATO's action. Political elites, however, were unmoved; the Communist Party was the only political party which was vocally opposed to siding with NATO partners.[80]

Four years later, with the U.S. led invasion of Iraq in 2003, Portuguese leaders faced a similar divergence between the imperative of alliance with the United States and public opinion. Notwithstanding strong opposition from the majority of the Portuguese population who demonstrated on the streets against the war, the Portuguese government hosted a planning summit with the United States, United Kingdom, and Spain on the Azores military base. The invasion of Iraq began four days later on March 20.[81] In contrast to the earlier Kosovo intervention, the Communists were not alone in loudly opposing the war in Parliament. The left opposition—Socialists, Communists, and Left Bloc—contested Portuguese involvement, and President Sampaio called the war illegitimate for lacking a UN mandate.

In siding with the United States in the Iraq invasion, a number of familiar concerns were at play, most importantly, the need to convince the United States of Portugal's continued strategic importance and the desire to stand out as a prominent and faithful ally. On Lisbon's view, when Europe is divided on whether to align with the United States, Portugal becomes all the more important a partner to Washington. In other words, in the midst of divergence amongst European partners, Portuguese loyalty counts more. In addition, with Spain at the forefront of support for the United States, prominent Portuguese support was all the more relevant. One of the country's main concerns is NATO's and Washington's conduct toward Spain. Portugal wishes to retain the status and the privileges gained as a founding member and keep NATO's command base near Lisbon. For that reason, it fears the consequences of distancing itself from the Alliance's main actor and the eventual replacement by its neighbor as the trustworthy Iberian ally.

The war in Iraq showed how important the relationship with the United States is for Portugal—the country's leaders were willing to endure reproach by major European partners in order to side with its Atlantic ally. Interestingly, Prime Minister Barroso justified Portuguese support for the invasion primarily in terms of the alliance's importance to the country—and not, as had been the case with his predecessor in regards to Kosovo, as a moral imperative. "This meeting in the Azores," he explained, "shows the importance of trans-Atlantic relations, and also shows the solidarity among our countries."[82]

Lisbon was also playing a pre-emptive card, as it suddenly saw itself surrounded by countries even more eager to be Washington's next "favorite" ally. Central and Eastern Europe have courted U.S. support, rendering Portugal (and its military bases) less significant than during the Cold War period, or even the 1990s. This "competition" in the country's relations with the single pole of the post-Cold War world has made Lisbon even more inclined to align with U.S. policies. Indeed, Portuguese support for the U.S. invasion of Iraq is not an isolated case or mere response to Bush's dichotomist threat of "either with us or with the terrorists." What Iraq or Kosovo suggest is Portugal's subscription to and conformity with American power projection in the post-Cold War world.

Other episodes support this view. Lisbon is suspected of collaborating in the Bush administration's rendition activities by allowing alleged stopovers at national airports by secret CIA rendition flights transporting terror suspects in 2004 and 2005.[83] Portugal was the first country to announce, in December 2008, that it was willing to receive prisoners from the U.S. prison at Guantanamo which President Obama has promised to close. Foreign Minister Luís Amado wrote a letter to other EU Member States and declared: "The time has come for the European Union to step forward. As a matter of principle and coherence, we should send a clear signal of our willingness to help the U.S. government in that regard, namely through the resettlement of detainees. As far as the Portuguese government is concerned, we will be available to participate."[84] This gesture, particularly appreciated in Washington, cleared the way for cooperation and led to a resettlement plan in Europe for those prisoners who, for security reasons, could not return to their home countries upon release. In August 2009, two Syrian nationals were transferred from Guantanamo to Portuguese territory. Lisbon has given broad political support to Washington's "War on Terror," even though its material contribution has been more limited, with troops in Afghanistan (105 as of February 2010) and a police force in Iraq (128 in 2003, withdrawn in 2005).[85]

Six centuries ago, Portugal's primary concern was loss of sovereignty at the hands of Spanish invasion—this motivated its alliance with Britain and the 1386 Treaty of Windsor. Today, contemporary international relations are less existentially dangerous for this European country. Lisbon's alliance with the superpower is therefore no longer primarily a response to immediate defense concerns. But nor is it simply a consequence of Portugal's membership in NATO. Rather, Portugal actively seeks to contribute to the construction and maintenance of a U.S.-led world order. As Walt points out, with the advent of unipolarity, weaker states "can (1) ally with each other to try to mitigate the unipole's influence, (2) align with the unipole in order to support its actions or exploit its power for their own purposes, or (3) remain neutral."[86] Lisbon feels comfortable in a world where U.S. power is predominant, benefiting from its close relationship with the hegemon. It is not threatened by American unilateralism and finds no reason to contribute to efforts to counterbalance the United States or to remain neutral. In so far as the unipole seeks to maintain the status quo—and thus its hegemonic position—Portugal, along with other smaller allies, contributes to sustaining and reproducing the current imbalance of power.

The possibility of corroding relations with the United States is perceived by Portuguese leaders as a source of great vulnerability—too great to be risked by taking stands contrary to U.S. policies at a given moment. Moreover, partnership with the United States also balances Portugal's relative unimportance in the European context: the stronger its relations with the superpower, the more leverage it gains within the continent. Following a realist approach, Portuguese governments have successively decided embracing American patronage bears more fruits than questioning it, even in the face of tension and disagreement, international law, or ethical problems—hence why recent Portuguese governments have been so unreservedly pro-American and will probably remain so in the near future.

Reconnecting with the Lusophone World

The Lusophone world has always held a special place at the heart of Portuguese foreign policy. Emotional attachment and instrumental interests seem to be intertwined in the perception of Portuguese-speaking countries as a "natural" space of interaction, where the former metropolis can expect a certain degree of familiarity and mutual understanding conducive to the establishment of beneficial relations. As with Britain or France—although not to the same extent— long-term family, cultural, political, and economic ties have underpinned this privileged bond between Lisbon and its former colonies. In a world divided in historical spheres of influence, Portugal was able to carve out a space in which it could seek to realize its foreign policy goals.

The reality, in the aftermath of the Revolution, proved, however, more complicated than the myth of an inevitable and spontaneous connection would have us think. Ranging from difficult interactions with the Portuguese-speaking African countries (PALOPs) throughout the 1970s, to nearly complete disconnection with East Timor while under Indonesian occupation, and a near absence of institutionalized relations with Brazil, Portugal took some time to extricate its colonial problems and redefine its role within this geographical space.

The dynamics and the inherent turbulence of the Portuguese revolutionary process had complicated the former African colonies' negotiated and "orderly" transitions to independence. The wounds resulting from the thirteen-year colonial war, along with the panicked and resentful exit of hundreds of thousands of Portuguese, left deep scars on both sides.[87] Mistrust prevailed and Lisbon's endeavors to formulate a coherent post-decolonization African policy were met with suspicion. Answering a question at a press conference on the possibility of creating a Luso-Afro-Brazilian community, Mário Soares stated the idea "had very unpleasant connotations for Africans, because they feel, when one speaks of such a community, that it is an attempt to establish, even if indirectly, a neo-colonialist situation in relation to their territories." He went on to say that the nationalist movements were "really allergic to formulas of that kind."[88] These problems were compounded by the Cold War and the regional context at the time: the involvement of the United States, the Soviet Union, Cuba, and apartheid South Africa in Angola and Mozambique left little room for Portuguese maneuver. Moreover, Europe came first in any calculation of the post-1974 governments, which made it difficult to place the newly independent states on the agenda. What had once been the "African vocation" was clearly marginalized in favor of the recently rediscovered "European vocation," which garnered the majority of attention, time, and resources. The pursuit of substantive relations between those countries once connected by the same rule was, hence, postponed.

It was not until the mid-1980s that perceptions and interests began to change, and relations finally normalized. By then, despite the absence of an institution to structure and further economic ties between Portugal and its former African colonies,[89] commerce between them—fostered mainly by individual entrepreneurship—had quadrupled, remaining favorable to the former colonial power.[90] Public opinion has proved very sensitive to the fate of the PALOPs. As had happened with other European metropolises, the imperial impetus for engaging with Africa was transformed into a discourse of responsibility and duty to help stabilize and develop the new sovereign states—a sentiment shared by both the general population and the elite, thus constituting an effective ideological foundation for mobilizing the necessary resources when the time came to delineate a coherent policy. A change of government from the Socialists, with a record of tense relations with the Liberation leaders, to the Social-Democrats, on the center-right, removed the last obstacle for rapprochement with the former colonies.[91]

The end of the Cold War opened a space ultimately conducive to more active Portuguese intervention. Attempts to negotiate the conflicts in Angola and Mozambique presented an opportunity for Lisbon's foreign policy to exhibit its comparative advantage over other countries. Capitalizing on a long common history, Portugal sent its diplomats to pave the way for negotiations, and at the same time, shine on the international stage. The personal involvement of the then Secretary of State for Foreign Affairs and Cooperation, José Manuel Durão Barroso, in the mediation of the Bicesse Accords in Angola (1991),[92] as well as Lisbon's role as an official observer of the Rome Accords (which put an end to the Mozambican conflict in 1992) are examples of how vested Portugal was, by then, in playing up its relevance as a former colonial power.

Also in the early 1990s, East Timor, a former Portuguese colony in Southeast Asia, became an international human rights issue. At the time of the Revolution, Portugal had entertained several options regarding the fate of this small territory miles away from the metropolis: maintenance of Portuguese rule with comprehensive autonomy, peaceful incorporation into Indonesia, and outright independence (although the latter was by and large considered unrealistic). Portugal was concerned that its sovereignty over the territory be respected, and that the right to self-determination of the East Timorese be assured. This was seen as a way of demonstrating the democratic nature of the post-Revolution regime. When Indonesia invaded and forcefully annexed East Timor on December 7, 1975, Lisbon broke diplomatic relations with Jakarta and brought the issue before the UN. Portugal, however, was incapable of reacting militarily or reversing the situation, and for the next decade, its foreign policy largely accepted the incorporation as a "fait accompli."[93]

Membership in the EC changed the balance of power. Vetoing the Community's decisions concerning Indonesia and putting the settlement of the East Timorese conflict on the agenda made Jakarta more willing to negotiate.[94] The Santa Cruz Massacre in 1991, which placed the East Timorese strife and Indonesia's widespread human rights abuses in the media spotlight, finally provided the window of opportunity Portugal was waiting for. Supported by moral outrage at both the international and domestic levels, and arguing how clear East Timorese rejection of integration with Indonesia had become, Lisbon acted swiftly and pressured its European partners and the United States to force Indonesia to the negotiation table. Portugal also instrumentalized its position as President of the EC from January to June 1992 to loudly advocate for the East Timorese right to self-determination. In addition to a surprisingly active stance on the part of its hitherto dormant diplomacy, Portugal further profited from the awarding of the 1996 Nobel Peace Prize to the symbols of the East Timorese resistance—Ramos Horta and Ximenes Belo—which brought international prominence to their cause.[95] The economic decadence of the Suharto regime and its replacement by the elected Habibie saw Indonesia ultimately cave into Portuguese demands for negotiations in August 1998, which culminated in the May 1999 New York agreements.

After twenty-five years, 78.5 percent of East Timorese were finally able to choose independence in a referendum held in August 1999. This, however, was followed by a grim period of violence at the hands of militias supported by the Indonesian army. Portugal voiced the international outcry—which demanded protection for the population and turned to its strongest ally—even threatening to leave NATO's operation in Kosovo in order to get Washington's support for a UN peace enforcement mission.[96] Diplomatic and political pressure from both Portugal and Australia was ultimately successful in sending a UN mission, INTERFET, to the territory. In 2002, East Timor became the first newly independent state of the twenty-first century. The East Timorese chose to adopt Portuguese as their official language, along with Tetum, thus expanding the number of Portuguese-speaking countries in the world.

Portugal had nothing to lose and only to gain in this particular endeavor of its foreign policy. Moreover, it was an excellent opportunity to act where national interests and values came together: recovering Portuguese influence in a former colony went hand in hand with defending an emotional attachment most Portuguese felt with the East Timorese and a strong sense of responsibility for their fate. Having garnered this consensus, it became a matter of deploying Lisbon's diplomatic apparatus, which, quite efficiently, rose to the occasion.

The 1990s became the decisive decade for Portugal's determined involvement with its Lusophone counterparts. A combination of popular support for rebuilding historically special ties, and economic elites looking to explore the potential of new markets, led Lisbon to strengthen and institutionalize both its bilateral and multilateral relations with this part of the world. Interest and predisposition, therefore, have generated a national consensus within Portuguese public opinion in support of the construction of a Lusophone community. Media, universities, NGOs, business, political parties, and human rights activists have all extensively promoted strong cooperation between Portuguese-speaking countries.[97]

Originally a Brazilian initiative, the CPLP, created in 1996, tapped into this Lusophone identity, based mostly on shared language, history, and interests, similar to that of the Commonwealth or the Francophonie.[98] A cohesion born of cultural affinities and the desire to promote the language manifested itself in common political goals: firstly, encouraging more intense relations amongst its members; and secondly, engaging with the international system from a stronger position, to be initially concerted at the CPLP level, and later presented internationally as a platform for further negotiations. This was particularly visible, for instance, at the time of Portugal's (1997-1998, 2011-2012), Brazil's (1998-1999, 2004-2005, 2010-2011), and Angola's (2003-2004) bids for the United Nations Security Council as non-permanent members. By pursuing together as a group, foreign policy goals in each other's interest, these countries manage to gain support for their projects and enhance their weight on the international scene.

Furthermore, the CPLP helps Lisbon establish its peculiarity within the European Union. As opposed to merely a small and peripheral state, Portugal brought to the table new connections, particularly relevant for a community eager to become a global player. It capitalized on having links to Latin America, Africa, and Asia and played out its fundamental comparative advantage within the context of the Union. Strengthening its role within the Lusophone geographical space meant, therefore, strengthening its role within the EU, and vice-versa. Conversely, Portuguese-speaking countries saw in Portugal an important intermediary for dialogue with Europe and believed it to be a reliable partner to act on their behalf within the Union.[99] They trusted Lisbon to boost their issues and concerns at meetings and negotiations, which it did quite successfully.

Portugal's first step was to raise the Lusophone identity as a specific group which should be targeted as such. The number of EC political statements relating to the Portuguese-speaking community in and of itself reflects the successful affirmation of its identity. In 1992, Brussels signed a program of cooperation with the PALOP and recognized them as a regional group under Lome IV, despite the discontinuity of borders.[100] Moreover, Portugal managed to mobilize political and financial support for the Angolan, Mozambican, and East Timorese peace processes and elections, as well as peacebuilding initiatives. Cape Verde's democratic transition and Guinea-Bissau's security sector reform also profited from the Union's interest and material support—once again a product of strong Portuguese advocacy. Portugal thus forced its former colonies onto the European agenda, an effort which then generated its own synergies: it locked Brussels' once loose commitment to this space and made Lisbon the most relevant speaker for the community. In addition, Portugal's accession to the EU allowed for additional funding for investment in its former colonies and, as a result, the country's cooperation policy gained structure and financial viability.

The CPLP includes today more than 220 million people around the globe and is seen as an important geopolitical player, especially given two of its members—Brazil and Angola. Portugal, along with Brazil, played a central role in establishing this prominence, benefiting both itself and the community. It helped put the CPLP on the map while also actively protecting it from the influence of its bigger neighbors.[101] Exploring the complementarity between Europe and the Lusophone world became the norm, putting an end to the "either/or logic" which had prevailed in the immediate aftermath of the Revolution.[102]

Nevertheless, the relationship between the members of the Portuguese-speaking community is still some way from being truly reciprocal. Portugal seems to think of this organization as an instrument to enhance its weight in the European and international scenes, and is far less interested in creating a symmetrical relationship. Lisbon has consistently sided with Europe in matters which divide North and South, supporting, for instance, European intransigence on issues ranging from Doha negotiations to Economic Partnership Agreements between the EU and ACP countries. Instead of taking these opportunities to fight for the best interests of the countries to which it purports to be deeply connected, Portugal has time and again chosen to align with its European partners. Both the content of agreements and tactics employed during negotiations betray a hollowness to pledges of a real partnership: threats of withholding aid or closing European markets to ACP products have been prominent in negotiations to which Lisbon was a party.[103]

In this sense, Portuguese foreign policy toward the Lusophone world is more about form than content. Over the years, Portugal has undoubtedly reinforced its position as an intermediary between Europe and the countries with which it has historic ties, focusing on organizing large and publically conspicuous events, such as the EU-Africa Summits of 2000 and 2007 and the EU-Brazil Summit of 2007. It has not, however, sought so far to forge a more equal relationship which might eventually change the rapport between North and South and lead to a more auspicious rapprochement.

Conclusion

Portugal staged an impressive comeback in the late twentieth century with the demise of the dictatorial regime and subsequent democratic consolidation. After decades of exclusion, the country re-engaged with the outside world and invested in developing those relations that had fallen victim to the country's status as an international pariah. Indeed, the two main goals of the post-dictatorship governments with respect to the country's foreign policy—integration and diversification—were successfully achieved. In just a few years, Portugal was fully involved in world affairs, becoming an active member of manifold multilateral organizations and, moreover, was able to expand its foreign connections to counter external overdependence on one particular partner.

Joining the EU, strengthening its relationship with the United States, and exploring its historical ties with the Lusophone world represented an extraordinary added value to Portugal's international profile, exceeding traditional expectations for a state of its size and might. Successive governments managed to tie the three main vectors of its foreign policy together in an ultimately productive and mutually reinforcing way, building on synergies that were favorable to the pursuit of what they perceived to be the country's national interests. In this sense, the democratic transition has definitively proven that the dichotomy between Europe and the Atlantic was always a false one.[104] Furthermore, Lisbon has sought to buttress these relations through institutionalization. Along with NATO, the EU and the CPLP have given the country's most important foreign connections their own space where negotiation, coordination, and decision-making formally take place. The process, and not just the content, of Portugal's external affairs thus underwent an interesting change in the recent decades.

Portugal enters the twenty-first century entirely integrated into the world's political, economic, military, and cultural institutions. The international community no longer fears a relapse into dictatorship or revolutionary government[105] and, above all, has welcomed Portugal as a Western democratic "mainstreamer." Moreover, Portugal's strategic relevance and the value of its traditional ties remain undiminished. As in the past, these assets facilitate Lisbon's attempt to secure tacit support—or at least complicit indifference—for the promotion of its national interests.

Nevertheless, the national consensus regarding Portuguese foreign relations, from which the first democratic governments profited, is no longer predominant. To be sure, key center-oriented foreign policies still gather significant agreement—indeed nowhere else is the "bloco central" (the two main parties' alliance) clearer than in foreign policy; however, now and then, debate over the country's Europeanism or Atlanticism still resurfaces in Portuguese political debate, especially when the country is seen as having to make a choice between siding with its European partners and standing in solidarity with the United States.

At present, the anchors on which Lisbon's foreign policy has so far relied might not suffice for a country whose poor economic performance of the past ten years leaves it inadequately positioned to face external pressures. Indeed, the dawn of the new millennium is not looking particularly auspicious: even though Portugal's international profile does not derive from vast economic resources— but from the country's historical legacy and geopolitical location—its current weaknesses have, in the present juncture, become paramount and are bound to restrain Lisbon's capacity to play a greater role in world affairs for the foreseeable future.

Notes

1. I would like to thank Tor Krever for comments on an earlier draft.

2. Alvaro Vasconcelos, "Conclusion, Portuguese Defense and Foreign Policy Since Democratization" ed. Maxwell, *Camões Center Special Report No. 3* (NY: Camoes Center, 1991): 83.

3. The European Union (EU) was created in 1957 with the official denomination of the European Economic Community (ECC) and, until the Maastricht Treaty in 1993, it was usually referred to as the European Community (EC). This chapter refers to both the EC and EU depending on the period (pre- or post-1993) in question.

4. "Europe Watches as Portugal's Economy Struggles," *New York Times*, February 9, 2010.

5. The literature on small states is extensive; see, for example, Annette Baker Fox (1959); David Vital (1967); Robert Rothstein (1968); Robert Keohane (1969); Maurice East (1973); Peter Baehr (1975); Michael Handel (1981); Christine Ingebritsen *et al.* (eds.) (2006).

6. Robert Keohane, "Lilliputians' Dilemmas: Small States in International Politics," *Small States in International Relations*, ed. Christine Ingebritsen, et al. (Seattle: University of Washington Press, 2006), 59.

7. Maurice East, "Size and Foreign Policy Behavior: A Test of Two Models," *World Politics*, vol. 25 , no. 4 (1973): 557-58.

8. Iver Neumann and Sieglinde Gstohl, "Introduction: Lilliputians in Gulliver's World?" *Small States in International Relations*, ed. Christine Ingebritsen, et al. (Seattle: University of Washington Press, 2006), 21.

9. Peter Baehr, "Review Article – Small States: A Tool for Analysis," *World Politics*, vol. 27, no. 3 (1975): 459.

10. Annette Baker Fox, "The Power of Small States: Diplomacy in World War II," *Small States in International Relations*, ed. Christine Ingebritsen, et al. (Seattle: University of Washington Press, 2006), 44.

11. East, "Size and Foreign Policy Behavior," 560.

12. David Vital, "The Inequality of States: A Study of the Small Power in International Relations," *Small States in International Relations*, ed. Christine Ingebritsen, et al. (Seattle: University of Washington Press, 2006), 79.

13. Vital, "Inequality of States," 87.

14. Michael Handel, "Weak States in the International System," *Small States in International Relations*, ed. Christine Ingebritsen, et al. (Seattle: University of Washington Press, 2006), 149; Christine Ingebritsen, "Conclusion," *Small States in International Relations* (2006b), 288.

15. Portugal has a territory of 92,090 sq km (91,470 sq km of land and 620 sq km of water) including both autonomous regions—Madeira and Azores—and a population of 10,707,924. July 2009 estimates: Data in *CIA World Factbook*, https://www.cia.gov/library/publications/the-world-factbook/geos/po.html (accessed August 2009).

16. Teresa Cravo and Maria Raquel Freire, "La politique étrangère du Portugal: européanisme, atlantisme, ou les deux?" *La Revue Internationale et Stratégique, Institut de Relations Internationales et Stratégiques (IRIS)*, Été, No. 62 (2006): 22.

17. Baldur Thorhallsson, "The Role of Small States in the European Union," *Small States in International Relations*, ed. Christine Ingebritsen, et al. (Seattle: University of Washington Press, 2006), 218.

18. Mark Stenhouse and Bruce George, "Defense Policy and Strategic Importance: The Western Perspective," *Portuguese Defense and Foreign Policy Since Democratization, Camões Center Special Report*, ed. Maxwell, No. 3 (New York: Camoes Center, 1991), 29; 35.

19. Vasconcelos, "Portuguese Defense and Foreign Policy," 88.

20. Esther Barbé and Alvaro Vasconcelos, "Portugal and Spain in EPC and CFSP: Committed Partners," *Synergy at Work: Spain and Portugal in European Foreign Policy*, ed. Algieri & Regelsberger (Bonn: Europa Union Verlag, 1996), 295.

21. The first two years of the post-Revolution regime were marked by grave political instability with six governments, two presidents, and two attempted coups.

22. Nuno Severiano Teixeira, "Between Africa and Europe: Portuguese Foreign Policy, 1890-2000," *Contemporary Portugal: Politics, Society and Culture*, ed. Costa Pinto (Boulder: Social Science Monographs, 2003), 114.

23. Paul Christophe Manuel, "Regime change, elite players, and foreign policy in Portugal, 1960-1991," *Perspectives on Political Science*, vol. 25, no. 2 (Spring 1996): 69-73.

24. The Portuguese Socialist Party had actually been officially created in the Federal Republic of Germany, in 1973, with the active support of Chancellor Willy Brandt.

25. Stenhouse and George, "Defense Policy and Strategic Importance," 45-46.

26. Tad Szulc, "Lisbon & Washington: Behind the Portuguese Revolution," *Foreign Policy*, no. 21 (Winter 1975-1976): 8.

27. Fox, "Power of Small States," 49.

28. Sebastián Royo, "From Authoritarianism to the European Union: The Europeanization of Portugal," *Mediterranean Quarterly* (Summer 2004): 108-109.

29. Maria João Seabra, "Portugal: Prudent Pragmatism," *Synergy at Work: Spain and Portugal in European Foreign Policy*, ed. Algieri & Regelsberger (Bonn: Europa Union Verlag, 1996), 279.

30. Henrik Larsen, *Foreign Policy and Discourse Analysis: France, Britain and Europe* (London: Routledge, 1997), 184.

32. Sebastián Royo and Paul Christopher Manuel, "Some Lessons from the Fifteenth Anniversary of the Accession of Portugal and Spain to the European Union," *Spain and Portugal in the European Union*, ed. Royo & Manuel (London: Frank Cass, 2003), 7.

33. Royo, "Europeanization of Portugal," 120.

34. António Costa Pinto and Xosé Núñez, "Portugal and Spain," *European Political Cultures: Conflict or Convergence?* ed. Eatwell, Roger (London: Routledge, 1997), 184.

35. The euro was fixed against the currencies of eleven European countries on January 1, 1999 (Austria, Belgium, Finland, France, Germany, Ireland, Italy, Luxembourg, Netherlands, Portugal, and Spain), and on January 1, 2002, the new European currency was circulating while the old currencies began to phase out. At present, the Euro has been adopted by Andorra, Austria, Belgium, Cyprus, Finland, France, Germany, Greece, Ireland, Italy, Kosovo, Luxembourg, Malta, Monaco, Montenegro, Netherlands, Portugal, San Marino, Slovakia, Slovenia, and Spain.

36. Franco Algieri, "Spain and Portugal in EPC and CFSP: Transformation and Correlation," *Synergy at Work: Spain and Portugal in European Foreign Policy*, ed. Algieri & Regelsberger (Bonn: Europa Union Verlag, 1996), 20-21.

37. Alvaro Vasconcelos, "Portugal: A Case for an Open Europe," *Synergy at Work: Spain and Portugal in European Foreign Policy*, ed. Algieri & Regelsberger (Bonn: Europa Union Verlag, 1996), 112.

38. Barbé and Vasconcelos, "Committed Partners," 300.

39. Algieri, "Transformation and Correlation," 23.

40. Teresa Cravo, et al. "Председательство Португалии в Европейском союзе:шаг вперед или отражение тупика?" [The Portuguese Presidency of the European Union: A Step Forward or the Expression of an Impasse?], *Europe: The Journal of the Polish Institute of International Affairs*, Vol. 8, No. 1(26) (2008): 7-34

41. Cravo, et al., "Portuguese Presidency of the European Union."

42. Seabra, "Portugal: Prudent Pragmatism," 283.

43. "José Cutileiro: Europe's Fledgling Defender," *The Economist*, August 1, 1998.

44. Barbé and Vasconcelos, "Committed Partners," 299.

45. Royo and Manuel, "Some Lessons," 5-7.

46. Costa Pinto and Núñez, "Portugal and Spain," 189.

47. Barbé and Vasconcelos, "Committed Partners," 302.

48. Observatório de Relações Exteriores-UAL (2002), "Bilateralidade e multilateralidade de Portugal e Espanha", *Janus*, http://www.janusonline.pt/2002/2002_3_2_8.html (accessed May 2009).

49. Seabra, "Portugal: Prudent Pragmatism," 288.

50. "Lonely at the top," *The Economist*, June 4, 2009.

51. Udo Diedrichs and Wolfgang Wessels, "From Newcomers to Mainstreamers: Lessons from Spain and Portugal," *Synergy at Work: Spain and Portugal in European Foreign Policy*, ed. Algieri & Regelsberger (Bonn: Europa Union Verlag, 1996), 315.

52. Seabra, "Portugal: Prudent Pragmatism," 282-283.

53. Seabra, "Portugal: Prudent Pragmatism," 280.

54. Seabra, "Portugal: Prudent Pragmatism," 289-291.

55. President Sarkozy's speech to the European Parliament, November 13, 2007, at http://www.ambafrance-uk.org/Discours-du-President-Sarkozy,9844.html (accessed May 2009).

56. Cravo et al., "Portuguese Presidency of the European Union."

57. Algieri, "Transformation and Correlation," 12, 26.

58. Royo, "Europeanization of Portugal," 124-125.

59. Costa Pinto and Núñez, "Portugal and Spain," 183.

60. The evolution of the right wing party—CDS (Center Democratic Social Party)—to an anti-European nationalist party (since 1993, adding the denomination of Popular Party), and its electoral results in 1995 (9 percent), was evidence of this shift in the Portuguese perception of Europe (Costa Pinto and Núñez, "Portugal and Spain," 185).

61. Royo, "Europeanization of Portugal," 123.

62. The extent of this compensation has always been a matter of disagreement, although Salazar was, in fact, extremely careful not to demand too much aid, in an attempt to retain some independence from the superpower (Maxwell, 1991: 6).

63. "Socratic dialogue," The Economist, April 30, 2009.

64. António Costa Pinto, "Twentieth Century Portugal: An Introduction," Contemporary Portugal: Politics, Society and Culture, ed. Costa Pinto (Boulder: Social Science Monographs, 2003), 43.

65. Severiano Teixeira, "Between Africa and Europe," 106.

66. Stenhouse and George, "Defense Policy and Strategic Importance," 32.

67. Severiano Teixeira, "Between Africa and Europe," 109.

68. This new policy was labeled "Tar Baby" in the Administration's National Security Study Memorandum 39.

69. Stenhouse and George, "Defense Policy and Strategic Importance," 33.

70. Witney Schneidman, Engaging Africa: Washington and the Fall of Portugal's Colonial Empire (Lanham, MD: University Press of America, 2004), 114-121.

71. According to Szulc, during the Nixon era, the United States sold TAP, the Portuguese airline, 707 Boeings that were used to transport troops to the African war theatre; jet fighter pilots trained in U.S. facilities in West Germany; and Portuguese officers had counterinsurgency training at the U.S. Army's Jungle Warfare School at Fort Gulick in the Panama Canal Zone. (Szulc, "Lisbon & Washington: Behind the Portuguese Revolution," 20-21).

72. Military intervention, in order to keep the Azores within Western orbit, was entertained; however, a Chilean-style intervention was too risky and out of the question while war continued in Vietnam. The Administration considered sponsoring the Azorean secessionist movement and even expulsion from NATO (even though the organization's charter did not contemplate this possibility). In an interview on May 23, 1975, President Ford stated, to the astonishment of most Allies, "I don't see how you can have a Communist element significant in an organization that was put together and formed for the purpose of meeting a challenge by Communist elements from the East" (quoted in Szulc, 1975-76: 42-43). Kissinger instructed the CIA to build up contacts with conservative factions in Portugal and transferred financial aid to non-Communist parties through Western European intermediaries.

73. Vasconcelos, "Portuguese Defense and Foreign Policy," 83.

74. Mário Soares, "Portugal's New Foreign Policy" (press conference given by Mário Soares at Palácio das Necessidades, Lisbon, Ministry of Foreign Affairs, September 13, 1974), 25, 47.

75. Kenneth Maxwell, "Portuguese Defense and Foreign Policy: An Overview," Portuguese Defense and Foreign Policy Since Democratization, ed. Maxwell, Camões Center Special Report, No. 3 (New York: Camoes Center, 1991): 2.

76. Ingmar Oldberg, "The Portuguese Revolution of 1974-75 and U.S. Foreign Policy," *Cooperation and Conflict*, XVII (1982):179, 180, 184.

77. There are currently 295 Portuguese troops serving in NATO's KFOR mission in Kosovo.

78. Quoted in Szulc, "Lisbon & Washington: Behind the Portuguese Revolution," 60.

79. NATO, "Statement by the Prime Minister of Portugal, Antonio Guterres," (NATO Council Meeting, April 23, 1999), http://www.nato.int/docu/speech/1999/s990423s.htm. According to the "Iraq Body Count" estimates, since 2003 the war has caused between 95,000 and 103,000 civilian deaths.

80. Vasconcelos, "Portuguese Defense and Foreign Policy."

81. Despite the prime minister's heavily pro-American stance, however, much of the world press thought of him secondary to Bush, Blair and Aznar, cropping him from most photos. A popular cartoon at the time even drew Barroso as a butler serving coffee to his guests, thus emphasizing Portugal's perceived subordinate role.

82. "Threats and Responses; Excerpts From Joint News Conference: 'Tomorrow Is a Moment of Truth," *New York Times*, March 17, 2003. An investigation was conducted by the European Parliament which concluded that more than 1,200 CIA flights used European airspace between 2001 and 2005 and accused fourteen European governments of complicity with CIA extraordinary rendition operations in the context of the "War on Terror."

83. Of course, the episodes discussed above also demonstrate Portugal's value as an ally for the United States, albeit on a completely different scale. This is still a case of, in Keohane and Nye's words, "asymmetrical interdependency" (2001).

84. "Unwanted Guantánamo Prisoners: Portugal Open to Accepting Detainees," *Spiegel Online International*, December 12, 2008.

85. Only in February 1991 was a Financial Fund to support cooperation between Portugal and the PALOP finally set up.

86. Stephen Walt, "Alliances in a Unipolar World," *World Politics* 61(1) (2009), 94.

87. Norrie MacQueen, "Re-defining the 'African Vocation:' Portugal's Post-Colonial Identity Crisis," *Journal of Contemporary European Studies*, Vol. 11 (2) (November 2003): 181-99.

88. Soares, "Portugal's New Foreign Policy," 70-71.

89. Portugal was part of the troika of observers of the peace process in Angola, along with Russia and the United States.

90. Adelino Torres, "Introdução," *Portugal—PALOP: As Relações Económicas e Financeiras*, ed. Torres (Lisboa: Escher, 1991), 23.

91. Ernesto Melo Antunes, "Vector Africano da Política Externa Portuguesa," *Portugal, os Estados Africanos de Língua Oficial Portuguesa e os Estados Unidos da América*, ed. Aguiar (Lisboa: Fundação Calouste Gulbenkian, 1987), 163.

92. Portugal is presently running for a non-permanent member's seat at the UN Security Council for the biennium 2011-2012.

93. Paulo Gorjão, "The End of a Cycle: Australian and Portuguese Foreign Policies and the Fate of East Timor," *Contemporary Southeast Asia: A Journal of International & Strategic Affairs*, Vol. 23, No. 1 (2001).

94. Teresa Sousa, "A opção europeia", *Janus* (1997), http://www.janusonline.pt/conjuntura/conj_1997_3_14_c.html (accessed May 2009).

95. Arnaldo Gonçalves, "Macao, Timor and Portuguese India in the Context of Portugal's Recent Decolonization," *The Last Empire: Thirty Years of Portuguese Decolonization*, ed. Lloyd-Jones and Costa Pinto (Bristol: Intellect Books, 2003), 61.

96. Gorjão, "End of a Cycle."

97. Miguel Santos Neves, "Portugal: A Promoter for Sub-Saharan Africa," *Synergy at Work: Spain and Portugal in European Foreign Policy*, ed. Algieri and Regelsberger (Bonn: Europa Union Verlag, 1996), 139-40.

98. Luís António Santos, "Portugal and the CPLP: Heightened Expectations, Unfounded Disillusions," *The Last Empire: Thirty Years of Portuguese Decolonization,* ed. Lloyd-Jones and Costa Pinto (Bristol: Intellect Books, 2003), 71.

99. Santos Neves, "Portugal: A Promoter for Sub-Saharan Africa."

100. Santos, "Portugal and the CPLP," 70.

101. Santos Neves, "Portugal: A Promoter for Sub-Saharan Africa," 146.

102. Santos Neves, "Portugal: A Promoter for Sub-Saharan Africa," 141.

103. Cravo et al., "Portuguese Presidency of the European Union."

104. Barbé and Vasconcelos, "Committed Partners," 297.

105. Stenhouse and George, "Defense Policy and Strategic Importance," 47.

10 Conclusion: The Portuguese Case in Comparative Perspective

Robert M. Fishman

Portugal can be viewed through two seemingly opposite perspectives: as a small country at the periphery of Europe which falls short of the level of well-being taken for granted elsewhere on the continent, or, as a nation that has left an unmistakable mark on the history and contemporary configuration of the world writ large. If the country's continuing challenges seem significant in their magnitude, so too are its cumulative achievements; Portugal has helped to shape the modern world through its language, political, and economic innovations and the basic demographic fact of sustained emigration to other nations. Portuguese is one of only *three* European-origin languages which is more widely spoken outside Europe than within the continent's boundaries, and of those three languages—the others being English and Spanish—it is Portuguese which has the most lop-sided imbalance between a relatively small number of native speakers in the country of origin and the massive number living in former colonial territories. Despite the great impact on world history reflected by that basic linguistic fact, the country is, today, the least wealthy in Western Europe and has often seemed a marginal exception to the main lines of political and economic advancement of the continent's most successful states. This fundamental duality of the country's stature in the world (the primary theme of one chapter in this volume and an "undercurrent" in the analysis found in several others) helps to capture the remarkable importance, and the intrinsic interest, of this country. The valuable chapters making up this volume shed light on this paradox and on the contours of the country's successes, as well as its continuing challenges and disappointments.

The study of any given country offers students and scholars a *privileged window* onto one or another set of problems and processes which have unfolded in that country. Students of the welfare-state look to small countries of northern Europe to see how the generous provision of social guarantees to all residents of a nation can be made compatible with sustained economic success. Analysts of political life in culturally pluralistic societies look to the Netherlands, Switzerland, and other cases to understand how democratic political institutions can survive and prosper in such heterogeneous settings. In the case of Portugal, the list of themes for which the country provides a highly useful vantage point is an especially long one, for reasons connected to the nation's history and continuing structural challenges. The study of Portugal provides insight into how empires arise and are dissolved, the ways in which democratic politics emerges and achieves consolidation (or fails to do so), mechanisms of integration into the European Union, and strategies for countries to "catch up" with more developed neighbors.

The list of themes for which Portugal offers scholars and students an interesting "test case" is a rather long one, perhaps helping to explain why so much social science work of broad relevance has focused on this case. One of the most important early conceptual breakthroughs in the scholarship on the late twentieth century's worldwide turn to democracy, Philippe Schmitter's "Liberation by Golpe" (1975) elaborated theoretical implications of the country's "Carnation Revolution" beginning on April 25, 1974.[1] A landmark study on the revolutionary route to modern democracy, Nancy Bermeo's *The Revolution within the Revolution* (1986) analyzes the forces at work in the collectivization of many large agricultural estates in the context of democratization.[2] Numerous prominent scholars in the fields of economics, political science, and sociology have examined the country's labor market in order to understand the dynamics leading to success or failure in the creation of employment. Students of European Union enlargement, and of European integration in a broader sense, have turned to Portugal's accession to the European community in 1986, and its aftermath, for lessons of relevance to countries that have entered the EU more recently. Scholars in such diverse fields as cultural studies, international relations, and political institutional analysis have found special interest in developments within Portugal.

The contributions found in these pages delineate and analyze the circumstances of contemporary Portugal, while also placing that enterprise within the broader effort to theorize cross-national institutional differences and causal pathways that shape the contemporary world. In that sense, this volume is strongly rooted in an approach to social science best articulated by the great master of historically-embedded comparative analysis, Max Weber, who classically insisted on the scholarly imperative of trying to understand both the *par-*

ticularities of specific cases and probabilistic regularities extending *across cases*, even though that effort inevitably involves the embrace of certain tensions.[3] The analyzes found in this volume have underscored the usefulness—indeed the indispensability—of such *historically embedded* investigation. The current and recent institutional parameters of Portuguese democracy, the country's economic and demographic challenges, and its international strategies are all best understood through an analytical perspective built off a fine-grained attentiveness to recent (or in some cases, not so recent) national history coupled with a reliance on theoretical insights elaborated within the context of broader social science literatures.

If the global stage—extending across continents—continues to be a relevant point of reference for the political and economic efforts of contemporary Portugal, it remains the case that the European Union and the country's larger Iberian Peninsula neighbor, Spain, hold special significance for Portuguese elites, ordinary citizens, and the scholars who study them. Much of the scholarly work collected in this volume addresses either the country's interface with the European Union, following its accession to membership in 1986,[4] or Portugal's record of development relative to that of its larger Iberian neighbor. Both of these comparative vantage points offer a somewhat mixed picture in which both successes and relative failures are evident—as is underscored in this volume's chapters. Yet the mixed character of the country's record should not obscure its very considerable triumphs—not only in the age of early modern European exploration of the globe, but much more recently in the years following the inauguration of the ultimately worldwide "Third Wave" of democracy on April 25, 1974, in Portugal.

The comparison with neighboring Spain, a theme taken up in Sebastián Royo's important chapter on economic divergence, and in a growing body of scholarship in several disciplines, holds special theoretical promise for social scientists as well as much intrinsic interest for the broader literate public for a rather obvious reason: the two countries of the Iberian Peninsula share a long list of historical parallels and structural similarities extending backward in time for centuries. Yet they diverged in fundamental ways at the time of their passage from right-wing authoritarianism to democracy in the 1970s through nearly polar opposite pathways of change. Whereas Portugal experienced a crisis of state power, rooted in the colonial wars in Africa, and as a result underwent a social revolutionary transition to democracy, post-Franco Spain experienced a consensus-oriented process of democratizing reform transforming the larger country's political regime, but leaving state structures and many other institutions largely intact.[5] Those thoroughly dissimilar roads to democracy, rooted in each case in historical circumstances shaping the choices open to political actors, have generated important enduring effects for the neighboring countries, leading to a series of new divergences in societal outcomes increasingly manifested after the 1970s.[6] In this comparative context, Portugal has enjoyed its relative successes along with some disappointments.

The intensive social revolutionary phase of the Portuguese road to democ-racy[7] proved relatively brief, and soon led to the forging of representative politi-cal institutions that fall within the range of variation characterizing contempo-rary democracies.[8] Democracy was established, but unlike many other new democracies, it was one rooted in a socio-political experience marked by rather thorough purges of old regime loyalists within numerous institutions.[9] The re-sulting political and economic system remained strongly marked for a time by the socialist project which predominated at the time of the Revolution;[10] but by the end of the 1980s, the country's two largest parties had reached a bipartisan consensus to re-privatize the firms nationalized in 1975 while maintaining the broadly shared commitment to the use of state policies to ameliorate social prob-lems such as poverty and unemployment. Survey research has established the basis in mass attitudes for such policies; Portugal stands as a world leader in the breadth of public support for governmental policies designed to reduce inequali-ties.[11] The distinctiveness of the country's passageway from dictatorship to de-mocracy, coupled with other crucial features of its recent political past,[12] has helped to set the stage for the specific stories related and analyzed in these pag-es, but other factors have also shared in shaping Portuguese realities.

The list of paradoxes and puzzles in the country's recent performance is a long one. Whereas Portugal scores relatively low, along with the rest of southern Europe, in PISA evaluations of the educational performance of high school stu-dents, recent work shows that the pattern of cultural consumption by young Por-tuguese born under democracy and educated in the new post-April 25 context is remarkably similar to that found in the most successful countries of northern Europe. Although the musical consumption patterns of Portuguese and Span-iards born and socialized under authoritarian rule are quite similar, a large cross-national divergence has emerged among those born *after* the democratic transi-tions of the 1970s, with young Portuguese being far more likely than their Span-ish counterparts to regularly listen to multiple genres of music, thus exhibiting the "omnivore" pattern of cultural taste which has attracted great interest among sociologists of culture.[13] Even though the country experienced a prolonged eco-nomic slowdown in the years after 2000, underperforming much of Europe by a considerable margin, its economic performance over the previous two decades compares favorably with other European cases. In the context of recovery efforts after the worldwide economic crisis beginning in 2007, Portugal enjoyed one of the two most rapid growth rates within the Eurozone during the first quarter of 2010 and managed to reassert a considerable advantage over neighboring Spain in the provision of employment. Although financial market contagion in the spring of 2010 substantially impacted Portugal—following the revelation that Greece had falsified public data on its official state debt—Eurostat data for 2009 showed that the Portuguese accumulated debt was far from the highest levels found in the European Union, placing the country sixth among EU member states in the magnitude of its sovereign debt relative to GDP.[14] Portugal's per-formance can be cast in a positive or critical light, with both perspectives identifying part of the overall complex reality manifested by the country's recent history.

The larger European "stage" constituted by the evolving institutions of the European Union provides not only a broad point of reference for analyzing the Portuguese experience but, even more importantly, a crucial context for the strategic efforts of Portuguese actors. The EU also quite obviously serves as a supra-national source of policies that directly shapes outcomes within Portugal. One cannot understand Portugal—or any other member state of the European Union—without taking fully into account its experience within the large supranational European institutional arena. Yet, that unmistakable relevance of the EU arena has not generated an easy consensus on exactly *how to characterize* the overall balance between positive and negative effects of European integration. The strictly economic impact of EU membership and of the euro may be taken as something of a "double-edged sword" for Portugal and many other participating states. The complex interaction between socio-cultural and political realities constructed within nation-states such as Portugal and the emergent reality of supra-national Europe resists easy or rapid theorization and calls out for the careful empirical analysis of strategic and expressive action by political, economic, and cultural actors.[15]

The interface between Portugal and the EU is, for this reason, one of the central themes for scholarship such as that found in this volume, but the growing salience of European institutions does not signify a decline in the relevance or distinctiveness of the national level. Indeed, European integration is "framed" and understood in differing ways, which vary by country for reasons rooted in national histories.[16] Volumes such as this one—focused on a particular national experience—continue to be absolutely essential to understanding European realities. Much of political, social, and economic life continues to be nationally bounded in ways shaped by complex histories, just as the chapters of this book so clearly show. Each of the chapters in the volume poses important questions that contribute to the readers' understanding of the broader Portuguese experience.

Ana Evans's carefully researched and theorized chapter on the changing affiliation strategies of elected members of the European Parliament (EP) provides telling evidence on the ability of Portuguese political elites—and parties—to successfully make use of European institutions to pursue their political ends. Evans shows how Portuguese party delegations to the EP elaborate their affiliation strategies—deciding which parliamentary group to join—in a fashion deeply marked both by the history and identity of their parties in Portugal and their analysis of the institutional incentives provided by alternative affiliation choices. Portuguese members of the EP—representatives chosen in a rather unusual democracy in which the largest center-right party calls itself "social-democratic" and once tried to affiliate to the socialist international—face difficult choices in which either elements of a party's domestic identity, or its strategic interests within the EU, may need to be compromised given the evident tensions between these two quite different considerations. Evans shows how Portuguese parties have contemplated multiple options, changing their affiliation in some instances. One of the results of this strategic thinking, rooted in Portuguese history but thoroughly willing to make adjustments calibrated to the supra-national institutional incentives, has been the extraordinary bipartisan success of Portuguese elites within the EU.

As of this writing, two Portuguese public servants hold positions of extraordinary authority in the European Union: José Manuel Durao Barroso (a former prime minister of the center-right PSD) serves as president of the European Commission, and Vitor Constancio (a former secretary general of the Socialist Party) serves as vice-president of the European Central Bank. Portuguese elites have not been laggards in their ability to work—and compete—successfully within the structures of the European Union. The chapter of Ana Evans provides readers with an understanding of the basis for that success and its paradoxical rootedness in the political history of the country.

Examining the other side of the ledger, António Goucha Soares locates shortfalls in the country's Europeanization, specifying disappointments in diverse fields such as education and the functioning of legal structures. That shortfalls of this general nature exist is uncontestable, and the critical spirit of Portuguese scholars such as Goucha Soares can be seen as a way to push the country toward greater successes. The complex nature of the mix between significant national successes and ongoing arenas of disappointment makes the assessment of the country's progress or stagnation an especially challenging venture.

Despite the undeniable importance of the European Union for Portuguese policy-makers and citizens, many of the country's external strategies and concerns extend well beyond the continent's boundaries. Teresa de Almeida Cravo's insightful chapter on foreign policy shows how Portugal's EU membership represents one fundamental component of a larger and complex set of international linkages shaped by the country's distinctive history and geopolitical location. Cravo builds a strong case that Portugal's commitment to Europe coincides with both a historic alliance to the United States and deep connections to the Lusophone world. This unique combination of international ties places Portugal in a position of substantially greater importance than the country's small size and economic stature might lead one to expect. Cravo shows how the Portuguese serve as a bridge between the Lusophone world and Europe in ways that, to varying degrees, serve the interests of all concerned.

Seen in this light, the Portuguese case is especially relevant for understanding how small states can carve out for themselves a role of significance in international affairs and how countries lacking substantial military resources can, nonetheless, gain influence on multiple continents. The large question which arises, as Cravo suggests, is whether this pattern will prove sustainable in a context of disappointing economic performance for the country. Yet by the same token, the Portuguese case may ultimately provide evidence of ways in which strategic geopolitical dexterity—and positive consequences of location—can promote new foundations for economic growth. With the advancement of Brazilian economic development, Portugal's position as a historic intermediary between Europe and South America's largest economy has assumed new importance, complemented by Lisbon's connections to Africa and Asia.

Thus, the economy emerges as an inevitable source of concern—and a major object of study—for this volume. Portugal's impressive record of economic development during the final decades of the twentieth century—spanning the last years of the authoritarian Estado Novo and roughly the first quarter century after the carnation revolution of 1974—gave way to substantial underperformance after the year 2000.[17] This forms the backdrop for Sebastián Royo's judicious and important contribution on the economic performance of Portugal and Spain in the EU. Royo carefully examines Portugal's serious underperformance from 2000 to 2007, precisely when Spain was outperforming not only Portugal but also many other EU member states. Yet, as Royo suggests, by the end of that period of time Portugal had shown some signs of overcoming problems faced by its economy. Moreover, as that chapter establishes, the verdict one draws on the relative success of Portugal and Spain depends on the years examined. Both Iberian cases have experienced periods of under and over performance. Royo's previous contributions on the political economy of the Iberian cases, establishing the complex record of triumphs and shortfalls in both countries, provide the background for this carefully documented examination of economic divergence after joining the European Union.[18]

If one focuses above all on the period of economic underperformance in Portugal, the country's experience appears especially troubling from the standpoint of an assessment of the EU's efficacy. After all, as Royo's chapter on economic divergence makes clear, Portugal has been a major recipient of EU funding; that financial support has represented a much larger share of GDP in Portugal than in Spain. Yet the country's experience in the EU—and above all in the new system of monetary union—appears disappointing. Exactly why the Portuguese economy performed poorly in the period from 2000 through 2007, when signs of recovery began to emerge just before the world as a whole entered a period of economic difficulty, is a question on which economists and economic historians will continue to work for some time. Yet, it is remarkable that in certain other respects the country has continued to do reasonably well, even as the economy stagnated, and in spite of what many see as a national tendency toward self-criticism.

That tendency toward national self-criticism and its paradoxical association with national pride is carefully documented by Baum and Glatzer in their thoughtful exploration of Portuguese national identity at a time of rapid change. Their essay identifies various complexities and paradoxes while also drawing a careful balance between positive and negative elements of the record amassed by Portugal in recent decades. These two scholars examine the Portuguese experience through a dual perspective informed by familiarity with societies—and scholarly debates—on both sides of the Atlantic. Their nuanced and textured analysis defies the opposition between celebratory and critical scholarship, offering readers a view of many Portuguese complexities, including the country's record in dealing with immigrant minorities.

The great question of how a society with a long and demographically massive history of emigration comes to terms with the rapid shift toward accepting large numbers of immigrants is taken up by Sebastián Royo in his careful analysis of the Portuguese experience. Royo's study gets to the heart of a fundamental theme in Portuguese identity and society, providing readers a valuable window onto broad features of the nation's contradictory tendencies and placement in the world. The basic demographic fact of large numbers of people exiting or entering a country is, in and of itself, of enormous societal and economic significance, but it also provides a vantage point from which to examine the historical processes which induce and channel the movement of people. Royo's analysis shows how the broad lines of the country's historical development have shaped—and then been reshaped by—migratory flows of people. The massive emigration of Portuguese to venues both within and outside Europe, including the United States and other points in the Americas, diminished the country's population but provided valuable remittances supportive of domestic economic development. The successive waves of immigration following the Revolution of the Carnations in 1974 partly reflected the country's growing prosperity, relative to economic circumstances in the countries of immigrant origin, but they also actively shaped Portuguese social and economic development under democracy. Moreover, the extraordinary worldwide range of sender countries underscores the salience of Portuguese ties to Asia, Africa, and the Americas, as well as Europe.

In the history of demographic movements, as in all the other themes taken up in this volume, one cannot escape the significance of the Portuguese state and its strategies for the unfolding of the country's history and social development. Some national histories can be written from a vantage point privileging the role of civil society but, in the Portuguese case, despite the significance of civil society, the state has played an especially important role in maintaining the country's independence from Spain, articulating the long-lived colonial venture, and partially reshaping society through revolution and republicanism.[19] All of this leads us back to politics and political institutions—themes which hold importance in any country but perhaps even more so in Portugal than in many other national cases. This in turn helps to explain the evident excellence of Portuguese political science, represented in this volume by António Costa Pinto, Marina Costa Lobo, and Pedro Magalhaes. Whether the theme of study is institutional, behavioral, or cultural, Portuguese political scientists have made fundamental contributions to knowledge about the country and to larger international literatures of a theoretical nature.

Octavio Amorim Neto and Marina Costa Lobo's chapter on semi-presidentialism persuasively establishes the continuing and multi-faceted significance of the presidency in the Portuguese Republic. With a strong basis in both empirical material on this national case and comparative theoretical debates on presidentialism and other institutional forms, they show that Portugal can be placed well within the middle range of presidential powers in contemporary semi-presidential systems. Their analysis examines both formal institutional powers and emergent forms of practice, such as the "open presidencies" initiated by Mário Soares, which underpin the continuing saliency of the presidency. The powers and the public visibility of the presidency in Portugal, as this chapter shows, are embedded in the substance of contemporary political life and its historical antecedents in a revolution which quickly generated a duality of power. Portuguese institutions have subsequently changed, but they have done so in ways which still show marks of their beginnings in a historically uncommon pathway to democracy.

Three of Portugal's leading political scientists—António Costa Pinto, Pedro Magalhaes, and Marina Costa Lobo—take up the broader makeup of the country's institutional configuration, offering a nuanced, yet clear examination of the emergence of Constitutional powers and political actors in the carnation revolution. They provide a compelling analysis of how institutions have been subsequently transformed, albeit in ways which still show marks of the context in which they initially came into being. Their authoritative analysis covers a wide expanse of institutional arenas and structures including the presidency, the party and electoral systems, and a great deal more. The descriptive and analytical components of the chapter will help to orient initiates seeking to learn the basic parameters of the system while also leading those familiar with the polity to rethink some of its characteristic features such as the repeated calls for institutional reform.

The larger picture created by the ensemble of important contributions found in this volume is one of a somewhat unusual national case which can—and must—be analyzed through analytical frameworks widely used in comparative analysis, but which must also be understood through the perspective provided by a rendering of the country's history and identity. Portugal's political parties, economic challenges, international strategies, public institutions, and demographic dynamics cannot be understood without careful attention to various specificities of this national case. Yet the Portuguese example also shows that countries with unusual histories and which face complex challenges can succeed in attaining widely pursued ends. Much of the substance of this volume is about Portuguese successes—often under difficult circumstances. Readers of the volume may well debate whether the country's successes or failures and disappointments weigh more heavily, and in doing so, they will find support for both positions in the chapters assembled here. But more fundamentally, readers will agree that this country, which contributed so much to the European exploration of the globe, continues to constitute a vital ground for the explorations and analyses of social scientists.

Notes

1. Philippe Schmitter, "Liberation by Golpe," *Armed Forces and Society* 2, no.1 (1975): 5-33.

2. Nancy Bermeo, *The Revolution Withing the Revolution* (Princeton: Princeton University Press, 1986).

3. Robert M. Fishman, "On Being a Weberian (after Spain's 11-14 March): Notes on the Continuing Relevance of the Methodological Perspective Proposed by Weber," in *Max Weber's 'Objectivity' Reconsidered*, ed. Laurence McFalls (Toronto: University of Toronto Press, 2007), 261-289.

4. Sebastián Royo and Paul Manuel, *Spain and Portugal in the European Union: The First Fifteen Years* (London: Frank Cass, 2003).

5. Robert M. Fishman, "Rethinking State and Regime: Southern Europe's Transition to Democracy," *World Politics* 42 (1990): 422-440

6. Robert M. Fishman, "Rethinking the Iberian Transformations: How Democratization Scenarios Shaped Labor Market Outcomes," *Studies in Comparative International Development* 43, no. 3 (2010).

7. See Nancy Bermeo, *The Revolution*; John Hammond, *Building Popular Power: Worker's Power and Neighborhood Movements in the Portuguese Revolution* (New York: Monthly Review Press, 1988); Ken Maxwell, *The Making of Portuguese Democracy* (Cambridge: Cambridge University Press, 1995); Durán Muñoz, 2000; and Palacios Cerezales, 2003.

8. See Paul Manuel, *Uncertain Outcome: The Politics of the Portuguese Transition to Democracy* (Lanham, MD: University Press of America, 1995); and Juan Linz and Alfred Stepan, *Problems of Democratic Transition and Consolidation: Southern Europe, South America, and Post-Communist Europe* (Baltimore: Johns Hopkins University Press, 1996).

9. Antonio Costa Pinto, "Settling Accounts with the Past in a Troubled Transition to Democracy: The Portuguese Case," in *The Politics of Memory: Transitional Justice in Democratizing Societies,* ed. Alecandra Barahona de Brito et al., (Oxford: Oxford University Press, 2001), 65-91; and Costa Pinto, "Authoritarian Legacies, Transitoinal Justice and State Crisis in Portugal's Democratization," in *Democratization* 13, no. 2 (2006): 173-204.

10. Boaventura de Sousa Santos, *O Estado e a Sociedade em Portugal (1974-1988)* (Porto: Edicoes Afrontamento, 1990).

11. Jorge Vala Villaverde Cabral and André Freire, *Desigualdades Sociais e Percepcoes de Justica* (Lisboa: Imprensa de Diencias Sociais, 2003).

12. Riag Fernandes, *Nem Ditadura, Nem Revolução: A Ala Liberal e o Marcelismo (1968-1974)* (Lisboa: Dom Quixote, 2006).

13. Robert M. Fishman and Omar Lizardo, "How Legacies of Macro-Political Transformation Shape Patterns of Cultural Taste: The 'Natural Experiment of Spain and Portugal,'" (paper presented at the annual meeting of the American Sociological Association in Atlanta, GA, 2010).

14. Data extracted online from the Eurostat website, April 20, 2010.

15. Refer to Royo and Manuel, *Spain and Portugal*; and Robert M. Fishman and Anthony Messina, *The Year of the Euro: The Cultural, Social, and Political Import of Europes' Common Currency* (Notre Dame, IN: University of Notre Dame Press, 2006).

16. Juan Diez Medrano, *Framing Europe* (Princeton: Princeton University Press, 2003).

17. Francesco Franco, *Challenges Ahead for the Portuguese Economy* (Lisboa: Imprena de Ciencias Sociais, 2008).

18. Refer to Sebastián Royo, *From Social Democracy to Neoliberalism: The Consequences of Party Hegemony in Spain, 1982-1996* (New York: St. Martin's Press, 2000; _____, *A New Century of Corporatism? Corporatism in Southern Europe: Spain and Portugal in Comparative Perspective* Westport, CT: Praeger, 2002; and _____, *Varieties of Capitalism in Spain: Remaking the Spanish Economy for the New Century* (New York: Palgrave Macmillan, 2008).

19. See Tiag Fernandes, *Patterns of Civil Society in Western Europe, 1800-2000: A Comparative and Historical Interpretation*, PhD Dissertation, Dept. Of Social and Political Sciences, European University Institute (Florance Italy, 2009).

Index

About the Contributors

Michael Baum is an associate professor and chair of the Political Science Department at the University of Massachusetts Dartmouth. His research on Portuguese political behavior and gender politics has appeared in journals such as the *European Journal of Political Research*, *South European Society & Politics*, the *Portuguese Journal of Social Science*, and *West European Politics* (forthcoming). He is also the author of numerous book chapters and co-chairs the Iberian Studies Group at Harvard University's Center for European Studies.

Teresa de Almeida Cravois an associate at Harvard University's Belfer Center for Science and International Affairs at the John F. Kennedy School of Government. She lectures in international relations at the Faculty of Economics at the University of Coimbra, Portugal, and is also a researcher at the university's Center for Social Studies. She is currently finishing her PhD at the Department of Politics and International Studies at the University of Cambridge. Her research interests include development aid, geopolitics, and peace and conflict studies, with a focus on Africa.

Ana Maria Evans is a post-doctoral research fellow at the Instituto de CiênciasSociais of the Universidade de Lisboa. She is the author of articles and chapters in the fields of comparative political economy and European institutions and politics.

Robert M. Fishman is professor of sociology and Kellogg Institute Fellow at the University of Notre Dame. His books include *Democracy's Voices* (2004), *Working-Class Organization and the Return to Democracy in Spain* (1990), and, with Anthony Messina, *The Year of the Euro* (2006). He is currently writing a book on the origins and consequences of divergent democratic practice in Portugal and Spain.

Miguel Glatzer is an assistant professor of political science at La Salle University. Glatzer's research focuses on the politics of globalization, democracy, and inequality in comparative perspective. He is the co-editor of *Politics Matters: Globalization and the Future of the Welfare State* (University of Pittsburgh Press) as well as *Portugal: Strategic Options in a European Context* (Lexington Books) and has also published in the journal *South European Society and Politics* and in edited volumes. His most recent work is on the politics of taxation and inequality as well as social policy under authoritarianism. In addition to courses on Europe and the developing world, his teaching interests include civic education, the media, and globalization.

271

Marina Costa Lobo is a political science researcher at the Social Sciences Institute of the University of Lisbon. Her research has focused on leader effects in new democracies and semi-presidentialism. She has been co-director of the Portuguese Election Study since 2001. Recent publications include *Portugal at the Polls* (with A. Freire and P. Magalhães) and academic articles in *Political Research Quarterly*, European Journal of Political Research, *Electoral Studies*,and *Party Politics*.

Pedro C. Magalhães is a researcher at the Institute of Social Sciences, University of Lisbon. His research interests include public opinion, political attitudes, voting behavior and judicial institutions. He has published in journals such as *Comparative Politics, Electoral Studies,Public Choice, West European Politics*, and others. He is one of the coordinators of the Portuguese Election Study.

Octavio AmorimNetois a lecturer in political science at the Graduate School of Economics (EPGE) at the Getulio Vargas Foundation, Rio de Janeiro, Brazil. He received his PhD from the University of California at San Diego in 1998. He is the author of *Presidencialismo e GovernabilidadenasAméricas* (2006). His research interests are comparative political institutions and Latin American politics, with a focus on Brazil.

António Costa Pinto is a research professor at the Institute of Social Science, University of Lisbon. His research interests include authoritarianism, political elites, democratization and transitional justice in new democracies, the European Union, and the comparative study of political change in Europe. He recently published, *Ruling Elites and Decision-Making in Fascist-era Dictatorships* (New York, SSM-Columbia University Press, 2009) and (with Leonardo Morlino), *Dealing with the Legacy of Authoritarianism: The "Politics of the Past"* in *Southern European Democracies* (New York, Routledge, 2011)

Sebastián Royo is an associate dean and professor of government at Suffolk University in Boston and director of the Suffolk University Madrid campus. Royo's articles and reviews on comparative politics have appeared in *Comparative Political Studies, European Journal of Industrial Relations, PS: Political Science and Politics, West European Politics, South European Society and Politics, Democratization, Mediterranean Quarterly, SELA,FP,Perspectives on Politics*, and other publications. His books include *From Social Democracy to Neoliberalism: The Consequences of Party Hegemony in Spain, 1982-1996* (2000), *A New Century of Corporatism? Corporatism in Southern Europe: Spain and Portugal in Comparative Perspective* (2002), *Spain and Portugal in the European Union: The First Fifteen Years* (with P. Manuel, 2003); *Portugal, Espanha e aIntegraçãoEuropeia: Um Balanço* (2005); and *Varieties of Capitalism in Spain* (2008). He writes a regular column for the Spanish daily

Cinco Dias. His research interests include Southern European and Latin American politics and economic institutions. Royo is an affiliate at the Minda de Gunzburg Center for European Studies at Harvard University, where he co-chairs the Iberian Study Group.

AntónioGouchaSoares earned his PhD degree in law at the EUI, Florence (1996) after graduating from Lisbon Law School (1985) and the College of Europe, Bruges (1987). He is Jean Monnet Professor of European Law at ISEG—Technical University of Lisbon and was a visiting professor at Brown University. GouchaSoares is the author of *A LivreCirculação de Pessoasna Europa Comunitária* (Fragmentos, 1990), *Repartição de Competências no DireitoComunitário* (Cosmos, 1996), *A Carta dos DireitosFundamentais da UniãoEuropeia* (Coimbra Ed., 2002), *A UniãoEuropeia* (Almedina, 2006). He has also published a number of scholarly articles in the fields of European law, European integration and competition policy in refereed journals such as *European Law Review, Liverpool Law Review, European Public Law, Perspectives on European Politics and Society, European Competition Law Review, Econômica, World Competition,* and *European Societies.*